Y0-AAO-285

Contemporary Physical Education

Contemporary Physical Education

George R. Colfer
University of Texas at San Antonio

Keith E. Hamilton
The Citadel

Richard A. Magill
Louisiana State University at Baton Rouge

B. Jean Hamilton
College of Charleston

ⓌⒸⒷ Wm. C. Brown Publishers, Dubuque, Iowa

Book Team

Edward G. Jaffe *Executive Editor*
Bonnie Roesch *Editor*
Raphael Kadushin *Assistant Editor*
Vickie Blosch *Production Editor*
Anne Magno *Designer*
Mavis M. Oeth *Permissions Editor*
Shirley M. Charley *Photo Editor*

wcb group

Wm. C. Brown *Chairman of the Board*
Mark C. Falb *President and Chief Executive Officer*

wcb

Wm. C. Brown Publishers, College Division

Lawrence E. Cremer *President*
James L. Romig *Vice-President, Product Development*
David A. Corona *Vice-President, Production and Design*
E. F. Jogerst *Vice-President, Cost Analyst*
Bob McLaughlin *National Sales Manager*
Catherine M. Faduska *Director of Marketing Services*
Craig S. Marty *Director of Marketing Research*
Eugenia M. Collins *Production Editorial Manager*
Marilyn A. Phelps *Manager of Design*
Mary M. Heller *Photo Research Manager*

Consulting Editor
Aileene Lockhart *Texas Woman's University*

Cover photograph by Bob Coyle

Copyright © 1986 by Wm. C. Brown Publishers. All rights reserved

Library of Congress Catalog Card Number: 85–72064

ISBN 0–697–00140–7

No part of this publication may be reproduced, stored in a retrieval system, or transmitted, in any form or by any means, electronic, mechanical, photocopying, recording, or otherwise, without the prior written permission of the publisher.

Printed in the United States of America

10   9   8   7   6   5   4   3   2   1

To my wife, Dorothy, son, Eddie, and daughter, Kathy
George R. Colfer

To our daughters, Julie and Joni
B. Jean Hamilton
Keith E. Hamilton

To my son, Jeff
Richard A. Magill

On December 30, 1984, Dr. Keith Hamilton, professor of Physical Education at The Citadel, died suddenly at the age of 42. Keith's life and career were a tribute to our profession. He was a teacher, scholar, practitioner, and example of what a physical educator should be. To those of us who knew him and called him friend, he will be missed. Keith's final professional contributions are part of this book. It is with great pride that we dedicate the book to him.

Contents

Preface

The purpose of this text is to provide you with a grasp of the total foundation of physical education. You can then use this foundation to build your performance and skills to become physical educators. The book presents a broad scope of information about the physical education profession in a contemporary, innovative approach. Organized to provide comprehensive coverage of the foundations of physical education, this text provides a useful resource throughout your professional career.

The text is divided into four parts. Fourteen chapters provide information on such topics as history and philosophy of physical education, personal fitness, the scientific foundations, careers evaluation, the allied fields, professional development, coaching and athletics, social foundations and roles, teaching, the student, curriculum, and contemporary issues and trends.

Part 1 studies primary influences that have shaped contemporary physical education, the impact that physical education has on today's society, and the relationship of physical education and science. Part 2 encompasses the diverse career opportunities in physical education with focus on professional preparation and development and personal fitness. Part 3 examines teaching because most of the careers that physical education majors will pursue involve teaching through skills, duties, responsibilities, curriculum, styles, and strategies. Part 4 examines the broad scope of physical education and its relationship to a number of other fields. The subjects of coaching, athletics, health, dance, recreation, and safety are covered, along with the current trends and issues shaping physical education.

This book provides the future physical educator with a wealth of current information and knowledge. It will serve as an effective orientation to what physical education is and what being a physical educator can be. Our purpose is to aid you in your orientation in an effort to maintain and improve the quality of the profession. Contemporary physical education is a diverse and complex field. With a grasp of the foundations of this field, you have the insight and information needed to lay the groundwork toward a successful career in physical education.

In writing this book, we gratefully acknowledge the assistance and patience of those who worked with us. We appreciate the encouragement and inspiration of our spouses. We are indebted to our typists, Andree Gingles and Margie Pyka. We especially thank our colleagues in the physical education field who reviewed the manuscript and provided valuable criticisms and suggestions: Professor Robert Curtin, Northeastern University; Professor S. Jae Park, Ball State University; Professor Robert A. Mechikoff, San Diego State University; Professor Nena Rey Hawkes, Brigham Young University; Professor Ronald Hyatt, University of North Carolina, Chapel Hill; and Professor Neil Schmottlach, Ball State University.

Contemporary Physical Education

The Foundations of Physical Education

1

Our goal for part 1 is to help you grasp the essence of this extremely complex entity we call *contemporary physical education.* We use a theme to assist you, the theme *humans moving dynamically.* In our study, we focus on the bases for contemporary physical education: the enhancement of vigorous movement of human beings, the study of movement's effects on individuals and society, and the efficient, acceptable ways studies can be conducted.

In chapter 1 we will study the primary influences that have shaped contemporary physical education. In chapter 2 we will examine the impact that physical education has on our society. Chapter 3 focuses on the relationship of physical education and science and explores the avenues of study created by this relationship.

Your study of part 1 should help you better understand the foundations of physical education and the roles physical education plays in our day-to-day lives.

Historical and Philosophical Foundations of Physical Education   *1*

Chapter outline

History and Philosophy
The Influence of the Need for Fitness on
  Physical Education
    Fitness for Militarism
    Personal Fitness
The Influence of Medicine and the
  Sciences
    The Swedish System of Ling
    Tests and Measurements
    Other Curricular Relationships
    Sports Medicine
The Influence of General Education
    Ancient Athens
    Medieval Religious Training
    The Renaissance
    The German System of Jahn
    Educational Developmentalism and
      John Dewey

The New Physical Education
The Influence of Sports and Games
    The Ancient Olympic Games
    The Modern Olympic Games
    Olympic Boycotts
    Sports and Games in the United States
    The Governance of Sport
    Sports and Education
    Exhibit 1.1 Why I Run
    The Rise of Women's Sports
The Influence of the Discipline Movement
The Influence of Play Education
Summary
Study Questions
Student Activities
Notes
Related Readings

Student objectives

As a result of the study of this chapter, the student should be able to

1. Discuss the two primary ways that fitness has been important to society and relate each way to ancient Greece and Rome, medieval times, and contemporary America.
2. Contrast the education of the male youth of ancient Sparta with his counterparts in ancient Athens and Rome.
3. Discuss the contributions of the following people to the fitness boom: President Eisenhower, Dr. Paul Dudley White, Dr. Kenneth Cooper, and President Kennedy.
4. Describe how the American Association for Health, Physical Education, and Recreation (AAHPER) Youth Fitness Test evolved and list the persons contributing to its development.
5. Compare the motives of Per Ling, Friedrich Jahn, and Pierre de Coubertin in the contributions they made to physical education.
6. Discuss the relationships between science, medicine, and physical education.
7. Describe the medieval concepts of *scholasticism* and *asceticism* and tell how each has influenced the development of physical education in the United States.
8. Describe the influences of *educational developmentalism* and John Dewey on education and physical education in the twentieth century.
9. Discuss the relationship between the *new physical education* and sports and explain how this relationship developed.
10. Describe the rise of the *discipline movement* in physical education.
11. Explain the justification for physical education as an integral part of the educational process, using the *padia-ludus continuum.*
12. Discuss the application of the recurrent theme of physical education, *humans moving dynamically,* to each of the influences on modern physical education described in this chapter.

The concept we term *physical education* has existed, at least informally, since humans began to move upon the earth. Cultural survival was dependent upon the ability of human beings to improve their movement capabilities; consequently, efforts to improve and understand the capacity for movement have never diminished in importance to any society. The emphasis on the particular aspects of physical education has shifted from time to time, but the constant thread, or theme, of physical education throughout history has been **humans moving dynamically.**

The first teacher of physical education might have been an elder in a tribe or community who excelled at hunting, fishing, manufacturing weapons, and providing for his family. Through an informal physical education process, he passed to the next generation important information that related to movement prowess: thus, his expertise and quality of movement contributed to a better life for the next generation. Similar processes of education have been a part of societies where humans have sought to improve and understand their movement.

Today, the nature of the dynamic movement of human beings has changed. More formalized physical education enables us to refine, improve, and understand movement—knowledge that is important to contemporary society for several reasons. First, we seek to improve the quality of our play lives by becoming more adept at activities that inherently satisfy us. Skill improvement is an integral part, an objective, of contemporary physical education. Second, all indicators point to improved health status through programs of vigorous physical activity. Formal physical education can provide the programs needed to attain this health objective. Third, formal physical education studies broaden our knowledge of ourselves and our capabilities. Formal physical education, then, is best presented by persons who are adept at what they do, understand the nature and scope of humans moving, possess the skills necessary to transmit their knowledge to others, and are diligent in continuing to delve into the phenomenon of humans moving dynamically.

HISTORY AND PHILOSOPHY

History is the record of past events that have influenced the world in which we now live. A study of history should include an understanding of the circumstances that caused these past events to occur. Primary circumstances include the perceptions and interpretations of persons in positions of leadership: it has often been human interpretation that has shaped history.

With its roots among the great thinkers of ancient Greece, philosophy expresses what humans have interpreted to be universal truths. As we know, humans often do not interpret the same things in the same way. Such is the case with physical education.

Contemporary physical education is the result of past events and interpretations. As you continue to study physical education, you will discover that physical education has no clear, universally accepted definition or statement of goals and objectives. As you study and learn, you should develop a personal philosophy about physical education that will guide your involvement throughout your career. What do you believe

Figure 1.1 The influences on contemporary physical education affect each other.

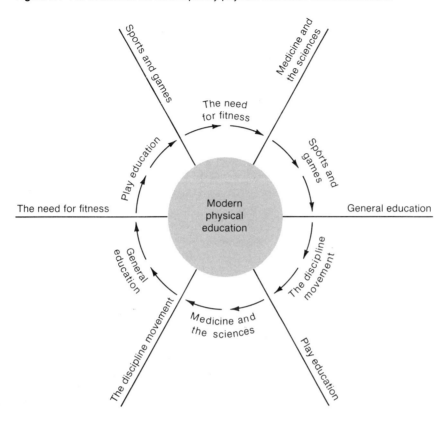

about physical education today? What has motivated you to this point to desire a career in physical education? Perhaps you have an affinity for sports and would like to teach and coach. Maybe you have worked at a summer camp and would like to continue similar experiences with children. Are you a dancer who would like to choreograph the performances of a dance troupe? Do you know a physical therapist, a cardiac rehabilitation technician, a community recreation director, or someone in the sporting goods or fitness promotion business who is doing what you would like to do? Perhaps your interest is in science, so that the challenges of an exercise physiology or motor learning laboratory appeal to you.

As diverse as these careers in physical education are, each has a direct relationship to contemporary physical education. Each stems from and is influenced by past events and philosophies that have broadened the scope of contemporary physical education. Factors influencing modern physical education include the need for fitness, medicine and the sciences, general education, sports and games, the discipline movement, and play education (see fig. 1.1). The influence of these factors is apparent not only in modern physical education, but on each other as well. Fitness and preventive medicine, for example, have a close relationship, as do sports and games and their influence on the goals of general education.

Organizationally, the remainder of this chapter is not a chronological account of the influences on contemporary physical education; rather, it is a historical and philosophical examination of each of six major influences independently. Because of the extreme interrelatedness of one influence to another, you should read the remainder of the chapter as a whole before you stop to examine each influence in detail.

THE INFLUENCE OF THE NEED FOR FITNESS ON PHYSICAL EDUCATION

The concept of physical education for fitness has historically been dichotomized into programs intended to serve militaristic ends and those designed for personal health improvement. Humans have long waged war on each other; thus, it has been important throughout history for nations to undertake rigorous training programs. The objective of such programs has always been to develop the physical capacities of soldiers, to prepare them to successfully engage in battles and endure the hardships imposed by war.

More recently, a resurgence of concern for health and well-being by a large segment of the public has prompted participation in a daily regimen of vigorous physical activity. Physical educators have responded to this concern by designing programs for developing personal wellness: the relationship of programs for personal wellness to the field of medicine is apparent here. We will attend to this relationship later in this chapter. For now, we will examine the influence of each aspect of the dichotomy of fitness.

Fitness for Militarism

At the Federal Institute of Physical Education and Sport in Moscow, Russia, a group of male and female students, dressed in combat fatigues and carrying assault rifles, charge down a stairway, along a hall, and through the exit door. They engage in military maneuvers on the playfields adjoining the Institute. School physical education in the Soviet Union emphasizes preparation for mandatory military service through drill and rigorous activity. The Soviet Union has an elaborate system of tests and awards for adults who maintain fitness as part of their readiness for defense and labor.

An Ohio high school physical education teacher marches his class to attention, checks the attendance roll by squads, and continues his lesson with a series of gymnastic stunts performed to a cadence. College students who have served in the armed forces may be given a waiver or have credit granted for physical education requirements. Emphasis on military fitness has recurred in physical education following the world wars and other conflicts where Americans have failed physical examinations, indicating a poor readiness for combat.

The United States and the Soviet Union have programs in physical education to strengthen military capabilities: these programs are a modern example of the historical

Figure 1.2 Combative training is important to students in military college.

relationship between physical education and militarism, where the objective has been to prepare humans to move dynamically in warfare (see fig. 1.2). Dominant in several cultures, this objective can be found repeatedly in different eras of history.

Ancient Sparta

A civilization that stressed physical development for its citizens was Sparta, a city-state of ancient Greece. Sparta is a clear example of a society whose emphasis on militarism was so pervasive that it led to the civilization's decay and downfall due to cultural stagnation.

Spartan civilization revolved around the development of obedient, stoic soldiers who dedicated their lives to the military service of the city-state. Spartan youth moved into crude military barracks at age seven to begin their training. Life was hard for Spartan soldiers. Provisions were often scarce, prompting soldiers to forage for or steal food. Soldiers caught in this act were severely punished, not for stealing, but for not being clever enough to get away with stealing. Love and support from the family unit was nonexistent. The greatest joy Spartan parents experienced was being notified that their children had given their lives in service of Sparta. Conversely, nothing brought greater dismay than the news that a child of theirs who was a soldier had demonstrated cowardice in the face of the enemy, an unthinkable act in Spartan culture.

This "never say die" attitude of the Spartan prevailed not only on the battlefield, but also in competition in the ancient Olympic Games. The pentathlon, for example, ended in a wrestling match. If one of the competitors was a Spartan, opponents knew that he would probably have to be killed in the match before he would yield victory. Spartans' rigorous military training led to success in athletic competition, evidenced by the fact that the majority of champions in the ancient Olympics were Spartans.

The emphasis on producing strong soldiers was so intense in Sparta that a baby who showed signs of being weak or deformed was left on a mountainside to die. Young women received physical training until the age of twenty. The purpose of this training was to condition their bodies to bear strong children. Adult women assumed control of the household while providing leadership for the government. The men were usually away at war.

The military training system of the Spartans consisted of wrestling, boxing, running, javelin and discus throwing, and long hikes to condition boys into hardened soldiers capable of withstanding terrible living conditions. Even dance took on military overtones, being choreographed to imitate the soldier's actions in battle. Hand-to-hand combat that systematically became more difficult as the soldier grew older was a basic aspect of Spartan training. The system also included difficult examinations that were administered by leaders to evaluate both citizenship and physical development. Youth who failed to measure up were punished and ostracized until they finally reached expected development.

Eventually, the Spartans' preoccupation with militarism and inattentiveness to other aspects of their culture created a static existence characterized by ultraconservatism and a lack of personal freedom. Education consisted only of military training and ignored intellectual development. The might of Sparta dissolved around 500 B.C. due to Spartans' dissatisfaction with a heavily militaristic way of life.

Ancient Rome

Like their predecessors in Sparta, the citizens of Rome considered service in the military to be their prime vocation. Unlike the Spartans, however, the male youth of Rome were part of close-knit families. Responsibility for the initial physical training of a youth fell to the male parent. Prior to formal induction into military service, the Roman youth was trained by his father to fight, swim, ride, and endure difficult circumstances. Occasionally, this training took the form of enjoyable games of skill not unlike our children's games of today.

Fun and enjoyment ceased abruptly when the male entered the military training ground near Rome, the huge Campus Martius. Field maneuvers and forced marches of great distances were common occurrences. A nation intent on establishing a mighty empire needed many quality soldiers. Obviously, their difficult military training paid dividends for the empire, for it enabled Rome to acquire and hold vast amounts of territory, creating one of the largest and wealthiest empires the world has ever known. The goal of the Roman educational system for militarism was fully realized.

Later, as a pervasive moral decline occurred in Rome, attention to physical training was curtailed. The Romans became spectators instead of participants in physical activities and, eventually, their attention focused on mental instead of physical development. Gladiators, captives brought to Rome from various conquests, competed as combatants in life or death struggles to satisfy the Roman thirst for excitement in their roles as spectators in great arenas. After the Romans conquered Greece and turned their attention solely to intellectual development, it was no great task for the barbaric tribes from Northern Europe to conquer Rome. The Romans' complete turnaround from physical training to intellectualism left the empire physically unable to defend itself, ushering in the historical period known as the Middle Ages.

A lesson of history should become apparent to us after a glimpse at two great civilizations whose decline and fall were caused mainly by their inflexibility. Sparta sought physical development for military might, ignoring the need for intellectual development to advance their culture. Initially, Rome had the same objective as Sparta, but later turned away from physical development to concentrate totally on intellectual development. For civilization to survive and advance, a balance was needed. These two extreme positions—total emphasis on physical development as opposed to total emphasis on intellectualism—needed to be tempered.

A tempering of the extremes occurred during the Middle Ages. The ultimate example of this tempering of positions, which we will examine later in this chapter, occurred in the *Golden Age of Greece* in Athens, a time in which a philosophy of development that sought *a man of action and a man of wisdom* as a necessary balance was emphasized.

Training for Knighthood

Feudalism was the name given to the social system that arose during the Middle Ages, the period from 500 A.D. to 1500 A.D. Kings held vast territories, dispensing portions of their land to noblemen, or *lords,* in exchange for allegiances. In a like manner, land was given to farmers, or *serfs,* by the lords for their mutual survival, with the lord receiving a percentage of the crops grown. Because this system was oppressive for the serfs and because stealing land was commonplace, bodyguards of sorts were needed to serve and protect the nobility. These personal armies of the noblemen, their knights, endured a two-phased training program prior to attaining knighthood.

At age seven, the training process began. As a **page,** the prospective knight entered service in the castle of his lord and began exercises for strength development. Along with learning how to handle weapons, his training might have included reading, writing, and the study of Latin. Because a strict code of moral conduct governed the knights, pages also received intense religious education as part of their training.

The page graduated to the status of a **squire** when he reached the age of fourteen. His training intensified, taxing the limits of his endurance as he exercised by riding, swimming, running, and jumping, often while dressed in full armor. The squire served a knight as a personal servant, attending to the knight's needs and wishes both during battle and leisure time. Games and mock battles sharpened the squire's fighting skills. He continued to serve others at court, perhaps entertaining them with song and dance, as he had when he was a page.

At age twenty-one, or earlier if the squire distinguished himself by a courageous act, he entered full service as a **knight.** Even in times of relative peace, knights prepared for and engaged in battle, either defending some point of honor that was felt to have been violated or by participating in tournaments, or jousts. These colorful affairs brought spectators from around the countryside to witness the knight's attempt to unseat his rival from his horse and engage him in hand-to-hand combat. Initially, these battles continued until one combatant was killed, but later they became more civilized, and blunt weapons were used to avoid serious injury.

As population centers grew and weapons, particularly those involving gunpowder, became more sophisticated, the need for knights diminished. The title still exists in Europe and is granted to persons performing outstanding service for their country.

With the diminished need for knights came a pronounced shift in the importance of military training in the educational process. The primary purpose of the training for knighthood was militaristic, but the training also included social and intellectual development. During the Renaissance and periods that followed, military training became only one aspect of the total educational process. Although emphasis on militarism rises briefly from time to time in modern eras, physical education for militaristic aims has diminished since the Middle Ages.

Personal Fitness

The rise in the popularity of distance running has been a spin-off from the **fitness boom,** a relatively recent phenomenon (see fig. 1.3). A field of two thousand runners in a marathon produces diverse testimonials about the joys of running. A young man tells of lowering his weight from well over 225 pounds to his current 145 pounds. With no previous athletic experience, he has become a national-class marathoner, breaking two hours and twenty minutes. A woman of 82 years and her great-granddaughter of 9 run the race together and exclaim that they plan to lower their times significantly in their next race.

It is extremely gratifying for physical educators to observe the many persons exercising, coming to know the health benefits derived from vigorous activity. Wishful thinking would lead those of us in physical education to believe that the health concerns of the American people and the resultant fitness boom are due to programs and promotional efforts in physical education. Although physical educators have long recognized the relationship between physical activity and positive health and have devised programs to promote this relationship, the current fitness boom must be credited to a number of factors.

Health is the oldest of the personal objectives of physical education. Testimonies about the value of exercise on the body came from such notables as Thomas Jefferson and Benjamin Franklin. More specifically, Catherine Beecher and Dr. George Winship devised programs of exercises that were supposed to promote good health in the early 1800s. From Catherine Beecher we derived *calisthenics,* while the program of Dr. Winship was structured around his view of equating good health with strength. The gymnastic systems created in Germany and Sweden, which comprised most of the physical education in the United States in the nineteenth and early twentieth centuries,

Figure 1.3 Many people have been encouraged to run competitively as part of the fitness boom. Pictured here is the Cooper River Bridge Run, held in Charleston, SC.

advocated health as a direct benefit of participation. Dr. Edward Hitchcock, a medical doctor, directed the first college physical education program in the United States. It was intended to help the students at Amherst College develop healthy bodies and minds. This program, which began at the start of the Civil War, continued under the direction of Dr. Hitchcock for the next half-century. Even the programs of Dr. Dudley Sargent, at Harvard, and those of the architects of the new physical education, while broader in their scope of objectives, maintained health development as their number one aim. These programs will be discussed later in this chapter.

After the Renaissance, humans were regarded as integrated entities. The medieval concept that the mind and body were separate was replaced by the thought that humans were comprised of complex interrelationships that created a *total unity* of mind and body. This concept, **holism,** led to the promotion of programs designed to foster

total fitness—fitness in physical, mental, spiritual, and social realms. These four aspects of total fitness were incorporated into the programs of the new physical education that replaced the rigid gymnastic systems in our schools early in the twentieth century. **Physical fitness** came to be the objective of programs for developing good health, but this term needed further defining. Was one really physically fit with the physique of a Mr. Universe? Were highly skilled athletes physically fit?

A natural definition occurred by separating the components of physical fitness into those thought necessary for good health and those thought to be necessary skill prerequisites for successful participation in sports. **Health-related components** included cardiovascular fitness, strength and muscular endurance, flexibility, and body composition. The **skill-related components** were identified as agility, balance, speed, power, coordination, and reaction time. (Chapter 7 of this text gives a detailed description of these various components of fitness.)

Until the middle of the 1950s, promotion of physical fitness was done through the occasional emphasis on militarism and through physical education programs in schools and colleges. Several important events occurred at that time. Each involved President Dwight D. Eisenhower and provided great impetus for physical fitness.

A test comparing the youth of Europe with their counterparts in the United States had tremendous ramifications for fitness. When the attention of President Eisenhower was called to the fact that American youth had performed more poorly on this physical fitness test than had the Europeans, a concerted effort was made to upgrade fitness programs in physical education in schools. The President's Council on Physical Fitness was created, with former Oklahoma football coach Charles "Bud" Wilkinson serving as its first director. A President's Award was given to students scoring well on the American Association for Health, Physical Education, and Recreation Youth Fitness (AAHPER)Test. This award motivated students to perform well, enhanced program development in the schools, and called public attention to the need for physical education. The test, designed by Dr. Paul Hunsicker of the University of Michigan, originally evaluated items more geared to skill-related aspects of fitness. The test was revised in 1981 to more appropriately measure health-related components.

The instrument that prompted these actions, the **Kraus-Weber test,** was probably not a valid measure of physical fitness between the two groups of young people. It did, nevertheless, create an awareness that if a global conflict should develop, the United States would have to go to war with young people of inferior physical capabilities. The resultant promotional efforts were somewhat militaristic in their fervor, but another incident involving President Eisenhower caused the fitness boom to take on more personal connotations.

As the nation turned its attention and concern toward Washington, D.C., because of the unstable health status of President Eisenhower, Dr. Paul Dudley White, the President's physician, began advocating exercise as a deterrent to heart disease. Dr. White contended that the President was able to survive his series of heart attacks because he was such an active person. The seed of awareness of the need for fitness through exercise was planted among the citizens of the United States. What was needed, then, was the method to achieve fitness.

Dr. Kenneth Cooper, at the time an Air Force officer and physician, published a book entitled *Aerobics*. Although he said essentially the same things about the value of exercise that physical educators had been saying for years, he put the information into a language that all readers could easily understand. By awarding a point value to various forms of physical activity and maintaining that earning twenty-four to thirty points per week would provide positive health benefits, Dr. Cooper's book became a best-seller. Cycling, swimming, and especially jogging became the means by which millions of Americans turned from being a nation of spectators to being a nation of participants.

Another boost for physical fitness came from former president John F. Kennedy. As a member of a vigorous, active family, President Kennedy called the nation's attention to involving itself in that kind of life-style. He promoted fitness through his famous fifty-mile hikes, in which he and his family took part. Despite a debilitating back problem, President Kennedy was an excellent model for the nation in regard to physical fitness.

The fitness boom, although predicted to be short-lived, has increased steadily. Commercially, health clubs and fitness salons have become tremendously lucrative. Educationally, *concepts* courses about the value of exercise and physical fitness are an integral part of the curricula of physical education programs in high schools and colleges. Personally, fitness takes on great significance for persons who find that by following certain guidelines they are able to be one of the humans moving dynamically who experience physical and psychological health benefits. For this reason, physical education will continue to be heavily influenced by the need for fitness.

THE INFLUENCE OF MEDICINE AND THE SCIENCES

In a South Carolina college gymnasium, a physical educator carefully monitors the progress of post-coronary patients engaged in an exercise program. This *rehabilitation* phase is part of a program conducted in association with a large medical university. Throughout the country, persons trained in physical education are assuming positions of leadership as directors of cardiac rehabilitation programs (see fig. 1.4). Such programs are examples of the strong relationship between physical education and medicine.

In a biomechanics laboratory in Pennsylvania, a physical educator applies the laws of physics to determine the causes of what appears to be an inefficient arm movement in the running pattern of a world-class marathoner. Elsewhere, a physical therapist manipulates the limbs of a young boy injured in a diving accident in an effort to restore the limb's usefulness. In an athletic training room on a college campus, the trainer, with a degree in physical education, supervises the efforts of a football player to rehabilitate a knee that was severely injured. These examples further illustrate current applications of medicine and science to fields with ties to physical education.

As mentioned earlier in this chapter, the medical relationship to the philosophy of physical education that advocates fitness for the sake of good health is a strong one. The broad scope of this relationship, however, can be attributed to persons and events that made physical education more comprehensive than the singular mission of fitness.

Figure 1.4 Continuous monitoring of patients is important in cardiac rehabilitation programs.

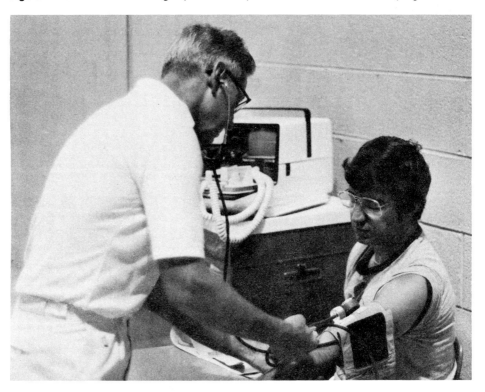

The Swedish System of Ling

When Sweden was forced to give up Finland to the Russians in 1808, the Swedes voiced a cry for a return to the glorious days enjoyed by their Scandinavian ancestors. A student of languages, Per Henrik Ling (1776–1839) responded. Ling shared with his compatriots the love of Swedish cultural heritage and desired to return Sweden to a position of might similar to that held when the Viking and Norse conquerors inhabited Scandinavia. Although his initial motivation was militaristic in nature, Ling's later interests were on the effects of exercise on the human body. Ling was influenced by gymnastics in Denmark during his course of study there. He found that exercise dramatically improved the condition of his crippled arm and he sought to discover the nature of this improvement.

Ling is reputed to have stolen bodies from graves and mortuaries in order to study the anatomical and physiological functions of humans. Within the limitations of the medical knowledge available in those days, Ling experimented with three types of exercises designed to improve physical problems. Active exercises were exercises practiced by the patient alone. Passive exercises were to be performed by a therapist, without resistance from the patient. Duplicated movements were done against a therapist's resistance. (These exercises are, incidentally, similar to those practiced by physical therapists in today's clinical settings.)

Ling divided his system of gymnastic exercises into four areas. *Military gymnastics* consisted of exercises designed for use by Sweden's armed forces. *Pedagogical gymnastics* were for inclusion in the schools of Sweden. Ling's son, Hjalmar Ling, developed pedagogical gymnastics after the death of his father. *Aesthetic gymnastics* were for posture improvement and the improvement of movement efficiency. Ling's efforts in what he termed *medical gymnastics* have proven to be outstanding.

Charles Bucher states that "Ling's greatest contribution is that he strove to make physical education a science."[1] In his attempts to take the guesswork out of the application of exercises to the body, Ling studied the circulatory, muscular, and nervous systems. By individualizing exercise programs, he was able to attend to the needs of a diverse population.

After Ling's system was refined by his successors, his gymnastics became the programs for both the military and the schools of Sweden. Another of his significant contributions was the founding of the Royal Central Institute of Gymnastics in Stockholm, one of the first teacher-training institutions for physical education in the world.

Through the efforts of philanthropist Mary Hemenway, of Boston, Ling's **Swedish gymnastics system** was brought to the United States. She provided the financial and political support necessary to include the Swedish system in the public schools of Boston. From there, the Swedish system proliferated and eventually rivaled German gymnastics for the dominant position in formal physical education in United States' schools.

Tests and Measurements

Ling's thoroughness in his work on the effects of exercise on physical development, coupled with the promotion of physical development for good health by medical doctors Edward Hitchcock and George Winship, caused the concept of testing and measuring physical development to grow rapidly in the United States. Just prior to the twentieth century, science established a foothold in physical education due, for the most part, to the relationship of science to medicine. Devices and tests for measuring strength became popular. Dr. Dudley Sargent, at Harvard, was known for the careful taking and recording of the measurements of the bodies of his students. A student's progress was indicated by the change in the dimensions of body parts as a result of exercising. These **anthropometric measurements** were popular among physical educators, especially when new statistical analysis procedures were applied. Charles H. McCloy, a pioneer in research in physical education, was one of the first to use statistics for the analysis of data related to physical education.

The strong emphasis on science in the training of doctors and persons in allied medical fields carried into physical education areas, and science became a cornerstone of the traditional curriculum for training physical educators. Since the end of World War I, the influence of science in physical education has justified science's inclusion in the curriculum. Physical education in the middle one-third of the twentieth century has been dominated by tests of general motor ability, sport skills evaluations, classification indexes, and, later, cardiovascular research. Athletic achievement tests indicating the relationship of physical education to sports were used extensively. One of the most popular of these tests, the Sargent Jump, was invented by Dr. Dudley Sargent to measure power. Its use continues today.

Other Curricular Relationships

Several other aspects of the curriculum designed for medical training have carried over into the training of physical educators. The medical field places strong emphasis on the physical sciences, particularly chemistry—sciences that are an integral part of the traditional curriculum in physical education. The life sciences, biology, zoology, and especially anatomy and physiology, are focal points of study both in medicine and physical education, reflecting the influence medicine and science have had on physical education.

These parent disciplines found in the curricula of medicine and physical education have also become fields of specialization within physical education. Exercise physiology has evolved from anatomy, physiology, and chemistry. Earlier in this chapter we saw an example of the application of the parent discipline of physics to kinesiology (biomechanics). Motor learning and sport psychology stem from the parent discipline of psychology. These fields within physical education, which are examined more specifically in chapter 3, have enjoyed significant progress within the *discipline movement* discussed later in this chapter.

Health, in the form of health education programs in schools and colleges, further illustrates the relationship of medicine to physical education, since health education has primarily been included as part of the physical education curriculum throughout the twentieth century.

Sports Medicine

The mix of politics and sports has had an impact in many areas, among them medicine and science. The incredible debut of the Russians in the Olympic Games in Helsinki, Finland, in 1952 caused the American sports community to reevaluate the role of science and medicine in sports. The Olympic success of the Russians prompted an examination of the Russian system, and it was determined that their application of medicine and science to sports was far ahead of that of the Americans. Shortly thereafter, in 1954, the American College of Sports Medicine was founded.

Since that time, the College—an association of physicians, physical educators, and other allied health scientists—has led the way in the advancement of training and rehabilitation techniques that have benefited America's elite athletes and the area of research and development in general medicine as well. Cy Young award winning pitcher Tommy John underwent radical surgery on his pitching arm that saved his career. In fact, John won his award after the surgery. Olympic slalom silver medalist Phil Mahre captured his medal at Lake Placid in 1980 only a year after shattering his ankle in a training run, evidencing near-miraculous rehabilitative techniques. He has gone on to win the World Cup in skiing several times and was the 1984 Olympic slalom champion. Science and medicine are continuing to play an important role in the development of athletes in the United States. Both are important departments at the Olympic development training site in Colorado Springs, Colorado, which opened late in the 1970s.

In conclusion, the quality of humans moving dynamically has been positively influenced and improved by the fields of medicine and science. As the body of knowledge in these two fields increases, physical education, too, will benefit due to the close historical relationships that have evolved since the days of Per Ling.

THE INFLUENCE OF GENERAL EDUCATION

Physical Education Public Information (PEPI) has been a continuous public relations venture that began in the early 1970s. Conceived and promoted by the American Association for Health, Physical Education, and Recreation, PEPI has established a network of information about physical education through various forms of media at the state, district, and national levels. Dr. Fay Biles, later the president of the American Alliance for Health, Physical Education, Recreation, and Dance (AAHPERD), served as the first project director of PEPI.

The PEPI movement has attempted to promote five concepts for public awareness concerning the value of physical education in our schools.

1. A physically educated person is one who has knowledge and skill concerning the body and how it works.
2. Physical education is health insurance.
3. Physical education can contribute to academic achievement.
4. A sound physical education program contributes to development of a positive self-concept.
5. A sound physical education program helps an individual attain social skills.[2]

In three of these five concepts the value of physical education is expressed by the contribution it purportedly makes to one's academic achievements, mental health, and social interaction skills. Physical education in the United States has been influenced by the goals of general education, and its expectations have been directed at education's goals. The philosophy of physical education developed in the twentieth century is probably the most entrenched—that physical education is a medium *through* which the goals of education can be realized.

Education underwent tremendous changes following the Renaissance, directly shaping the course of this philosophy of physical education. Historical roots of this philosophy, however, can be traced to five centuries before the birth of Christ.

Ancient Athens

No civilization has ever paid closer attention to the balance of physical and intellectual development than the ancient Athenian Greeks. Their ideal was to "encourage the individual to develop all capacities of his mind and body into a well-proportioned and harmonious personality capable of serving the state effectively in both war and peace."[3]

Physical educators point with pride to this civilization where physical education played an important part in the lives of citizens. Physical education's importance was evidenced by its place in the Athenian ideal. Like the contemporary philosophy that assumes a role for physical education in general education, the Greeks' philosophy saw physical education as part of a larger educational system. Van Dalen and Bennet state that, for the Greeks, physical education's role "was not the cultivation of the physical alone, but rather the development of individual qualities through the physical."[4] The Greek love of beauty was portrayed not only in their art, music, and literature, but also in their quest for the development of a well-proportioned body capable of moving with good form and skill. Great feats of physical performance were not esteemed as highly as the fluid movement of a beautifully proportioned body.

Although attended primarily by slaves, Athenian children were reared among family until the age of seven. Their formal educational training reflected the Greek ideal of "a sound mind in a sound body." Intense study in literature, mathematics, and music occurred at the *didascaleum,* or grammar school. At the *palaestra,* or wrestling school, physical development was nurtured. Progressing from simple exercises to promote general physical conditioning, male children later began to practice many of the events that were part of the ancient Olympic Games. These included javelin and discus throwing, wrestling, foot races, and the *pancratium,* a combination of boxing and wrestling.

All of the children's activities were supervised by the teachers at the palaestra and by the *pedagogues,* wise slaves responsible for the welfare of the Athenian boys. Of utmost importance was the fostering of sound moral character; young boys were severely chastised for any deviations from this standard. At age eighteen, sons of citizens became citizens of Athens and served two years of compulsory military service.

Because Athenians were motivated to possess high degrees of physical, mental, and spiritual character, they earnestly continued their programs of daily exercises in the gymnasia in Athens after completing their military service. Eventually, these gymnasia became assembly points for citizens to listen to the great teachers and philosophers for which the ancient Greeks are noted. As time passed, attention focused on the "man of wisdom," forsaking the "man of action." Self-indulgence replaced the desire for the state to progress. Despite warnings and pleadings from such proponents of physical development as Plato, Socrates, and Aristophanes, the importance of physical development declined. Eventually, the Athenian Greeks were swallowed up by the mighty Roman Empire.

Medieval Religious Training

Young men of noble birth had two vocational options during the Middle Ages: knighthood or the religious life. Training for and becoming a knight was the more popular of the two, but because the Roman Catholic church exerted such power and control over the people of this period, religious training was considered an important and desirable choice.

Even though physical education played no part in the training of monks and priests, two concepts that grew out of medieval religious training have influenced physical education in the United States. Although **asceticism** and **scholasticism** promoted intellectual development, their influence has had negative overtones for physical education.

Humans were regarded as dualistic entities by the religious monastics; that is, they considered the mind and the body to be separate. From dualism came the religious principle that the mind was good and the body was evil. Development of the mind through intellectual pursuits was the purpose of the monks as they labored for their monastery, meditated and prayed continuously, and dedicated themselves to their ideals of patience, obedience, and chastity. Part of the theology of the age dictated a purging of those things that were of the body. Since desires of the flesh were thought to be from the devil, those in religious training actually tortured themselves by such acts as wearing shirts made of hair and driving nails into or burning their flesh. The idea that idleness led to evil was derived from this medieval concept of asceticism, and its influence later impeded the development of physical education in the United States.

The Puritans embraced the idleness-to-evil notion and, in reaction, lived a lifestyle that emphasized the value of work. When the Puritans came to America, they brought this value, known as the Puritan work ethic, with them. The Puritan work ethic suppressed leisure-time pursuits, especially in New England. The Puritans believed that idle hands committed evil acts, and they severely punished any behavior considered frivolous. This negatively influenced the development of programs in physical education in New England states; the Southern states, not having this profoundly negative influence, were far advanced in the position that recreational pursuits enjoyed in their culture.

A second concept from medieval times, scholasticism, is still prevalent. After the oppressive control of the church eased in the latter part of the Middle Ages, intellectualism was enthusiastically embraced. Great universities were established to serve the number of students seeking knowledge about the liberal arts, law, and medicine. Scholasticism, from the *scholastics* who began this intense intellectual pursuit, meant that the development of the body was ignored and condemned for the sake of the intellectual development of the mind.

A humorous yet pitiful twentieth century statement made by a university president intent on having his institution focus on intellectualism was that whenever he felt like exercising, he would lie down until the feeling went away. This statement reflects the current narrow view held by some administrators and faculties of colleges and universities. Departments of physical education are sometimes repressed and placed on the defensive by the scholastic attitude of those educated in the liberal arts who contend, like their medieval counterparts, that physical education has no place in the process of education.

The Renaissance

A *rebirth,* or *reawakening,* of the human spirit occurred in Europe between the fourteenth and seventeenth centuries. By focusing their attention on the classical eras of ancient Greece and Rome, the intellectual leaders of the Renaissance rekindled a belief in human dignity and potential. The desire to learn was enhanced by books that became available following the invention of the printing press. With such intellectual leaders as John Locke, John Milton, and, later, Jean Jacques Rousseau lending support to physical education as a means of elevating the spirit through total development of body and soul, the Athenian Greek ideal of a sound mind in a sound body was promoted. The religious influence of asceticism was countered by leaders of the Protestant Reformation, especially Martin Luther, who advocated physical education. The Renaissance belief that humans were holistic entities set the stage for the development of the gymnastic systems that comprised American physical education for nearly fifty years.

The German System of Jahn

Many contemporary physical educators have misunderstood the work of Friedrich Ludvik Jahn (1778–1852). He emphasized **nationalism,** the attitude of strong, fervent love and dedication to one's homeland, but his purpose was not, as some believe, to develop a strong German youth capable of casting off by military force the oppressive yoke of Napoleonic domination. Instead, Jahn sought to use his system of gymnastic exercises to create "liberty-loving, social, and independent-thinking men by strengthening degenerated muscle groups that made him feeble and liberating man from an environment that allowed his muscles, and consequently his mental vigor, to decay."[5]

Jahn was able to draw upon the work of Guts Muths, an early teacher at Germany's Schnephenthal Institute, for ideas concerning exercise, apparatus, and purposes. Jahn devised a system he called *Turnen* and expressed its objective as follows: "Turnen shall recover the lost balance of human education. It shall add to a one-sided intellectualism the true physical basis, and establish for a man a necessary counterbalance against over-refinement. In welding body to mind we aim to create a whole and forever youthful being."[6]

Jahn's gymnastic exercises were incorporated into the operation of the *Hasenheide,* the playground near Berlin that Jahn founded. The system grew in popularity throughout Germany and was expanded to include the aspects of fencing, swimming, dancing, and skating to the other exercises of walking, running, balancing, climbing, throwing, and those performed on apparatus like the beam, horizontal bar, and parallel bars.

The influx of German immigrants during the nineteenth century to the United States and the work of three of Jahn's former students, Charles Follen, Charles Beck, and Franz Lieber, promoted the German system in this country. Turnvereins, German gymnastic societies, were privately established in many areas where the immigrants settled. Beck introduced the system into the Round Hill School of Massachusetts, where he was a teacher. The people of Boston, desiring a public gymnasium, hired Follen and, later, Lieber to direct it. Both used the German system exclusively in the gymnasium, with Lieber opening a swimming school next door.

The advocates of German gymnastics lobbied long and hard to have their system included in the curricula of the public schools. Their success was limited primarily to public schools in areas where large populations of Germans settled, particularly in the Midwest. The **German system** of Jahn and the Swedish system of Ling competed for placement in the public schools from about 1885 until they were replaced by the new physical education.

Educational Developmentalism and John Dewey

A new emphasis on what should be taught to children prefaced the progressive steps made in education in the United States. Very little had been done earlier in attempting to understand children and their needs. The intellectual awakening that occurred during and after the Renaissance, however, brought about the development of many new fields, one of which was psychology.

The brilliant Dr. G. Stanley Hall, a product of the tutelage of the "father of American psychology," William James, intensely studied children and their behavior. Dr. E. L. Thorndike devised *laws of learning* about children that proved to be the framework for the development of educational psychology. As the field of psychology broadened to include diverse theories about how children learned, so did the search for ways to assist children with their development.

The "father of American education," John Dewey, expressed in his book *The School in Society* and in other writings the need for schools to provide an environment where children could develop ideal social behavior and where each child could realize his or her potential through appropriate planning by the schools.

The fact that Drs. Thorndike and Dewey worked at Teacher's College of Columbia University in New York had a great deal to do with the founding of the new physical education. One of its architects, Clark W. Hetherington also taught at Teacher's College and was directly influenced by these two doctors. Hetherington had earlier studied under G. Stanley Hall. The thought that physical education could be a means *through* which children could develop to their optimum potential physically, mentally, and socially in educational settings prompted drastic changes for physical education and assured its inclusion in the schools of America.

The New Physical Education

Toward the end of the nineteenth century, Dr. Dudley Sargent, an early leader in physical education at Harvard, stated program aims that encompassed more than physical development for good health. His inclusion of an *educative aim* for the cultivation of the special powers of the mind and body, a *recreative aim* for restoring vital energies for daily work, and a *remedial aim* for correcting disturbed functions gave breadth and depth to the purpose of physical education. Dr. Sargent's broader view of the role of physical education combined with a growing lack of interest in the drab exercises of the gymnastic systems to set the tone for a change in philosophy and programs. In addition, persons attending the Boston Conference of 1889 to debate the merits of the gymnastic systems came away thinking that the United States should develop its own program of physical education.

Two physical educators, comprehending the new mission Dewey had set for the schools and the changes wrought by educational developmentalism, devised the philosophy of physical education that has had the greatest impact on physical education in the twentieth century. Dr. Thomas D. Wood, a physical educator at Stanford University, and one of his brilliant students, Clark Hetherington, determined that physical education should contribute to one's total education. An outspoken critic of the gymnastic systems, Dr. Wood argued that good health should not be the singular goal for physical eduation, but a value derived from participation in enjoyable physical activity. Students in schools and colleges were conveying what they felt these physical activities should be, since sports and games were enjoying tremendous popularity at the beginning of the twentieth century. Clark Hetherington, an articulate spokesperson for what he termed the **new physical education,** stated four objectives for programs in physical education. He said that they should develop a person organically, promote the development of efficient motor ability, and develop one's character and intellectual ability.

Hetherington expressed this view near the start of the twentieth century. Charles Bucher reinforced Hetherington's objectives nearly fifty years later, which illustrates the longevity of the new physical education.

Objectives for Programs in Physical Education

1. Physical development objective: The objective of physical development deals with the program of activities that builds physical power in an individual through the development of various organic systems of the body.
2. Motor development objective: The motor development objective is concerned with making physical movement useful and with as little expenditure of energy as possible and being proficient, graceful, and aesthetic in this movement.
3. Mental development objective: The mental development deals with the accumulation of a body of knowledge and the ability to think and to interpret this knowledge.
4. Social development objective: The social development objective is concerned with helping an individual in making personal adjustments, group adjustments, and adjustments as a member of society.[7]

Further support for the new physical education came from three of the *Seven Cardinal Principles* of education, established by the Educational Policies Commission in 1918. These three—health, worthy use of leisure time, and ethical character—were strongly tied to the objectives of the new physical education. In 1938, the Educational Policies Commission reduced the seven principles to four, further justifying the place of the new physical education in the schools of America.

1. Self-realization, which includes the skills of speaking, reading, writing, and arithmetic; *desirable health knowledge and action; participation and observation of sports and pastimes; mental resources for use of leisure;* and responsible direction to one's own life.
2. Human relationships, which include *those practiced as a friend and neighbor and in the home and family.*
3. Economic efficiency, which includes the individual both as a consumer and producer.
4. Civic responsibility, which includes defenses against propaganda, unswerving loyalty to democratic ideals, *respect for honest differences of opinion, and cooperation as a member* of the world community.[8]

These goals and the singular recent one, *self-realization,* reflect the impact of educational developmentalism and John Dewey on American education. Physical education has followed the same path by being thought of as a process *through* which the goals of general education can be attained. Wood and Hetherington as first generation proponents, Luther Gulick, Jay B. Nash, and Jesse F. Williams in the second, and, more contemporarily, Delbert Oberteuffer and Charles Bucher have been outstanding leaders of physical education in this century. Each subscribed to the philosophy of physical education that Jesse Feiring Williams defined as "education *through* the physical." The proponents of this philosophy share a unique common bond. Each has either taught or studied at Teacher's College or New York University. Consequently, the thread of this philosophy has been easily passed, while being strengthened, from generation to generation through the hands of these dynamic leaders.

That each child should have the opportunity to realize his or her optimum potential is a feature of **Public Law 94–142,** enacted in 1975. This law guarantees that handicapped children will have their needs met within the structure of free, public education. Of particular importance to physical education is the facet of the law that has led to the concept of **mainstreaming.** By placing the handicapped child in the regular physical education class and adapting the situation for the maximum benefit of this child, mainstreaming meets the requirements of the law. The special training physical educators require under the mandate of Public Law 94–142 has affected teacher education curricula, with the addition of courses in adapted physical education and physical education for the handicapped now being essential.

The validity of the education through the physical philosophy has been the subject of recent criticism. Some have referred to Wood and Hetherington as opportunists who rode the tide of change in American education by tying physical education to the goals of general education, assuring it a place in the educational structure. Some have regarded the objectives of this philosophy as placing physical education on the defensive, since the achievement of the objectives is difficult to verify. Whether we have built our "modern house on a foundation of sand" remains speculative, but, as adamant critic Dr. Daryl Siedentop has stated, the education through the physical philosophy has benefited us in three ways.

1. The idea solidified a young profession that needed solidarity in order to grow in breadth and depth.
2. The infusion into physical education curricula of a broad variety of physical education activities has been a benefit.
3. An accomplishment of education through the physical has been the broad acceptance of physical education as a legitimate part of school programs.[9]

Applying the philosophy of education through the physical to our recurrent theme of physical education means that humans moving dynamically in selected activities develop physically, mentally, emotionally, and socially.

THE INFLUENCE OF SPORTS AND GAMES

A Soviet fencer and his coach are disqualified from the 1976 Olympics in Montreal because an electronic device was tampered with to show a "touch" when none had actually occurred. A twenty-two-year-old professional basketball player signs a twenty-five year contract for one million dollars per year. Collegiate athletic programs are rocked by scandals early in the 1980s. Transcripts are altered and credits for nonparticipants in summer-term courses are awarded in an effort to ensure eligibility of athletes.

That Americans could "stand a little taller" following the American defeat of the Russian ice hockey team at the 1980 Lake Placid Winter Olympic Games is an example of the importance of sport in society. Such is the state of affairs in the world of

Figure 1.5 Sports have been the focus of physical education in the twentieth century.

national and international sports, reflecting the awesome impact that sports have on those who compete and those who watch (see fig. 1.5). We will examine the sociological implications of physical education and sports in chapter 2, but for now let us examine the evolution and influence of this phenomenon.

The Ancient Olympic Games

In his *Iliad* and *Odyssey*, the Greek poet Homer told of contests of speed, strength, and bravery that were part of funeral celebrations held in honor of deceased warriors. Later, these celebrations grew to a position of great importance in the lives of the ancient Greeks. Every four years, games were held at Olympia to pay homage to Zeus, the supreme god of the Greeks.

The date recorded for the first Olympics was 776 B.C., the year Coroebus, a sprinter, was declared the first official Olympic champion. Originally, the games included contests of oratory, singing, and flute playing, but they eventually became purely athletic contests. Running, jumping, wrestling, and boxing competitions were held, pitting the best athletes in each event from the city-states of ancient Greece against each other. Discus and javelin throwing were also part of the program. As mentioned earlier in this chapter, these events were regularly practiced as part of the physical education programs of the men in Athens, while the training received by the Spartans enabled them to dominate.

An *Olympiad* was a calendar designation of the Greeks that specified the four-year period between games. Winning became important enough that various city-states, in an effort to add to their prestige, hired professional athletes. The city-state provided for the needs of these athletes while they trained. An Olympic victory was well-rewarded, and an athlete who won could expect to live comfortably for the rest of his life.

Even after Greece was conquered by Rome, the Olympic Games continued to flourish. The Romans even adopted some of the contests and used them as part of the spectacles of their arenas. Chariot racing was a particular favorite, since it often resulted in collisions and serious injuries. Later, however, the Olympics came to be regarded as pagan festivals by the Christian emperor Theodosius, who abolished them in 394 A.D.

The Modern Olympic Games

An attempt to establish a strong youth and a spirit of nationalism, similar to earlier attempts by Jahn and Ling in their respective countries, occurred in France late in the nineteenth century. The humiliation of France after the Franco-Prussian War was felt by Pierre de Coubertin (1863–1937). To help France become strong, de Coubertin launched a campaign to rebuild the bodies and spirits of youth through sports. De Coubertin was enthralled with Olympia and, relying heavily on what he knew about the classical period of ancient Greece, sought a way to recreate its games. In 1890 he visited the estate of Dr. William P. Brooke in England. Brooke's "Olympics" were outings for the British aristocracy that recreated many of the events practiced by the ancient Greeks. These events enabled de Coubertin to see the potential for games in international competition which could, as he conceived them, promote world peace.

At a conference held in France to examine the principles of amateurism in sport, de Coubertin added a proposal to the agenda to restore the Olympic Games. The delegation unanimously approved this proposal, and the first of the modern Olympic Games was held in Athens in 1896. The second and third Olympics were a part of World's Fairs in Paris and St. Louis, respectively. After the Games of St. Louis, however, the newly formed International Olympic Committee, with de Coubertin as president, voted to never again hold the Olympics in conjunction with another event.

Early in the Olympic movement, de Coubertin recognized potential problems and forbade nations to march together in military fashion. He thought this to be an excessive show of nationalism and was especially critical of the German gymnastic societies. He was dismayed, too, at the partiality of the British judges in the London

Games of 1908, which prompted the subsequent use of international judges for all events. Later, over the protests of de Coubertin, the International Olympic Committee permitted women to participate, beginning with the Games of 1920. The Winter Olympics were added in 1924.

In explaining his motivation to establish physical and moral development in the youth of France and the world, de Coubertin wrote,

> Why have I restored the Olympic Games? In order to ennoble and strengthen sports, in order to assure their independence and duration and thus to set them better to fill the educational role which devolves upon them in the modern world. To exalt the individual athlete, whose very existence is necessary for the involvement of the community in athletic sports, and whose achievements provide an example to be emulated.[10]

In light of the purity of his intentions in founding the Olympic Games, Baron Pierre de Coubertin would surely shudder at the twisting of his original ideal today.

The Berlin Olympics of 1936 was the scene of many Olympic firsts. Sophisticated electronic timing devices, pomp and ceremony, the carrying of the torch via relay runners from Olympia to the host nation's stadium, and political intrigue were integral parts of these "Nazi Olympics." Hitler wished to showcase the return of Germany to a position of world power under his national socialist movement and to show the world the superiority of the Aryan race. Even the persecution of the Jews ceased as an act of good will during the Games. The success of the American black, Jesse Owens, diminished Hitler's aim to some degree, but political appeasement of Hitler occurred when two Jewish members of the United States' 400 meter relay team were replaced at the last minute. Hitler's propaganda motives were realized, as the participating nations came away from Berlin in awe of Germany's might.

Following the example set during World War I, when Olympic Games were not held, no Games were held during World War II. De Coubertin's dream of world peace was shattered, but a successful reestablishment of the Olympics in London in 1948 helped to heal some wounds from the war.

Olympic Boycotts

The term *boycott*, relative to the Olympic Games, struck the United States for the first time when President Jimmy Carter ordered the move following the Russian invasion of Afghanistan in 1980 and for the second time when the Soviet bloc countries boycotted the Los Angeles Games in 1984. Boycotts can, however, be traced back several Olympiads, to the Melbourne Games of 1956. The Dutch and Spanish teams refused to participate due to the Russian invasion of Hungary. Egypt boycotted because of differences in the Middle East over the Suez Canal. Mainland China refused to compete because Taiwan's participation was permitted. The Olympic Games had become such a focal point of international attention that they became a political arena.

Other examples of the intrusion of political concerns include the water polo match between Russia and Hungary in 1956, just after the Russian invasion of Hungary. Observers claimed that the pool literally turned red from the blood of the contestants. The demonstrations by American blacks on the award stands in 1968 and 1972 over racial discrimination, the African boycott of the Montreal Games of 1976 over South

Africa's apartheid policies, and blatant partiality by officials in boxing, diving, and basketball in Munich in 1972 are yet more examples of political intrusion. The worst horror, to date, was the kidnapping and killing of the Israeli athletes by the Black September terrorists in Munich. Lord Killanin, former president of the International Olympic Committee, said, "The future of the Olympic Movement is, I believe, assured, although we shall always have our problems. Among these are the immense growth of the Games, amateurism and eligibility, political interference, and the use of scientific advances in medicine."[11]

The United States Olympic Committee, cognizant of the Olympics as a reflection of political and military might, has undertaken an Olympic development program. A national training site has been established in Colorado. National Olympic Academies offer summer conferences on the Olympic movement, while the International Olympic Academy, at Olympia, brings delegates together from all over the world. Both conferences are designed to advance the ideals of the Olympic Games.

Sports and Games in the United States

Depending upon where the early colonists settled along the East Coast and what their motives were for leaving England, sports and games had either great importance or no place in the lives of America's settlers. The Puritans, as mentioned earlier, discouraged leisurely physical activity. In the Middle Atlantic and Southern states, however, the rich traditions of English sporting activities flourished. Hunting, fishing, falconry, and horseracing were some of the traditions brought from England.

After the Revolutionary War, settlers moved West. Activities that provided diversions from the rigors of pioneer living were popular and served a utilitarian function. The necessities of skills in shooting, knife and axe throwing, foot racing, and horseriding were important to the survival of the pioneers and also provided their amusements during less serious circumstances. Quilting bees and barn raisings served two purposes: they were needed for the welfare of pioneer families and brought together many people in a spirit of fun and celebration. Bearbaiting, cockfights, and dogfights also spread to the West.

The Civil War indirectly promoted sports and games. Both Northern and Southern soldiers occupied their time between battles playing games. After the war, they returned to their homes and continued their participation in games.

The most pronounced growth of sports and games in the United States occurred in the period after the Civil War to 1900. Immigrants poured into the United States during this period, bringing with them the sports indigenous to their homelands. The growth of colleges and universities was rapid, and the attractiveness of sports to students gave birth to the rise of intercollegiate athletics. The English influence continued, with the London rules of soccer, Canadian rugby, and rules that varied from college to college combining to establish American football. Baseball, too, underwent a complete change from the English game of cricket to become "America's pastime." New games were created, including basketball, invented by Dr. James Naismith in 1892, and volleyball, invented three years later by William Morgan. Mary Outerbridge brought the game of tennis to New York following her exposure to this British game in Bermuda. Golf courses were constructed along the East Coast and, eventually, this popular Scottish game moved westward. Track and field grew rapidly in the colleges and became especially entrenched in the private athletic clubs that were formed in the nineteenth century. As competition increased between these various organizations fielding teams, so did excesses, prompting the need for sports legislation.

The Governance of Sport

With direction in athletics being provided by students and alumni, the hiring of athletes with no affiliations to colleges, disputes over rules, and disfiguring injuries and death became commonplace in athletics. These factors led to faculty control and the eventual formation of athletic conferences. President Theodore Roosevelt recognized the problems associated with football and called a meeting of college presidents. This meeting led to the founding of the **National Collegiate Athletic Association (NCAA)** in 1910. These same abuses were occurring in high schools, necessitating the establishment of state federations to control them. In 1922, the state federations combined to form the **National Federation of State High School Athletic Associations.** An effort to legislate private sports clubs led to the formation of the **Amateur Athletic Union (AAU)** in 1879. Eventually, these governing bodies attempted to exert control over each other's purported domains. Federal mediation has often been required to solve the resultant rifts. Problems between the NCAA and AAU, which usually arose over the selections of Olympic participants, lasted over fifty years. Currently, the **National Junior College Athletic Association (NJCAA)** and the **National Association for Intercollegiate Athletics (NAIA)** legislate their respective members. All governing bodies of intercollegiate athletics currently reflect faculty control.

Sports and Education

Media exposure added greatly to the development of sports at the turn of the century. William Randolph Hearst's expansion of the sports pages of his New York newspaper influenced sports in several ways. First, it helped to dispel the misconceptions people had about professional athletes. The misconception that professional athletes were people of "low moral character" was exploded by the portrayal of their sporting exploits in the sports pages, which endeared them to the reading public. Secondly, it created sports *fans* (from *fan*cier of sport and, more recently, *fan*atics about sport), since the sports page permitted people to follow every move of the professional, college, or high school team to which they affiliated themselves. The resulting popularity of sports provided the founders of the new physical education with the means to advance their philosophy of education through the physical. Van Dalen and Bennett state that "the newer concept of physical education fully recognized the popular movements of play and athletics. As outlined by Wood, the content of physical education was to be found in play, games, dancing, swimming, outdoor sports, athletics, and gymnastics."[12] Assumed in the promotion of these activities was that they inherently provided the participant with desirable characteristics, thereby contributing to general education. The philosophy that sports built sound moral character through physical, mental, and social development in its participants attached sports to physical education programs.

exhibit 1.1

Why I run

At this point in my life my feelings about competitive distance running are really quite ambivalent. I recognize the benefits of athletics: the attainment of a degree of physical fitness, a sense of dedication and self-discipline; a knowledge of physical abilities and limitations; a respect for raw courage and a feel for nitty-gritty competition.

When on a long run, I often question my reasons for participating in track at all. Is the time and effort worth it? Is it worth the fatigue you live with? And the short temper you develop as a consequence of that fatigue? Is it worth the weekends one relinquishes to studying—the payment for climbing into bed before midnight during the week?

With certain reservations, the sacrifice of athletics *is* worth the discomforts. It provides the opportunity to achieve a self-satisfying performance in an area where I may never again have such an opportunity.

Certainly, I have my doubts about just what running will ever do for me, in the sense of furthering a career, but I see in competing a "chance to excel" in the truest meaning of those words. I can never promise anyone, or myself, that I'll win a race or even run what I consider a "good" race; but I would like to think that I possess the self-discipline to train myself with rigor and diligence, and to struggle against the opponent with the greatest tenacity, to the point of genuine exhaustion.

Running is proving to myself that I am able, in a certain way, to resist the easy temptation to crack, to quit, to give up, to run away from a situation that involves placing every psychological comfort I have right on the firing line.

I think that a lawyer does the same thing when he argues a life-or-death case; or a doctor when he performs a sensitive operation; or a military commander when he decides to "damn the torpedoes."

I think that running, like all these actions, takes just a little courage.

Source: Courtesy *The Talon,* the United States Air Force Academy.

Since much of our sports heritage comes from England, we can speculate that so, too, did this relationship between sports participation and character development. Sally Magnusson, in her biography of Eric Liddell, the 1924 Olympic 400 meter champion and missionary to China, discussed the concept of *Arnoldism* that was pervasive in the schools of England early in the nineteenth century. Dr. Thomas Arnold founded the famed Rugby School in England. He believed that sports were "an essential contribution to manliness, patriotism, moral character building, stoicism, courage, and team spirit."[13] This belief became entrenched in the philosophies of the schools in England and was extensively accepted internationally. The play and recreation movements spearheaded by Dr. Luther Gulick sought to include athletics in physical education for the value they provided for participants in leisure-time activities. Dr. Elmer Mitchell strove to develop sports for all through the establishment of intramural athletics.

Since this time in the 1920s, sports and games have typified programs in physical education. Because of the popularity sports enjoy, their relationship to physical education has, at times, been overwhelming. Some physical educators resent being called coach or resent being asked what sports they coach when they identify themselves as physical educators. Administrative expectations of physical educators have been that they be hired to coach and teach, with emphasis usually in that order. As a result, the desire to appease fans by producing winning athletic teams (and thus improve job security) has often been at the expense of quality physical education programs. Hiring practices, design of facilities, and allocation of money for equipment are currently in favor of athletic programs.

The Rise of Women's Sports

Activities that were accepted within the concept of femininity comprised sports for women in the late nineteenth century. Cycling, a "genteel" game of tennis, croquet, and hiking were popular, and basketball later became a favorite. Championships in track and field, archery, and golf took place at the turn of the century. Fearful that the popularity of sports among women would follow the same excesses as sports for men, a Women's Athletics Committee was appointed in 1917. At the same time, a women's division of the National Amateur Athletic Federation, headed by Mrs. Lou Henry Hoover, the wife of President Herbert Hoover, was founded. Both groups promoted *play days* and discouraged intense competition. At the high school level, however, competition between teams of girls grew rapidly.

In the early 1930s, a reorganization of existing regulative bodies formed the National Section on Women's Athletics, which published rule books for a wide variety of sports. This era saw very little change in the status of competition between women's teams. In fact, an association of college physical educators stood in opposition to proposed national tournaments for women. It was late in the 1960s and early 1970s before a dramatic change in that stance occurred (see fig. 1.6).

The governance of women's athletics has, until recently, been under the auspices of the **AAHPERD** (see chapter 6 for an explanation of the functions of this body). A division of that organization, the Division of Girls' and Women's Sports, formed the Commission on Intercollegiate Athletics for Women that, in turn, created the **Association for Intercollegiate Athletics for Women (AIAW)**. Seventeen national championships were sponsored by the AIAW. Recently, a number of large universities with women's athletic teams have aligned themselves with the NCAA. After the AIAW was disbanded, women's collegiate athletics became governed by the NCAA and NAIA. These bodies now conduct women's national championships.

The stereotypical roles that society expected of men and women precluded the participation of women in sports because such participation was considered unfeminine. Playing aggressively or perspiring while playing did not fit the role society dictated for women. Early in the 1970s, women began to inquire why the educational benefits men were receiving from sports participation could not apply to them as well. This challenge, coupled with the feminist movement, brought needed attention to the role of sports for women. Society adopted a more liberal attitude toward women and

Figure 1.6 Intensity typifies sports competition for women and men.

Historical and philosophical foundations of physical education   **33**

discarded some of its oppressive stereotypes. The success and media exposure of out-standing female athletes, headed by tennis champion Billie Jean King, helped to dispel the attitude that sports detracted from femininity. Federal legislation prohibiting dis-crimination against women's athletics followed in 1972.

Title IX ensures that equal opportunity for participation shall be afforded members of both sexes at institutions receiving financial assistance from the federal government. Although this act was initially confusing and sometimes caused hostility between men's and women's athletic programs, the fact that women should be given practice time, equipment, and money on an equal basis and receive athletic scholarships has gained acceptance. The challenge for the future will come from attempts to continue to conduct competitive men's and women's programs in an era of high inflation rates and diminishing athletic budgets.

The popularity of sports and games is likely to continue indefinitely. Many problems face administrators, coaches, and physical educators in their attempts to maintain sanity in an era of sports hysteria. James Michener, in his book *Sports in America,* points out some of the major problem areas:

Children are being introduced into highly organized sports too young.

Girls and women are unjustly deprived of an adequate share of the sports budget.

The popular contention that sports are an escape hatch for ghetto youth is overstated.

Most medium-sized universities are spending too much money trying to maintain big-time football programs and many should de-escalate to something more manageable.

Large universities with successful big-time programs should finance them more realistically.

The recruiting of high school athletes is a national scandal.

Television threatens to engulf many of the inherent values of sports.

The media, up until recent years, have been delinquent in reporting the facts about sports.

It is improper for political units like cities, counties, and states to use public money to pay for large stadiums which are then turned over to professional teams for a fraction of a realistic rental.

The federal government may have to intervene to provide guidance for national sporting programs, including supervision of professional contracts with players, the awarding of franchises to cities, and the sponsorship of our Olympic teams.

Throughout our sports program there is an undue emphasis on violence.

Even if, as some charge, the excesses of sports merely reflect the excesses of our society, that is no justification. Sports, as an idealistic exercise, should transcend any meannesses in our society and offer a more responsible ideal.[14]

Humans moving dynamically in sports and games have shown human nature and capabilities at their best and at their worst. The influence of sports and games on physical education is strongly felt today and requires physical educators to shape a philosophy designed to maintain sports in their proper context in our society.

THE INFLUENCE OF THE DISCIPLINE MOVEMENT

What had been the department of physical education at a large university in New England is now the *Department of Exercise Science.* Two universities on the West Coast have renamed their's *Departments of Kinesiology.* In an effort to broaden the scope of their curricula, the departments of some colleges and universities have *professional preparation* divisions and divisions in which the *art and science of human movement* is studied. These are recent moves away from traditional departments that prepare teachers of physical education. The early part of the 1960s was characterized by the need to reconceptualize a theoretical framework for physical education; the need was spurred by reactions to a piece of legislation in California and by a dissatisfaction with the state of affairs in physical education.

The stage was set for a "revolution" in physical education early in the 1950s. Eleanor Metheny, at the University of Southern California, and Camille Brown and Rosalind Cassidy, at the University of California at Los Angeles, led a move away from the heavy emphasis on teacher education. They sought to redefine physical education. By replacing the term *physical education* with **human movement,** these leaders dedicated themselves to formulating a framework in which scholarly inquiries into the uniqueness of human movement could occur. Prompted by the contributions of noted dance theorist Rudolph Laban, human movement was regarded by these West Coast leaders as having a unique **body of knowledge.** That human movement is the means by which expression is given to emotion, mood, gesture, and communication in temporal and spatial relationships became the basis for scholarly investigations in the what, where, and how aspects of the body moving.

The passage of the Fisher Bill in California in 1961 gave impetus to the formulation of the body of knowledge unique to human movement. The bill differentiated between academic and nonacademic curricula of colleges and universities in the California system, with physical education considered nonacademic. Because administrative positions could be filled only by persons from academic areas and teacher certification could evolve only from academic departments, a redefinition of physical education took place. Physical education departments were eventually able to change their status by showing that their programs came from the sciences, history, philosophy, psychology, and sociology. Since that time, research in physical education has been directed at expanding the body of knowledge unique to each of these diverse areas that comprise contemporary physical education.

Franklin Henry proved to be another strong voice from the West Coast. In 1964, he defined an academic **discipline** as "an organized body of knowledge collectively embraced in a formal course of learning."[15] Today, the field of physical education is comprised of specialists in exercise physiology, motor learning, sports history, sports psychology or sociology, and kinesiology (biomechanics), among others. The expansion of research in each of these areas of physical education fit Henry's definition of an academic discipline perfectly. From this has come specialization in undergraduate as well as graduate programs. Many of these specialists contribute to the body of knowledge unique to each of these areas to enable humans to more thoroughly understand the impact of physical education and sport on their lives. These research efforts are pure or basic in nature and are not necessarily intended to be applied by practitioners to teaching and coaching.

A final impetus for the discipline movement came from dissatisfaction with the scope and direction of physical education. The contribution of physical education to general education was firmly entrenched as a philosophy, causing departments of physical education to devote themselves to preparing teachers and coaches. Upon examination, professional preparation curricula was found lacking in substance and failing to achieve its intent. The leaders of the discipline movement believed that professional physical education was a poor risk as a foundation on which physical education should develop. Consequently, these leaders added depth and breadth by developing the academic areas within physical education. The assumption that a program offering a series of courses ranging from history to exercise physiology and exposure to courses in sciences and methods, culminating in student teaching, would produce a qualified teacher was found wanting. The lack of expertise of graduates of these programs justified a move away from the traditional emphasis on teacher preparation programs to the academic discipline movement.

One direct benefit of the subsequent movement toward the discipline has been the upgrading of professional preparation programs. Inductive analyses of teaching have led to the formulation of a new discipline within physical education called **pedagogy.** Pedagogy can be defined as the science of teaching. The study of the behavior of teachers that affects the behavior of students began late in the 1960s and early 1970s. This new study of teaching has prompted a careful scrutiny of curriculum and experiences that contribute to the development of a teacher. Many research efforts in pedagogy are intending to discover how teachers can best effect student learning, a subject more thoroughly examined in chapter 8.

Although many physical educators have argued from a position of *the profession versus the discipline* of physical education, such positions need not be at odds. John Cheffers and Tom Evaul, in their book *Introduction to Physical Education: Concepts of Human Movement,* express the relationship involved: "If human movement is the discipline that incorporates a body of knowledge about human beings in motion, then physical education is a profession that applies that knowledge."[16] In the future, the best kind of professional preparation may be that which incorporates the ability to contribute to and draw from the body of knowledge unique to all areas in physical education and to be able to apply that knowledge toward the improvement of the quality of humans dynamically moving.

THE INFLUENCE OF PLAY EDUCATION

Recently, in a college classroom of physical education majors, the purpose of physical education was being discussed. Following the usual discourse on the merits of physical education for health and fitness, character development, and its unique body of knowledge, the professor asked the students for their reactions to the notion of physical education being the process that teaches people to **play.** After thinking for several minutes, one student emphatically stated that physical education serves a purpose much more important than that. This student added that "kids play naturally" and do not need physical educators to teach them. Later, through a study of *physical education as play education,* the class became aware of the significance of play in all cultures. This philosophy, recently advanced by Dr. Daryl Siedentop at Ohio State University, considers the sociological, psychological, and anthropological implications of play. Although the cultural importance of play has been recognized for some time, the relationship of play to physical education has occurred in the twentieth century as part of the philosophy of the new physical education. The concept of physical education as play education was formulated early in the 1970s and, because of its logical presentation, is rapidly gaining acceptance.

Siedentop defines physical education as "any process that increases a person's tendencies and abilities to play competitive and expressive motor activities."[17] Perhaps an interpretation of this definition would be of help in understanding this philosophy. The part referred to as "any process" means that physical education need not occur only in school settings. An interchange between a "teacher" and a "learner" resulting in a positive attraction of the learner to the activity being taught can result in the process of physical education. The enjoyment a child experiences from fly-fishing may have come from a parent who taught the child the intricacies of that activity. The peculiar action of a tennis serve may be the server's attempt to imitate the serve of another tennis player. Each example, according to Siedentop, would be included in the process called physical education.

In the definition, the phrase "that increases a person's tendencies and abilities" refers to the fact that the process is attractive: the participant is not bored learning the new activity but desires to learn as much as possible about the activity in order to perform better and thus enjoy the activity more. Since we tend to be attracted to activities in which we excel, skill learning becomes an important part of the process. Our desire to play is directly related to our ability to play. Siedentop urges physical educators in formal settings to strive to make the physical education environment one that children will desire to enter. In chapter 8, we will use the play education model as the framework for the skills needed for successful teaching.

"To play" is the theme of the definition. A rationale for playing does not have to be given by the player or by anyone attempting to explain the motivation to play; the intrinsic satisfaction experienced by those at play is sufficient for the play to be of worth. Play is simply the medium of expression and satisfaction for the player. The parameters of play include "competitive and expressive motor activities." Activities that match player against player or team against team are competitive. Sports best personify competitive motor activities. "Expressive motor activities" usually refers to dance or gymnastics, but any activity that gives vent to one's internal motivation to be a player would certainly qualify. Skydiving, hang gliding, mountain climbing, and white water canoeing are activities through which players express themselves in inherently meaningful experiences. "Motor activities" implies that **movement is dynamic** and separates these activities of play from play activities such as gambling or chess, which are largely nonphysical in nature.

According to Siedentop, education is the process by which a player moves from the level of casual participant in an activity to the expert level in the play world. Drawing from many sources, Siedentop gave structure to this process he calls the *padia-ludus continuum* (fig. 1.7). *Padia* is the left end of the continuum and connotes the carefree spontaneity of child's play. Rightward progression along the continuum adds complexity to an activity in the form of increased skill, rules, strategies, customs, training

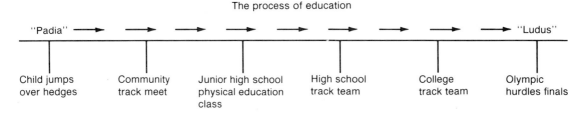

Figure 1.7 The padia-ludus continuum. The player is moved along the continuum by the process of physical education, which takes the player from a child at play to an expert at play.

methods, and sophisticated equipment, with each adding enrichment to the play experience for the player. Players whose "tendencies and abilities to play" enable them to reach the extreme right, the *ludic* end, enter the play world of the expert, the world of Olympians and Super Bowl participants. Siedentop believes that since education is the process involved, the physical educator is charged with the responsibility of advancing the player along the continuum in an educational setting, therefore, Siedentop contends, physical education has a justifiable place in the schools.

Siedentop's aim of physical education is "to increase tendencies and abilities to play competitive and expressive motor activities."[18] Figure 1.8 illustrates the direction and structure of this aim as represented by the objectives of levels 1, 2, and 3. An in-depth analysis of this aim and these objectives occurs in chapter 8.

Siedentop contends that play is important enough to be a legitimate educational concern for two reasons. "First, it must be made clear that a person's play life is as important as any other part of his life," and that it "must be understood that play is not synonymous with child's play."[19] Siedentop indicates the importance that various forms of play take in different cultures beyond the level of child's play. One need only to note the hysteria of the Super Bowl and the Pee Wee football championships, the scope of the community fun run or the New York City Marathon, or the politics of a high school booster club and the Olympic Games to determine our affinity for players at different levels of play.

In his second reason, Siedentop argues that physical education does not have to be a means to serve a greater purpose. He considers art and music to be, along with sport, simply different species of play:

> In play education we can let our subject matter be just what it is—institutionalized forms of play that are of fundamental importance to the culture within which we live and grow. Art therapy has become a legitimate method for helping mentally and emotionally disturbed people to gain skills in living, but that fact does not mean that painting should be taught in schools because it promotes psychological growth. Painting should be taught because art is a valuable part of our culture. Should the violin or French horn be taught because playing in an orchestra promotes discipline and good citizenship? No! Like art and music, physical education activities can be used to reach other goals, but this does not mean that they should be so used in school programs of physical education. And there is always the danger that in using the activities for other purposes, a person might never come to know what we know—the joy, frustration, and a wholeness of being a player.[20]

Figure 1.8 The aim and objectives of physical education as play education provide a model for teacher education.

Aim: To increase tendencies and abilities to play competitive and expressive motor activities.

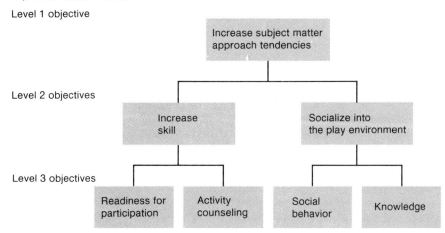

Within the scope of our recurrent theme of physical education, we can state that physical education adds the complexity that increases the meaningfulness for humans moving dynamically at play.

SUMMARY

What is physical education and what are its goals and objectives? Although physical education has historically involved the dynamic movement of human beings, the basis for this involvement has been motivated by various philosophical reasons.

Contemporary physical education is the summation of a number of diverse influences. A historical relationship has been established between physical education and the need of society for fitness, from both a militaristic and a personal standpoint. In addition, medicine and science are two fields that have significantly influenced physical education: career opportunities in physical education reflect this relationship, as does the curricula designed to prepare physical educators.

The most widely held philosophy is that the goals of education can be attained through physical education, with sports and games providing the medium for these goals to occur.

More recently, a dissatisfaction with the status of physical education has led to the discipline movement. This movement involves studies in various disciplines associated with human movement in an effort to contribute to the body of knowledge unique to physical education.

During the 1970s, Dr. Daryl Siedentop contended that physical education is play education and should enrich the play lives of individuals by giving inherently meaningful experiences to people entering play environments.

Physical education has many definitions, and its goals and objectives are great in number. Contemporary physical education is diverse and complex, owing to the influences that have given it its current dimensions. What will be important as you continue to study physical education is the development of a personal philosophy, a statement about what you believe physical education is, that will guide your involvement in physical education in the future.

STUDY QUESTIONS

1. Define the following terms.
   a. total fitness
   b. physical fitness
   c. health-related fitness
   d. skill-related fitness
2. How did the German and Swedish gymnastic systems develop in their respective countries? How did these systems happen to come to the United States?
3. What are the similarities between the objectives of physical education stated by Clark Hetherington and Charles Bucher and the five concepts of PEPI?
4. How did the relationship between the new physical education and sports and games develop?
5. What is an academic discipline? How does physical education qualify as an academic discipline?
6. Why does Dr. Daryl Siedentop object to the education through the physical philosophy of physical education?

STUDENT ACTIVITIES

1. Now that you have examined the major influences affecting modern physical education and the philosophies of physical education that have resulted, do you feel more comfortable with one or two of the philosophies than you do with the others? Write a paragraph explaining your affinity for one of these philosophies. Do your career aspirations have a bearing on the philosophy you prefer?
2. Interview three members of the faculty of your department of physical education. Ask them how they would define physical education and what they think the purpose of physical education ought to be. Do their areas of specialization coincide with their statements?
3. Refer to the four principles of education found in the section entitled The New Physical Education, under the heading The Influence of General Education. Note the portions of the principles that are italicized. Match the italicized portions with the philosophies of physical education from this chapter to which they most closely relate.

4. Refer to your high school or middle school physical education experiences. Can you list some concrete examples of how your classes or experiences on a team improved your fitness, character, and playing ability? Did you ever have to "study" for physical education? How many personal improvements on your list can you attribute to physical education classes? To athletic teams?

5. Author James A. Michener has listed thirteen problems facing contemporary sports in America. Choose one of Michener's thirteen problems and write a paragraph on how you think the problem ought to be dealt with.

NOTES

1. Charles A. Bucher, *Foundations of Physical Education* (St. Louis: C. V. Mosby Co., 1975), 106.
2. Fay Biles, "The Physical Education Public Information Project," *Journal of Health, Physical Education and Recreation,* 54 (1983).
3. Deobold Van Dalen, Elmer Mitchell, and Bruce Bennett, *A World History of Physical Education* (Englewood Cliffs, NJ: Prentice-Hall, Inc., 1953), 55.
4. Deobold Van Dalen and Bruce Bennett, *A World History of Physical Education* (Englewood Cliffs, NJ: Prentice-Hall, Inc., 1971), 47.
5. Leopold Zwarg, "Historical Review of the Development of Apparatus Exercises," *International Gymnast Technical Supplement No. 7,* 2, no. 3 (September 1981): TS–34.
6. Ibid.
7. Daryl Siedentop, *Physical Education: Introductory Analysis* (Dubuque, IA: Wm. C. Brown Pubs., 1980), 67.
8. Van Dalen and Bennett, *A World History of Physical Education,* 479–80.
9. Siedentop, *Physical Education,* 71.
10. Lord Killanin and John Rodda, *The Olympic Games* (New York: Macmillan Co., 1976), 139.
11. Ibid., 11.
12. Van Dalen and Bennett, *A World History of Physical Education,* 460.
13. Sally Magnusson, *The Flying Scotsman* (New York: Quartet Book, Inc., 1981), 24.
14. James A. Michener, *Sports in America* (New York: Random House, 1976), 16–17.
15. Siedentop, *Physical Education,* 105.
16. John Cheffers and Tom Evaul, *Introduction to Physical Education: Concepts of Human Movement* (Englewood Cliffs, NJ: Prentice-Hall, Inc., 1978), xii.
17. Siedentop, *Physical Education,* 253.
18. Ibid., 266–67.
19. Ibid., 258.
20. Ibid., 259–60.

RELATED READINGS

Abernathy, Ruth, and Maryann Waltz. "Toward a Discipline: First Steps First." *Quest,* monograph 2 (1964).

Dulles, Foster Rhea. *A History of Recreation.* New York: Appleton-Century-Crofts, 1965.

Hart, M. Marie, ed. *Sport in the Socio-Cultural Process.* Dubuque, IA: Wm. C. Brown Pubs., 1972.

Henry, Franklin. "Physical Education: An Academic Discipline." *Journal of Health, Physical Education and Recreation* (September 1964).

"Learning How to Play." *Quest,* monograph 26 (1976).

Lockhart, Aileen S., and Betty Spears, ed. *Chronicle of American Physical Education, 1855–1930.* Dubuque, IA: Wm. C. Brown Pubs., 1972.

Mandell, Richard D. *The Nazi Olympics.* New York: Macmillan Co., 1971.

Metheny, Eleanor. *Movement and Meaning.* New York: McGraw-Hill Book Co., 1968.

Siedentop, Daryl. *Physical Education: Introductory Analysis.* Dubuque, IA: Wm. C. Brown Pubs., 1980.

Spears, Betty, and Richard A. Swanson. *History of Sport and Physical Activity in the United States.* Dubuque, IA: Wm. C. Brown Pubs., 1978.

"Sport in America," *Quest,* monograph 27 (1977).

Van Dalen, Deobold and Bruce Bennett. *A World History of Physical Education.* Englewood Cliffs, NJ: Prentice-Hall, Inc., 1971.

Vanderzwaag, Harold J. *Toward a Philosophy of Sport.* Reading, MA: Addison-Wesley Publishing Co., 1972.

Social Foundations and Roles

2

Chapter outline

Student objectives

As a result of the study of this chapter, the student should be able to

1. Discuss how sports and organized recreation can legitimately be considered social institutions.
2. Identify various social factors that influence an individual to get involved in sport and physical activity.
3. Provide evidence indicating that people look to participation in sport as a means for upward social mobility and that such a view is not very realistic.
4. Discuss how attitudes have changed about women's involvement in sports and physical activity and how attitudes concerning what activities are considered "appropriate" for women have been slow to change.
5. Identify various factors related to establishing group cohesiveness and how these factors apply to the physical education teacher or coach.
6. Define *social loafing* and discuss how it relates to group behavior.
7. Discuss the characteristics of an effective leader.
8. Present several ways a physical educator can effectively educate the public concerning physical activity.
9. Identify four social situations in which physical educators can assume leadership roles.
10. Discuss how the physical educator can provide leadership in the four social settings.

Most people will agree that physical activity has an important place in our society. The evidence for this is readily apparent in a variety of social situations, such as the frequency of the use of sport or physical activity terminology in people's daily conversations. A businessperson may state that he or she is giving you a "ball park figure" to indicate an amount of money he or she will pay for something. A student may describe another student as being "way out in left field" about some issue. An associate may claim that his or her partner "played dirty pool" in a recent deal. During a period of arbitration, one side may sit back and wait for the other side's response because the "ball is in their court." Problems get "tackled"; bosses like to be known as the "quarterback" of the "team"; a person may not feel "up to par"; and a difficult decision is a "tough call."

The abundant use of sport-related metaphors in our daily speech is just one way of exemplifying the position that sport and physical activity have in society. Other indicators include the amount of time devoted to televising sports events or news; the amount of advertising that is approached from a physical activity slant; the amount of money that a family, church, or community spends on recreation or sports; and the status given to sports stars in our communities. Each of these situations attests to fact that from society's point of view, physical activity is an integral part of our daily routine and our social well-being.

While it may not be necessary to convince you, a physical education major, of the importance sport has in our society, it is important to make you aware of the implications of that status for you, the physical educator, for physical education itself, and for society in general. In this chapter we will consider some of the social factors that help establish the foundation which supports the existence of physical education and sports programs. We will also suggest some areas of social concern for physical education and sport that deserve attention.

Obviously, this chapter cannot cover every possible social issue related to physical education and sport. Our primary purpose here is to introduce you to this important element of physical education. You are preparing to enter a profession that can directly and profoundly influence society, and vice versa. It is important for you to be aware of this social influence at the outset of your professional education. Further detail and more in-depth study will be available to you as you progress through your education experiences.

It should be noted that while the term *sport* is commonly used throughout this chapter, the term implies more than just organized, competitive sports. We are considering this term in its broadest scope to include all forms of physical activity, recreational or competitive.

SOCIAL FOUNDATIONS OF PHYSICAL EDUCATION AND SPORT

A social scientist is interested in establishing the social impact of social institutions. To the social scientist, social institutions are typically defined as structures that are established and evolve "to regulate and channel the behavior of people in order to achieve collectively shared goals."[1] Organized recreation and sports are obvious candidates as social institutions since organized programs develop to provide people with a way to

Table 2.1

Kenyon's Model of Some Social Roles Associated with Primary and Secondary Modes of Sport Involvement

MODE	PRIMARY	SECONDARY				
		CONSUMER		PRODUCER		
		Direct	Indirect	Leader	Arbitrator	Entrepreneur
ROLE	Contestant	Spectator	Viewer	Instructor	Members of —sports governing body	Manufacturer
	Athlete		Listener	Coach	—rules committee	Promoter
			Reader	Manager	Referee	Wholesaler
	Player			Team leader	Umpire Scorekeeper Other officials	Retailer

Source: Loy, J. W., Jr., Kenyon, G. S., and McPherson, B. D.: *Sport, Culture, and Society*, 2d. edition. Lea and Febiger, Philadelphia, 1981.

collectively share their goals by either participating in or observing physical activity. As social institutions, organized recreation and sports command the attention of people interested in determining the influence of these institutions on the society they serve. Social scientists are clearly among those having such an interest.

In this section, we will look at recreational activity and organized sports through the eyes of the social scientist. We will do this by looking at some important social aspects of physical activity that indicate the need for physical education in society and that help provide a better understanding of the social nature of physical activity. To accomplish this, we will consider a few topics that might be investigated by a sport sociologist or sport psychologist and that are particularly significant in portraying the social basis of physical education.

Socialization into Sport

If sports have such a pervasive influence in our society, then it should be helpful to understand what seems to motivate people to get involved in sports in the first place. Because sports have a social basis, it is reasonable to expect that certain social factors are strongly related to why people participate in sport.

What Is a Participant in Sport?

Before answering this question, it will be helpful to establish what we mean by *participating* or *being involved* in sports. This has been nicely addressed by Gerald Kenyon, an internationally known sport sociologist. Kenyon considers involvement in sport as either *primary involvement* or *secondary involvement*.[2] Table 2.1 illustrates the differences in these two forms of involvement by identifying the role played by an individual in each of these modes. The primary mode of involvement is essentially active

participation in sport or physical activity. People who are joggers, members of local softball teams, and golfers, for example, are considered as being involved in sport in the **primary mode.**

The **secondary mode,** on the other hand, includes people who are either consumers or producers of sport (see table 2.1). These people are not physically active in competition or activity but are active by being spectators, coaches, officials, and sporting goods retailers, for example. They are actively involved in sport and physical activity but in a different way from those who are associated with primary involvement.

As a physical educator, you will teach people who will be involved in sport in various ways in both primary and secondary forms. You should be aware of these different types of involvement so that your views or expectations will not be improperly limited with regard to the influence you might have on those you teach.

While the consideration of why people get involved in sport or physical activity as either primary or secondary participants is an interesting and important study, we will limit ourselves to discussing primary involvement. This will effectively serve to introduce you to this issue and to exemplify an interesting form of social research. You can more fully investigate motivational issues later in your education career by taking sociology of sport or psychology of sport courses. For now, however, we can gain sufficient understanding of this social issue by directing our attention to discussing what is known about why people get involved in sport and physical activity as active, primary participants.

Table 2.2

Results of Responses to the Question, Who was Responsible for Your First Becoming Interested in Sport? (Numbers are in percent of responses)

SEX	FATHER	MOTHER	MALE FRIENDS	FEMALE FRIENDS	SCHOOL PE TEACHER OR COACH	OTHER*	TOTAL N
Male	10.9	9.8	24.7	1.5	25.1	28.0	275
Female	5.7	14.6	1.0	13.8	33.8	29.1	717
Total	71	132	75	117	311	286	992

*Includes brothers, sisters, other relatives, classroom teachers, club or recreational agency personnel, and "other." These categories were collapsed after statistical manipulations.

Source: Michael D. Smith, "Getting Involved in Sport: Sex Differences," in *International Review of Sport Sociology* 14 (1979): 93–101. © 1979 R. Oldenbourg Verlag, Munchen, West Germany. Reprinted by permission of the publisher.

Social Influences for Initial Involvement

Among the leading candidates in society that influence people to initially get involved in sport or physical activity are family, school, peers, and the community. Within each of these various social institutions, certain elements can be singled out as being especially significant in influencing sport involvement. The primary influencing social agent is typically not one individual or one social group; instead, the source of primary influence is more typically a combination of these social agents.

In a review of research on this topic, Kenyon and McPherson reported that when college athletes, Olympic athletes, and youth athletes are interviewed, it is difficult to isolate one primary influencing social agent.[3] The results of these studies are consistent in showing that while family, teachers, coaches, and friends may have varying degrees of influence for certain individuals, in general all of these interact so that their influential roles must be considered together.

To illustrate this, let us consider a study in which 1,011 athletes, ages 12 through 19 years old, from the United States and Canada, were surveyed by Michael Smith. A part of this survey included the question "Who was responsible for you first becoming interested in your sport?" The group that was surveyed consisted of athletes involved in gymnastics, badminton, basketball, field hockey, figure skating, synchronized swimming, table tennis, and modern dance.[4] Results of the response to this question are presented in table 2.2.

Interestingly, the range of individuals who were considered by these athletes to be influential also fit well into the framework of influential individuals presented by Kenyon and McPherson. Another point to note in these results is that one-fourth of the boys and one-third of the girls were influenced initially by their physical education teacher or coach.

In addition to individuals, other significant social influences have been identified. For example, the type of community in which a person lives can influence an individual to get involved in sport or physical activity. If the community regards sport participants with a high degree of stature, the incentives to get involved in sport in that community are greater than if sport participation is not regarded as giving a person any special status in the community.

If we take the question about initial involvement in sport one step farther, we might ask about the social influences related to a person's getting involved in a specific sport or activity. In this case, while the same social agents are influential, community-related factors seem to take on an added significance. Such things as the ethnic composition of the community, the rural or urban nature of the community, the availability and accessibility of facilities, the availability of a particular sport group, and the status given to a particular sport all become important factors in influencing a person's decision to get involved in a particular sport or physical activity. If you want to learn and play tennis, but your community has no tennis facilities, no one to teach you tennis, or nobody to play against, chances are you will not play tennis. Involvement in ice hockey would not be expected in an area where no ice is available. Conversely, if football players are community heroes, then there is a strong incentive for boys to go out for football rather than some other sport.

For the Physical Educator

As a physical educator, you will be a significant influential social agent for getting people involved in sport. This influence appears to be a pervasive one and should not be taken lightly. You will find that as a physical educator you will not only have a direct influence on individuals to get involved in sport, but you will also indirectly influence many by having a key role in determining what physical activities are taught or made available in a community. It is worth noting also that research concerned with identifying influences for secondary involvement in sport also indicates the significant role played by the physical education teacher.

Taken together, this research suggests that your potential influence on the students you will teach goes beyond that of helping them learn skills or develop physical fitness. Your influence as a physical educator may also make a significant contribution to a person's decision of whether or not to become involved in sport or physical activity as a primary participant—an active participant—or a secondary participant—as a consumer-spectator or producer of sport.

Social Mobility

Socioeconomic status has been identified as being related to particular types of involvement in physical activity and sport. For example, a 1974 survey by the President's Council on Physical Fitness and Sport found that male adults' involvement in exercise activities could be linked to their education and income. A summary of some of the results of this survey are presented in table 2.3. Similar relationships have been found for secondary involvement in sport. This seems especially so for the sports people choose for participation as spectators. Eitzen and Sage, for example, present this situation this way: "For the very rich, there are sports like polo, yachting, and sports-car racing. The middle classes enjoy watching or playing tennis, golf, sailing, and skiing. . . . Among the lower classes, there is a distinct preference for such sports as bowling, pool, boxing, automobile racing, arm wrestling. . . ."[5]

Table 2.3

**Male Adult Participation in Exercise Activities According
to Their Socioeconomic Status (SES)**

SES LEVEL	ACTIVITY					
	Walking	Swimming	Bicycling	Calisthenics	Jogging	Weight Training
Education						
Less than high school	36%	7%	9%	6%	3%	2%
High school	34	16	15	11	8	5
Some college	47	30	28	23	16	10
Occupation						
Manual	31%	12%	13%	8%	5%	8%
Craftsmen	27	18	15	13	6	8
Managerial	38	24	23	19	6	9
Professional	53	33	30	25	12	18
Income						
Under $5,000	46%	7%	6%	5%	4%	4%
$7,000–9,999	30	16	14	11	7	5
$15,000 or over	44	27	29	19	13	6

Source: D. Stanley Eitzen and George H. Sage, *Sociology of American Sport*, 2d ed. © 1978, 1982 Wm. C. Brown Publishers, Dubuque, IA. All rights reserved. Reprinted by permission.

We will now briefly address an issue related to the study of who participates in or spectates at various types of sport or physical activity: this is the issue of social mobility via sport. Since socioeconomic classes tend to get involved in certain types of sports, do people in these social strata see sport as a means of moving out of their present social class and into a higher level?

Is Sport Viewed as a Social Mobility Vehicle?

Research has been fairly consistent in showing that people tend to view sport as a viable means of social mobility. This seems especially evident from studies where educational aspirations are compared to athletic participation by high school students. For example, in a study comparing 254 rural and 630 urban high school students, Picou and Curry looked at various factors that might influence educational aspirations. For both groups, participating in athletics was significantly related to their desire to seek further education. Interestingly, however, this relationship was stronger for the rural students than for the urban students. When level of performance or achievement in athletics was considered in this study, the desire for higher education was even stronger. This held for both rural and urban students.[6]

In another study, 386 male high school varsity athletes, grades ten to twelve, from ten different high schools were surveyed by Lee. Of the 386 athletes, 75 (19.4%) indicated they expected to finish high school, compete in college athletics, and become a professional athlete. An additional 201 (52.1%) indicated they expected to finish high school and compete in college athletics. Thus, 71.5% of these high school athletes expected to be involved in college athletics. This study also attempted to determine what might be the source of motivation behind these expectations. Possible candidates here were such things as coaches' encouragement; race; athletic participation; parental encouragement; achievement; and socioeconomic status. For the total group, coaches' encouragement was by far the strongest predictor of athletic expectations.[7]

These results are typical of many others. Involvement in athletics seems to be a source of motivation for seeking higher education. Why this occurs is an interesting problem. Undoubtedly, one of the reasons is that athletes see college athletics as providing them an opportunity to get into professional athletics. What is important to note from these studies is that the coach plays a very significant role in these expectations of athletes.

Another approach to investigating this question of whether or not people view participation in athletics as a vehicle for upward social movement is by comparing income expectations of current athletes and nonathletes. Typical of studies reporting income expectations was one in 1968, conducted by Emil Bend. He found that active high school athletes expected to have, in fifteen years, incomes that were approximately fifty percent to fifty-five percent higher than expected by their nonathlete classmates.[8]

The expectations seem clear. Athletes generally expect to improve their social status by being involved in organized sports. Sport is commonly viewed as a viable vehicle for social mobility. While this may be a common view, how correct or valid is such a view?

The Reality of Sport as a Social Mobility Vehicle

The question of how realistic the expectations are about sport as a means of improving one's social status is a complex one. The immediate problem we confront here is the attention given by the media and society to highly paid professional athletes. The public apparently sees these multimillion dollar salaries as indicative of the general nature of incomes for professional athletes.

There are, however, more appropriate ways of viewing this situation. First, it is important to realize that the multimillion dollar athlete is the exception, not the rule. A look at the median income of professional athletes will quickly reveal this. Second, although the multimillion dollar salary is not representative of the typical professional athlete, it could be argued that even the lowest paid professional athlete tends to make more in a year than the typical American worker. While this may be so, it should also be pointed out that the average longevity of professional athletes is quite short; thus, the amount of time that a person is making the pro athlete's salary is not very long. After the athletic career is over, the athlete must find a means of livelihood by some other occupation.

Let us consider these points further by first examining how realistic the expectation is for being a college or professional athlete. A *New York Times* columnist reported in 1974 that while 200,000 high school seniors were playing high school basketball, only 5,700 college seniors were playing ball. To make matters even less encouraging, only 211 of those college seniors were drafted by the pro basketball teams that year, with only 55 actually making the final pro team selection.[9] If we calculate all of this, we find that of the high school senior players, only 2.9% were still playing ball as college seniors and only 0.0003%, or approximately 3 out of every 10,000, of high school senior basketball players realized a professional career.

Similar results were reported in a 1977 article in the *St. Louis Post-Dispatch*. In that article, it was reported that 700,000 boys were playing high school basketball, while 18,000 were playing college ball. However, only 264 players were on pro teams, 41 of whom were rookies.[10] The results are quite consistent with the *New York Times* report from 1974 in that only 0.0004%, or 4 of every 10,000, of high school basketball players ever make it in the pros. Thus, the first essential point to consider here is that the expectations typically found in high school athletes about playing college or professional athletics are not very realistic. Only a very select few ever realize either goal.

How long are the careers of those who are successful enough to make it into professional athletics? Eitzen and Sage report results of several studies that provide some evidence about this.[11] The typical professional baseball career is seven to eight years. In football and basketball, the average career is only five years. So even though the professional athlete's average salary looks and is attractive, it does not last very long for the typical pro. Even the pro athlete must be prepared for alternative forms of employment.

Social Mobility after Sports

We have considered social mobility and sports involvement by looking at educational and income expectations of high school athletes and by considering how realistic those expectations actually are. Now we shall go one step farther in our investigation of the reality of sports as a vehicle for social mobility by examining what happens to college and professional athletes after they complete their sports careers. Do they tend to achieve the socioeconomic status they aspired to as college athletes and do they maintain the status they achieved as pros?

The few studies investigating this question are not very encouraging. For example, a study by Dubois found that when comparing former college athletes and nonathletes several years after college graduation, athletic achievement or participation was not significantly related to either occupational prestige or earnings. In fact, academic average and amount of education were the strongest predictors of occupational prestige while age and number of work years were the best predictors of earnings.[12]

In a study of British former professional soccer players, Houlston found that they actually tended to experience downward occupational mobility after completing their pro careers. In this study, forty-two of fifty-two former soccer players had jobs of lesser status or income levels than what they had as pro athletes. The really unfortunate note in this study is that only fifteen of the fifty-two players pursued education while pros or sought training in an alternative occupation.[13] Similar findings have also been reported for American professional athletes.

A Realistic Conclusion

We have studied the social bases of sport and physical activity and have looked at the popular notion that sport is a viable means of achieving upward social mobility. The results of this investigation have not been very encouraging. First, we found that the view of sport as a means of social mobility is indeed a common one. We have found also that involvement in sports can help individuals achieve improved socioeconomic status. However, we have also found that there is a need to strongly qualify the reality

exhibit 2.1

Striking a balance: Some thoughts from a pro

There must be some way to assure that the 999 who try but don't make it to pro sports don't wind up on the street corners or in the unemployment lines. Unfortunately, our most widely recognized role models are athletes and entertainers—"runnin' " and "jumpin' " and "singin' " and "dancin.' " While we are sixty percent of the National Basketball Association, we are less than four percent of the doctors and lawyers. While we are about thirty-five percent of major league baseball, we are less than two percent of the engineers. While we are about forty percent of the National Football League, we are less than eleven percent of construction workers such as carpenters and bricklayers.

Our greatest heroes of the century have been athletes—Jack Johnson, Joe Louis and Muhammad Ali. Racial and economic discrimination forced us to channel our energies into athletics and entertainment. These were the ways out of the ghetto, the ways to get that Cadillac, those alligator shoes, that cashmere sport coat.

Somehow, parents must instill a desire for learning alongside the desire to be Walt Frazier. Why not start by sending black professional athletes into high schools to explain the facts of life.

I have often addressed high school audiences and my message is always the same. For every hour you spend on the athletic field, spend two in the library. Even if you make it as a pro athlete, your career will be over by the time you are 35. So you will need that diploma. . . .

I'll never forget how proud my grandmother was when I graduated from UCLA in 1966. Never mind the Davis Cup in 1968, 1969, and 1970. Never mind the Wimbledon title, Forest Hills, etc. To this day, she still doesn't know what those names mean.

What mattered to her was that of her more than thirty children and grandchildren, I was the first to be graduated from college, and a famous college at that. Somehow, that made up for all those floors she scrubbed all those years.

Source: Arthur Ashe, "Striking a Balance; Some Thoughts from a Pro," *New York Times,* 6 February 1977, sec. 5, p. 3. Copyright © 1977 by The New York Times Company. Reprinted by permission.

of such achievement. While many have expectations to achieve more education, greater income, or increased social standing through sports, very few actually realize these goals as a direct result of being involved in sports.

For you, the future professional physical educator, this discussion is especially relevant. Physical education teachers and coaches commonly are called on by their students and athletes to serve career counseling roles. It is imperative, therefore, that you be aware of the validity of the advice you provide. The numbers are not very encouraging. Few high school athletes become successful athletes in college. Even fewer achieve professional athletic careers.

Lest you come away from reading this section feeling that we are being very negative about all of this, let us remind you of this section's main point. Sport can be a viable means of achieving improved socioeconomic status. However, the chances for such achievement are very slight. The need, then, is for you to accept the responsibility to provide accurate and realistic advice; that is, while you should encourage a young athlete to try for a college scholarship or a professional career if you feel he or she has that potential, you must also encourage that individual to adequately prepare for an alternative career.

Women in Sport and Physical Activity

A social phenomenon that continues to influence sport and physical activity is the increasing number of females taking active, primary participant roles. This can be validly labelled a social phenomenon in that the impact of this increased involvement has influenced not only sport but society and social attitudes as well. Our views of what women can do, what is considered "feminine," and what roles women should play in society have been expanded as a direct result of this increased involvement.

Rather than discuss at length the social issues related to the topic of women in sport, we will try to make you aware of some of the issues that may have direct bearing on your early career development. As a professional physical educator, you will have a great deal of social influence with regard to the role of women in sport and physical activity and the attitude of society about women involved in these activities. We hope to enlighten you about some of these issues in an attempt to stimulate you to think about these issues and think about your involvement with them.

While there are several possible directions we could take this discussion, we will limit it to just two issues: social attitudes about the participation in sport and physical activity by women and sex roles as related to sport participation. We will let other courses in your curriculum address other, equally important issues.

Attitudes Concerning Women in Sport

One of the most interesting and enlightening approaches that can be taken to the study of attitudes concerning women in sport is to consider the changes in attitudes that have occurred in our history. By doing this, we can get a better perspective on our current attitudes as well as gain a better understanding of what might be expected about these attitudes in the future.

We do not have to go back very far in history to get a flavor of the discrimination directed toward the active participation in sport by women. For example, Hogan reported that in 1970–71, there were only 294,000 girls playing high school sports compared to 3,666,000 boys.[14] In other words, only 7% of the high school athletes in the United States in that year were girls. In university sports, in 1976–77, the budgets for women's athletics at the Big Ten universities ranged between 3.5% and 11.1% of the total athletic budgets for the universities.

Comparisons of numbers of participants and sizes of budgets are interesting comments on the discrimination of women in sport. However, these comparisons often lead to more arguments than they solve. Other examples of discriminative attitudes may be more revealing.

One approach is to take a look at various comments by distinguished individuals that reveal past attitudes about the participation in sport by women. For example, in 1928, Ethel Perrin, chairperson of the Executive Committee of the Women's Division of the National Amateur Athletic Federation, argued that women should be barred from participating in the Olympics. Perhaps even more surprising, surveys by Mabel Lee in 1924 showed that 60% of the women surveyed believed that physical harm could result from participation in intercollegiate sports by women.[15]

Current attitudes are definitely changing. Not only are there increased opportunities for women to participate in sport and physical activity, but attitudes about this participation are also improving (see fig. 2.2). A 1982 survey by Woodford and Scott is most revealing about current "improved" attitudes. They interviewed 353 men and women, ranging in ages from 18 to 84, in Oklahoma City, Oklahoma. Only 11.6% of these people agreed that "women ought to stick to cheerleading and leave participation in organized sports to men." Only 11.7% agreed that "participation in organized sports only takes time away from the other important things a woman ought to be doing." And only 10.8% agreed that "a woman cannot be a good athlete and a truly feminine person." However, lest we become complacent about current positive attitudes, 27.2% agreed that "women are likely to develop unsightly muscles if they exercise regularly." Interesting, though, when the responses to the "unsightly muscles" statement were considered in terms of the respondents' education levels, 37% of the no-college respondents agreed with it, while only 16.9% of college educated respondents agreed.[16] Obviously, education is a positive influence on attitudes about women in physical activities.

The discussion of why these kinds of positive attitude changes have occurred in recent years we will leave for the courses you may take in sport sociology or sport psychology. For our purposes, it is sufficient to understand that attitudes have changed and that change has been typically in a more positive acceptance of women's involvement in sport and physical activity. This does not, however, mean that no further improvement is necessary: quite the contrary. But at least most indicators suggest that the progress made in recent years has moved us a great distance.

Sex Roles Associated with Sport

Even though there seems to be greater acceptance and promotion of participation in sport and physical activity by women, there remains an interesting twist to this issue. We have been considering participation in sport in general, but what about attitudes about participation in specific sports or activities?

Discussion and research about this issue are generally labelled sex typing or sex role identification in sport; that is, are certain sports or activities labelled more "masculine" or more "feminine," or are some activities more "acceptable" than others for female participation?

One of the earliest views of this situation was given to us by Eleanor Metheny. In a book entitled *Connotations of Movement in Sport and Dance,* she presented lists of activities that society viewed as "categorically unacceptable," "generally not acceptable," and "generally acceptable" for participation by women. Sports that involved direct body contact, the application of bodily force, or the projection of the body through space were typically labelled "categorically unacceptable." These included such activities as wrestling, judo, weightlifting, high hurdles, distance races, and many team sports. "Generally not acceptable" were sports similar to but not as intense as the

Figure 2.2 Attitudes toward women's participation in sport are becoming more positive and opportunities for women's participation are increasing.

exhibit 2.2

Myths on women and athletic participation

Negative Stereotypes

A number of myths traditionally prevalent in American society have supported sport as an exclusively masculine activity.

Myth 1: Athletic Participation Masculinizes Females

One of the oldest and most persistent myths throughout sport, and a main deterrent to female sports participation, is the notion that vigorous physical activity tends to masculinize the physique and behavior of girls and women. For centuries, women of physical competence were stigmatized as "masculine" by persons who believed that women who had excellent physical ability were unfeminine. "Masculine," used in this sense, refers to body structure and behavioral patterns, not to biological considerations. Every culture defines what is appropriate and inappropriate, ideal male and female appearances and behaviors (and these vary from culture to culture), and establishes severe negative sanctions for those who do not meet cultural standards of masculinity and femininity. . . . The notion that women become masculinized from sports participation is a hoax used to enforce cultural traditions, and women are increasingly rejecting it. Indeed, in recent years some women have completely repudiated the traditional definitions that identify muscles with masculinity, and female body building is a rapidly growing sport. . . .

Myth 2: Sports Participation is Harmful to the Health of Females

Another well-entrenched myth is that sports are harmful to female health. Principally concerned with physical injury to the reproductive organs and the breasts, effects on the menstrual cycle and pregnancy, and on the psychological well-being of females, the literature of the past 100 years is laden with opinions of how competitive sports are harmful to females. At one time, physicians and other professionals made a convincing case that a pregnancy and a female's reproductive capabilities would be hampered by stressful physical activity. . . .

aforementioned sports. For example, shot put, javelin, low hurdles, and short distance races were included here. Finally, "generally acceptable" sports did not require body contact and were typically "aesthetically pleasing." Here, such activities as badminton, archery, golf, figure skating, bowling, and volleyball were included.[17]

Have these attitudes changed since the mid-60s? The results of a 1975 survey of 500 adults in Toledo, Ohio, by Snyder, Kivlin, and Spreitzer provides some insight into this question. These adults were asked to respond to several questions concerning women's participation in sports. Table 2.4 provides the results from two of their questions. Obviously, we still harbor strong attitudes about what is feminine and what sports enhance or detract from that femininity.

While physicians and educators were able to convince the public of the health dangers of sports for females, no substantial evidence supported their claims. Research, when it has been done, suggests that the health hazards were imaginary. The internal reproductive organs have a most effective shock-resistant system. The external genitalia of females is less exposed than those of men and can be easily protected with safety equipment. Strenuous competitive activities do not delay the onset or regularity of menstruation, and, indeed, females may participate in sports during menstruation. In fact, menstruating athletes have set national and world records. . . .

Myth 3: Women Are Not Interested in Sports and They Do Not Play Well Enough to Be Taken Seriously

Contempt for the female athlete is shown by the contention that women are not really interested in or not very good at sports. Those who make this point refer to the paucity of women in sports, and claim that their best performances are inferior to those of men. The list of reasons that has been used to describe or explain the differences between male and female athletes is remarkable. . . .

Perhaps Simone de Beauvoir, one of the most esteemed writers in the world, best described the absurdity of comparing male and female sports performances:

> In sports the end in view is not success independent of physical equipment; it is rather the attainment of perfection within the limitations of each physical type; the featherweight boxing champion is as much a champion as is the heavyweight; the woman skiing champion is not the inferior of the faster male champion; they belong to two different classes.

Source: D. Stanley Eitzen and George H. Sage, Sociology of American Sport, 2d ed., © 1978, 1982. Wm. C. Brown Publishers, Dubuque, IA. All Rights Reserved. Reprinted by permission.

These sex type attitudes are not limited to our adult population. A study by Herkowitz revealed that when various motor activities, depicted on slides, were shown to 360 preschool, second, fifth, eighth, and eleventh grade students and to university sophomores, definite distinctions between what were labelled boy's activities and girl's activities were made.[18]

A Word to the Physical Educator

Attitudes are difficult to change in a society. Social conditions are difficult to improve, and immediate effects are seldom seen. However, in time we may see positive benefits from efforts directed at bringing about real change. Physical educators, while only one

Table 2.4

**Perceptions of the General Population Concerning the Effects
of Athletic Participation on Female Characteristics**

QUESTIONNAIRE ITEM	PERCENT RESPONDING "YES"
In your opinion, would participation in any of the following sports enhance a girl's/woman's feminine qualities?	
Swimming	67
Tennis	57
Gymnastics	54
Softball	14
Basketball	14
Track	13
In your opinion, would participation in any of the following sports detract from a girl's/woman's feminine qualities?	
Track	30
Basketball	21
Softball	20
Gymnastics	6
Tennis	2
Swimming	2

Source: E. E. Snyder, J. E. Kivlin, and E. E. Spreitzer, "The Female Athlete: An Analysis of Objective and Subjective Role Conflict." In D. M. Landers, ed., *Psychology of Sport and Motor Behavior II.* Penn State HPER Series No. 10. The Pennsylvania State University, 1975. Permission to reprint granted.

part of society, must endorse and initiate actions to bring about changes in attitudes about women and physical activity. Through the appropriate and effective use of their influence in society, physical educators can effect positive attitude changes.

Group Dynamics and Sport

One of the many interesting social aspects of sport and physical activity is the group nature of these activities. Organized sports and recreational activities involve groups. If we look at team or individual sports and activities, such as baseball, volleyball, golf, aerobic dance classes, boating groups, or jogging groups, we see the interaction of individuals functioning together in group activity.

To the social scientist, groups are an important focus of study for gaining a better understanding of the structure and function of society. By looking at various aspects of how groups organize, what groups do to keep or lose members, and how groups achieve their goals, for example, it is possible to gain insight into social processes that can be useful in developing effective social change.

As a physical educator, this aspect of social science is especially pertinent. Whether you will be teaching physical education in an elementary or secondary school, coaching

Figure 2.3 Group dynamics are an interesting social aspect of sport and physical activity.

an athletic team, running a health and fitness club, teaching dance classes, or administering a recreation program, you will be involved with groups. Through the study of group structure and function processes, you can be better prepared to interact in these situations and, as a result, more effectively perform your duties.

In this section, we will introduce you to the study of groups by considering some of the many topics included in the study of **group dynamics** (see fig. 2.3). Group dynamics is an area of study in the social sciences devoted to advancing our knowledge about the nature of groups. This field of study is important to include in our development of the social foundation of physical education because physical education typically involves group participation. In this introduction, we will briefly discuss three areas of study within group dynamics to help establish some basic knowledge of group behavior that should be especially pertinent to you at this stage of your career.

Group Cohesiveness

The term *group cohesiveness* is generally defined as the degree to which members of a group want to be together (see fig. 2.4). In an article devoted to presenting how cohesion-related research can be done in sport, Carron stated that "cohesion can be viewed as the tendency to stick together and remain united . . . cohesion is the construct used to represent the strength of the social bond with the group."[19]

One of the difficulties in understanding cohesiveness is the problem of identifying the characteristics that would be considered indicators of the degree of cohesiveness of a group. One way to reduce this problem is by looking at tests designed to identify the amount of cohesiveness in a group. In terms of sport, a test that is gaining popularity for this purpose is the **Sport Cohesiveness Questionnaire.** To measure cohesiveness of a sports team, this questionnaire considers seven aspects about the team: (1) the degree of friendship among team members; (2) the relative power or influence among team members; (3) the sense of belonging each individual feels toward the team; (4) the value each individual gives to being a member of the team; (5) the degree of enjoyment each individual derives from being on the team; (6) the amount of teamwork each individual perceives as being present on the team; and (7) the degree of closeness each individual feels is present among team members.[20]

While these seven points represent what is involved in cohesiveness for a group, we need to know how these points relate to performance of a group and how any of these, if essential to group performance, can be developed. Let us consider some general conclusions that can be drawn from our present knowledge about cohesion and group or team performance.

Typically, research related to sports teams indicates that cohesiveness within a team will contribute to team success. However, successful team performance can also lead to increased team cohesiveness. For example, Karen Ruder and Diane Gill found that members of a winning intramural women's volleyball team rated all seven aspects of cohesiveness from the **Sports Cohesiveness Questionnaire** higher than did members of losing teams. In terms of the influence exerted by the winning or losing of a game, Ruder and Gill found that cohesion tends to increase more for winners than it decreases for losers. For the losers, the primary aspect of cohesiveness that was affected was the feeling of the degree of teamwork among team members.[21]

Results like these are fairly typical of the research investigating the relationship between team performance and team cohesiveness. On the basis of results like these, then, it would be helpful to have some information about how group cohesiveness can be increased. Obviously, it would not be very beneficial to wait until the team was successful to build cohesion, since team success is usually the desired outcome of increasing cohesion.

Figure 2.5 summarizes characteristics generally found in a cohesive group. These characteristics indicate important aspects of group behavior that should be enhanced if cohesiveness is to be increased. This applies to a broad range of situations, such as physical education classes, sports teams, and fitness groups for example, in which you might eventually find yourself. How each of these characteristics can be developed will be related to the particular situation. However, certain basic principles can be applied across many different types of group situations. For example, if a group has a specific

Figure 2.4 Group cohesiveness is demonstrated by the degree to which a team functions effectively and with little dissent.

Figure 2.5 Characteristics generally found in a cohesive group.

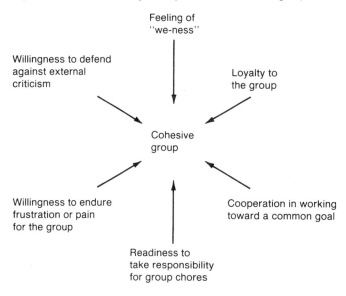

goal and each member of the group is in agreement that this goal is worthy of his or her time and effort, then it is likely that there is a high degree of cohesiveness within the group. Similarly, if all members of the group are willing to get involved and take responsibility for the work that must be done to achieve that goal, then cohesiveness will also be positively influenced.

Social Loafing

In our discussion of group cohesion, we indicated that an important factor in the level of cohesion of any group was the degree to which members of the group exerted effort in performing their individual responsibilities. One of the interesting social phenomena related to this situation is labelled **social loafing;** that is, when individuals work together on a particular task, the total effort expended is not as great as the sum of all the individual effort possible. In other words, three people working together do not exert the amount of effort equal to the total of what each person in the group could exert alone. For example, six members of a tug-of-war team do not pull on the rope with the same force that would be expected if the amount of force possible from each of the six members pulling individually was totalled. In fact, research shows that with an increase in the number of members working together comes a decrease in the proportional amount of work contributed by each member.

A recent study with cheerleaders shows results typically found in investigations of social loafing. Hardy, Prestholdt, and Hall had high school cheerleaders cheer, for five seconds alone, with one other, and with two other cheerleaders. While groups of three cheerleaders yelled louder than groups of two, and groups of two yelled louder than single cheerleaders, the individual efforts were lowest when the girls were in groups of three and next lowest in groups of two. These same effects were found when the cheerleaders performed together with cheerleaders from their own squad as well as from other squads.[22]

The interesting question here seems to be why this social loafing phenomenon occurs. One suggestion is that social loafing is motivated by individuals wanting to minimize their own energy output. When working alone, people work hard because their effort can be easily evaluated or measured. However, as the size of the group increases, the likelihood that any individual's effort can be readily evaluated decreases. The individual effort gets "lost in the crowd." The motivation to work is decreased and so the amount of effort expended diminishes as well.[23]

Most people do not seem to be consciously aware of actually decreasing their individual effort when in a group. Thus, the social loafing phenomenon does not appear to be the result of devious behavior by group members. Although social scientists are continuing their attempts to determine the cause for social loafing, it is sufficient for our purposes to simply be aware of this phenomenon. Physical educators are regularly involved in situations where teamwork is critical; thus, as a physical educator, your knowledge of the social loafing phenomenon should provide you with some useful insights into what you might expect in situations requiring teamwork.

Leadership

A consistent characteristic of group behavior is that if a leader is not designated for a group, or if a designated one is weak and ineffective, a leader will generally emerge from the group. This does not mean that the group will then automatically be successful. Group success is dependent on the interaction of many variables and cannot be attributed to a single factor. However, that a leader will likely emerge is an indication of how important leadership is for any group.

As a physical educator, you will automatically, by the very nature of your job, be in a group leadership position. How effective you are in that capacity is dependent on several things. In this section, we will consider a few of the factors related to effective leadership. This consideration is important for you at this stage of your career development because it can help you begin to effectively develop your own leadership skills.

While many efforts have been directed toward identifying the personality characteristics of an effective leader, these efforts have provided little useful information. The adage "leaders are born, not made" is only partly correct. Many social scientists, in fact, would argue that only a very small part of that adage is correct. The effective leader seems to be one who possesses the appropriate personal characteristics for the conditions of the situation in which he or she must lead. It is very possible that a person who is a successful leader in one situation will be a failure as a leader in another situation.

This view of the need to match the appropriate personal characteristics of a leader with the situation takes away the importance sometimes given to the question of what leadership type is best. Traditionally, leadership types fall into these three categories: **autocratic,** where the leader exercises totalitarian, autonomous control; **democratic,** where the leader directs according to the wish of the majority of group members; and **laissez-faire,** where the leader acts more like a guide who keeps the group on course.

Arguments about which of these or other leadership types is best seem irrelevant when we consider that different situations demand different leadership styles.

With regard to sports, it has been suggested that players performing as individuals need more direct support from the coach than do players performing as a team.[24] In other words, team sport groups seem to require a coach or leader who can be considered as **task-oriented** as opposed to **people-oriented,** while the opposite may be the case for the coach of an individual sport team.

This distinction of task-oriented and people-oriented leaders comes from the theoretical work by Fred Fiedler. Fiedler suggested that, given different situations, the leader must adapt his or her leadership to focusing on the task or on the group members. Task-oriented leadership is concerned more with structuring conditions to accomplish a particular goal. The interpersonal feelings among group members or the feelings of members toward the leader are of secondary concern here. For the people-oriented style, interpersonal feelings are of primary concern while the achievement of the goal by the group is secondary. Accordingly, then, the demands of the situation should dictate the leadership style that should be most effective.[25]

Support for these suggestions was provided in a study by Anne Marie Bird. She studied college volleyball teams from highly competitive intercollegiate women's volleyball divisions. Teams with coaches who were more task-oriented typically had more successful seasons than those with coaches who were people-oriented.[26]

The conclusion that one leadership style is best for all situations simply does not have support. Effective leaders possess characteristics that enable them to assess the needs of the group members and to determine how the group should function to achieve the group goal. Further, the effective leaders are able to establish appropriate priorities for group members as well as for themselves. It is apparent, then, that effective leaders learn how to lead in the situation in which they find themselves.

SOCIAL ROLES OF PHYSICAL EDUCATORS

In the first section of this chapter, we considered various aspects of physical education that provide evidence for the social basis of physical education. In our discussion of that evidence we established a substantial social foundation on which physical education can be built. Now we will develop an essential part of the physical education structure by considering one of the important implications of our social foundation; that is, what social roles should the physical educator be prepared to play in society?

While a wide range of roles could be identified, we will limit our discussion to two. These have been singled out because of their immediate significance to society and because of their importance in your early training to be a physical educator. We will label these roles **educating** and **leading.** Thus, two essential roles of physical educator in society are to *educate people* in terms of the essentials about physical activity and to *provide professional leadership* for society in physical activity-related programs.

These roles may be carried out within the context of the physical educator's professional position or in a setting not directly related to that job. Where these roles are performed is not the critical issue here. The critical point is that these roles should be performed by physical educators since they are trained professionals capable of carrying out such tasks. If physical educators fail to perform these functions, you can be assured that others will. Society has historically sought out people to take on these educating and leadership roles. Too often, however, those who have accepted the roles have not been properly or adequately trained to perform such responsibilities.

Educating People

It may seem somewhat strange to you that we should single out educating people as one of the social roles of the physical educator, especially since an implicit part of any job you take will involve teaching. In this section, we want to emphasize some important concerns that need to be considered and reinforced. While you are well aware that teaching will be an essential part of your professional work, you may not be as aware of the exact scope of your responsibilities as an educator.

Whom Should You Educate?

When we say that an essential part of your professional responsibility to society is educating people, the first question is who in society should receive this education. One way to look at this question is to consider the various types of jobs you could take as a physical educator. As you do this, think about the different types of people with whom you could come into contact. Some could be children, others adults. You might work in an economically depressed or disadvantaged area or in a wealthy area. You may be in a rural environment or an urban one. Regardless of where you work or who you teach, as a physical educator you will be educating people.

As a physical educator, you will be viewed as an "expert" in a variety of issues related to physical activity. Whether or not you have the expertise will not keep people from looking to you as one who can provide some wisdom on related matters. One responsibility here, then, is to not go beyond your own boundaries of knowledge when asked to provide information. On the other hand, do not be hesitant to offer your professional advice when you have supportable advice to give. If you want to help eliminate any "dumb jock" attitudes about physical educators, this is certainly one way to do it. However, professional advice-giving carries with it a responsibility to be knowledgeable about issues related to your profession.

The people you will educate are not limited to those you teach, coach, or work with every day. These people will include the many with whom you interact socially as well. You will be requested to provide a wide range of people with information that will increase their own understanding about performing physical activities. Our admonition to you, then, is to prepare yourself to be a worthy representative of both your professional self and your profession.

What Education Should You Provide?

In an article concerned with the roles of physical education, Linda Bain argues that "the goal of physical education is to socialize the student into the role of the participant"; that is, it is important that physical education provide students with "the opportunity to learn the skills, strategy, customs, expectations, and folklore surrounding specific movement activities which he/she finds enjoyable."[27]

As you will see emphasized in various parts of this book, physical education offers subject matter that is unique to the rest of the school curriculum. We, then, are responsible for providing education about the need for, benefits of, and procedures for learning movement activities. As a professional physical educator, you will have the background to provide this type of education to people with whom you have contact, and they will benefit from your expertise.

In nonschool settings, you will find that people will ask you endless questions. "What are some good exercises to do to get into shape?" "How can I improve my golf game?" "What kind of sports activity is best for me?" "How can I know if I'm in shape?" "How can I play my best in a game?" All the questions have in common a searching for information about physical activity. In fulfilling the role of a physical educator, you are saying that you are a professional with regard to physical activity and that you have more information about questions like these than does the layperson.

Unfortunately, a lot of incorrect information is available about physical activity. As people continue to get involved in various forms of sport and physical activities, the desire for information about matters related to that involvement will also increase. There will always be a lot of educating to do.

Providing Professional Leadership

The importance of physical activity continues to grow in our society. One line of evidence for this comes from research that shows that *leisure satisfaction* has become a more significant contributor than *work satisfaction* to *life satisfaction*. Table 2.5, from a study by Spreitzer and Snyder, provides data supporting this trend. In other words, there is a growing tendency in this country for people to rank what they do in their leisure time as more important to their feeling of satisfaction with life than what they do for a job.

This movement away from the dominance of the work ethic in what we consider important in our lives has tremendous implications for the physical educator. Since much of leisure time is filled with physical activity, the demands for people to assume leadership roles to provide for those needs will increase. This brings us to an interesting point with regard to physical educators. What level of involvement will physical educators take in these roles? Will physical educators sit back and let others provide the necessary leadership or will they assume a level of direct responsibility as trained professionals concerned about the physical well-being of society? The latter should be the more common response.

In this section we will provide some direction here. What are some leadership roles that physical educators can assume? How can these roles be carried out? While we will not provide an exhaustive list of possible roles, we will focus on a few that are representative of the kinds of leadership responsibilities the physical educator can readily assume.

Table 2.5
Attitudes Toward Work and Leisure as Related to Adult Participation in Sports

PERCENTAGE AGREEING	RUNNERS (N = 316)	RACQUETBALL (N = 201)	GENERAL POPULATION (N = 112)
"I find that my lesiure activities are more satisfying to me than my work."	61%	62%	48%
"My personal identity is realized more in my work than in my leisure activities."	38%	42%	61%
"If I were to describe myself, you would get a better understanding of me through my leisure activities than through my work."	48%	48%	26%

Source: Elmer Spreitzer and Eldon E. Snyder, "Correlates of Participation in Adult Recreational Sports." In *Journal of Leisure Research* 15: 27–38. © 1983 *Journal of Leisure Research*. Reprinted by permission.

Health and Fitness Programs

A snowballing industry in this country is the commercial health and fitness business. This is evident by a quick survey of your own community. The emergence of health spas, fitness centers, aerobic dance classes, sports centers, and the like has been overwhelming. While this boom is good news to the physical educator in that it reflects a concern about the physical condition of our society, there is another side of this phenomena that gives some cause for concern. This concern stems from the general lack of professional training in physical education-related areas by many who are administering or directing these programs. Too often these businesses are established on the basis of a profit motive rather than on a motive of genuine concern about the health and well-being of the public.

Physical educators can play a significant role here. While they cannot lead a crusade to close down poorly run businesses, they can help to make certain that the public is being educated with regard to health and fitness-related matters. An informed public has always been an excellent source for eliminating the imposter. This informing can occur in various ways. Physical education teachers can provide this type of information in classes they teach. Trained fitness directors can provide this information to their clients or students. College and university teachers can make sure that all physical education majors and minors receive appropriate instruction in health and fitness matters.

Each professional physical educator can take a leadership role in the health and fitness business. Some will take a direct role by being the instructors or owners in these businesses. Others will take more indirect roles by ensuring that there is an informed public that can distinguish legitimate, worthwhile programs from those that are not.

Youth Sports Programs

Recent estimates suggest that as many as 17 million children between the ages of 6 and 16 are participating in nonschool sports programs. Any study of the history of participation in these programs reveals an unfortunate tale of physical education's role.

To make a long story short, that role can be labelled a hands-off approach. In fact, the physical education profession went on record in the 1930s condemning youth sports programs.[28]

An excellent series of reasons why physical education's attitude must change concerning the existence of youth sports programs has been provided by Daniel Gould. First, these programs are more popular than ever and they are growing. Second, involvement by children in these programs has important implications for the development of physical skills and attitudes. Third, children are intensely involved in these programs.[29] For example, sports appear to be one of the most valued activities for adolescents.[30] Finally, it is becoming increasingly evident that the effects of nonschool sports on children are not inherently good or bad.

This line of reasoning suggests that we can no longer sit back and argue whether or not these programs should exist. While this may be interesting from a philosophical perspective, it will have little, if any, impact on the existence of these programs. The need, then, is for physical educators to provide leadership in youth sports to ensure that the programs in operation are run with the best interests of the participants, not the adults, in mind.

To accomplish this leadership the physical educator can get involved in at least five possible ways, according to Gould.[31] First, physical educators can get directly involved as volunteer coaches or officials. Second, they can serve as league or agency administrators. Third, they can provide training for volunteer coaches. Fourth, physical educators can get involved as researchers of youth sport issues. Finally, teachers or coaches can be good role models for volunteer coaches.

Youth sports provide an excellent opportunity for the physical educator to apply his or her professional expertise in a leadership capacity. This can only happen by getting involved. We can no longer wash our hands of the problems; we must do something about them.

Programs for the Aged

As the life expectancy of our population increases, there will be increasing demands to take care of the needs of our senior citizens. One of these needs is physical activity. Evidence of this need was recently reported in a survey of 565 Floridians over the age of 55, conducted by Ragheb and Griffith. Results of that survey indicated that leisure satisfaction and leisure participation were highly related to their life satisfaction. In fact, participation in leisure activities was more highly related to life satisfaction than any other factor.[32]

Evidence like this supports the need to provide older persons in our society with leisure opportunities and experiences (see fig. 2.6a). The question, however, that must be addressed is who will take the leadership responsibilities necessary to provide for these needs? We would like to argue that one source of that leadership must and can come from the ranks of physical educators. This leadership can be provided by college and university professors, who can teach courses that offer information about appropriate physical activities for older persons.[33] Physical education majors and minors can also get involved by considering work with senior citizens as a potential area for their professional career. All in all, leadership in this critical social need can be provided by physical educators.

Figure 2.6 Physical activity represents a need of our senior citizens and the handicapped.

a

b

exhibit 2.3

Children's bill of rights in youth sports

1. Right of the opportunity to participate in sports regardless of ability level
2. Right to participate at a level that is commensurate with each child's developmental level
3. Right to have qualified adult leadership
4. Right to participate in safe and healthy environments
5. Right of each child to share in the leadership and decision making of their sport participation
6. Right to play as a child and not as an adult
7. Right to proper preparation for participation in the sport
8. Right to an equal opportunity to strive for success
9. Right to be trained with dignity by all involved
10. Right to have fun through sport

Source: Thomas, J. R., ed., *Youth Sports Guide.* © 1977 by The American Alliance for Health, Physical Education and Dance. Reprinted by permission.

Programs for the Handicapped

Perhaps one of the most critical pieces of legislation related to physical education and the handicapped child was enacted in 1975 in the form of PL 94–142, the Education For All Handicapped Children Act. In this law, physical education was singled out from all curriculum areas as a required part of all special education programs. Other laws have been passed which mandate equal opportunities for handicapped children to participate in physical education, recreation, intramurals, and athletics.

One effect of these laws has been that mildly handicapped students have been mainstreamed into regular physical education classes in the public schools. Another effect has been to increase the need for effective adapted physical education classes for the moderately and severely handicapped (see fig. 2.6b). Both of these effects have had an impact on physical education. Not only has there been a need for changes in curricula and facilities, but there has also been a similar need for changes in the training and attitudes of physical education teachers.

Here, then, is a social issue where the need for leadership in physical education is clear: this need has been mandated by both federal and state laws. What can *you* do? If you intend to become a physical education teacher in the public schools, be sure to include experiences in your curriculum for working with mainstreamed, handicapped children. You can even go a step farther by orienting your teacher preparation program to certify you to become an adapted physical education teacher. The important point is, that as a physical educator, you must take a leadership role in ensuring that our handicapped citizens receive adequate opportunities to experience the benefits of sport and physical activity.

SUMMARY

In this chapter, you have been introduced to several topics that, when taken together, provide evidence for the social foundation of physical education and the roles that can be played by the physical educator in society. Physical education is essential to society because it provides opportunity and training in activities designed to improve the quality of life of its citizens. As an integral part of the social system, then, physical education can be looked at in terms of its social nature. This is what we have done in this chapter. We examined this social nature by considering four social issues important to our understanding of physical education and its place in the social system. First, we investigated the social factors that are related to getting people involved in physical activity and sport. The most significant among these are family, peers, school, and the community. Second, we looked at how people view sport and physical activity as a potential vehicle for upward social mobility. We found that while it is possible to increase one's social status through sport, the likelihood of realizing such a goal is very small. Third, we considered society's view of women in sport and physical activity. We saw that attitudes about women's involvement have changed in a more positive direction over the years, while attitudes about what activities were appropriate have been slow to change. Finally, we viewed sport and physical education as a means of group interaction and as a source to help us better understand how society functions when people must work together for a common goal. We did this by discussing three aspects of the study of group dynamics: group cohesiveness, social loafing, and leadership.

In our section on the social roles that can be performed by the physical educator, we limited our discussion to two general categories: educating people and providing leadership. As professional physical educators, we have a responsibility to society to use our training and experience to educate society in matters related to physical activity. Similarly, we have a responsibility to be the leaders in society in areas related to our profession. We discussed some examples of these areas, namely, health and fitness programs, youth sports programs, activity programs for senior citizens, and physical education for the handicapped.

STUDY QUESTIONS

1. What are some of the influences that motivate people to get involved in sports for the first time?
2. What are some of the reasons for stating that it is unrealistic to depend on sports as a means for achieving upward social mobility?
3. What evidence can be provided that society's attitudes about women in sports are changing?
4. What are three areas of study in group dynamics related to sport and physical activity? How do each of these provide information that can be useful for sports teams or physical education classes?
5. In what ways can physical educators educate the public?
6. What are some ways in which physical educators can take effective leadership roles in society?

STUDENT ACTIVITIES

1. Organize two debate teams to debate the resolution "Women's teams should not be granted equal status with men's teams in college sports."
2. Interview several different coaches concerning how they try to establish cohesiveness, or group togetherness, on their teams. Present a report that compares and contrasts these approaches.
3. Have a "wheelchair day" for your class where members of the class must spend an entire day in a wheelchair. Present individual reports on what your experiences were and how your awareness of needs of wheelchair-bound individuals was affected.
4. Discuss in a group the pros and cons of organized youth sports. Take your lists and visit several youth sports games. Write a report on how many of the pros and cons from your lists were observed in these games.

NOTES

1. Eldon E. Snyder and Elmer Spreitzer, *Social Awareness of Sports* (Englewood Cliffs, NJ: Prentice-Hall, Inc., 1978), 40.
2. Gerald Kenyon, "Sport Involvement: A Conceptual Go and Some Consequences Thereof," in *Sport, Culture, and Society,* 2d ed., eds. John Loy, Gerald Kenyon, and Barry McPherson (Reading, MA: Addison-Wesley, 1981), 33–38.
3. Gerald Kenyon and Barry McPherson, "Becoming Involved in Physical Activity and Sport," in *Sport, Culture, and Society,* 2d ed., eds. John Loy, Gerald Kenyon, and Barry McPherson (Reading, MA: Addison-Wesley, 1981), 217–37.
4. Michael D. Smith, "Getting Involved in Sport: Sex Differences," *International Review of Sport Sociology* 14 (1979): 93–101.
5. D. Stanley Eitzen and George H. Sage, *Sociology of American Sport,* 2d ed. (Dubuque, IA: Wm. C. Brown Publishers, 1982), 269.
6. J. Steven Picou and Evans Curry, "Residence and the Athletic Participation Educational Aspiration Hypothesis," *Social Sciences Quarterly* (December 1974): 768–76.
7. Courtland Lee, "An Investigation of the Athletic Career Expectations of High School Student Athletes," *The Personnel and Guidance Journal* (May 1983): 544–47.
8. Emil Bend, *The Impact of Athletic Participation on Academic and Career Aspirations and Achievement* (Pittsburgh: American Institutes of Research, 1968).
9. Steve Cady, "Sports Recruiting: For Every Winner, A Hundred Losers," *New York Times,* 13 March 1974, p. 46C.
10. Joe Lapointe, "Pro Sport: Is It the Best Way to Escape the Ghetto?" *St. Louis Post-Dispatch,* 7 June 1977, p. 13A.
11. Eitzen and Sage, *Sociology of American Sport,* 2d ed., 269.
12. Paul E. Dubois, "The Occupational Attainment of Former College Athletes: A Comparative Study," *International Review of Sport Sociology* 15 (1980): 93–107.
13. David R. Houlston, "The Occupational Mobility of Professional Athletes," *International Review of Sport Sociology* 17 (1982): 15–28.

14. Candace L. Hogan, "Title IX: From Here to Equality," in *Sport in Contemporary Society: An Anthology,* ed. D. Stanley Eitzen (New York: St. Martin's Press, 1979), 420–24.

15. Eitzen and Sage, *Sociology of American Sport,* 2d ed., 269.

16. Robert C. Woodford and Wilbur J. Scott, "Attitudes Toward the Participation of Women in Intercollegiate Sports: Evidence from a Metropolitan Area Survey," in *Studies in Sociology of Sport,* eds. Aidan O. Dunleavy, Andrew W. Miracle, and C. Roger Rees (Ft. Worth, TX: Texas Christian University Press, 1982), 203–19.

17. Eleanor Metheny, *Connotations of Movement in Sport and Dance* (Dubuque, IA: Wm. C. Brown Publishers, 1965).

18. Jacqueline Herkowitz, "Sex Role Expectations and Motor Behavior of the Young Child," in *Motor Development: Issues and Applications,* ed. Marcella V. Ridenour (Princeton, NJ: Princeton Book Company, 1978), 83–98.

19. Albert V. Carron, "Cohesiveness in Sport Groups: Interpretations and Considerations," *Journal of Sport Psychology* 4 (1982): 124.

20. Rainer Martens and James A. Peterson, "Group Cohesiveness as a Success and Member Satisfaction in Team Performance," *International Review of Sport Sociology* 6 (1971): 49–61.

21. M. Karen Ruder and Diane L. Gill, "Immediate Effects of Win-Loss on Perceptions of Cohesion in Intramural and Intercollegiate Volleyball Teams," *Journal of Sport Psychology* 4 (1982): 227–34.

22. Charles J. Hardy, Perry H. Prestholdt, and Evelyn G. Hall, "I Can't Let the Team Down . . . Or Can I? An Example of Social Loafing" (Paper presented at the annual conference of the North American Society for the Psychology of Sport and Physical Activity at the University of Maryland, May 1982).

23. Stephy G. Harkins, Bibb Latane, and Kipling Williams, "Social Loafing: Allocating Effort or Taking It Easy?" *Journal of Experimental Social Psychology* 16 (1980): 457–65.

24. Bryant J. Cratty, *Psychology in Contemporary Sport* (Englewood Cliffs, NJ: Prentice-Hall, Inc., 1973).

25. Fred E. Fiedler, *A Theory of Leadership Effectiveness* (New York: McGraw-Hill, Inc., 1967).

26. Anne Marie Bird, "Leadership and Cohesion Within Successful and Unsuccessful Teams: Perceptions of Coaches and Players," in *Psychology of Motor Behavior and Sport* 2, eds. Robert W. Christina and Daniel M. Landers (Champaign, IL: Human Kinetics Publishers, 1976): 176–82.

27. Linda Bain, "Socialization into the Role of Participant: Physical Education's Ultimate Goal," *Journal of Physical Education and Recreation* 51 (September 1980): 48.

28. Jack W. Berryman, "The Rise of Highly Organized Sports for Preadolescent Boys," in *Children in Sport,* 2d ed., eds. Richard A. Magill, Michael J. Ash, and Frank Smoll (Champaign, IL: Human Kinetics Publishers, 1982), 2–15.

29. Daniel Gould, "The Role of the Physical Educator in Nonschool Youth Sports," *The Physical Educator* 38 (1981): 99–104.

30. Deborah Feltz, "Athletics and the Status System of Female Adolescents," *Review of Sport and Leisure* 3 (1978): 98–108.

31. Gould, "Role of the Physical Educator," 99–104.

32. M. G. Ragheb and C. A. Griffith, "The Contribution of Leisure Participation and Leisure Satisfaction of Older Persons," *Journal of Leisure Research* 14 (1982): 295–306.

33. William F. Price and Lesley B. Lyon, "Fitness Programs for the Aged," *Journal of Physical Education, Recreation and Dance* 54 (February 1983): 42–44.

RELATED READINGS

Aufsesser, Peter M. "Adapted Physical Education: A Look Back, A Look Ahead." *Journal of Physical Education, Recreation and Dance* 52 (June 1981): 28–31.

Cleaver, Vicki, and Henry Eisenhart. "Stress Reduction Through Effective Use of Leisure." *Journal of Physical Education, Recreation and Dance* 53 (October 1982): 18–21.

Duquin, Mary E. "The Importance of Sport in Building Women's Potential." *Journal of Physical Education, Recreation and Dance* 53 (March 1982): 18–21.

Greendorfer, Susan L. "A Challenge for Sociocultural Sport Studies." *Journal of Physical Education, Recreation and Dance* 54 (March 1983): 18–20.

Ibrahim, Hilmi. "Immigrants and Leisure." *Journal of Physical Education, Recreation and Dance* 52 (October 1981): 36–37.

Wakat, Diane, and Sarah Odom. "The Older Woman: Increased Psychosocial Benefits from Physical Activity." *Journal of Physical Education, Recreation and Dance* 53 (March 1982): 34–35.

Scientific Foundations

3

Chapter Outline

Establishing the Scientific Foundation
    Identifying the Components of the
      Foundation
    The Value of Studying the Sciences
    The Scientific Method of Inquiry
The Scientific Disciplines
    Scientific Disciplines Outside Physical
      Education

Scientific Disciplines Within Physical
    Education
Summary
Study Questions
Student Activities
Notes
Related Readings

Student Objectives

As a result of the study of this chapter, the student should be able to

1. Define the term *scientific foundation* and indicate how it is related to physical education.
2. Explain why having a knowledge of the disciplines in the scientific foundation is of value to the physical educator.
3. Explain what is meant by the *scientific method of inquiry.*
4. List the scientific disciplines that are included in the scientific foundation of physical education.
5. Differentiate the scientific disciplines that are outside and within physical education.
6. Give a brief description of some of the topics typically contained in each of the scientific disciplines within physical education.
7. Give examples in physical education activity situations that indicate how each of the scientific disciplines within physical education provide essential information to the physical educator.

As you are undoubtedly aware by now, physical education is a very complex area of study. Part of the reason for this complexity is the nature of physical education itself. Rather than being a unique scientific discipline (that is, an area of study that has a distinct body of knowledge), physical education owes much of its body of knowledge to information provided from a wide range of disciplines. For example, in physical education we know that if people practice hitting a golf ball often enough and under appropriate instruction and practice conditions, they can hit a golf ball off a tee, from the rough, from the fairway, out of a sandtrap, from behind a tree, and so on. While we might consider this kind of knowledge as unique to physical education, since it involves the performance of a physical activity, the roots of this knowledge are actually in a variety of disciplines. For example, knowledge gained from such areas of study as anatomy, physiology, and physics all interact to provide the basis for our understanding of what is involved in an efficient and effective golf swing. From the study of psychology, especially the study of learning, we are provided a basis for understanding what the instruction and practice conditions must be to achieve the desired result of being able to hit the ball from a variety of surfaces.

ESTABLISHING THE SCIENTIFIC FOUNDATION

The preceding discussion pointed out that what we know in physical education is heavily based on several scientific disciplines. These disciplines provide us with valuable information about the people with whom we, as physical educators, must regularly interact. For example, we can discover information about specific physiological or psychological characteristics of these individuals. This could include information such as which muscles act in causing a particular movement, how muscles work, what causes muscles to act, what influence exercise or work has on the muscles of the heart, what happens when a person learns, and how a person remembers what he or she is supposed to do during a movement. Additionally, these disciplines also provide us with information about how these people interact with the conditions or situations in which they must practice and perform. Here we can discover such things as the best ways to provide information to help these people learn, how practicing or performing in front of other people will influence the performance, how this person will act when interacting in a group activity as compared to doing something alone, what influence this person's involvement in sports or recreational activities will have on how this person moves in society, and the like. All of this useful information helps physical educators design and provide effective instruction.

These examples are indicative of the great debt physical education owes to the knowledge available in a variety of scientific disciplines. While these examples have seemingly suggested that scientific disciplines exist only outside of physical education, it is important to note that physical education has within it some scientific areas of study. Such areas as exercise physiology, biomechanics, and motor learning, while not exclusively belonging to physical education, provide the basis for courses that are typically found only in physical education-related curricula. These courses are representative of an essential scientific foundation within physical education itself. These disciplines are intimately related to their parent disciplines, which are found outside of physical education, while remaining closely allied with physical education by focusing on problems unique to human movement and sport.

This alliance between the physical education scientific disciplines and their parent disciplines can be illustrated with some examples. **Physiologists** have provided important basic information about the function of the cardiorespiratory system. In physical education, **exercise physiologists** use that information as they seek to determine the effect of exercise or training on that important system. **Physicists** have given us the basic laws of motion and, in physical education, the study of **biomechanics** relates these laws to better understanding skilled performance in sports. **Psychologists** have given us some basic knowledge about what influences our ability to remember. In physical education, this knowledge has been applied to learning movement skills by researchers in **motor learning.** In these and other ways, physical education interacts with a variety of other scientific disciplines to establish a solid base on which to operate.

Identifying the Components of the Foundation

The logical question that arises from our discussion so far is, what are the scientific disciplines that form an important foundation for physical education? In this chapter, we will categorize these disciplines into two general groups: those typically *within physical education* and those typically *outside physical education.* This arrangement will help keep in perspective where the various disciplines fit in the scientific foundation of physical education. Within each grouping, specific scientific disciplines can be identified. These are presented in figure 3.1, along with a hierarchical structure that exists among these groupings and the principles and practices of physical education. From this structure, you can see how the scientific disciplines outside physical education form a foundation for the scientific areas of study within physical education, and together, they form a solid foundation for the principles and practices of physical education.

Within physical education, the scientific disciplines are kinesiology and biomechanics, exercise physiology, motor learning and motor control, motor development, sport psychology, and sport sociology. Each of these is related to one or more of the scientific disciplines labelled as being outside physical education. These are biology, anatomy, physiology, mathematics, chemistry, physics, psychology, and sociology. While it could be argued that there are others or that these labels are too broad, the discussion of these disciplines will adequately serve our needs to establish a basic awareness and understanding of the scientific roots of physical education. As depicted in figure 3.1, these disciplines provide the essential knowledge structure on which the scientific areas within physical education base their research and knowledge and on which physical education methods and practices ultimately should be based.

The Value of Studying the Sciences

Before more closely examining the various scientific disciplines, let us consider the value of studying these disciplines for physical educators. We would certainly expect that there is merit in such study or we would not see so many courses related to these disciplines as required parts of most physical education curricula. While there may be

Figure 3.1 Hierarchy of the scientific disciplines related to the principles and practices of physical education.

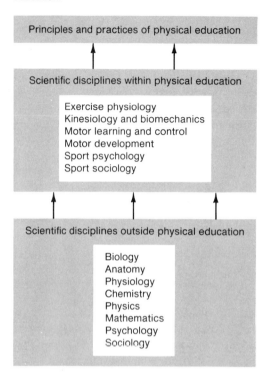

many reasons for studying these scientific areas, we will focus on only two. These should effectively make you aware of some of the benefits you will gain from studying these disciplines.

First, physical educators should know *why* they do certain things as they teach or coach. Consider, for example, why you would choose to teach shooting a jump shot in basketball in a certain way, or why you would have your class follow a specific practice routine for learning to dribble a basketball, or why you might feel so confident that a certain technique for shooting free throws is better than any other technique. Teachers with a good foundation in the sciences have a confidence and assurance that their teaching practices can be readily justified and substantiated as effective. These individuals are secure in the knowledge that while there are other methods that could be used, the method they employ is best for their students and situation. The reason for using a particular teaching method is more than simply, "I do it this way because I was taught this way," or "That's the way my coach did it," or "I read in a book that this method worked for an Olympic champion."

Second, consider the following problem. What happens if the way you have been teaching something for a long time suddenly fails to give you the usual results with a particular class? You have relied on this method because it was recommended by your teacher and, until now, it has worked very well for you. What do you try next? How do you go about developing an alternative strategy? The critical point here is that the physical educator who has a solid foundation in the scientific disciplines has developed a broad range of principles that can serve as the basis for developing an effective approach to handle this new situation. Here, then, is an important benefit for physical educators who are firmly grounded in the scientific disciplines: there is a wealth of information from which to draw. As a result, these physical educators have the capability to be more than technicians who can only mimic what they have been taught. You can be a skilled professional who can readily adapt, with confidence, to new situations as they arise.

The Scientific Method of Inquiry

One of the things common to all of the scientific disciplines you will study in this chapter is the approach taken to gathering information. This approach has been labelled the **scientific method of inquiry.** It is based on the need for objective observation of what is occurring in the world (see fig. 3.2). Objective information is information that is not based on what several people think or feel; it is information based on evidence that, when considered by several different people, will lead each of them to similar conclusions. The point is that information that describes and explains our world cannot be based only on an individual observer's opinion. While the scientist is indeed an observer, he or she follows as closely as possible the scientific method of inquiry to help ensure that the observations made would be made by anyone who was in the same situation and followed similar procedures.

In the scientific method, a primary means of observation, or gathering information, is the **experiment.** The essential purpose of an experiment is to provide a controlled and objective method for obtaining reliable information. There are several ways in which this can be done. One way is for the scientist to simply describe the actions while they naturally occur. For example, the sport psychologist may wish to observe how the anxiety levels of athletes before a game relate to performance during the game. This information could objectively be obtained by administering a test of anxiety to the players before the game and then comparing that information to how the players actually performed in the game. As such, the sport psychologist is observing behavior as it naturally occurs in a particular setting.

If the sport psychologist was interested in the effect of a relaxation training session on some of the players, then he or she would observe these players after the relaxation training session and compare players' performances in games not preceded by relaxation training. Using this approach, the sport psychologist has added a new dimension to the information gathering process. A comparison was made between a group of people who received relaxation training and those who did not. Here, rather than simply observing behavior as it naturally occurred, the researcher actually manipulated something in the situation and then observed its influence.

Experiments can be carried out in almost any setting. Laboratories generally offer the greatest amount of control for the scientist. Natural settings, such as classrooms, playgrounds, and athletic events, generally permit less control but allow for more practical kinds of observations. Experiments can be concerned with basic, or theoretical, problems that have no direct or immediate relevance to practical situations: because

Figure 3.2 The scientific method of inquiry is based on objective observation.

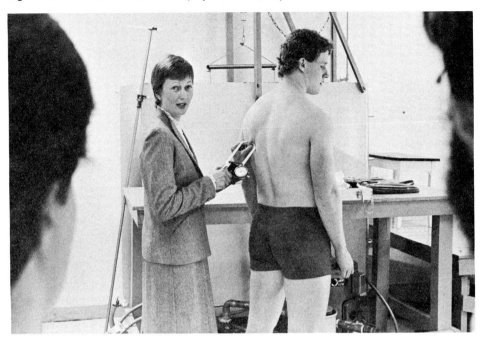

of this lack of immediate relevance, research investigating these types of problems is known as *basic research.* Experiments can also be concerned with gathering information that can be directly related to practical applications: research of this type is usually called *applied research,* due to the applied, or practical, nature of the research.

The gathering of objective information is essential to all scientific disciplines. While these disciplines may differ somewhat in their information gathering techniques, you can be certain that the use of the scientific method is common to all the disciplines. As a result, we can be confident that the knowledge transmitted by these disciplines is based on objective and verifiable information.

THE SCIENTIFIC DISCIPLINES

In the remainder of this chapter, we will look more closely at the various areas of study that comprise the scientific foundation of physical education. Rather than give you a minicourse in each of these subjects, our intent is to provide you with a general feeling of (*a*) what information is typically contained in these subject areas and (*b*) how each area provides the physical educator with useful knowledge. Many physical education curricula require courses in most of these subjects. This section will, hopefully, give you a better understanding of why these courses are in your curriculum and will whet your appetite for more complete information in these important foundational areas of study.

Scientific Disciplines Outside Physical Education

At the base of the scientific structure supporting the principles and practices of physical education are the scientific disciplines outside of physical education. You will recall that we are labelling these disciplines as *outside* physical education because they are basic sciences in their own right. The courses you will take in these sciences are generally not taught in the physical education department, although there are exceptions. Even though some of these courses may be taught in the physical education department, similar courses usually exist in the college or university department having the parent discipline. These are scientific disciplines, then, that are *based* in a college or university department other than the physical education department.

Each discipline is presented here in a broad, general way. As you take the various science courses of your program, you will become aware of the many subdisciplines and specializations within each discipline. As you read about each of the scientific areas of study in this section, try to think of some situations in physical education or sports or of some questions that could possibly be related to or benefit from the knowledge and information in that discipline.

Biology

If a cornerstone exists in the scientific foundation of physical education, biology may be the leading candidate. Not only is biology an essential base to several of the scientific disciplines within physical education, but it is similarly critical to many of the parent disciplines outside physical education. As the **study of living organisms,** biology provides a basis as well as a framework for the investigation of questions that are concerned with the origins, structures, and functions of living organisms. Thus, biology provides information that is relevant to anatomy, physiology, chemistry, physics, psychology, and sociology, all of which are essential parts of the scientific foundation we are considering for physical education. Within physical education itself, the more specialized scientific disciplines, such as exercise physiology, motor learning, and sport psychology, ground much of their knowledge structure, theory development, and research directions on a biology-based foundation.

If biology is so essential as a part of the scientific foundation for physical education, then what kinds of topics will a typical introductory course in biology involve? While courses vary widely, most seem to include certain basic topics. These topics generally consist of discussions related to the structure and function of cells; the form and structure (morphology) of plants; the physiology of plants; the naming and classification of animals; the origins and evolution of life; genetics; and ecology. The depth of study of these topics and the inclusion of other topics will depend on the individual instructor's orientation to teaching biology.

Within biology itself are many specialized areas of study that have emerged as scientific fields of study in their own right. These are typically divided into two major subdivisions, **zoology** and **botany.** Within zoology are such disciplines as anthropology, the natural history and physical development of humans; mammology, the study of mammals; ornithology, the study of birds; icthyology, the study of fish; herpetology, the study of snakes; entomology, the study of insects; and protozoology, the study of protozoa. Botany includes such disciplines as pteridology, the study of ferns; mycology, the study of fungi; virology, the study of viruses; and bacteriology, the study of bacteria. The disciplines in both zoology and botany that are concerned with life that can be investigated only with the microscope are also considered parts of **microbiology.**

We could go farther with identifying specialized areas of study within biology; however, such detail would not add to the intent of this discussion. As you progress through your physical education studies, you will increasingly find that the strength of your biology base will be very influential in your success as a physical education student as well as in your attitude about your experiences in the physical education program. For example, as you study many topics in exercise physiology, you will find that you will often rely on information you learned in biology. Being able to draw from your experience in biology will help you develop a better understanding of the concepts you study in exercise physiology. A background in biology, then, will help you see how many of the courses in your curriculum fit together to provide you with a good base of support for your role as a physical educator.

Anatomy and Physiology

In many colleges and universities, basic courses in anatomy and physiology are taught separately, while in others these topics are combined into one course. Regardless of how your college or university handles this, you should be aware of the importance of both anatomy and physiology. These areas of study are not only substantial elements in the scientific foundation of physical education, but they also provide knowledge that can be used daily by the physical educator. For example, a knowledge of anatomy and physiology is required when preparing exercise routines, establishing physical fitness plans, deciding whether or not to let a child throw a curve ball, and caring for and preventing injuries, among many others. The intent, then, in this brief discussion of anatomy and physiology, is to introduce you to the study of these topics so that you can get a better understanding of why this study is an important part of your training as a physical educator.

Anatomy of the human involves the study of the **structure** of the body and its parts. In this study, the goal is to describe as completely and as accurately as possible the shape and structure of the entire body (see fig. 3.3). **Physiology,** on the other hand, is concerned with the **functions** of the body and its parts. Whereas anatomy provides the identification of body parts, physiology goes a step farther by identifying how these parts function or operate in the human body.

Anatomy is generally studied from two perspectives. One perspective is gross anatomy, the study of body parts visible to the naked eye. Microscopic anatomy, the second perspective, involves the study of body part structure by means of the microscope. An important advance in this area of research has been the development of the electron microscope. Since each of the various parts and systems of the body can be studied from either a gross or microscopic perspective, the level of understanding desired by the individual, as demanded by his or her profession, will generally determine which perspective will be taken.

Within the study of physiology are several branches of study. These branches are identifiable as areas of specialized study of a particular body system. For example, cellular physiology is concerned with the functions of the cell and its parts in the various tissues of the body; cardiology involves the study of the functions of the heart and

Figure 3.3 Anatomy is the study of the structure of the body.

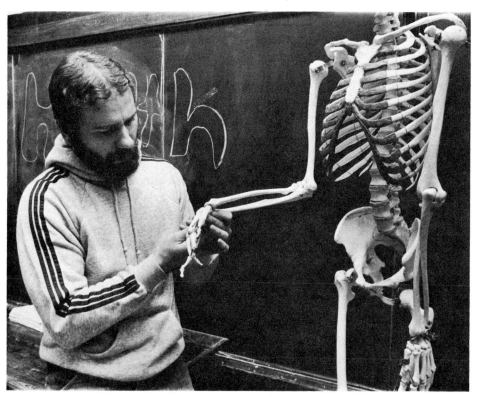

related elements; and endocrinology is the specialized study of the endocrine system. The many specializations within physiology illustrate both the breadth and depth of the study of human physiology.

For the physical educator, knowledge about the structure and function of the human body is essential. The physical educator is involved in teaching or helping people perform skills that require movement. To adequately perform this function, the physical educator must be aware of the parts of the body involved in movement and the capabilities and limitations of these body parts. For example, the teacher or coach must have a working knowledge of the body parts and their functions in order to know how movements should be done to correctly perform a skill, how to develop proper teaching techniques, or how to properly care for injuries.

The study of anatomy and physiology not only forms an essential part of the base from which sound teaching practices emanate, but it also is an important component in the foundation on which the study of many of the scientific disciplines within physical education are built. Exercise physiology, kinesiology and biomechanics, motor learning, motor control, and sport psychology all have roots firmly planted in these two disciplines. In fact, researchers in any of these scientific disciplines in physical education would be very limited in their investigations without a good base of knowledge in the anatomy and physiology of the human body.

Chemistry

As you progress through your development as a physical educator, you will discover that much of what you study includes discussions involving the basic properties of matter and energy. Matter is anything that has mass and occupies space. Energy is the capacity to do work. A science that is concerned with the **study of matter and energy** is chemistry. Through the study of chemistry, we can get to know something about the important substances on which life is based and to know how and why these substances act as they do. In addressing these concerns, chemistry has developed laws and methodologies that enable us to know more about ourselves and our world.

In physical education, there are many instances where the science of chemistry is important. For example, understanding how food is transformed into energy in the body, or how muscles respond to exercise, or what changes take place in the cell as a result of an extended exercise program all require some basic knowledge of chemistry. Consequently, physical education students who have a good base in chemistry find themselves at an advantage over students who do not have this background.

Chemistry is usually divided into general chemistry, organic chemistry, inorganic chemistry, and biochemistry. **General chemistry** considers the essential ingredients of the study of chemistry. Here, the study of such things as atoms, the periodic table of elements, chemical bonds, chemical reactions, solutions, gases, and nuclear activity are included. **Organic chemistry** focuses on organic compounds, which are compounds formed with the element carbon as an essential ingredient. These compounds are the foundation of all living things. Since our own bodies, as well as the food we eat, the clothes we wear, the fuel we put in our cars, and the medications we use to make us well, consist of organic compounds, the study of organic chemistry is of critical concern to all of us. **Inorganic chemistry** is concerned with inorganic compounds, the compounds that do not have a carbon-base. Such compounds as acids, bases, salts, and water are inorganic. Studying the structure, properties, and behavior of the different classes of compounds is an essential part of the work of both the organic and inorganic chemist.

Biochemistry involves the study of development of life from molecules and the developing of molecules from life. At the heart of biochemistry is the study of nucleic acids, which contain the "brains" of the living cell. Two important nucleic acids, DNA and RNA, are critical to the control and regulation of the reproduction of life. Other important concerns of the biochemist include the study of proteins, carbohydrates, and fats. Biochemists are interested not only in the composition of these, but also in the roles these play in the support of life.

An example of an important interest shared by the biochemist and the physical educator is respiration. To the biochemist, respiration is the burning of fuel by cells to obtain energy. To the physical educator, respiration is a critical component of physical performance. Answers to questions about respiration, such as what in the cell is involved with respiration, how do cells harvest the energy from respiration, and what can affect respiration, are of interest to both the biochemist and the physical educator.

To the physical education teacher, these examples may seem to suggest that the only people who benefit from studying chemistry may be the ones preparing to become researchers rather than teachers or coaches. While the researcher in the various scientific disciplines in physical education will obviously benefit from the study of chemistry, the teacher of physical education can likewise benefit. Many foods and liquids designed to aid athletic performance, weight control programs, and the like have their advertising benefits described in terms of chemical or biochemical benefits. If physical educators are unable to interpret these ad claims, then they, like many people, are at the mercy of the advertiser.

Physics

If biology can be considered the cornerstone of the scientific foundation of physical education, then physics must be considered the discipline that most permeates the other sciences in that foundation. There is scarcely a scientific discipline in existence that has not been directly or indirectly influenced by the fundamental science we know as physics. Research methodologies and techniques as well as fundamental concepts of physics have typically been adapted by the scientific disciplines being discussed in this chapter.

Like chemistry, physics is a science concerned with matter and energy; however, the approach to studying these concepts differentiates physics from chemistry, although the two sciences are interrelated in many areas. The physics approach to the study of matter and energy began with a systematic investigation, conducted by such men as Galileo and Newton, of the mechanical motions of large bodies. Later, investigations were directed toward the study of electric and magnetic forces and the nature of light. Modern physics has extended these interests by delving into the world of the atom.

In a typical introductory physics course, you will consider such topics as motion, with interest in such things as time, velocity, vectors, and acceleration; forces, with concern for mass, weight, and Newton's Laws; energy, with discussion of kinetic and potential energy and power; matter under stress; fluids under pressure; thermal energy; waves; electricity and electronics; optics; and the atom and its nucleus.

Human movement cannot be considered apart from its relationship to physics. Whether you will be involved in teaching movement skills or in research investigating various issues related to human movement, you will benefit by having your practices grounded in the sound base that physics provides. For example, as a teacher or coach, you will be concerned with such things as velocity, motion, and forces. These things are essential in such skills as running, jumping, hitting a ball, and throwing a ball. As such, principles of physics are essential to the effective and efficient performance of these and many other skills you might teach. Regardless of your specific professional aspirations as a physical educator, you will find that physics provides an essential part of the foundation on which you will base your work.

Mathematics

It is difficult to imagine anyone going through an ordinary day and not needing to use mathematics in some way. The need to count your change, balance your checkbook, determine how long you can or should work out, calculate your weight change from yesterday, or measure a strip of paper all require some basic mathematics skill. For physical educators, a good mathematics base beyond that needed for routine chores is essential: in your career, you may be required to calculate the proper dimensions for building a new baseball field, estimate the physical fitness levels of students in your classes, determine whether a class you taught using one teaching method did better than another class you taught a different way, or even determine the optimum angle for the release of the discus to help your star discus thrower. The list could go on. But these few examples offer you a view of some of the direct applications of mathematics in your role as a physical educator.

Mathematics can be considered the **science of quantity and space.** These two elements, quantity and space, are more typically labelled **arithmetic** and **geometry.** Arithmetic is concerned with numbers and rules for operating with numbers. Geometry, on the other hand, is concerned with spatial measurements. The various topics you may confront in mathematics, such as trigonometry, algebra, and calculus, are interrelated.

Each of the scientific disciplines within physical education has a direct link to the world of mathematics. Problems must be solved, logic must be applied to developing testable hypotheses as well as valid conclusions, quantities must be appropriately measured, and so on. There is no way in which the research that must be conducted within each discipline can be carried out without depending on the essentials of mathematics.

How much mathematics you should take is difficult to predict. The level of mathematics a person needs is in many ways dependent on the kind of work in which the person will get involved. Individuals who wish to become researchers in any of the scientific disciplines within physical education will find that advanced mathematics such as calculus and matrix algebra as well as work in experimental statistics are essential. The professional who opts for public school teaching or coaching, on the other hand, may find that such an extensive background in mathematics is not necessary. However, due to the nature of physical education itself, we would strongly encourage every physical education major to have at least advanced algebra, geometry, and trigonometry as minimum mathematics competencies. This enables physical educators to adequately study many of the subjects in their curriculum as well as be adequately prepared for their roles as professionals. Kinesiology and biomechanics, for example, provide a major source for our understanding of how we effectively and efficiently move. These disciplines involve describing human movement on the basis of mathematics and physics. As such, they will enable you to more effectively function as a physical educator.

Psychology

When you hear the word *psychology,* what usually comes to mind? Probably you think about mental and emotional problems and how to deal with such problems. While psychology is involved in this, it includes much more. Psychology is a term that literally means *the study of mind.* As an aid to helping you know what psychology really is, however, this literal definition does not help very much. Perhaps a better way is to indicate some of the topics that are typically included in the study of psychology. These topics are generally labelled clinical psychology, experimental psychology, perception, developmental psychology, physiological psychology, industrial psychology, school psychology, as well as a few others. Each of these subdisciplines of psychology focuses on a particular aspect of behavior.

As a scientific discipline, psychology does not have a very long history. While ancient civilizations were concerned about many issues that we now include in psychology, the approach to investigating or dealing with these issues was more from a philosophical perspective. It was not until the mid-nineteenth century that scientific research became a part of the process of seeking answers to questions relevant to psychology. Since that time, psychology, as a scientific discipline, has grown tremendously throughout the world.

Researchers in psychology use a variety of methods to investigate the wide range of concerns within their discipline. The methods used are typically determined by the question being investigated. For example, a clinical psychologist may investigate the effectiveness of a particular therapy technique by using individual case studies, where the psychologist obtains as much information as possible about the effects of a particular treatment on the behavior of an individual. For the psychologist interested in human learning, experimental methods of research, where hypotheses are established and tested in controlled settings, will generally be used to describe or predict learning-related effects. The social psychologist may find that surveys, psychological tests, interviews, and questionnaires are the best research methods to use in their search for answers about social issues related to human behavior. Because of the scope of the issues involved in the study of behavior, psychology has found that this search for understanding cannot be considered its exclusive domain; rather, interdisciplinary research is important to this endeavor. The study of perception, for example, can involve the researcher who collaborates with the physiologist or physicist. Social psychologists find themselves interacting with sociologists, anthropologists, and physiologists. Such interdisciplinary approaches are encouraging as well as essential.

As a physical educator, you will find that the study of psychology will be valuable to you, both as an individual and as a professional. Since you will be interacting with people in a variety of ways, such as helping them learn, leading groups, and even dealing with their emotional problems, a basic knowledge of some principles of psychology will aid you in handling these situations. Also, as a physical education teacher or coach, you will be working with children and youth who are in the process of rapid psychological development. The study of developmental psychology will better enable you to deal with these individuals in positive and beneficial ways. Psychology, then, becomes an essential part of the scientific base on which physical education is built by being a primary source for the knowledge physical educators need to effectively function.

Sociology

The science of sociology involves the **study of the interactions of individuals and groups in their various social environments.** The sociologist investigates social life as it exists in the family, school, community, working place, culture or subculture, and other social units. One of the main tasks of the sociologist is to explain society and social behavior. To do this, the sociologist is often involved in conducting descriptive research that will provide information concerning the nature of a society and its elements and about the nature of social behavior, or the behavior of individuals as they function within the various units of a society.

Within sociology are certain sources of social interaction that are given particular attention. Among these are the family, religious institutions, economic institutions, and government. Each of these social units provides sociologists a source for observing the structure of the organization and the ways people behave in these various social contexts. Other studies that intrigue the sociologist include the study of culture. Customs, laws, folklore, moral codes, languages, institutions, play and work characteristics provide sociologists with an abundant supply of information about the cultures themselves, their unique characteristics, and their similarities to other cultures.

The study of population is also of interest to the sociologist. How is a population distributed? Where do different races live? How and why do different cultures exist in certain geographic locales? Why and how do immigrants migrate? What is the nature and cause of population density? What is the rural-urban distribution of a population and what causes any change in this distribution? These few examples illustrate the intriguing questions that a sociologist uses to guide his or her study.

Issues that concern the sociologist also affect the realm of the physical educator. It is difficult to think of a typical physical education situation that does not involve the interaction of individuals in a particular social environment. Consider children playing on the school playground, or playing on a soccer team in a local youth league, or being involved in Special Olympic competition. Each situation involves a different social climate and organization. Understanding the differences and similarities of these climates and organizations as well as their influences on behavior occurring within them is of interest to both sociologists and physical educators.

Scientific Disciplines Within Physical Education

In the preceding section, you were briefly acquainted with the sciences that are the parent disciplines to the scientific areas of study within physical education. As pointed out at the beginning of this chapter, these disciplines are not the exclusive domain of physical education. Do not be misled by the title *within physical education;* it is used here primarily as a convenience to aid in the discussion of the entire scientific foundation of physical education. In your program, you will likely take courses related to these disciplines in your physical education department. However, the study of these areas is not limited to physical education departments but is also carried out in departments where the parent and related sciences are located. As such, it is easy to see that physical education is truly an interdisciplinary field of study.

To acquaint you with the disciplines in this section, several points of discussion will be presented. Included in each discussion will be a brief description of what the discipline is concerned with and how the discipline is related to physical education. There will also be a table presented that will include a list of topics and questions typically addressed in an introductory course in that discipline. Additionally, each discussion will present some examples of the types of research typically done in the discipline; the examples will show the kinds of questions that form the basis of research in that discipline or some experiments that might be conducted. Again, the goal is to briefly introduce you to the typical content of each discipline and to help you to be aware of why you will undoubtedly take a course related to this scientific discipline.

Physiology of Exercise

Although the study of the physiology of exercise (or, as it is typically called, exercise physiology) involves a wide range of topics, deVries indicates in his popular textbook that this study can be divided into two general topics that are of primary interest to the physical educator. First is the **enhancement of health and fitness** of the general population. Second is the **optimizing of performance** in the various types and levels of competitive athletics from a physiological standpoint.[1] Most physical educators will undoubtedly be confronted with either one or both of these issues, as you will see during your study of this section.

Exercise physiology differs from physiology in that the basic physiologist is primarily concerned with the functioning of the various systems of the body while the body is at rest: the exercise physiologist, on the other hand, is similarly interested in the functions of body systems, but from the viewpoint of these functions while the body is exercising or working. Thus, it is easy to see that exercise physiology is strongly dependent on the biological and natural sciences to provide a solid scientific base from which to develop knowledge.

When applied to the concern of health and fitness, exercise physiology focuses on such things as the understanding of what physical fitness is; how to best measure and evaluate physical fitness; the contribution of physical conditioning to the health and well-being of individuals; successful methods for controlling and reducing weight; the evaluation of physical conditioning programs; the influence of exercise on the aging process; and the role of exercise in preventing and recovering from coronary problems.

Exercise physiologists concerned with the training and conditioning of athletes are interested in such issues as strength development, endurance training, muscle efficiency, warming up, and the influence of environmental factors such as altitude or heat on performance. While these issues have relevance to the general population, they are of particular importance to developing optimal performance for the athlete. Thus, the exercise physiologist, when working with athletes, takes special interest in these topics as they apply to athletic performance.

To gain knowledge about this wide variety of issues, the exercise physiologist uses a vast array of research equipment and techniques (see fig. 3.4). The research methods employed will be dependent on the nature and goal of the problem under investigation. One example of this can be seen when the exercise physiologist collects samples of expired air from a person who is running on a treadmill for a specified amount of time. The expired air is then measured and analyzed to determine the fitness level of that individual. In this way, the exercise physiologist is involved with problems that can be investigated using gross physiological measures and procedures. At the other extreme, the investigation may involve the analysis of intracellular conditions, as would be the case when the research concerned the influence of certain training techniques on metabolic processes.

To help you gain a better understanding of what exercise physiology involves, let us consider a couple of other examples of research concerns in exercise physiology. For each concern, we will consider both a basic research and an applied research example. The first will come from the study of muscle physiology, the second from cardiovascular physiology. Keep in mind that these are only two examples of many areas of study in exercise physiology.

Figure 3.4 Students learn about the body's reaction to exercise stress in the exercise physiology laboratory.

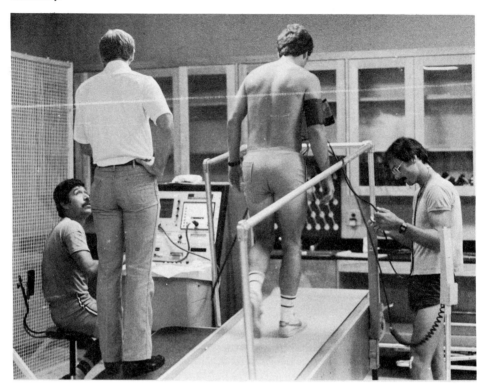

Muscle function is a common interest to many exercise physiologists. The approach taken to study muscle function will depend on the researcher's interest. The researcher who is interested in muscle function from a more theoretical perspective might be interested in determining the intra- or intercellular changes that take place in the muscle tissue as a result of exercise or work. Through the use of isolated muscle preparations that allow the researcher to observe changes within the cellular structure of the muscle, the researcher is able to observe these changes and make certain conclusions about how muscle functions under various conditions. For the exercise physiologist interested in muscle physiology from a more applied, or practical application, perspective, the interest could be related to muscle fatigue. Here the interest might be in determining such things as what causes muscle fatigue, what types of work loads lead to the fastest muscle fatigue, or what kinds of "cool down" routines provide the best recovery for the muscle from its fatigued state.

Another example of research in exercise physiology can be taken from the study of cardiovascular functions. Here, the interest involves the influence of exercise on the functions of the heart and circulatory system. The more applied physiologist might be interested in describing how various types of individuals differ on such parameters as blood flow, heart rate, or blood pressure. An example of the results of this type of

Figure 3.5 An important concern in exercise physiology is the relationship between a person's physical condition and heart rate during exercise. This graph shows this relationship for two persons, one who is well-conditioned and one who is poorly conditioned. Notice that for the same amounts of work (work load), the heart rates for these individuals differ significantly, especially as the work load increases.

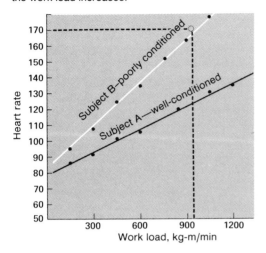

investigation is presented in figure 3.5. In this example, individuals have been compared on the basis of their heart rates at various amounts of work (work loads). On the other hand, the exercise physiologist involved in more basic research might also focus on blood flow but might direct the investigation to determine how blood flow gets distributed to the various organs of the body in response to different levels of exercise.

These examples serve only to illustrate some of the many concerns in the study of exercise physiology. A more complete view of the topics included in exercise physiology is provided in table 3.1. From this table, you can get a good idea of the topics and the types of questions you may address in the exercise physiology course you will probably take as a physical education major. The types of questions included in this table indicate the range of concerns confronting the physical educator that are addressed by exercise physiology. Each time you prepare a lesson plan, an exercise routine, or a schedule of practices for an athletic team, you will find that the principles learned in your study of exercise physiology have enabled you to successfully carry out these tasks.

Kinesiology and Biomechanics

An important part of skilled performance is the efficiency of movement. In fact, efficiency of movement can be one way to distinguish a beginner from an advanced individual for almost any physical activity. Since the efficiency of movement is so critical to physical skills, the physical educator must have a basic understanding of what efficient movement is and what its basis is. This will be useful information to the person who is teaching beginners in a skill or highly skilled athletes. For teachers working with beginners, knowledge of what skilled performance is will provide a model to direct teaching strategies to help beginners learn. For teachers working with skilled athletes, a basic knowledge of efficient movement is essential for providing effective instruction to these individuals, who are in need of skill refinement. When answers to questions

Table 3.1

Topics Included in Exercise Physiology

TOPICS	EXAMPLES OF QUESTIONS INVESTIGATED IN THESE TOPICS
The cardiovascular system and exercise	How is heart rate affected by exercise?
	How is exercise related to the prevention of heart disease?
	How is blood flow related to exercise?
	What chemical changes occur in the blood as a result of exercise?
Respiration and physical work capacity	How are the lung volumes related to exercise?
	What are the training effects on respiratory processes?
	What role does oxygen play in exercise?
	What sets the limits of aerobic capacity?
	What is oxygen debt?
Muscular function	How do muscle fiber types relate to sport performance?
	Why do certain training procedures lead to increased strength and/or endurance?
Physical conditioning	What is the benefit of interval training?
	What is the best way to measure physical fitness?
	What type of exercise programs will provide effective rehabilitation following a heart attack?
	What are the benefits of warming up or cooling down?
Environmental factors related to exercise	What are the effects of air pollution on the cardiorespiratory system during exercise?
	How does altitude affect the ability to exercise?
	How are heat and humidity related to exercise?
Nutrition	What foods relate to high-level endurance performance?

related to describing effective and efficient movement are sought, one of the places to look is the study of the basic laws of motion as applied to human movement. This is known as kinesiology and biomechanics, the study of the **anatomical and mechanical bases of movement of the human body.**

Actually, the terms *kinesiology* and *biomechanics* should not be used interchangeably. **Kinesiology,** while generally defined as the scientific study of human motion, is used more specifically to indicate the study of **anatomical kinesiology;** that is, the understanding of such things as the planes and ranges of motion possible at the various joints of the body, the interaction of forces between muscles, the influence of gravity on the motion of the joints, and so on. For example, if you were a physical therapist, you might be interested in knowing the possible range of motion of the shoulder joint. This would be valuable to you so that you would be able to develop an appropriate therapy that would lead to an effective recovery of the patient's use of this joint or so that you could determine the progress being made by your patient.

Biomechanics, on the other hand, is used to denote the study of **mechanical kinesiology.** This is the application of laws of physics to human movement, particularly in terms of the study of the effect of forces on motion. Understanding biomechanics is dependent on a knowledge of anatomical kinesiology. For example, an effective study of the influence of forces on motion would be difficult if the kinds of motions made possible by the various joints and segments of the body are not known. In physical education, the usefulness of knowing biomechanical principles can be seen when the teacher is instructing a class about proper forms of throwing. Effective throwing involves the movement of the body and limbs through specific planes as well as the appropriate generation of forces. A knowledge of such information can aid the teacher's development of appropriate techniques for teaching an effective throwing pattern.

Two important areas of study in biomechanics are the kinematics and kinetics of movement. **Kinematics** refers to the study of motion without reference to the forces causing the motion. Here the concern is what characterizes the outcome of motion. Such things as speed, velocity, acceleration, rotation, center of gravity, and trajectories are involved in the study of kinematics. **Kinetics,** on the other hand, incorporates forces into describing motion. Here, such things as momentum, power, moment of inertia, centripedal force, and the loss of energy are studied.

The study of kinesiology and biomechanics has led to the development and use of a variety of techniques that enable the researcher as well as the teacher or coach to observe and analyze human motion. Some of the most commonly used methods of observation include electromyography, cinematography, and free body diagrams. **Electromyography** (EMG) involves the electrical stimulation of a muscle and the recording of the muscle's electrical activity in response to the stimulation. In this way, a single muscle or group of muscles can be observed in terms of their involvement in a particular movement. **Cinematography** involves the use of film in the observation of movement. Here, high-speed filming of an individual performing a movement permits observation of the actions of body parts in small time segments when frame-by-frame observation of the films is seen. Cinematography is a very useful means of kinematic analysis of movement to help depict external forces and torques exerted. **Free-body**

diagrams involve first drawing simple sketches of the body and then drawing arrows that represent the external forces on the body and/or the external torques exerted on the body during movement.

The three methods of analyzing movement just considered are all types of **quantitative** analysis; that is, methods that will allow the use of numbers in the analysis. Using these methods, joint angles can be measured, forces can be calculated, velocities and momentum can be determined, and so on. Figure 3.6 presents another example of the use of quantitative analysis. Here, a hurdler is shown in action, as analyzed by limb segment action from graphs developed from film sequences.

There is another method of analysis that does not involve the application of numbers and mathematics. This method is known as **qualitative** analysis and involves the analysis of movement and identification of what is occurring throughout the movement in verbal rather than numerical terms. This method of analysis can be especially useful to physical education teachers who may not have the necessary background to use quantitative analysis methods. Cinematography, which was identified as an effective tool for quantitative analysis of movement, can also be effectively used for qualitative analysis. Rather than using the filmed action as a means of calculating various kinematic and kinetic measures, the film is used as the basis for observation and verbal identification of the performance being analyzed. For example, a track coach may be attempting to determine how to improve his or her star hurdler's performance. A frame-by-frame analysis of that hurdler's performance can be a valuable means of identifying problems and determining effective corrective measures. This analysis will be greatly aided by a working knowledge of biomechanical principles related to skilled hurdling performance.

The list presented in table 3.2 represents topics and questions you may address in a course on kinesiology or biomechanics. It becomes obvious as you study this list that a good working knowledge of anatomy, mathematics, especially algebra and trigonometry, and mechanical physics is critical to the study of kinesiology and biomechanics. Since physical educators are involved in improving performance, they must have the ability to analyze skills. A basic knowledge of kinesiology and biomechanics provides this ability.

Motor Learning and Motor Control

An important concern for every physical educator is which teaching strategies most effectively help people learn motor skills. Regardless of whether the student is a child or an adult, a beginner or advanced, in a group or alone, the need for effective instruction is always present. An important underlying component for developing this type of instruction for physical activities is a knowledge of how people learn motor skills and what affects how they learn. To establish this base, the study of motor learning and motor control has incorporated information from psychology (with particular reference to the psychology of learning and physiological psychology) as well as from physiology (especially neurophysiology) and biomechanics. From this wide assortment of information, researchers in motor learning and motor control have developed their own research directions to enable them to better understand what influences the learning and control of motor skills.

Figure 3.6 After the sequence of an athletic performance has been filmed, the biomechanist analyzes the sequence by a variety of methods. These two graphs show one means of analyzing the filmed sequence. Graph *a* shows the lower limb segments (by heights) of a hurdler as the hurdler approaches the hurdle (the O point on the horizontal axis). You can see the interrelationships of three points of the lower limb as the hurdle is approached. Graph *b* illustrates a similar type of analysis, but for a discus throw. Here the arm, lumbar-thoracic area, and pelvic area are plotted in terms of their angular velocity during the throw. Of interest here is the point in the throw at which maximum angular velocity was attained for each of the three body segments.

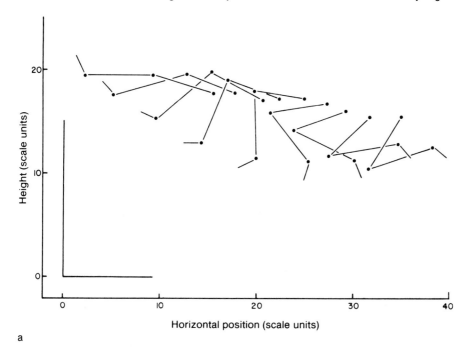

a

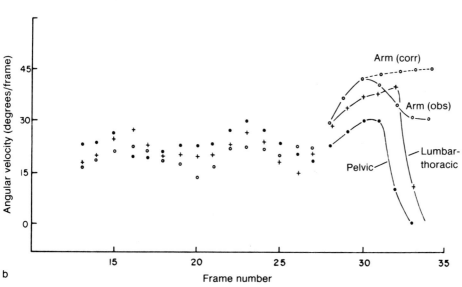

b

Table 3.2

Topics Included In Kinesiology and Biomechanics

TOPICS	EXAMPLES OF QUESTIONS INVESTIGATED IN THESE TOPICS
Anatomical kinesiology	What are the primary muscles and joints involved in running?
	Describe how the joints are involved in throwing a ball for distance.
	A well-executed golf swing travels through what planes?
Mechanical principles applied to fundamental movement skills	Describe the role of the body's center of gravity in executing the long jump.
	What forces are involved in a well-executed tennis serve?
	What is the relationship of lift, drag, and thrust to speed in a crawl stroke in swimming?
	How can a crew team best utilize information about force and fluid mechanics to improve their team performance?
	Describe the summation of forces in a world-class javelin throw.
Techniques for biomechanical analysis of movement	Describe the hitting of a baseball by using the following biomechanical methods:
	Cinematography Segmental analysis Electromyography Free-body diagrams

Motor learning is concerned primarily with what is involved in learning or acquiring a motor skill. Here, such topics as memory, attention, feedback and knowledge of results, practice conditions, and transfer of learning are included (see fig. 3.7). An example of the use of motor learning information can be seen in the situation where the physical education teacher is helping a student learn how to hit a golf ball. The teacher may watch the student hit a few balls and then give the student some advice on how to improve his or her swing. A problem for the teacher is that the beginner will make many mistakes on each practice attempt and the teacher must determine what to tell this student. It is not uncommon to hear a frustrated teacher say, "Where do I start?"

In the study of motor learning, an important topic directly related to the problem of what the teacher should tell the student is termed *knowledge of results,* or KR. Broadly defined, KR is the information a student receives about a response that will

Figure 3.7 The modeling effect generated by video observations helps the student develop motor skills.

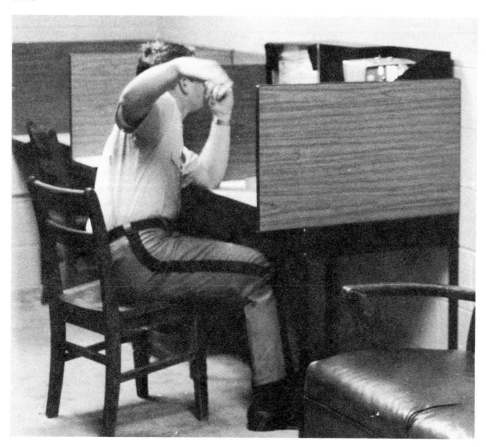

be helpful in improving the response on the next practice attempts. KR is generally thought of as information that comes from a source other than the student, such as a teacher, coach, videotape, and the like. Research related to KR and the learning of a motor skill can provide the physical educator with information about the kind of KR information that should be given, how much the student should be told, at what point KR should be given after a practice attempt, and so on. For example, figure 3.8 presents a diagram that represents the problem of when the next practice attempt should occur after KR has been given. This figure indicates that there is some optimal period of time during which the next response should occur. One of the areas of research in motor learning, then, is concerned with studying characteristics of this optimal period of time.

Motor control is the study of how we control the actions involved in performing a motor skill. Motor control researchers have taken different approaches to investigating this complex area. One approach is to study the neuromuscular basis of how we control

Figure 3.8 Intervals of time related to KR during the acquisition of a skill.

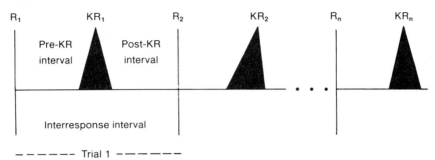

movement. Here, movement control is investigated by looking at how the nervous system interacts with the muscles and joints to produce and control movement. Another approach involves studying the control of movement in terms of the biomechanical basis of the movement. Here, a movement is analyzed in terms of how movement relates to biomechanical principles.

These two approaches have been used to address a number of motor control questions. For example, most theorists agree that after a lot of practice, we seem to be able to perform a motor skill "automatically." When you ride your bicycle, you do not think about what to do in order to stay balanced and to go where you want. Those things seem to happen automatically. The motor control researcher's interest here involves trying to explain how this automatic performance occurs. Questions such as, What happens in the nervous system to let this automatic performance occur? and What controls this type of movement? are the basis for research studies into understanding this situation.

Table 3.3 is a list of topics and questions that might be addressed in a motor learning or motor control course. At this point in our study of the scientific foundation of physical education, we should be able to see that these areas of study have their roots in several of the scientific disciplines discussed earlier. Also, as you study this listing of topics and questions, you should be able to see that the solution to many of the problems and situations you will encounter as a physical educator can be obtained from an understanding of motor learning and motor control principles. Since every physical educator is involved in one way or another in helping people learn, motor learning and control become essential components in the foundation for developing effective and efficient teaching practices.

Motor Development

By far, the greatest number of physical educators are involved with students in grades K through 12. Since these years represent very critical years in the growth of the child, the teacher of physical education should be knowledgeable about the characteristics and changes associated with this growth. This knowledge is important so that motor skills that are appropriate for the age of student are taught, and so that the teaching methods or techniques used by the teacher are appropriate for the children. Physical

Table 3.3

Topics Included in Motor Learning and Control

TOPICS	EXAMPLES OF QUESTIONS INVESTIGATED IN THESE TOPICS
The stages of learning	What distinguishes a beginner from a skilled performer?
	Can we predict how well students will do in a class based on their first day's practice?
Memory and motor performance	What influences how well a person will remember how to perform a skill?
	How well are motor skills remembered compared to verbal skills?
	What kinds of strategies will help a person remember what should be done when practicing a skill?
Motor control	How does the nervous system control coordinated movement?
	What are motor programs and what are they like?
	How does vision help to control movement?
	What influences a person's ability to catch a ball?
Knowledge of results	After students have practiced a skill, what should the teacher tell them that will provide the most help for improvement?
	When should the teacher tell students what they have done incorrectly when practicing a new skill?
	How often should the teacher provide information about what a student has done incorrectly?
Practice conditions	Should a gymnastics stunt be practiced as a whole unit or in parts?
	How can mental practice help when learning to spike a volleyball?
	Will practicing while fatigued affect a person's ability to learn a motor skill?
	What is the best way to practice the tennis forehand to be able to effectively use it in a game?

educators who are not aware of how children differ from adults as well as from each other in terms of age and sex will have difficulty in accomplishing the goals they have established for themselves and their students. One of the objectives of motor development research is to provide these types of information to the physical educator.

It is essential that physical educators realize at least two things about children's growth and development. First, children grow and develop at very different rates. It is not uncommon to have a sixth grade student who is physically more similar to a ninth or tenth grader and to have another sixth grader who is physically more like a third grader. Both of these children are in the same class and will be taught physical education together. How will the teacher handle these differences? The teacher cannot ignore such differences, as they are characteristic of all growing children.

Second, the physical educator must realize that children are not simply miniature adults. Teaching styles and techniques that work very well in high school or college should not necessarily be accepted as appropriate for the fourth grade student. The teacher must develop instruction that is appropriate for the age of the child being taught.

The following examples of areas of inquiry in growth and development should help physical educators better understand the type of motor development information they will need to know. First, consider the question of what differentiates how a 5-year-old kicks a ball from how a 15-year-old kicks a ball? One approach to looking at this question is seen in figure 3.9, where boys and girls ages 5 through 8 and 9 were compared on two kicking skills, kicking for velocity and for distance. Distinct age and sex differences can be seen from the results of this study. From this type of information, the motor development researcher can conduct further investigations into questions about why these differences exist and what these differences mean to the physical education teacher. For teachers, answers to questions like these will provide the basis for developing guidelines for establishing appropriate motor skill experiences in the physical education curriculum for the various grade levels.

Second, consider the problem of how we remember what we do. In the psychology literature, this problem is included in the study of memory. For the motor development researcher, a question of concern here is how children differ across age groups in memory-related characteristics and how these developmental differences relate to motor skill performance. How much information can a 7-year-old child remember compared to a 16-year-old? What will a 5-year-old child do, compared to a 12-year-old, to help him or her remember how to make a particular movement he or she has just been shown? If children are simply miniature adults, then we can use teaching techniques with children that have been proven effective with adults. Research in this area has shown, however, that this is not the case. Children approach memory situations differently from adults. There are even observable differences when children are compared at different ages.[2]

Answers to problems such as these relate cognitive development to the development of motor skills and can provide a solid basis on which the physical education teacher can build effective teaching techniques. In the instances just considered, developing these effective instructional strategies will relate to using methods and techniques that will lead to optimum learning and performance for the age group being taught.

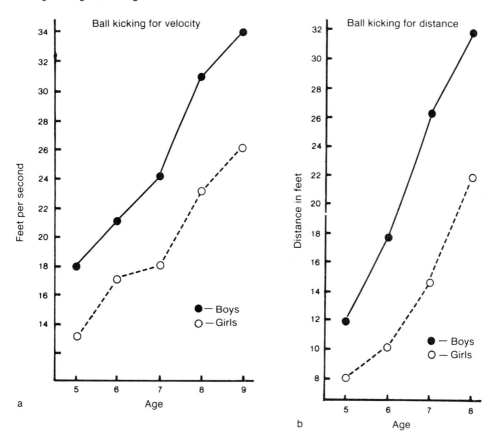

Figure 3.9 These graphs show the development of ball-kicking skill in young boys and girls. Graph *a* shows the average change in kicking for velocity (feet per second). Graph *b* shows the average change in kicking for distance.

For physical educators to understand how to accommodate the demands of the growing child in the teaching of physical skills, the study of motor development is essential. To help you see this in more detail, a list of topics and typical questions that can be investigated in the study of motor development is presented in table 3.4. At the end of this table is an issue that has become increasingly more common in the study of motor development, children's involvement in organized sports. As we discussed in chapter 2, youth sports programs have grown to such a magnitude in the United States that an estimated 20 million children, ages 6 to 16, participate in organized youth sports programs. For the motor development researcher, the questions that can be asked here are numerous. When are children old enough or ready to get involved in these programs? What psychological benefits or detriments will result from this type of competitive experience? What physiological effects will result from youth sport participation? Will involvement in competitive sports affect the child's academic performance?

Table 3.4
Topics Included in Motor Development

TOPICS	EXAMPLES OF QUESTIONS INVESTIGATED IN THESE TOPICS
Heredity vs. environmental influences in motor development	Is walking a learned skill or is it acquired through heredity? Can early training influence how well a child will be able to throw?
Relationships between age and sex and motor performance	What is the average age when a child begins to walk? run? throw? Do boys differ from girls in their development of motor skills?
Fundamental motor skill development	What performance stages can be described for running? When does arm-leg opposition start to appear in the throwing pattern?
Perceptual-motor development	Describe the development of eye-hand coordination. How is vision related to the development of motor skills? Is the development of perceptual-motor skills related to success in reading?
Intelligence and motor performance	Is a child's IQ related to how quickly motor skills are developed? Can a child's IQ be enhanced by practicing certain motor skills?
Cognitive processes and motor performance	Do children use strategies as adults do to help them remember? Can children deal with as much information at one time as adults?
Physical fitness and children	How do children differ from adults in cardiovascular characteristics? Can children benefit from exercise programs?
Youth sports participation	Will youth sports programs have negative effects on the child? At what age should a child participate in tackle football?

The list could go on. Physical educators should be aware of some of these concerns related to youth sport participation and be prepared to provide justifiable answers to as many of these issues as possible.

Sport Psychology

While the term *sport psychology* might seem to indicate the general application of the scientific discipline of psychology to sport, the current use of the term, especially in the United States and Canada, has narrowed the extent of that application. Sport psychology typically involves the study of social and clinical psychology-related topics to sport as well as to all movement settings. At the international level, however, the term *sport psychology* is used in a broader way to include these topics as well as the study of motor learning, motor control, and motor development. For our purpose, we will limit the discussion in this section to considering sport psychology as an area of study of the application of social and clinical psychology-related issues to organized sport and physical activity in general.

Sport psychologists are interested in determining why people behave as they do in various sport and physical activity settings. To investigate the various issues related to this interest, sport psychologists may direct their research efforts to describing psychological behavior during participation in sport or physical activity, to explaining the psychological bases for such behavior, or to developing appropriate techniques or strategies that can lead to optimizing performance in a sport or physical activity situation. Some sport psychologists, then, are interested in better understanding sport-related behavior from a psychological perspective. Other sport psychologists are more interested in improving sports performance of individuals.

Psychological factors play an important role in the performance of physical activities. To be physically prepared (that is, to be prepared in terms of adequate levels of physical fitness and skill) is only a part of the total preparation demands for physical activity performance. The individual must also be psychologically prepared. Involved in this psychological preparation are such factors as the individual's level of anxiety, his or her desire or expectation to excel or win, self-confidence, emotional stability, and the like. These, as well as other factors, interact to form the psychological component of physical activity. The following examples of sport psychology research should help you see how questions are investigated in this scientific discipline. They should also help you become more aware of what the study of sport psychology can do for you as a physical educator and why this study is an important part of your preparation to become a physical educator.

Athletes and coaches alike want maximum performance during an athletic event. A critical part of this level of performance is the level of anxiety of the performer at the time of the event. Research in psychology and sport psychology has shown, for example, that too low or too high states or amounts of anxiety can lead to poor performance. Each sport skill seems to have its own optimum anxiety (sometimes referred to as arousal) level for maximum performance. This research revealed that anxiety levels and performance levels are related and that techniques have been developed to alter the anxiety, or arousal, state to help ensure maximum performance.

Figure 3.10 This figure shows the relationship between skill performance and the presence of an audience. The presence of spectators can have either a positive effect or a negative effect, depending upon the complexity of skill and the individual's level of learning.

The nature of the skill influences whether negative or positive effects are the result of exposure to onlookers.

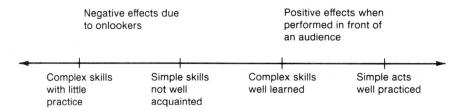

In the situation just described, an excellent opportunity exists to demonstrate how the basic researcher, the applied researcher, and the physical educator or coach can interact in developing and utilizing scientific information. For the basic researcher, interest in anxiety and performance leads to the development of research that provides a better understanding of how we deal with our world around us. The applied sport psychology researcher uses this information in the sport setting to determine how successful different techniques designed to alter anxiety levels are in regard to performance. The coach benefits from all of this information by being able to use the knowledge about anxiety and performance in a setting that requires its immediate use.

The second example of sport psychology research is taken from a psychosocial orientation to sport psychology. A topic of interest in this area of study has been the influence of spectators' observations of a performance on the level of performance that results. To study this influence, performance levels of athletes or nonathletes are observed under conditions of both no spectators or spectators present. The researcher may, for example, vary the number and types of individuals being used as spectators. The results of this research have been very interesting and typically have shown that more skilled individuals are positively influenced by the presence of spectators while beginners are negatively affected. This relationship, presented in figure 3.10, has been illustrated by Cratty.

For researchers interested in psychosocial theory, this type of study provides an excellent opportunity to add to the body of knowledge concerning how social interactions and behavior interact. For applied sport psychologists, the approach to the study of psychosocial interactions and sports performance provides valuable information for better understanding the influences on maximum performance. This knowledge is also useful to coaches because they can use it to develop appropriate coaching strategies to enhance their teams' performances.

These examples of sport psychology research, one from a more clinical psychology orientation and the other from a psychosocial perspective, are only two of many topics studied by sport psychologists. The list of topics and typical questions of interest presented in table 3.5 gives you a better picture of the broad range of topics studied in sport psychology. As you study this table, you should be able to see how each topic, since it adds to our understanding of human behavior, is a valuable element in the scientific foundation of physical education.

Table 3.5
Topics Included in Sport Psychology

TOPICS	EXAMPLES OF QUESTIONS INVESTIGATED IN THESE TOPICS
Competition and competitiveness	What is the effect of competition on the psychological well-being of an individual?
	Will being in a competitive situation lead to better or poorer performance than being in a noncompetitive situation?
Aggression	Do aggressive individuals make better athletes?
	Does participating in sports lead to making people more aggressive?
Anxiety and sports performance	How is anxiety related to sports performance?
	Will relaxation training lead to improved performance during a game?
	How can a person's level of anxiety be measured before a game?
Motivation and sports performance	What can be done to motivate a team to play its best?
	What can be done with a player who is not motivated to play?
	How influential are personal goals to performance?
Personality and sport	Do certain types of personalities play certain sports better than others?
	Can successful athletes be predicted on the basis of their personalities?
Social facilitation	What is the influence of spectators on performance in sports?
	Is jogging with a friend better than jogging alone?
The elite athlete	What are the psychological characteristics of the world-class athlete?
	What types of psychological training will help world-class athletes give their best performance during a championship event?

Sociology of Sport

As you saw in chapter 2, sport and physical activity are important parts of our society. Televised football on Monday nights has changed many regular patterns of behavior. Saturday afternoon or night football games are major social events on most college and university campuses. Many business deals are culminated in locker rooms of racquet clubs or on the golf course. A person's popularity among schoolmates can be dramatically influenced by success on an athletic team. The list of examples could continue far beyond these few. We will stop here, however, because these varied examples, in addition to the discussion in chapter 2, should be sufficient to get you thinking about sport's pervasiveness as a social influence.

The scientific discipline devoted to the study of sport's influence on society is known as the **sociology of sport.** As a specialized branch of sociology, as well as of physical education and sport studies, the study of the sociology of sport has had a strong impact in making people aware of sport as a social influence. Through research techniques developed in sociology, sport sociologists investigate a wide range of issues related to both society and the individual. With regard to sport in society, the sport sociologist may investigate such issues as the social and cultural influences related to the development of sport in our society, sport and religion, sport and education, and sport and politics.

For example, consider the role of sport in our society. One question that could be asked is, how important is sport in our society? To answer this question, the sport sociologist may conduct interviews, search through newspapers, and develop and send out questionnaires, among many other research methods. One example of a research study that investigated one aspect of this question is presented in figure 3.11. In this study, individuals were surveyed to determine the types of recreational activities in which they participated. From this type of information, the sport sociologist can help establish some understanding of the importance of sport and other recreational activity in our society as well as the types of activities that seem to attract the most interest.

When the sport sociologist's interests are directed at the individual level, the following example illustrates the type of research that can be conducted. In recent years, the role of women has changed with regard to involvement in sport. A sport sociologist who is interested in this topic could approach this study in several ways. For example, the issue could be approached by investigating what society in general views as the role of women in sport, or how various segments of society view women's involvement in sport, or how involvement in sport has affected women's place or status in society, or why women's role in sport has gone through the changes it has. Each question takes the researcher a different direction in the investigation of the issue of women's role in sport. However, each question becomes a critical piece in a rather large and complex puzzle that the sport sociologist needs to address.

Table 3.6 will help you get a better understanding of the types of issues and questions addressed by the sport sociologist. You may have noticed from our discussion and from studying the list of topics and questions in this table that there appears to be some overlap between the subjects that sport sociologists and sport psychologists investigate. In many cases this is an accurate observation. However, what differentiates these two researchers, and thus the areas of study themselves, is the approach taken

Figure 3.11 This figure indicates the number of individuals, age seven and older, who participated in a wide range of recreational activities.

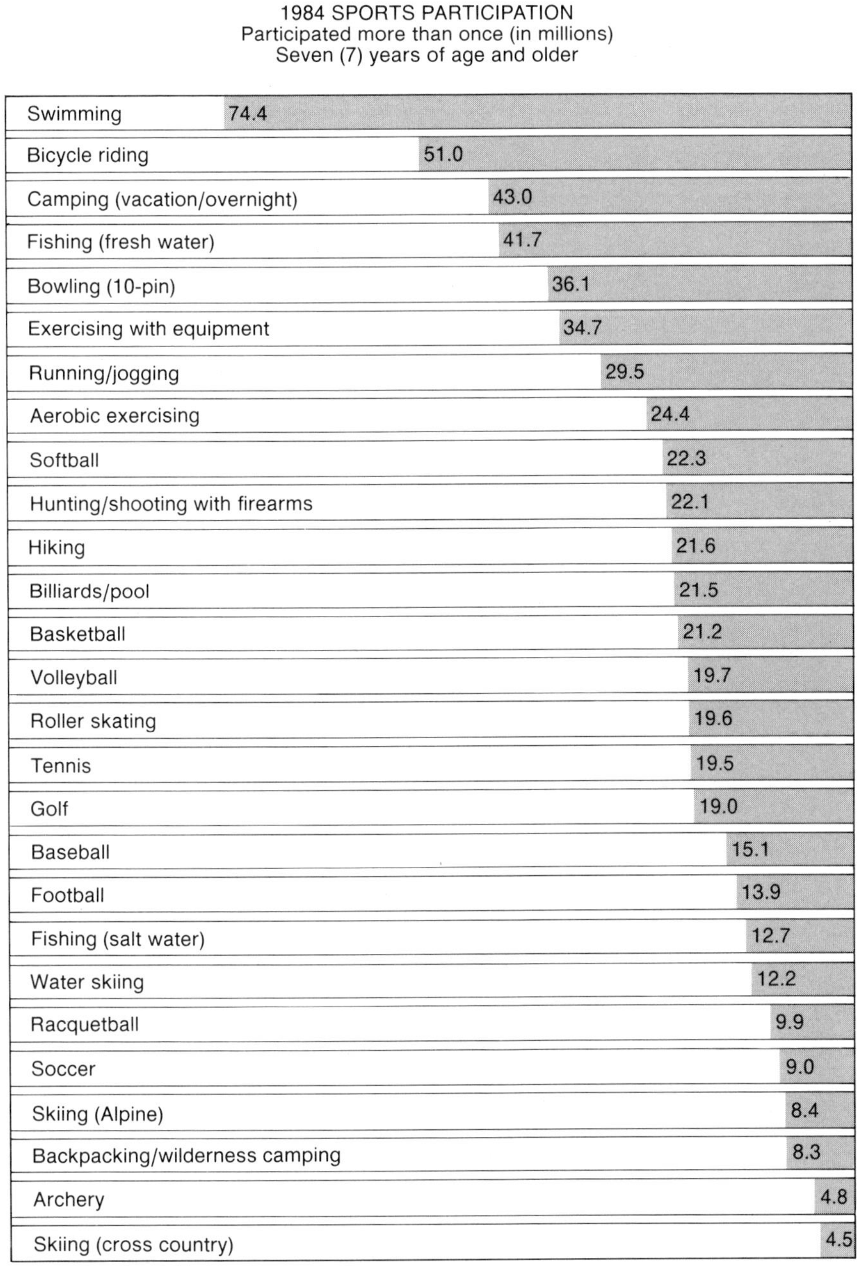

1984 SPORTS PARTICIPATION
Participated more than once (in millions)
Seven (7) years of age and older

Swimming	74.4
Bicycle riding	51.0
Camping (vacation/overnight)	43.0
Fishing (fresh water)	41.7
Bowling (10-pin)	36.1
Exercising with equipment	34.7
Running/jogging	29.5
Aerobic exercising	24.4
Softball	22.3
Hunting/shooting with firearms	22.1
Hiking	21.6
Billiards/pool	21.5
Basketball	21.2
Volleyball	19.7
Roller skating	19.6
Tennis	19.5
Golf	19.0
Baseball	15.1
Football	13.9
Fishing (salt water)	12.7
Water skiing	12.2
Racquetball	9.9
Soccer	9.0
Skiing (Alpine)	8.4
Backpacking/wilderness camping	8.3
Archery	4.8
Skiing (cross country)	4.5

Table 3.6
Topics Included in Sport Sociology

TOPICS	EXAMPLES OF QUESTIONS INVESTIGATED IN THESE TOPICS
The role of sport in society	How popular are sports in this country?
	Does participation in sports influence a person's social status?
Becoming socialized into sports	How influential are parents and relatives in a child's getting involved in sports?
	Do certain things influence a person to go out for football and others influence their going out for golf?
Sport and education	How do athletes compare with nonathletes in academic performance?
	How does the graduation rate of athletes compare to that of nonathletes in college?
Sport and economics	What role does success in football have in alumni giving?
	How much money is spent on sports and recreation each year?
Social class and social mobility	Do high school athletes look at sports as a means of achieving a better social status than their parents have?
	What is the success rate of athletes who have improved their social and economic status because of sports?
	What happens to athletes after they stop competing in athletics?
Ethnicity and sport	What percentage of professional athletes are black or hispanic?
	What is the history of racial discrimination in sports?
Women in sports	How has women's involvement changed during the past twenty-five years?
	What impact has involvement in sport by women had on how women are perceived in society?

to investigate these issues. The sport psychologist, coming from a social psychology view of sport, approaches an issue in terms of the individual, whereas the sport sociologist approaches the same issue from a perspective that stresses factors external to the individual. As such, the sport psychologist and the sport sociologist provide a much needed interdisciplinary view of human behavior and sport.

For physical educators, the study of the sociology of sport can be an important influence on professionalism. When a person is aware of the impact he or she can individually have on society, the person has a tendency to more carefully evaluate the practices put into use. Additionally, the study of the sociology of sport helps physical educators get a better view of where sport or physical activity fits in a society or culture. This enables physical educators to have a more realistic perspective of their role. While other benefits could be described, these should indicate to you how familiarity with sport sociology can aid you in your professional career as a physical educator.

SUMMARY

In this chapter, you have been introduced to a wide range of topics that, when taken together, form the scientific foundation of physical education. Without this foundation, the principles and practices of physical education would be a collection of experiences, myths, and unsubstantiated anecdotes. However, because of this foundation, we can be secure in the knowledge that a base of scientific evidence supports the structure of physical education. In this chapter, then, we have taken a look inside that foundation and briefly viewed its components.

Before looking at those components, however, we considered two important points that are helpful in better understanding the nature of the scientific foundation itself. First, we discussed the value of studying the sciences that make up the foundation. The focus here was on the benefit of establishing a base of understanding regarding why physical education teaching practices are effective and should be done. Second, we looked briefly at the primary means of gathering information in the scientific disciplines. This method, termed the scientific method of inquiry, is employed by researchers in all the disciplines. The strength of this method lies in its ability to provide information that is based on substantiated evidence.

Inside the foundation itself, we found that its components could be divided into two groups, each defined by whether its subject matter was essentially based outside or inside a physical education department. Scientific disciplines identified as outside physical education are biology, anatomy, physiology, chemistry, physics, mathematics, and sociology. These disciplines are also considered to be "parent" disciplines to those labelled as within physical education, which include physiology of exercise, kinesiology and biomechanics, motor learning and motor control, motor development, sport psychology, and sport sociology.

Before leaving this discussion, you must keep two things in mind about these disciplines. First, each area of study has its own body of knowledge that continues to grow as researchers find new information. Second, each discipline holds information that can be used by physical educators to help them perform their jobs in an effective manner. In this way, these scientific disciplines become an essential part of the physical educator's training.

STUDY QUESTIONS

1. What is the distinction between scientific disciplines labelled as outside physical education and those labelled as within physical education?

2. How are the scientific disciplines related to the principles and practices of physical education?

3. What are two benefits of having the principles and practices of physical education based on scientific knowledge?

4. What is the scientific method of inquiry?

5. Name five of the scientific disciplines *outside* physical education and indicate one way each discipline relates to a problem that might be confronted in physical education.

6. Name four of the scientific disciplines *within* physical education and for each identify one physical education-related question that could be addressed by that particular discipline.

STUDENT ACTIVITIES

1. Visit the laboratory of one of the scientific disciplines outside physical education. Notice what kinds of research are being conducted and what procedures are used in that laboratory. Develop a list of questions or problems related to physical education that you think could be addressed by the research done in this lab.

2. Visit the laboratory of one of the scientific disciplines within physical education. Notice what kinds of research are being conducted and what procedures are used in that laboratory. Develop a list of questions or problems related to physical education that you think could be addressed by the research done in this lab.

3. Volunteer to be a subject in an experiment being conducted by a faculty member or student in one of the scientific disciplines in your physical education department.

4. Select one scientific discipline within physical education and list ten specific questions for which you might want to know the answer if you were a physical education teacher or coach. Get into a small group and discuss possible answers to these questions.

NOTES

1. Herbert A. deVries, *Physiology of Exercise for Physical Education and Athletics,* 3d ed. (Dubuque, IA: Wm. C. Brown Publishers, 1980).

2. Jerry R. Thomas, "Children's Motor Skill Development," in *Motor Development During Childhood and Adolescence,* ed. Jerry R. Thomas (Minneapolis: Burgess Publishing Company, 1984), 91–104.

RELATED READINGS

American Alliance for Health, Physical Education, Recreation, and Dance. *Basic Stuff Series I.* Reston, VA: AAHPERD Publications, 1981. (Information booklets for exercise physiology, kinesiology, motor learning, motor development, psychosocial aspects, and humanities)

Coakley, Jay J. "From Elites to Everybody: A Changing Agenda for Sport Sociological Study." *Journal of Physical Education, Recreation and Dance* 54 (March 1983): 21–23.

Dillman, Charles J. "Applied Biomechanics Research for the United States Ski Team." *Journal of Physical Education, Recreation and Dance* 53 (January 1982): 27–29.

Duda, Joan L. "Future Concerns for Applied Sport Psychology." *Journal of Physical Education, Recreation and Dance* 53 (November/December 1982): 51–52.

Gallagher, Jere Dee. "The Effects of Developmental Memory Differences on Learning Motor Skills." *Journal of Physical Education, Recreation and Dance* 53 (May 1982): 36–37, 40.

Pollock, Michael L. "How Much Exercise is Enough?" *Physician and Sports Medicine* 6 (1978): 50–64.

Schmidt, Richard A. "Schema Theory: Implications for Movement Education." *Motor Skills: Theory Into Practice* 2 (1977): 36–48.

Involvement in Physical Education

By now, we think you will agree that physical education, past and present, is complex. Physical education encompasses diverse career opportunities, providing a variety of ways that one can become professionally involved.

Chapter 4 examines career options that someone with a background in physical education may be capable of assuming. Chapters 5 and 6 are designed to acquaint the potential professional with formal and informal processes one must go through in order to obtain and enhance one's professional status.

In chapter 7 the focus is on an item of personal development—personal fitness—that may help the professional assume a desired role.

We hope that your study of part 2 will acquaint you with the many career opportunities available in physical education and the processes necessary to achieve a desired professional status to help make your career choice a rewarding one.

Career Planning

Chapter outline

Student Objectives

As a result of the study of this chapter, the student should be able to

1. State the usefulness of a degree in physical education.
2. List and explain various career opportunities that are available to the physical educator.
3. State the importance of teaching ability in both teaching and non-teaching careers.
4. Describe a variety of teaching careers.
5. Describe a variety of coaching careers.
6. Describe a variety of non-teaching careers.
7. Explain the reasons for your choice of an initial career in physical education.
8. Develop an understanding of the importance of preparing for your anticipated career selections.
9. List the necessary preparation, whether degrees, certifications, or experiences, to be qualified for your career selections.
10. Understand that career planning is a matter of preparation, experiences, and a series of continuous decisions to be made throughout one's lifetime.

Life is a matter of continuous decisions. Your selection of physical education as a course of study was one decision. You will make many more decisions before your choice of a professional career is established. Most prospective physical educators enter professional preparation with the anticipation of teaching and coaching careers. Some already are planning future endeavors regarding the master's and doctoral degrees. Others involved in intercollegiate athletics pursue the quest of professional sports, with intentions of becoming highly paid players.

One's goals and ambitions should never be taken lightly, but what happens when all of the pieces to your plan of life do not fit? Let us note some specific examples. Teaching and coaching in the public schools were your goals in life since the time you really began to admire your high school coach. Now, after several opportunities to observe and participate in practice teaching experiences, you find yourself dreading the thought of a full semester of student teaching. Or you have just completed student teaching and definitely do not want to pursue teaching any farther. Yet you have invested four years of your life working toward that degree in physical education. What do you do? Your all-state credentials brought to you an athletic scholarship, but college athletics are much more competitive than you anticipated. You are not selected in the draft nor do you receive the opportunity to play professional sports. What do you do?

The answer to both examples seems simple, yet is complex in detail. The answer is preparation—preparation for certain situations that may never occur, but if they do, you are prepared to handle them. Again, let us be specific. You have decided a teaching career is not for you even though this was your goal originally. Rather than dwell on the aspect of failure, you should ask, "What can I do with my physical education degree?" There are many options, and one should search self to identify personal interests and then pursue those various avenues of interest. However, prior to this experience you should have totally examined the teaching profession and its career opportunities. This knowledge of career opportunities will enable you to be prepared to explore your options. The other example regarding the athlete who was planning a professional playing career lies in the same category, with one exception. How serious did the athlete consider the physical education preparation? Some athletes choose physical education as a major course of study because it seems a "natural" for a physically active person. Yet many times the professional preparation is regarded lightly as to learning experiences for the future. Has the athlete ever seriously considered teaching and coaching as a career? Has a thorough examination of the various career opportunities within the profession been done? In both examples, if the individuals were aware of the career opportunities, the task of seeking an alternative to their former plans would be much easier.

The purpose of this chapter is not to try to change your mind concerning your future goals or ambitions, nor is it to imply in any way that one career opportunity is better or more lucrative than another. The purpose is to examine the total scope of career opportunities that may be available to physical education majors (with and without advanced training or higher education) so that you—the physical educator of the future—can make rational, logical decisions concerning your place in the profession.

A TEACHER FIRST

The majority of professional preparation programs in physical education are teaching-oriented. After four years in preparation to be a physical education major, you will undoubtedly have been exposed to a variety of teaching methods, techniques, and subject matter that will offer you the basic qualifications to teach physical education at various levels. It is important to remember that all teaching in physical education does not take place just in our school systems. There are numerous teaching opportunities outside of the school situation.

What this should mean to you at this stage in your professional preparation is to place a value on the teaching aspects in your courses of study. In return, this knowledge should prove valuable to you. Most people in other occupations go through their professional training and do not receive instruction on how to teach. Even in the realm of business, regarding sales and promotion, teaching ability is highly valued. Whether you are teaching people about a product or about the state of a healthy body, education is still taking place. To be more specific, let us quickly look at a number of career opportunities in physical education and relate them to teaching ability.

Athletic coach—A good teacher is always a good coach.

Athletic trainer—The trainer not only helps heal, but also teaches athletes how to stay fit and healthy.

Military officer—Teaches military knowledge and strategy to the troops.

Fitness instructor—Health spas and private fitness clubs depend upon good teaching to ensure that their patrons get the best results.

Sporting goods representative—Must teach the public about equipment and products in order to be successful.

Sports instructor—A good tennis or golf pro depends upon teaching. People will not pay for private lessons without good teaching that shows results.

Professional scout—Teaches the team and staff about the opponents they will play.

Sport nutritionist—Must teach people how to stay healthy through nutrition.

Pharmaceutical representative—Educates physicians and medical staff about products. Teaching ability possibly rates above sales ability.

Television sports analyst—The TV "color" person or analyst actually assists the sports commentation by teaching or educating the viewing audience about the technical aspects of the game or contest.

The list of career opportunities could go on, but the point is that, regardless of your career choice, teaching may be a part of it.

As a physical educator you are trained as a teacher first. Thus, the teachers training you have a certain amount of responsibility to you, the student. First of all, good teachers are competent in their knowledge of subject matter, regardless of what the subject may be. Further, good teachers become "students of the game" by constantly adding to and improving their knowledge through various resources that are available. Second, the presentation of subject matter is done through teaching methods and techniques; therefore, your teachers should strive to utilize the best possible methods and techniques to enhance your presentation and teaching competency. Third and possibly most important, you must develop your own **teaching personality** in order to be effective as a teacher yourself. Since people are different from one another, teaching personalities will vary also. Your teaching personality should be a reflection of yourself. This takes time and practice to develop. A simple rule to follow is to emulate the styles of successful persons in your field and synthesize those characteristics with your personality traits. The result should be your specific teaching personality which should add to your success as a teacher in any career.

Review of these three responsibilities indicates that knowledge of subject matter, the presentation of subject matter, and one's teaching personality are important in demonstrating teaching competency in any field. These responsibilities are part of your professional preparation in physical education. Take them seriously in your courses of study and they will be of great benefit to you in the future. This training is one of the strengths in your professional preparation that makes your physical education degree attractive to employers. Finally, always keep in mind that as a physical educator, you are a teacher first.

INITIAL CAREER SELECTION

The first factor that will help determine your initial career selection is the factor that motivated you to become a physical education major in the first place. The second and possibly the more influential factor will be the professional experiences in physical education and athletics as well as your courses of study. The four years spent in professional preparation will shape your interests or change your initial goal. A major point here is that to get the most out of your education, you must give it your best effort. You must become knowledgeable about your future profession.

The majority of physical education majors enter professional preparation with the anticipation of becoming teachers and/or coaches in the public school systems; thus, it is important to analyze some of the various reasons for this selection. The three reasons that are probably most common are as follows:

1. I like sports and physical activity.
2. I admired my physical education teachers and coaches throughout my scholastic career.
3. I would like to teach boys and girls in the same subject that I enjoyed so much.

All three are valid reasons, but they need further explanation so as not to cause any false impressions. First, the enjoyment of sports and physical activity does not necessarily imply that you will enjoy teaching these activities to others. Teaching and coaching do not involve you directly in the doing or participation of such activity. Second, a person you admire may make an excellent role model, but you may need to clarify the reasons or characteristics for that admiration and then analyze yourself to see if you possess the same or similar traits. The third reason is probably the most valid reason for entering the teaching and coaching profession. The teaching of values and other intangible qualities along with the teaching of sports or physical activities of your choice is also a part of the third reason.

Some other reasons for selecting the teaching and/or coaching professions, such as fame, prestige, wealth or supplemental income, the association of excitement and glamour, or the enjoyment of one particular sport in which you may have participated, may be questionable if they are not accompanied by a sincere interest in working with boys and girls. Few teachers and coaches attain wealth, power, or lasting fame. Many of your rewards in the profession are intrinsic. Any teacher or coach who is dependent upon extrinsic rewards probably is not going to stay in the profession for any length of time. Even for those to whom fame comes, that fame may not be permanent. A teacher or coach cannot rest upon the laurels of yesterday. In a profession that is people-oriented, it is the present—not the past—that counts, both in performance of duties and success.

CAREERS IN PHYSICAL EDUCATION

As mentioned previously in this chapter, teaching careers may take place outside of the school setting. The acquisition of a variety of teaching skills and subject matter makes the physical education major a candidate for various career opportunities.

This section is broken into five different areas in an attempt to categorize the numerous opportunities that await the physical education graduate. Some careers may overlap into more than one of these five areas. The basis for inclusion is, generally, where the emphasis on the job lies. As an example, a career as a fitness instructor for a health spa or fitness center would fall into teaching careers as well as business careers. While teaching people the skills of fitness, among other things, the instructor must have sales ability in order to secure memberships. Because most of these positions are paid on a commission basis, success is equated with sales and promotion. The instructor who is a skilled teacher, however, will have more opportunities for sales due to the teaching ability demonstrated with prospective members and from referrals by present members who are happy with their programs.

The purpose of this section is to enlighten you as to the scope of career opportunities open to a person with a physical education degree. The section is not a comprehensive listing of opportunities; your degree may benefit you in other areas as well. If certain careers interest you, do not wait until your degree is imminent to begin exploration into that field. Start now, while your professional preparation is in its beginning stages. You may find that a particular career may require additional training or focus into other areas that your present preparation does not supply. Use the following guidelines to begin your search into the various career opportunities that may interest you.

1. Contact your local or state professional organizations as to their information on various careers.
2. Contact AAHPERD about various sources of information into the area of career opportunities.
3. Read professional journals, magazines, newspapers, and books that may offer information on careers. Your college or university library may be the best place to start.

4. Request information from various organizations that sponsor or serve as professional associations or management associations within various career fields.

5. Once you have explored the career(s) that are of interest to you, contact a successful person in that field and ask if he or she can arrange to discuss the career field with you. Make sure you have some knowledge, through reading or other study, about the career prior to this meeting; otherwise, such a discussion may not benefit you and may waste valuable time for the person granting you the meeting.

Teaching Careers

Most public and private schools throughout the nation have instructional programs and requirements for physical education. To teach, you must obtain a valid teaching certificate in the state in which you select to teach. If requirements are unknown, write to the State Board of Education or State Education Agency for the necessary information. More than likely, your present college or university will be fully aware of your state certification requirements.

Student teaching should reinforce your desire to teach or may indicate that teaching in the schools is not for you. More than likely, once you begin teaching you will not be content with your bachelor's degree and, as you gain experience in teaching, will want to pursue your master's degree and possibly specialize in either an activity or a scientific area. However, many practicing professionals complete their master's degree in general education areas and pursue specialization in the doctorate degree program.

Teaching positions are not noted for unusually high salaries, but most teachers can live well, and if a person enjoys the work, teaching can be a most rewarding and satisfying career (see fig. 4.1). Job prospects in teaching physical education are usually classified as fair to average. However, good teachers are always needed and the turnover rate in education is relatively high. If you limit your job search to a particular locale, your chances of employment will not be as high as those of the person who is flexible to move wherever the opportunities arise. A great advantage of teaching is the ten to twelve week summer vacations, as well as liberal vacation time throughout the academic year. This gives many people the opportunities to attend graduate school, supplement their incomes, or do "their own thing." It also allows for rejuvenation, giving teachers time to prepare for the next year, which is important to the teaching-learning process.

Coaching Careers

Interest in a coaching career runs high for the young physical educator. Many enter the profession solely with the intent of success in coaching the sport of their choice. However, coaching is a very demanding and time-consuming career, and there are a few obstacles in the way of the future coach's ambitions. First, most coaches will start at the assistant level, but very few will want to stay at that level. Almost all coaches aspire to be head coaches, yet not everyone will make it, especially in the spectator-oriented sports.

Figure 4.1 Teaching physical education in the public schools is a challenging and rewarding career.

Most beginning coaches lack experience beyond that as high school or college athletes. This experience is valuable, but an understanding of the age and skill level of the youngster they will coach is also important. Playing in a highly competitive college situation does not enable athletes to automatically understand the ability level of a ninth-grade student. Further, any prospective coach must become a student of the game. This means you must read, comprehend, and prepare to implement the teaching of the skills of the sport (the head coach is usually responsible for strategy); therefore, a good coach must first be a good teacher!

Coaching is done at every level, from elementary to the professional ranks. However, most coaching done below the junior high school level is not performed by full-time teachers and coaches. You may or may not have ambitions to move from high school to college and to the professional ranks. Each has its advantages and disadvantages. Remember, the higher you intend to go, the harder it will be to get there and stay there (see fig. 4.2). The competition for highly paid coaching jobs is intense. Success at these levels is equated only with *winning*. Even in many public school situations,

Table 4.1

Teaching Careers

CAREER	BRIEF JOB DESCRIPTION	USUAL MINIMUM DEGREE REQUIREMENTS	ADVANCED TRAINING	EXPERIENCES NECESSARY
Elementary teacher	Teach children kindergarten through sixth grade in a variety of activities.	Bachelor's degree with elementary or all level certification.	Master's degree helpful.	Student teaching; movement education background.
Secondary teacher	Teach children seventh through twelfth grade in a variety of activities. Coaching duties may also be involved.	Bachelor's degree with secondary or all level certification; ability to coach athletics.	Master's degree helpful; necessary in some states.	Student teaching; coaching experience helpful.
Junior or community college teacher	Teach a variety of activities in general programs; professional preparation courses in associate degree programs. Activity specialization sometimes required; coaching duties may be involved.	Master's degree.	Activity specialization requirements if necessary.	Successful teaching and coaching experience.
Four-year college or university teacher	Teach activity courses to general student body; teach professional preparation courses to major students; student teaching supervision. Coaching duties may be involved.	Master's degree.	Doctorate degree with emphasis in area of specialization.	At least three years successful teaching experience. Proven publishing and research background helpful.
Sports instructor (private club such as tennis and golf)	Teach specialized skills in a particular activity to all age segments of population. Usually associated with a country club, private club, and the like; commonly called "the pro."	Bachelor's degree with activity specialization requirements.	———	Proven competitive playing experience; high skill level in activity.
Dance instructor	Teaching of dance, theory, and dance activities in various settings such as schools, dance studios, and agencies.	Bachelor's degree in dance or dance emphasis. Skill and fitness level.	———	Professional dance experience helpful.

Table 4.1 *Continued*
Teaching Careers

CAREER	BRIEF JOB DESCRIPTION	USUAL MINIMUM DEGREE REQUIREMENTS	ADVANCED TRAINING	EXPERIENCES NECESSARY
Acquatics instructor	Teaching of acquatic activities in a school, private club, or agency setting. Coaching duties may also be involved.	Bachelor's degree with life saving and water safety instructor rating.	Additional acquatic certification ratings.	Practical experience in all areas of expertise. Swim team participation helpful.
Adapted physical education teacher	Teaching physical education to students with physical handicaps, emotional problems, mental retardation and learning disabilities	Bachelor's degree with a specialization in adapted physical education.	Master's degree helpful.	Some experiences or training in special education.
Agency recreation leader/ instructor	Organizes and teaches a variety of activities for a public or private agency, such as the YMCA, Boy Scouts, community agencies, and church agencies.	Associate (two-year) or bachelor's degree with emphasis in recreation.	———	Recreational experiences and organization helpful.
Outdoor education instructor	Teach and organize outdoor education programs within the school setting or agency setting. Possibility exists to also work as instructor for the various outdoor education certification schools and programs.	Bachelor's degree, related certification as necessary.	Additional certification as needed.	Outward bound. National outdoor leadership schools, adventure schools, and the like.
Correctional facilities instructor	Teach and organize activities in correctional facilities and institutions.	Bachelor's degree, some sociology background helpful.	———	Some knowledge of criminal justice helpful.

a coach must win or lose the job; job security in the coaching profession comes from constantly being a winner.

All coaches are not physical education teachers. Some teach in other subject areas and some are part-time coaches. In most states, teaching certification is required, and some states also have a coaching certification requirement. Coaching jobs appear to be plentiful, but not always with physical education as the teaching field. Thus, if coaching is your primary goal, you may want to become certified in some other teaching field to help your chances of employment.

Table 4.2
Coaching Careers

CAREER	BRIEF JOB DESCRIPTION	USUAL MINIMUM DEGREE REQUIREMENTS	ADVANCED TRAINING	EXPERIENCES NECESSARY
Assistant coach, high school, junior high school level	Teach skills of sport to student-athletes. Carry out any other duties assigned by head coach. Scouting.	Bachelor's degree with teaching/coaching certification as necessary.	Coaching clinics.	Coaching experience in youth sports, volunteer coach, and the like are helpful. Playing experience.
Head coach, high school, junior high school level	Accept responsibility for the overall preparation of the school's sport, including skills and strategy. Supervise assistant coaches; public relations with community.	Bachelor's degree with teaching/coaching certification as necessary.	Master's degree helpful.	Prior assistant or head coaching experience. Successful record as coach.
Assistant coach, college level	Duties involving skills, strategy, and scouting, plus the recruiting of prospective athletes.	Master's degree.	———	Successful public school or college coaching experiences.
Head coach, college level	Accept responsibility for the overall preparation of the college's sport, including skills, strategy, and recruiting. Staff and program organization and public relations with media, alumni, and college personnel.	Master's degree.	———	Success in coaching and ability to withstand pressure.
Assistant professional coach	Usually a specialist in some area of skills and/or strategy. Scouting opponents and evaluating future personnel may be part of the duties.	No degree requirement.	Many professional coaches have bachelor's and master's degrees.	Successful college coaching experience is usually the key factor in obtaining the position.
Head professional coach	Responsible for the overall preparation and performance of a professional team. Public relations very important. Organizational ability to direct staff and players and to work with management.	No degree requirement.	Many professional coaches have bachelor's and master's degrees.	Successful college and/or professional coaching experiences. Helps to be a well-known personality.

Table 4.2 *Continued*
Coaching Careers

CAREER	BRIEF JOB DESCRIPTION	USUAL MINIMUM DEGREE REQUIREMENTS	ADVANCED TRAINING	EXPERIENCES NECESSARY
Specialty coach, college or professional level	Assist the college or professional programs in areas such as strength, conditioning, exercise physiology, and the like. The specialty coach works with the players directly to help improve their potential for performance. This may be a part-time position in many situations.	No degree requirement.	Any necessary certification for area of expertise. Many specialists have bachelor's, master's, and doctorate degrees.	Success in your area of expertise as participant, teacher, coach, and the like.
Athletic trainer	Responsible for the health, welfare, conditioning, and overall physical state of the athlete. Includes prevention, rehabilitation, and diet, among other areas.	Bachelor's degree plus NATA and state certification. Some states require teacher certification for the public schools.	Many trainers who want to move to the college and professional ranks will obtain a physical therapy degree or certification.	The trainer should be able to get along well with all types of people. Student training experience is very helpful.
Sports official	Officiate, referee, umpire, or judge at various sports. Usually is a part-time job. Most officials move to higher levels as a result of success and experience at various levels.	No degree requirements.	Officiating schools. Any certification that is necessary.	Participate in a broad range of officiating experiences before concentrating on one sport.
Sports camp director	Organize and administrate youth sports camps (mainly in the summer) for skill level improvement and fun of campers.	No degree requirements.	————	Usually, a well-known, successful player or coach is the sports camp director or sponsor.
Scout	Evaluation of potential personnel or observing opponents in preparation for competition. Freelance scouts usually work at the professional level. Most college scouts are coaches. Freelance scouting can be a part-time position.	No degree requirements.	————	Usually former highly skilled player or coach. Reputation as an excellent assessor of talent and game analyzation helpful.

Coaching is also a very rewarding and satisfying profession. Good coaches build good citizens as well as good athletes. Athletics should be fun, and you, as the coach, are the primary source of that fun. It is extremely important for the young coach to prepare to teach values as well as skills. Before you will be a well-rounded coach you must gain experience, usually working as an assistant coach. Be willing to learn and become a doer. Most head coaches do not have time to train an assistant once the season has begun. Keep in mind that even good coaches do not always make it to the top. Athletics are ruled by the abilities of the players as well as by good coaching. The old saying, "You have to have the horses to win," is basically correct. Success in coaching is a combination of good athletes and good coaching! Further study of the coaching profession and athletics appears in chapter 12.

Administrative Careers

Careers in the administrative areas of physical education and sport usually follow successful careers in the teaching and coaching professions. Administrators rarely, if ever, start at the top. Experience may be the key to future administrative careers, but other factors are also involved. Leadership qualities are most important. One also must be well organized, have integrity, be fair in dealing with others, and be willing to accept responsibility and its consequences.

If you think an administrative career is to your liking, do not wait until age forty to prepare for it. Like any profession, preparation is essential to future success. For example, it is important to gain various experiences during your professional career that may be considered "building blocks" to become an administrator. Advanced degrees also may be prerequisites. Your abilities are often governed by your experiences. If you desire to become a college or university physical education administrator, you will need to acquire teaching experience in the public schools; a master's degree; leadership experiences in physical education; college teaching experience; a doctorate degree; more college teaching and leadership experiences at the college level; and, finally, await the opportunity for which you may be qualified. This is not to say that every college physical education administrator has had that exact experience, but this pattern would parallel the career experiences of many. A similar pattern pertaining to athletics would be followed by the future athletic administrator.

While administrative positions appear to be lucrative both in salary and prestige, they also have their headaches. Some may be very confining, require long hours, and receive pressure from various aspects of the work itself. Administrators also must bear responsibility for the programs they administrate and may take much criticism. Administrative jobs are not for everyone, but if responsibility and organization, among many other various factors, appeal to you, administration may be one of your future goals. Table 4.3 summarizes various administrative careers in physical education and athletics.

Table 4.3
Administrative Careers

CAREER	BRIEF JOB DESCRIPTION	USUAL MINIMUM DEGREE REQUIREMENTS	ADVANCED TRAINING	EXPERIENCES NECESSARY
Athletic director, high school	Responsible for the total interscholastic program and its development. Includes personnel, scheduling, facilities, equipment, public relations, and budgeting, among many other duties.	Bachelor's/ master's degree.	Any necessary state certification. Athletic administration background helpful.	Usually many years of successful teaching and coaching experience.
Athletic director, college level	Responsible for the total intercollegiate program and its development. Includes supervision of coaches, business office, sports information, trainers, equipment and facilities, scholarships, conference and national affiliations, and scheduling.	Bachelor's/ master's degree in sports management or athletic administration.	Business training or background helpful.	Proven administrative ability. Usually has strong background in coaching and athletics.
Physical education director/ supervisor, public school level	Responsible for the curriculum, staff, and development of the total physical education program in the public school system.	Master's degree.	Any necessary state certification.	Successful teaching and administrative experiences.
Physical education director/ coordinator, college level	Responsible for the physical activities and professional preparation program for the junior college, college, or university. Program development, personnel, budget, and curriculum in the college setting.	Doctorate degree.	———	Successful teaching, leadership, and administrative experiences necessary. Scholarly activities helpful.
Intramural director	Responsible for the organization, administration, and development of the intramural activities program. This position usually exists full time only at the college level.	Master's degree.	Recreation training helpful.	Successful organizational and development ability. Strong leadership and motivation necessary.

Table 4.3 *Continued*

Administrative Careers

CAREER	BRIEF JOB DESCRIPTION	USUAL MINIMUM DEGREE REQUIREMENTS	ADVANCED TRAINING	EXPERIENCES NECESSARY
Camp director	Responsible for the total camp program and its development. Includes staffing, recruitment, program content, facilities, and equipment, as well as supervision during the camp sessions. May be with private camp or agency camp. Full- and part-time positions are available.	Bachelor's degree.	Recreation, outdoor education, and business training helpful.	Agency camps: successful teaching and camping experiences. Leadership ability. Private camps: same criteria plus years of successful experience at the camp in other capacities.
Athletic conference administration	Responsible for the organization, development, and enforcement of a college athletic conference, its laws, and its regulations. There are also many supportive-type positions below the commissioner or director level.	Bachelor's/ master's degree.	Varied, depending on the type of position.	Successful leadership experiences in athletics or other related areas.
Professional sports administration	Various positions in supportive roles for professional sports. Examples: player personnel director, public relations director, administrative assistant, business manager, and minor league or farm team officials.	Bachelor's/ master's degree.	Varied, depending on the type of position.	Successful leadership experiences in athletics or related specialty skills. Many jobs are related more to the business aspects of professional sports.

Non-teaching Careers

Non-teaching careers have surfaced in recent years for two main reasons. The first is that teaching and coaching jobs are not always plentiful, and necessity becomes the guide for an alternate career. Second is that the physical education major is diverse and often has skills that with little or no additional training may qualify the individual for various jobs. For example, many famous coaches leave the profession to obtain media careers. Health and fitness centers offer the opportunity to apply one's skills

with more salary potential if one has good sales ability as well as the personality to work with club members (see fig. 4.3). Insurance companies solicit coaches and physical educators for insurance sales. Most people in our profession are outgoing in personality and are somewhat aggressive and competitive by nature and from athletic experiences. These are also the qualities of a potentially good salesperson.

Many non-teaching careers come after physical educators have applied their skills as teachers and coaches. Obviously, success in coaching is one way to gain public exposure and other opportunities. The same may be said for the professional college or university physical educators who publish frequently or write books in accordance to their professional expertise. Professional athletes also can reap many career opportunities if they carefully manage their resources and are well advised in a business sense. Others in physical education and coaching actively prepare or seek alternative careers while they are teaching and coaching. The reason for this usually is the lack of high salaries and the amount of time necessary to be a successful teacher and coach.

What about persons who never prepare for a teaching or coaching career and yet desire a major in physical education? First, sport is big business in our society today. There are endless opportunities in sport. Further, some like the active, physical life

exhibit 4.1

Officer preparation: A degree in physical education

Physical education was a vehicle that enabled me to obtain a commission as an Officer of Marines. During my military career my physical education background has helped many times in planning and conducting physical training programs for the marines. This, of course, is expected of military leaders. Due to my knowledge of physical education I was able to emphasize the value of physical training and explain to Marines the objectives and benefits of exercise. After completing my degree in physical education, I believe there was no type of exercise or training program I was not able to perform and teach correctly. I understood the principles of exercise and how to plan programs for development, maintenance, and remedial physical training. I have always remembered that for a man to be effective in combat he must be physically ready, which means he must have stamina, be mentally ready, and have confidence. Physical training creates stamina and builds confidence, which in turn creates mental discipline and emotional stability in critical situations. Probably the most important benefit I have received from my professional preparation in physical education is the development of leadership skills. A military officer must be a leader of men, and my courses of study in physical education offered me the opportunity to practice these skills.

Major John S. Dill III, USMC
(degree in physical education from St.
Bonaventure University, New York)

that awaits the physical education major or feel that due to their participation in college athletics such a major is natural. One example is that of a career military officer who was an athlete and physical education major in college. By his own admission he was not going to teach, wanted a military career, and felt physical education was the best preparation he could obtain for his military career ambitions. Physical education has always had somewhat of a mystique that draws people without ambitions to teach into the major field. The appeal may be physical activity, exercise, or sport itself. Fortunately, due to the sport and fitness boom of the seventies, the career opportunities are available. Tables 4.4 and 4.5 summarize various non-teaching careers. However, this list is by no means complete. The opportunities are many more in number than stated here. One can search almost any profession and find someone who started in that field with a degree in physical education.

Whether it be in business, government agencies, allied professions, media, or free enterprise, the physical education major is there. However, one must realize that advanced training, on-the-job training, and other experience is often necessary to obtain non-teaching careers. In retrospect, this is not as bad or as time-consuming as it may sound. Actually, public school teaching and coaching are among the few professions

Table 4.4
Non-teaching Careers in Sport

CAREER	BRIEF JOB DESCRIPTION	USUAL MINIMUM DEGREE REQUIREMENTS	ADVANCED TRAINING	EXPERIENCE NECESSARY
Sports journalist	Newspaper, journal, and magazine reporting, editing, and writing. Reporters should be generalists in sports but may have one specialty sport.	Bachelor's degree with journalism experience.	Summer or part-time jobs in the journalism field.	Successful writing experience, usually beginning during the college years.
Sports photographer	Photographer for newspapers or magazine publications. Also may be self-employed as freelance photographer.	No degree requirement.	Courses and experience in photography, usually freelance or part-time jobs in the photography field.	Skill and successful experiences in producing top quality photographs.
Sportscaster	Announcing and informing the public about sporting events. Television and radio announcers broadcast news coverage, the actual sporting event, and provide "color" coverage for the public.	Bachelor's degree with communication experience and an excellent speaking voice.	Employment in the media field and technical training for radio and television career.	Successful broadcasting experience and public appeal.
Sports information director	Public relations specialist for athletics at the college level. Various responsibilities involving the press, media, and public.	Bachelor's degree with communications and journalism experience.	Employment in the media field, with writing and speaking skills involving sports.	Successful experience in journalism and other media and sports knowledge.
Professional athlete	Highly skilled individual who makes a living by participation in sport. Very competitive.	No degree requirement, although the majority of professional athletes attend college.	Ability to improve or maintain skill level and conditioning throughout career.	Proven skill and performance in competitive situations.

Table 4.4 *Continued*
Non-teaching Careers in Sport

CAREER	BRIEF JOB DESCRIPTION	USUAL MINIMUM DEGREE REQUIREMENTS	ADVANCED TRAINING	EXPERIENCE NECESSARY
Equipment manager	Responsible for purchase, selection, safety, care, handling and transportation of sports equipment, usually at the college and professional level.	No degree requirement, although this is a growing profession for degreed persons.	Obtain thorough knowledge of sports equipment and its repair.	Sports equipment training as a student manager at the college level or related experiences in the sports industry.
Facility manager and maintenance	Preparation and care of sports facilities, usually at the college or professional level. However, some positions are available at the high school level.	No degree requirement.	Usually on-the-job training involving the particular facility.	Employment in facility maintenance and management skills.
Business manager	Responsible for handling the business aspects of organized sports, such as tickets, concessions, travel expenses, accounting, and the like, usually at the college or professional level.	Bachelor's degree with business or accounting experience.	Obtain courses in business and accounting.	Proven skill in business aspects and involvement in organized sports.
Sports artist	Artist-illustrator for sporting events. Usually a freelance or part-time position.	No degree requirement.	Artist training as necessary.	Skill and successful experiences in painting and drawing sports events and personalities.
Sports agent or representative	Represent professional athletes in contract negotiations as well as serve as financial consultants for the players. Intermediate between the player and the team.	Bachelor's degree.	Advanced training or degrees in law, business, or accounting.	Money management experiences and negotiating skills. Knowledge of legal procedures.

Table 4.4 *Continued*
Non-teaching Careers in Sport

CAREER	BRIEF JOB DESCRIPTION	USUAL MINIMUM DEGREE REQUIREMENTS	ADVANCED TRAINING	EXPERIENCE NECESSARY
Sports promoter	Promote and organize sporting events. Promoters operate at various levels. Generally associated with boxing and wrestling, but other sports have promoters also.	No degree requirement.	Some business, advertising, and management training necessary.	Successful experiences in public relations, negotiations, and promotion. Knowledge of sport important.
Public relations director	Public relations specialist for athletics at the professional level. Various responsibilities involving all aspects of the media and public.	Bachelor's degree with communications and journalism experience.	Employment in the media field and public relations skills training.	Successful experience in journalism and other media and sports knowledge.
Personnel director	Responsible for the recruiting, procurement and general well-being of professional athletes on a team. Position is sometimes combined with other responsibilities such as general manager and the like.	Bachelor's degree.	Business or public relations training helpful.	Successful experience as athlete or coach in the sport. Ability to discriminate and recognize talent in prospective players.
Sporting goods sales	Sell, promote, and distribute particular or general sport products. Varies from wholesale to retail levels.	Bachelor's degree.	Sales training.	Successful sales or athletic experiences as a player or coach. Helpful to be a well-known personality.

Table 4.5

Non-teaching Careers in Allied and Related Areas

CAREER	BRIEF JOB DESCRIPTION	USUAL MINIMUM DEGREE REQUIREMENTS	ADVANCED TRAINING	EXPERIENCE NECESSARY
Physical therapist	Rehabilitation of injury or illness. May be associated with hospital, clinic, or have private practice.	Bachelor's degree with license as physical therapist.	Master's degree helpful.	Clinical experience in performance of therapy skills.
Sports medicine physician	Medical doctor who specializes in athletic injuries. Team physician examines players, designs rehabilitation programs, and determines whether or not players are capable of participation. Emergency treatment at games. Other physicians who are not team doctors also specialize in sports medicine for the general public.	Bachelor's degree, doctor of medicine degree, and license as a physician.	Sports medicine and exercise physiology. Most sports medicine physicians are orthopedists.	Successful experiences in working with athletes and athletic injuries. Knowledge of sports and athletic conditioning.
Sports podiatrist	Specializes in injuries to the foot and leg. A sports podiatrist concentrates on injuries and conditions that result from athletic events such as running as well as team sports. (See fig. 4.4.)	Bachelor's degree, doctor of podiatry degree and license as doctor of podiatric medicine.	Sports medicine and exercise physiology.	Successful experiences working with injuries to the foot and leg.
Sports nutritionist	Nutrition specialist who is responsible for the overall diet and meal planning for an athletic team or institution. Sports nutritionists are usually associated with a college team, professional team, or clinic.	Bachelor's degree.	Specialization and training in nutrition.	Successful experiences in nutrition planning. Knowledge of sports is important.
Sport and exercise physiologist	Specialist in the area of human performance in sport and exercise. Usually work at university or college level and consult for various organizations in sport and physical fitness.	Master's degree.	Doctorate in exercise physiology.	Knowledge and experiences working with a variety of sports and fitness activities is helpful.

Table 4.5 *Continued*

Non-teaching Careers in Allied and Related Areas

CAREER	BRIEF JOB DESCRIPTION	USUAL MINIMUM DEGREE REQUIREMENTS	ADVANCED TRAINING	EXPERIENCE NECESSARY
Sports medicine technician or assistant	Assist physician, physical therapist, or exercise physiologist in a variety of capacities in the performance of their skills, including clerical duties.	Bachelor's degree.	Sports medicine training.	Knowledge and interest in sports medicine.
Health/fitness center director	Overall responsibility for health spa or fitness center operations. Includes hiring staff, equipment, programs, sales, management, and advertising.	Bachelor's degree.	Sales and management training.	Successful experience as fitness instructor; sales and management skills.
Health/fitness center instructor	Responsible for the administration of programs to the members and for sales of memberships.	No degree requirement. Bachelor's degree helpful.	Exercise and fitness training; sales training.	Knowledge and interest in physical fitness. Instructor should demonstrate fitness by example.
Corporate fitness	Responsible for the health and fitness levels of personnel working for the hiring agency. Job responsibilities vary as to the company or organization. Usually included are stress testing, fitness testing, programs for exercise and fitness, recreational activities, consultations on diet, nutrition, and other related subjects. Agencies range from large corporations to hospitals.	Bachelor's degree to doctorate degree, depending on job description.	Exercise physiology.	Successful experiences in exercise physiology.
Military officer	Organize and coordinate sports activities and programs for physical activity at military installations. Often referred to as Special Services, Athletic, or Physical Training Officer. Coaching sports may also be part of position.	Bachelor's degree.	Master's degree helpful.	Background in sports as player and coach. Experiences in organizing programs of physical activity.

Table 4.5 *Continued*

Non-teaching Careers in Allied and Related Areas

CAREER	BRIEF JOB DESCRIPTION	USUAL MINIMUM DEGREE REQUIREMENTS	ADVANCED TRAINING	EXPERIENCE NECESSARY
Pharmaceutical sales	Sales, promotion, and education of consumers for pharmaceutical products. Clients usually include hospitals, doctors, clinics, and pharmacies.	Bachelor's degree.	Sales training usually arranged by hiring company.	Knowledge of pharmaceutical products. Sales experience helpful.
Insurance sales	Sales and promotion of various types of insurances. Physical education majors and coaches are considered good prospects for insurance sales because of outgoing personality and aggressive, competitive attitudes from sports participation.	Bachelor's degree.	Sales training usually arranged by hiring company.	Knowledge of insurance business. Sales experience helpful.
Textbook sales	Sales and promotion of textbook and other publications for major publishing companies. Sales are usually for the college market but other outlets are also possible.	Bachelor's degree.	Sales training usually arranged by hiring company.	Knowledge of textbook markets and subject matter in sales areas.
Publisher/editor for professional publications	Responsible for content and quality of various publications. Examples would be national and state journals, coaching publications, textbooks, and audiovisual materials.	Bachelor's degree.	Journalism and communications training. Some sales and management training.	Successful experiences in the journalism and publishing fields. Knowledge of sales market and subject matter in sales areas.
Government careers	Many career opportunities are offered by federal and state government. Examples would be the National Park Service, United States Department of Agriculture (Forest Ranger), Fisheries and Wildlife, Game Management, Peace Corps, and federal jobs overseas, including teaching positions.	Bachelor's degree.	Special training as required for specific positions.	Successful experiences and skills to qualify for various positions.

Figure 4.4 Care for injured athletes is provided by a person having a career in sports medicine, such as a podiatrist.

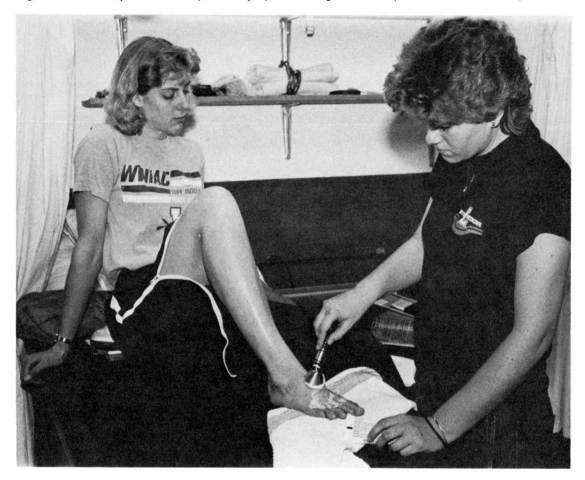

where the persons start performing their skills as soon as they are hired. Many other professions and careers call for lengthy and extensive training and retraining experiences before workers start performing their job skills.

If you decide to choose a non-teaching career either at the completion of your degree or after teaching and coaching for awhile, keep in mind that your opportunities are not limited if you are open to obtaining the necessary skills or qualifications for such a career.

SUMMARY

Successful career planning is a matter of preparation and continuous decisions. Numerous opportunities await the professional physical educator. Now, in the early stages of your professional preparation, you should thoroughly examine all possible career opportunities and investigate the qualifications and training necessary for career options that are of interest to you. The purpose of this chapter was to inform you about the total scope of career opportunities in order for you to make rational and logical decisions. No attempt was made to make one career appear more attractive than another. However, keep in mind that the majority of professional preparation programs in physical education are teaching-oriented. This is an asset in almost any selected field, for teaching skills are essential in many careers.

Your initial career selection will more than likely be motivated by the reason you chose physical education as your major. When the time comes for you to seek employment, you should reflect on your training and education, and evaluate your qualifications for jobs you desire. Career decisions are based upon numerous factors. Most people should anticipate a change in job description as they increase in age. Finding and selecting a new career opportunity is often exciting, but only to those who have made careful preparations. Careers for the physical education major are varied, ranging from teaching and coaching to administrative positions and non-teaching careers, which are limitless and diverse for the person willing to accept the responsibility to seek advanced training and job skills when necessary. The sport and fitness boom of the seventies is somewhat responsible for the existence of many new career selections. When the time comes for you to make career decisions, the knowledge gleaned from this chapter and the appropriate preparation should help you make informed, accurate choices.

STUDY QUESTIONS

1. What are your present reasons for becoming a physical educator?
2. State your present goals for the physical education profession.
3. Examine the advantages and disadvantages of a teaching or coaching career. Discuss both within your class.
4. Examine the advantages and disadvantages of a non-teaching career. Discuss both within your class.
5. Explain what is meant by the phrase, "A teacher first"?
6. What is the value of teaching ability in any career choice? Also, how does one develop a teaching personality?

STUDENT ACTIVITIES

1. Prepare a resume that could be used for summer or part-time employment in the areas of physical education, sport, or the like. Analyze your present strengths and weaknesses. State the professional experiences you need to enable you to be qualified for your present choice of careers.

2. Compile a list of references that you would include when applying for a position in physical education. Investigate the services that are offered by your college's or university's career placement services.

3. Interview any person actively employed in teaching physical education or coaching and ask her or him the following questions:
   a. What personal and professional qualities does the beginning physical education teacher need most to become a competent teacher?
   b. Do advanced degrees enhance teaching knowledge in the public schools? Of what value are the degrees?
   c. If you had your choice, would you teach/coach at the public school level or the college level?
   d. Make up questions of your choice.

4. Interview any person with a physical education degree who is employed in a non-teaching career and ask him or her the following questions:
   a. Has your physical education degree been a help to your present profession? How?
   b. Why did you not pursue a career in teaching? If you did teach, what were your reasons for leaving?
   c. If you were to begin your college career over again, would you still major in physical education?
   d. Make up questions of your choice.

RELATED READINGS

American Alliance for Health, Physical Education, Recreation, and Dance. *Alternative Professional Preparation in Physical Education.* Washington, DC: AAHPERD Publications, 1979. For information, write to AAHPERD Publications, 1900 Association Drive, Reston, VA 22091.

————. *Dance: A Career for You.* Washington, DC: AAHPERD Publications, 1977.

————. *Infusing Career Education into Physical Education and Sport, Selected Writings.* Washington, DC: AAHPERD Publications, 1977.

Corrigan, Gary J. "Ten Consequences of Career Change." *Phi Delta Kappan* 62, no. 6 (February 1981).

Heitzmann, William Ray. *Opportunities in Sports and Athletics.* Skokie, IL: National Textbook Company, 1980.

Pisana, John A. "The Job of Job Hunting." *Phi Delta Kappan* 62, no. 6 (February 1981).

Ryan, Kevin, et al. *Biting the Apple: Accounts of First-Year Teachers.* NY: Longman Inc., 1980.

Women's Sports Careers Guide. San Francisco: Women's Sports Foundation, published annually.

Professional Preparation

5

Chapter outline

The Professional Preparation of a
  Teacher
    Factors Affecting Professional
      Preparation
    Approaches to Teacher Education
    Exhibit 5.1 A Framework for Change
    Laboratory and Field Experiences
Professional Preparation in Non-Teaching
  Areas
    Athletic Coaching

Athletic Training
Exercise Science
Physical Therapy
Leisure Services
Summary
Study Questions
Student Activities
Notes
Related Readings

Student objectives

As a result of the study of this chapter, the student should be able to

1. Differentiate between formal courses of study for professional preparation and other factors affecting professional development.
2. Explain the functions and purposes of NCATE and NASDTEC.
3. Describe the influence exerted by state departments of education and their certification requirements on the professional preparation curricula for a teacher.
4. Define *reciprocity* and list the conditions under which reciprocal agreements between states usually occur.
5. Explain the impact of the AAHPERD professional preparation conferences on teacher education in physical education.
6. Describe the ways in which a teacher education institution exercises some latitude in its program and give an example of this *semi-autonomy.*
7. List and describe the three major approaches to teacher education programs.
8. List the characteristics that define a teacher education program as *behavioral* or *humanistic* in its approach.
9. Explain *competency-based teacher education* and its impact on professional preparation during the last decade.
10. List and explain the kinds of *field experiences* widely used in professional preparation programs.
11. State the current trends in professional preparation programs available in careers other than teaching in physical education.

In chapter 4, we examined a diversity of career opportunities in physical education. Undergraduate and graduate courses of study comprise the formal educational processes designed to prepare an effective professional for these careers in physical education. Courses in professional curricula are intended to meet the demand for specialization needed for each career, as well as meeting certain requirements imposed by other influences, which we will examine later in this chapter. It should be understood that formal courses of study, the subject of this chapter, represent only one avenue in preparing for a career in physical education.

In chapter 6, which deals with professional development, we will take a look at another avenue for professional preparation. Unlike curricular requirements imposed in formal courses of study at the undergraduate level, your involvement in and study of your profession is purely voluntary and contingent upon your own initiative (see fig. 5.1). Active participation in professional organizations, attendance at professional meetings, and study of the available literature related to one's career in physical education, all of which are mentioned in chapter 6, serve to greatly enhance formal professional preparation.

Only recently has professional preparation been considered for careers other than for the education of a teacher. Demands for the skills possessed by physical educators have come from other public and private sectors of our society, providing for numerous non-teaching career opportunities. Professional preparation programs designed to meet these demands are still in their infancy compared to teacher education programs. Formal non-teaching professional preparation programs will grow and develop in scope and quality when subjected to the same close scrutiny as teacher education programs have been over the years.

Teacher education represents the avenue pursued by the majority of the students entering physical education professional preparation programs. If this is currently your choice, have you closely examined your college catalog or spoken with your advisor relative to the course of study? Perhaps you have been bewildered by some requirements or have expressed doubts that certain courses could help you become a good teacher. As you will determine as we begin our examination of professional preparation, formal courses of study are the result of a number of trends and influences, including those affecting the professional preparation of a teacher.

THE PROFESSIONAL PREPARATION OF A TEACHER
Factors Affecting Professional Preparation

As mentioned earlier, the formal course of study for the professional preparation of a teacher is not the result of whims or a combination of philosophies of faculty members of the institution of higher education charged with preparing teachers. The college or university is permitted latitude for professional input only after certain standards and requirements are met. Among these are standards established by national accrediting agencies and certification requirements established by each state.

Figure 5.1 Professional physical educators continually strive to increase their knowledge. Here, a group of field hockey coaches learn techniques from a master British teacher and coach.

National Accrediting Agencies

Recognized by the United States Commissioner of Education and authorized by the Council on Post-Secondary Accreditation, the National Council for the Accreditation of Teacher Education (NCATE) is charged with adopting standards and procedures for accreditation and determining the accreditation status of institutional programs for preparing teachers.[1]

In order to facilitate the accreditation process, a team comprised of teachers and administrators from elementary, secondary, and higher education visits the college or university seeking NCATE accreditation. A report, prepared by the host institution, is made in response to the standards for each area of inquiry. It is the purpose of the visiting team to make an on-sight assessment of whether or not each standard is met. Subsequently, accreditation is either granted or denied. This accreditation process lends credibility and respectability to the institution and its teacher education programs. Since many employers hire only graduates of NCATE-accredited programs, this process is equally important to the prospective teacher.

Another agency granted accreditation powers by an association of state departments of education is the National Association of State Directors of Teacher Education and Certification (NASDTEC). In addition to investigating the status of an institution in meeting general standards similar to NCATE's, NASDTEC has also established specific standards for the various disciplines preparing teachers.

Because NCATE and NASDTEC accreditation teams are faced with the awesome task of evaluating all teacher education programs in a college or university, some physical educators believe that the teacher education programs in physical education are not examined in enough detail. It has been suggested that a logical accrediting agency for physical education would be the American Alliance for Health, Physical Education, Recreation and Dance. Since standards would have to be agreed upon by the AAHPERD membership, however, it might prove impossible to arrive at an agreement as to what ought to be the standards for teacher education programs. Should this factor not prove insurmountable, visiting teams, empowered by and armed with standards established by AAHPERD, could provide a logical future step in stabilizing teacher education programs among colleges and universities.

State Certification Requirements

State departments of education often have a division of teacher education responsible for coordinating certification requirements between the state and the colleges and universities within that state having teacher education programs. Such coordination involves receiving applications, transcripts, medical forms, and, possibly, scores from the National Teacher's Examination (NTE) from the college and prospective teacher. Following an evaluation of these materials to determine if state certification requirements are met, the state may grant certification that authorizes the person holding the proper credentials to teach in that state. Furthermore, it is the responsibility of this division to evaluate possible changes in the type of certification granted to a teacher. Factors that can change the type of certification include graduate credits earned, military experience, and teaching experience. Most beginning teachers are on some form of probationary certification. As evidence of teaching competence is obtained through evaluations and additional course work is taken and experience is earned, professional and permanent certification can be obtained. Some states may require additional course work during the life of a certificate in order for the certificate to be renewed. Usually, six to eight hours of relevant course work every five years is sufficient.

Changes occur frequently in teacher certification requirements. Such changes are the result of legislative mandate, lobbying by professional organizations, input from local and district school boards, and suggestions brought to the attention of supervisors within the state department of education. Professionals from the field of education are often consulted by the state departments to determine the feasibility of a change or to formulate a plan of action in bringing about a change. The fact that some states have not changed their certification requirements since the requirements were first formulated in the 1930s indicates that changes in traditional teacher education programs and certification requirements are, in some instances, resisted.

Reciprocity

Many states have joined in accepting the credentials earned by a teacher in one state as valid for teaching in another state. This *reciprocal agreement,* or **reciprocity,** allows for the waiver of specific course requirements. Most state boards of education accept this agreement only where the certifying state has been accredited by NCATE or NASDTEC.

exhibit 5.1

A framework for change

How long are we going to continue to certify physical educators who are unskilled—some of whom show little aptitude for learning physical skills? Do music programs certify students who have no musical talent? Do mathematics programs certify students who cannot do mathematics? Students who major in art have to demonstrate performance capabilities in several media, such as painting, printmaking, sculpting, and potting. While they most certainly do and should study such things as methods of teaching art and even the psychology of art, the bulk of their undergraduate training is spent in developing art skills—doing the subject matter of art. The subject matter of physical education is games, sport, exercise, and dance, and the more quickly that notion is reflected in the undergraduate curriculum the more quickly will that curriculum better prepare the potential teacher to contribute to the upgrading of school programs in physical education.

Source: Daryl Siedentop, "A Framework for Change" (Paper delivered to the Central Western Zone of the New York State Association for Health, Physical Education and Recreation, Rochester, New York).

Input from the Profession

The American Alliance for Health, Physical Education, Recreation and Dance has held national conferences devoted to the subject of professional preparation. Each reflected trends in teacher education and certification consistent with the times. The first, held in 1962, emphasized the *knowledge* model (discussed later in this chapter) by stressing course offerings in *general* education, *general professional* education, and *specialized professional* education. The 1962 conference recognized the need for time to accumulate knowledge in the aforementioned areas of education and suggested a need for a five-year professional preparation program. In addition, this conference focused on the need for professional laboratory experiences and field work to enhance the preparation of a teacher of physical education.

The 1973 New Orleans conference was an effort to upgrade recommendations from the earlier conference, as well as an attempt to identify **teaching competencies.** At this time, the emphasis on teacher accountability, the use of performance (behavioral) objectives, and the competency-based programs were gaining support. Task forces derived concepts and competencies to be acquired from the professional education of a teacher, a move away from course-oriented professional preparation curricula. Specifically, the move was away from general skills and abilities that teachers should possess to demonstrated competencies thought to be important for a teacher to utilize.

While colleges and universities continue to revise professional preparation curricula under the constraints of accreditation and certification standards, the impact of these two AAHPERD conferences have proven very valuable. Continuing efforts to upgrade professional capabilities have, in many cases, resulted from consulting the published AAHPERD standards for professional preparation, against which an institution can measure itself.

Institutional Requirements

Depending upon the nature of the institution of higher education, teacher education programs may vary significantly. Once the minimum credit-hour and course requirements have been met, each institution is permitted latitude to add courses it deems appropriate for a teacher. These additions may take the form of required courses, approved or guided elective courses, or may emphasize a specific area of the curriculum of study in professional preparation.

Departments of physical education in large universities, for example, may be under the direction of the College of Education or they may be autonomous. In either case, there is generally more emphasis on courses taken in the professional block in education or physical education. Small liberal arts colleges with physical education departments often emphasize the liberal arts curricula during the first two years of study, with course work in the humanities, sciences, and mathematics being the primary focus. The remaining two years are usually devoted to the professional curriculum in an attempt to meet certification requirements. As an illustration, a foreign language may be required of all graduates of a liberal arts college, but may not be required in a teacher education program in a large university. A foreign language is rarely required for the certification of a physical education teacher.

Some institutions may place additional qualifications on students entering a teacher education program. Some departments, for example, may require a fitness test or sport's skills assessment as prerequisites for entry, or they may withhold certification until the criteria of acceptable performance is met by the student. Other institutions require a particular grade-point ratio before a student is allowed to enter into or continue in a teacher education program. These requirements represent some of the ways the respective institutions of higher education assert themselves in the process of educating and certifying a teacher.

Approaches to Teacher Education

The Traditional Approach

Despite the cry for renovation of teacher education programs during the 1960s and 1970s and the support this criticism generated throughout the nation, in actuality, little has changed in the process of preparing teachers during the twentieth century. Granted, shuffling has occurred in the **traditional, knowledge-based approach** to teacher education; courses have been moved to the junior year instead of the freshman year or prerequisite courses have been established, but the model is essentially the same. This excerpt, from a state certification manual, is fairly representative of the traditional and wide-spread model for teacher education:

> The college preparation leading to the degree must include three categories as follows:
> (1) **Basic preparation** (general education). The basic program is to be composed of general courses usually from liberal arts or courses of common value to all teachers.

(2) **Specialized preparation.** This includes a minimum preparation in fields in which teachers are to teach. (3) **Professional preparation.** Courses or programs of professional education must include an understanding and an appreciation of the children who are to be taught, a knowledge of sound ways to teach these children, and a familiarity of the work of the schools in relation to the state and the nation.[2]

In most cases, the courses' credit hours, which must be accumulated before certification will be granted, are specified in each of these three categories. The student teaching experience is usually the final requirement, although some states require a satisfactory score on the NTE, which tests cognitive skills over courses taken, before eligibility to teach is granted.

Specifically, for physical education, this traditional model usually emphasizes these three categories in the following manner: **basic preparation** is to include courses in English, biological and physical sciences, social studies, and health. **Specialized preparation** in physical education is structured around credit-hour requirements in foundations (history and philosophy), organization and administration, human anatomy and physiology, and techniques for teaching activities ranging from rhythmics to team sports (see fig. 5.2). Some departments may also require additional specialized courses such as sports psychology or sports sociology within this category. **Professional preparation** courses include child and adolescent development, principles and practices of teaching, philosophy or history of education, and student teaching.

The underlying assumption in the traditional model is that exposure (the accumulation of cognitive experiences) to these areas of preparation, which are deemed appropriate "knowledge" for the teacher to have, enables one to teach effectively. Whether this approach represents a sound one or not has been the subject of debate over the last several decades. Nevertheless, the traditional approach is an approach that is thoroughly in place in the United States. This was confirmed at a meeting held prior to the 1982 AAHPERD National Convention in Houston, Texas, to discuss trends in teacher certification throughout the nation. A representative from each of the six districts that comprise AAHPERD spoke to certification policies in the states making up each district. With very few exceptions, the traditional, knowledge-based model was firmly entrenched, despite the fact that many states advocated a different model during the eras of criticism. The southern district was identified as a district where some states were moving away from the traditional approach to one that contained features of the competency-based teacher education model.

The Behavioral Approach

One departure from the *knowledge* emphasis, found in the traditional model for teacher education, has been the emphasis on *performance* as the focus of the behavioral model. This model assumes the following beliefs regarding teacher education:

1. Learning is a change in behavior.
2. The primary justification for education is that it should lead to functional, practical, and useful end products.
3. End products can be and should be pre-defined by some group of experts.
4. Teaching can be broken down into sequences of specifically defined behaviors.

5. Teachers should achieve proficiency in a predetermined set of skills.
6. Teacher training involves a series of activities designed to produce desired behaviors.
7. Anything worth doing is worth measuring.
8. If it can't be measured, it probably doesn't exist.[3]

The application of these beliefs has led to the development of *competency-based teacher education,* a model that features an inductive approach to deciding what the student is to learn. The process then involves working toward training the teacher to maximize the possibility that the teacher possesses the capabilities to teach those identified items.

Competency-Based Teacher Education
In chapter 9 we will examine teaching skills that are necessary for efficient teaching performances. The need for identifiable teaching skills, or competencies, grew from a widespread dissatisfaction, which began in the 1960s, with the American educational

system. Out of this dissatisfaction evolved the concept that the schools and their teachers must be accountable to the public for what is or is not occurring in the schools. If students are not being properly educated, what are the reasons? In attempting to answer that question, a public scrutiny of the abilities of our nation's teachers followed. Feeling the pressure, many state legislatures began mandating stronger requirements for teachers through institutions of higher education that conducted teacher-education programs within each state.

A method that attempted to provide stability for this new emphasis on teacher accountability was **competency-based teacher education** (CBTE).

The Background of CBTE   The genesis of CBTE programs can be traced to a project funded by the United States Office of Education, the Elementary Teacher Education Models Program. The task of this project was to reconceptualize both preservice and in-service elementary teacher education. Ten funded institutions developed the basic specifications for their models. Each model used the systems approach to design and operate the programs, and each was competency-based.[4]

The proponents of the CBTE movement offered this program as a solution to the shortcomings of the so-called traditional knowledge-based model.[5] A preservice teacher would be expected to follow the format suggested by the CBTE programs, which include focusing on specific skills the prospective teacher will demonstrate, providing instructional alternatives to facilitate his or her progress, and holding each teacher trainee accountable for the attainment of the target objectives.[6]

The Nature of CBTE   The teacher is assessed or evaluated by both performance (actually demonstrating the desired teacher behavior while teaching) and consequence (the students perform well as a result of the teacher performing well) assessment channels. Objectives that are as explicit as possible form the competencies to be attained and comprise three areas: (1) cognitive objectives, which, in teacher education, may include subject matter knowledge, psychological theories of learning, educational strategies, and other matters pertaining to intellectual skills; (2) performance objectives, which require the prospective teacher to actually demonstrate an ability to perform teacher-related tasks; and (3) consequence objectives, which are expressed in terms of the results of the teacher's actions. Consequence assessment is usually made as a result of the accomplishments of the students under the direction of the preservice teacher.

The major point of emphasis for CBTE programs is that objectives and criteria are unambiguously specified. A teacher's competency can be measured against specified criteria, which are as explicit as possible. Consequently, the teacher demonstrates competency against these criteria rather than on course work taken, as in the traditional programs.[7] During its infancy, CBTE programs gained high acclaim, with state after state mandating competency-based certification for their teachers. Much of this early enthusiasm was curtailed, however, as the task of identifying the competencies an efficient teacher needed to possess was undertaken. In addition, critics of CBTE were appalled that these programs should be so readily adopted with no research base to determine if this process of educating a teacher was better than the traditional method.[8]

Concurrent research in the late 1960s and early 1970s that focused on the behaviors of teachers and resultant behaviors in students has made the identification of desirable teacher competencies less awesome. Since this research permitted the identification of teaching skills that actually facilitated student learning, competency-based teacher education programs were allowed to progress beyond the level of philosophical desirability concerning teacher education to a level of better understanding of the teaching-learning process. What has followed are more efficient curricular frameworks for the preparation of teachers.

The Contemporary Status of CBTE   CBTE programs rarely exist in their purest theoretical forms today. Subsequent modifications, however, have made them amenable to a number of diverse philosophies existing among institutions of higher learning that educate teachers. Unlike many "bandwagon" approaches in education in general and in teacher education in particular, that sound terrific when presented at professional meetings or "look good" on paper, the legacy of CBTE programs appears to be that their effects will be around for some time to come. Educators have been forced to closely examine their course offerings to determine the material's relevance to teaching.

Teacher competence has become a common term. The extensive use of objectives is commonly found in many teacher education programs. Curriculum revisions have become a matter of course in seeking to find better ways of preparing teachers. Field experience programs, which permit actual teaching experiences in efforts to establish desired competencies, are now found extensively. Many states continue to grapple with massive changes in their certification programs, owing to the influence of CBTE programs. Those states adopting modifications of CBTE programs fully intend to certify only those who have successfully demonstrated specified competencies in a teaching situation. Under the dictates of a public law in South Carolina, for example, a student must demonstrate in a "showcase lesson" certain behaviors that have been identified as essential to the act of teaching (see fig. 5.3). Failure to demonstrate these competencies results in time spent in remediation. Repeated failures result in termination from the program, illustrative of the fact that those demanding teacher accountability "mean business."

CBTE: An Example of Its Contemporary Influence   Some institutions are utilizing what has been termed, a *block approach* as opposed to traditional courses intended to prepare teachers. *Blocks,* or areas, are identified as important to teaching. These blocks include input from the various disciplines comprising physical education, providing the cognitive skills the prospective teacher needs to meet specific objectives. Performance objectives are included that specify what the teacher trainee is to actually do. Incorporating these objectives into field experiences (which are examined later in this chapter) provides the opportunity for a prospective teacher to practice the skills in a realistic setting. An example of identified areas and the competencies the teacher trainee needs that relate to each of these areas follows.

Figure 5.3 Undergraduate students learn games and activities they will one day teach to children.

Area 1: Motor skill assessment, including:

A. Assessment of efficient movement patterns
B. Assessment of inefficient movement patterns
    1. Devising a plan for remediation
    2. Devising a plan for readiness to participate

Area 2: Human dynamics, including:

A. Improving movement efficiency
    1. Assessment and analysis techniques for fitness components
       a. Strength and endurance of muscles
       b. Flexibility
       c. Cardiovascular endurance
       d. Body composition

B. Techniques for improving motor performance
   1. Planning
   2. Motivation: contingency management
   3. Strategies
      a. Behavior shaping/maintenance
      b. Criterion referencing
   4. Feedback
      a. Rate
      b. Quantity
      c. Quality
   5. Activity selection

Area 3: Preparing to teach/coach, including:
A. Establishing a learning environment
   1. Management skills
   2. Organization
   3. Rule establishment
B. Developing interpersonal relationships
   1. Controlling antecedent events
   2. Use of positive reinforcement
   3. Non-verbal communication skills
   4. Extinction
   5. First name use
C. Personal development
   1. Speaking ability
   2. Professional involvement
   3. Modeling
   4. Fitness

Desired Competencies: Areas 1 and 2

1. For each activity selected, the student will be able to list efficient and inefficient movement patterns and suggest improvement where inefficiency exists.
2. Where inefficiency is due to physical restriction, the student will devise remedial or developmental programs for each fitness component, including assessment and evaluation procedures.
3. The student will attain skill levels at a criterion-referenced level established by the instructor for each activity taken.
4. Given a situation where a common athletic injury exists, the student will initiate and carry out treatment procedures.
5. For each activity selected, the student will devise a unit plan that meets the established criteria, including pre- and post-evaluation procedures.
6. The student will construct detailed lesson plans that include explicit performance objectives and further meet the established criteria.
7. Given a situation, the student will organize a class consistent with desired outcomes that best takes advantage of available equipment and facilities.

8. Students will devise techniques and strategies for developing the following in improving human performance:
   A. Motivation: contingency management
   B. Skill
      1. Behavior shaping and behavior maintenance
      2. Criterion-referencing for assessment
      3. Feedback skills
         a. Rates
         b. Quantity
         c. Quality
9. Given different variables, the student will devise methods for evaluating students and activities in an effort to match students with activities, including the atypical student.
10. Given a situation with a handicapped person, the student will design and implement a program for the mainstreaming of that person.

Desired Competencies: Area 3

1. The student will exhibit verbal ability free of distracting mannerisms and loud enough to be heard consistent with the established criteria.
2. The student will become a member of the state and national HPERD associations/alliance and will attend one professional meeting per year.
3. The student will demonstrate desirable behaviors at play consistent with behaviors to be exhibited that model a proper role for students.
4. The student will attain knowledge of the ludic elements for each activity selected that meets the criteria established by the instructor of the activity.
5. Students will demonstrate the ability to administer physical education and athletic programs, including all component features designated, at a criterion level established by the instructor.
6. The student will establish a learning environment where the percent of active participation is above fifty percent and the percent of appropriate behavior above eighty-five percent.
7. The student will devise, in behavioral terms, rules of conduct for pre-class, in-class, and post-class behavior of pupils.
8. The student will devise a method of roll-taking that can be accomplished in less than one minute.
9. The student will organize the class so that no more than twenty percent of class time is spent in management.
10. Where percents of management time, active participation, and appropriate behavior fall below desired levels, the student will devise contingency management plans to return these to desired levels.

11. The student will demonstrate the ability to initiate and conduct interpersonal relationships by performing each of the following at the established criterion level:
    A. Controlling antecedent events
    B. Using positive reinforcement
    C. Using non-verbal communication
    D. Using extinction
    E. Using vicarious reinforcement
    F. Learning and using first names

In chapter 8, much of the terminology used here and a description of the skills needed to teach effectively are presented.

Humanistic Teacher Education

Self-actualization has served as the goal of education in the United States for over a quarter of a century. The intention of self-actualization has been to utilize the educational system to help a child develop his or her fullest potential by recognizing that each child is an individual and, therefore, unique, and that each unique individual is highly valued. Educational experiences should be designed to permit the child to feel good about his or her individuality, resulting in what has been termed a *positive self-concept*.

Proponents of the **humanistic approach** to education argue that the formal structure of traditional education, with its heavy emphasis on discipline and its absorption of the value systems of teachers and administrators, deterred the goal of self-actualizing the children. As a result, by borrowing from the psychological teachings of Jean Piaget, Carl Rogers, and Abraham Maslow, humanistic teacher education approaches have been developed not so much as models of teacher education programs, but more as outgrowths of a specific philosophy of how teachers should be educated to suit a specific educational philosophy. One of the leading proponents and developers of humanistic teacher education, Arthur Combs, states that

> No teacher's college can make a teacher. The best it can do is provide students with problems, resources, information, and opportunities to explore what they mean. Beyond that the student is his own pilot and must find his own best ways of working.[9]

The humanistic approach to teacher education emphasizes self-discovery by those preparing to teach, as well as their abilities to facilitate similar discovery in their students. Being creative and utilizing problem-solving techniques and activities leading to self-actualization is the means by which the teacher is prepared under the philosophy of humanistic teacher education (see fig. 5.4). An effective teacher, according to Combs, is "a unique human being who has learned to use himself effectively and efficiently to carry out his own and society's purposes in the education of others."[10] Personal development, rather than learning specifics on how to teach teacher behaviors, appears to be the emphasis in humanistic teacher education.

> If we adapt this "self as instrument" concept of the professional worker to teaching, it means that teacher education programs must concern themselves with persons rather than competencies. It means that individualization of instruction we have sought for the

Figure 5.4 Humanistic physical education aims to help students feel good about themselves and their movement capabilities.

public schools must be applied to these programs as well. It calls for the production of creative individuals, capable of shifting and changing to meet the demands and opportunities afforded in daily tasks. Such a teacher will not behave in a set way. His behavior will change from moment to moment, from day to day, adjusting continually and smoothly to the needs of his students, the situations he is in, the purposes he seeks to fulfill, and the methods and materials at his command.[11]

Andrew has listed seven factors that are inherent in the humanistic teacher education approach.

1. Learning by personal experience. Experience, to proponents, seems to be limited to personal emotional experience and individual, physical participation. There is often aversion to research theory, past experience, or consideration of other people's ideas. The personal nature of meaningful experience implies that a common experience for all prospective teachers may not be relevant. One implication for teacher education would be to minimize traditional course work and maximize individualized practical experience.

2. Primacy of feelings and needs of the individual. This emphasis not only applies to teachers, but to children in school as well. There is a close relationship of this philosophy in teacher education to child-centered educational models.

3. Idiosyncratic, individual nature of learning. Allied with a requirement for personal experience, this characteristic forces a personalized curriculum. Behaviorists would settle for individualization, e.g., varying the rate and, sometimes, the approach by which persons acquired desired competencies; but the humanists would require a curriculum individualized in content as well as method, with the student having major voice in choice of both.

4. The value of indirect, long range, and often immeasureable outcomes and devaluation of short range, highly specific outcomes.

5. Positive view of man tending toward development and growth and able to change basic attitudes and behavior patterns.

6. Need for open communication.

7. Need for continual self-examination and redefinition.[12]

Proponents of the humanistic approach to teacher education regard the competency-based model with disdain. They abhor such terms as performance skills, systems approaches, and input as being mechanistic ways of determining outcomes of the educational process. They view education as an individualized facilitating of growth and development through personalized experience, the results of which cannot be objectively measured.

Applying this philosophy of teacher education to physical education means that a teacher with a strong belief in his or her identity can, as Hellison states, "devote major attention to the student instead of to self."[13] In addition, the teacher would need to be acutely aware of each child's reaction to the results of interactions in the play environment to ensure that adverse circumstances do not occur. Assuming that a game or skill can only be performed a teacher's way would not be consistent with the humanistic teaching environment. What would be sought is the child's creativeness in finding his or her way to perform. In other words, the child can learn to explore his or her unique capabilities within the play environment and find joy through such participation in a nonthreatening situation, leading to a love of activity and further self-awareness as participation continues. Movement education in elementary schools has proved to be a good illustration of this philosophy of teaching as it relates to an actual program in physical education, although the approach can be carried out in all physical education and athletic settings.

Laboratory and Field Experiences

The contemporary focus on skills needed for effective teaching has been mentioned elsewhere in this chapter and is the basis for chapter 9. If *skills* do prevail in teaching excellence, certain variables affecting skills must be considered in the professional preparation of a teacher. Knowledge of results, KR, provides information for the performer about the quality of the performance. A tennis serve that lands outside the service area on the opponent's side of the net "informs" the server that a correction is needed. Augmented feedback, from a teacher or coach, permits the performer to know that the ball was tossed improperly, causing a poor serve. This important information is provided in the hope that future attempts will be more efficient. Modeling, through the efficient performance of a skilled server or observing such performance on film or videotape, can assist in the learning of effective serving. One can assume that the tremendous serves of John McEnroe and Martina Navratilova took hours and hours of practice time to perfect. Practice time, then, is another variable affecting skill development.

The purpose of **laboratory and field experiences** in the professional preparation of a physical educator is to allow for these variables to be utilized to improve teaching skills. Laboratory experiences such as analyzing teaching performances as they occur in the school or on videotape assists in the identification of skills needed for effective teaching. Learning to utilize observation instruments like the Flander's Interaction Analysis Scale, Cheffers' Adaptation of the Flander's Interaction Analysis Scale (CAFIAS), or the many adaptations of the Ohio State University Teacher Behavior Rating Scale permit meaningful observation of teaching performances. Information generated from such instruments allows for deficiencies in teaching to be identified, remediations to be accomplished, and objective evaluations to take place. Observing skilled teachers provides a modeling effect essential to improving one's teaching skills.

Field experiences generate time to practice one's teaching skill (see fig. 5.5). Information from an instructor or trained classmates furnishes the feedback necessary to improve subsequent teaching performances. The use of videotape analysis permits self-evaluation of teaching performance to assist in determining those teaching skills needing improvement, a *knowledge of the results* of teaching.

The importance of field experiences and recognition of this importance has resulted in several innovations in adding these valuable experiences to teacher education programs. One important aspect of the following forms of field experiences is that each demands supervision and feedback in order to be effective. At the very least, each teaching performance should be videotaped and subjected to analysis to provide information about the current status and relative improvement of teaching experiences.

Tutoring
Tutoring is a teaching-learning encounter between a single teacher and a single student and focuses on a single component skill of a game or sport. Tutoring may serve as an effective screening device. If the prospective teacher lacks the skills necessary to work with a single person, this may indicate failure when working with large groups of students. Those who succeed in and enjoy the tutorial experience have probably developed the healthy self-concept needed about their teaching ability, indicating readiness for an actual teaching situation.

Micro-Teaching
This field experience is designed to provide opportunities for self-evaluation and for trying various teaching strategies on a small scale. This experience between a single teacher and three to five students is conducted for a relatively brief period of time. The

Figure 5.5 An undergraduate physical education major can develop teaching skills through working in a summer camp.

actual teaching-learning situation is videotaped for later analysis by the teacher trainee and the instructor, with the feedback received providing a basis for making alterations in subsequent lessons.

Simulations

These experiences provide a "game" between a teacher and a group of students who are assigned roles to "act out" in an effort to determine the ability of the teacher to cope with unusual or trying circumstances. It may include the use of videotape analysis and may also include the more traditional approach of the prospective teacher teaching his or her college or university classmates as if they were public school students. This type of field experience is termed **peer teaching.**

Variations of these and other innovative methods have provided the prospective teacher with the means to practice teaching before the culminating field experience for all professional preparation programs in teacher education, student teaching.

Student Teaching

This experience has been defined as "a period of supervised induction into teaching, scheduled usually during the fourth year of college study as part of a bachelor's degree program."[14] Armed with knowledge obtained in *methods* classes and more than a little trepidation, the student teacher begins what Oestreich terms "the professional osmosis phenomenon."[15] Theoretically, this experience, of varying length and intensity, provides the setting for the development of teaching skills by the close proximity of the student teacher to the *cooperating teacher*. Too often, the student teacher is forced to emulate the behaviors of the cooperating teacher during this experience. Success or failure, therefore, is often predicated not on the individual capability of the student teacher, but on how well he or she can duplicate the procedures and methods of the cooperating teacher or college supervisor. Efforts to assist student teachers to function as entities unto themselves have evolved from the identification of desired competencies expected by student teachers as they perform in the day to day routine of this field experience.

The Fifth-Year Internship

A result of the controversy that continues over the "how to teach" versus "what to teach" argument has been the fifth-year internship program. Believing that the traditional four-year bachelor's degree preparation is insufficient to master subject matter and methodology, proponents of the fifth-year internship advocate adoption of this European model whereby the prospective teacher could utilize the normal four-year preparation for subject matter study and a fifth year to learn *pedagogy*. Opponents argue that, given the extra time needed and the extra expense for the fifth-year internship before certification can be granted, this proposal is doomed to failure because teachers are not properly compensated for this additional training. Should a surplus of teachers continue along with the public dissatisfaction with the preparation of teachers, this proposal may gain in strength of support in the future.

PROFESSIONAL PREPARATION IN NON-TEACHING AREAS

Careers allied with physical education have been examined in chapter 4; a few are illustrated here to document the continuation of knowledge-based approaches in preparing to meet the demands for professionals with backgrounds in physical education. Non-teaching career options and professional preparation programs for each option are relatively new directions in physical education, with specific competencies in these options to be developed as analysis of the effectiveness of such preparation becomes available.

Athletic Coaching

From time to time, professional organizations in physical education push for the certification of athletic coaches, but very few states have adopted this. Primarily, a person certified to teach in a state is automatically certified to coach. A trend may be developing that will further negate demands for coaching certification. Some states are experiencing a shortage of athletic coaches and are meeting this shortage with persons without professional training as coaches. Parochial schools have done this for some time, but public schools are just now adopting this policy. The danger inherent in this lies with having persons serving as coaches who are ill-equipped to deal with youngsters in making the athletic environment a positive one and, at the same time, who lack the capabilities to properly condition athletes or deal with emergency situations.

Athletic Training

The National Athletic Trainer's Association has adopted certain course and service-hour requirements intended to prepare interested persons for careers in dealing with preventive and rehabilitative aspects of injuries derived from athletic participation. Curricular emphasis lies in psychology and science coupled with extensive practical experience under the supervision of a qualified athletic trainer. The makers of training supplies have conducted training workshops in the summer to help prepare students to be effective trainers in schools.

Exercise Science

The demand for persons knowledgeable in physical education, particularly in the areas of exercise physiology and fitness prescription programming, has prompted career opportunities in hospitals and clinics and in commercial and industrial fitness. Curricular emphasis in the biological and physical sciences is intended to provide knowledge and skill to the designers of programs for fitness development and remediation to help people derive health-related benefits from physical activity.

Physical Therapy

Most physical therapy programs are in conjunction with medical training in medical schools and are of a two-year duration. Becoming a registered physical therapist involves two years of undergraduate preparation heavily weighted in the sciences, followed by specific curricula at a medical school that trains physical therapists. This preparation usually culminates in an extensive in-service experience in a hospital or clinic in an effort to prepare persons to assist the disabled.

Leisure Services

As Americans continue to become more physically active, the demand for persons qualified to assist in developing programs of activity will increase. Community fitness and recreation programs are booming, and the public seeks professional help for participation, from purchasing needed athletic equipment to advice on weight reduction or relieving the pain from shin splints. This all-encompassing avenue for careers requires a knowledge of sociology, business and personnel management techniques, computer skills, and specific skills for motivating and guiding persons through well-designed programs of activity. Although no particular curricula are specified, the broad nature of careers for enriching leisure time demands diversity.

SUMMARY

One's professional preparation and development stems from curricular experiences in formal undergraduate teacher education programs and from involvement in the profession. Formal undergraduate programs are strongly influenced by a number of factors including requirements set by national accrediting agencies, state certification requirements, input from the profession, and institutional requirements.

The traditional, knowledge-based approach to teacher education has been under fire for several decades. Attempts at improving the professional preparation of teachers has come from the behavioral, or competency-based, approach and from the philosophy of humanistic teacher education.

Since teaching skills are needed for effective teaching, variables affecting skills, such as knowledge of results, modeling, and practice time, must be accounted for in the education of a teacher. Field experiences, from analysis of teaching through observations to actual practice culminating in student teaching, are ways that these variables are utilized in the development of teaching skills in professional preparation programs.

Since professional preparation in careers other than teaching are currently in existence in many undergraduate teacher education programs, curricula and experiences are being designed to produce effective professionals in areas allied with physical education.

STUDY QUESTIONS

1. What are the factors affecting undergraduate professional preparation programs? What are some of the historical relationships in existence (see chapter 1) that affect undergraduate curricula?

2. What are the essential features of the traditional, knowledge-based programs in teacher education? Competency-based programs? Humanistic teacher education?

3. What is reciprocity? What reciprocal agreements are included across state boundaries in regard to teacher education? What are some conditions under which reciprocity can occur?

4. What are field experiences designed to accomplish? What conditions make field experiences more valuable?

5. What are some strengths and weaknesses in student teaching experiences? What could be done to make these experiences better?

6. What are the professional preparation programs currently in effect focusing on in the preparation of professionals in careers other than teaching in physical education? What factors will make these programs more viable in the future?

STUDENT ACTIVITIES

1. Most teacher education faculties represent the diversities of philosophy concerning professional preparation. You probably have someone on the college faculty who advocates the humanistic approach and another supportive of the behavioral perspective. Using the following questions to generate discussion, conduct an interview with these persons and record and present their responses.
   a. Can the humanistic approach satisfy those who are demanding teacher accountability?
   b. Why is there such a lack of an empirical base to justify the movement to competency-based teacher education?

c. Why is the behavioral approach considered "inhumane," "dehumanizing," and mechanistic?

d. Can there possibly be an approach to teacher education labeled "behavioral humanism"? What would be involved in such an approach?

2. Scan your college catalog and see if you can classify the courses you "must" take into the three major categories required by the traditional state certification requirements and the knowledge-based model for teacher education.

3. Determine if reciprocity exists between your home state and the state in which you are enrolled in college. If you are an "in-state" student, is reciprocity established with the state you might consider as an "ideal" geographical area in which to teach?

4. Consult with the upper-level majors in physical education (juniors and seniors) and find out the kinds of field experiences they have had prior to their student teaching.

5. Have you or will you have, during your undergraduate professional preparation, any courses that are considered "competency-based"? Make a list of the characteristics of such courses.

6. Determine the non-teaching career options available to you through your physical education department and its professional preparation programs. List the ways these differ from the "teaching track." What does a student do in lieu of student teaching in a non-teaching option?

NOTES

1. National Council for Accreditation of Teacher Education, *Standards for Accreditation of Teacher Education* (Washington, DC: NCATE, 1977), 1.

2. South Carolina Department of Education, *Requirements for Teacher Education and Certification* (Columbia, SC: SC Dept. of Ed., 1976), i.

3. Michael D. Andrew, *Teacher Leadership: A Model for Change,* bulletin 37 (Washington, DC: Association of Teacher Educators, 1974), 11–12.

4. Dan W. Anderson et al., *Competency-Based Teacher Education* (Berkeley, CA: McCutchan Publishing Co., 1973), v.

5. W. Robert Houston and Robert B. Howsam, ed., *Competency-Based Teacher Education* (Chicago, IL: Science Research Associates, Inc., 1972), 3.

6. Anderson et al., *Competency-Based Teacher Education,* 54.

7. Houston and Howsam, *Competency-Based Teacher Education,* 5.

8. W. David Maxwell, "PBTE: A Case of the Emperor's New Clothes," *Phi Delta Kappan* 55, no. 5 (January 1974): 306–11.

9. Arthur W. Combs, *The Professional Education of Teachers: A Perceptual View of Teacher Education* (Boston: Allyn and Bacon Co., 1974), 9.

10. Ibid., 8.

11. Ibid., 9.

12. Andrew, *Teacher Leadership,* 13.

13. Donald Hellison, *Humanistic Physical Education* (Englewood Cliffs, NJ: Prentice-Hall Inc., 1973).

14. Edgar W. Tanruther, *Clinical Experiences in Teaching for the Student Teacher or Intern* (New York: Dodd, Mead and Co., 1965), xvii.

15. Arthur H. Oestreich, "The Professional Growth of the Student Teacher," *Phi Delta Kappan* 55, no. 5 (January 1974): 335–37.

RELATED READINGS

Bahls, Viola et al. "Dual Endorsement: Teacher Job Insurance." *Journal of Physical Education, Recreation and Dance* 52, no. 5 (May 1981).

Caskey, Sheila R. "The Mastery Approach to Teacher Education." *Journal of Physical Education, Recreation and Dance* 52, no. 9 (November/December 1981).

"Competency-Based Education: Its Implications for Physical Education." *Journal of Physical Education and Recreation* 49, no. 9 (November/December 1978).

"Competency/Performance-Based Teacher Education." *Phi Delta Kappan* 55, no. 5 (January 1974).

"Excellence in Physical Education." *Journal of Physical Education, Recreation and Dance* 54, no. 7 (September 1983).

Forker, Barbara, and Warren Fraleigh. "Graduate Study and Professional Accreditation." *Journal of Physical Education and Recreation* 51, no. 3 (March 1980).

Gratto, John. "Competencies Used to Evaluate High School Coaches." *Journal of Physical Education, Recreation and Dance* 54, no. 5 (May 1983).

Lambert, Charlotte. "What Can I Do Besides Teach?" *Journal of Physical Education and Recreation* 51, no. 9 (November/December 1980).

Levy, Joseph. "Toward a Humanistic Approach to Sports and Leisure: Implications Beyond 2001." *Journal of Physical Education, Recreation and Dance* 54, no. 4 (April 1983).

Seker, Jo. "Are We Preparing Teachers for the Reality of Unionism?" *Journal of Physical Education and Recreation* 51, no. 4 (April 1980).

Siedentop, Daryl. *Developing Teaching Skills in Physical Education.* (Palo Alto, CA: Mayfield Publishing Co., 1983).

Turner, Robert B., and William Purky. "Teaching Physical Education: An Invitational Approach." *Journal of Physical Education, Recreation and Dance* 54, no. 7 (September 1983).

Professional Development

6

Chapter outline

Why Pursue Additional Training?
Educational Development
    In-Service Training
    Graduate Education
    Professional Organizations
    Exhibit 6.1 The American Alliance for
      Health, Physical Education,
      Recreation and Dance
Research in Physical Education
    Defining Research

Research as a Means of Professional
    Development
    Exhibit 6.2 Why This Research?
    Types of Research in Physical
      Education
Summary
Study Questions
Student Activities
Notes
Related Readings

Student objectives

As a result of the study of this chapter, the student should be able to

1. Distinguish the term *professional development* from *professional preparation.*
2. Identify several different forms of in-service training.
3. Identify and discuss the various graduate degrees that are available in physical education.
4. Discuss what AAHPERD is and what your role as a student can be in it.
5. List several discipline related academic organizations and discuss their various purposes and functions.
6. Define the term *research* and discuss how research is important to physical education.
7. Discuss how involvement in research activity can serve as a means of professional development.
8. Identify and discuss three different types of research that are prevalent in physical education.
9. Identify various research journals where research done in physical education is published.

In chapter 5 you studied what is involved in being an undergraduate physical education major. You discovered the kinds of experiences that will qualify you to be a professional in the exciting and varied field of physical education. In this chapter, we will take you an additional step by considering you as a graduate of your college or university and employed as a physical educator.

While it may seem a bit premature for you to consider this topic, there are some important reasons for discussing this issue at this stage of your career. First, you must realize that your education will not stop with the completion of your bachelor's degree. Your undergraduate training is actually only one important step in your professional career. What we want to consider here are the additional steps that should eventually be taken to allow you to continually develop your professional skills and knowledge. Second, if you are aware of what is expected of you or what is available to you when you become a professional physical educator, you will be better able to plan and take advantage of undergraduate opportunities. Third, becoming aware of what is expected of you in the future will give you better insight into evaluating your career choice.

WHY PURSUE ADDITIONAL TRAINING?

Before going any farther, you may want to first address a question that might be in your mind right now: *why* should you want to pursue additional education after your undergraduate degree is completed? First note that when we use the term *education* in the context of discussing professional development, we do not limit the meaning to formal, degree-oriented education. While seeking advanced degrees is included in the kinds of professional skill enhancement opportunities presented in this chapter, we are not limiting our discussion to that aspect of professional development.

Second, consider a statement made earlier in this discussion: the undergraduate degree represents only one step in your professional career. That degree includes the minimum requirements for you to become a professional physical educator. It does not indicate that you are now completely knowledgeable about the profession and discipline. There is much more information for you to pursue and incorporate into your level of understanding. This information may help you know more about how to more effectively do your job or it may help you to know more about the characteristics, capabilities, or limitations of the people with whom you work on a daily basis. Whatever the type of information, the result should be a more knowledgeable, more qualified professional physical educator.

Third, since physical education is such a varied discipline, the knowledge base on which it rests is continually expanding. The only way for you to be aware of that expansion and to subsequently enhance your own knowledge and skills is to pursue opportunities for learning more about the discipline to which you have devoted your professional career. In this chapter, we will present a few of the ways in which you can do this.

Finally, a strong incentive to continue professional development after the bachelor's degree is provided by many state teacher certification laws. The laws require it! State education agencies recognize the need for continuing professional training. As a result, they incorporate training into their certification requirements.

EDUCATIONAL DEVELOPMENT

In-Service Training

The term *in-service training* refers to educational opportunities that working professionals can take advantage of without having to quit their jobs and pursue advanced degrees. In this section, we will discuss some of the opportunities afforded the professional physical educator as means of in-service training. Note that some of these opportunities are provided by the employer, such as the school or school district, while others are provided by related agencies, such as local colleges or universities. Some of the opportunities require classroom experiences, while others provide experiences that are more "hands-on" in nature. We will even discuss some in-service training experiences that you can pursue individually.

Workshops and Short Courses

Among the most popular forms of in-service training are workshops or short courses. These are related in that they both last for short periods of time. Workshops usually have a broader range of how long they continue. A workshop may last for an hour, day, weekend, or several weeks. A short course, on the other hand, generally lasts for several hours, which may be arranged over days or weeks.

The primary difference between a workshop and a short course is the approach taken to address a particular topic. A workshop is usually a more applied, hands-on type of experience. For example, a school district may sponsor a workshop entitled "Cooperative games for elementary physical education," or "The care and prevention of playground injuries." A short course, on the other hand, is more like a shortened version of a college or university class. In fact, many colleges and universities give degree credit for short courses. Examples of some short courses are "Principles of physical fitness" or "The application of motor learning principles to teaching physical activities."

Both workshops and short courses are directed toward specific topics. This provides an opportunity for physical educators to focus attention on one particular area of study or concern that is of interest to them without having to sift through many other topics that may or may not be of much interest. An important advantage of the workshop or short course format is that it provides an opportunity for developing knowledge or skills in a topic of interest in a short period of time.

Professional Conferences and Conventions

In a later section of this chapter, we will present a discussion of some of the professional organizations in which physical educators can become involved. One of the advantages of involvement in professional organizations is that the organizations usually have conferences and conventions, which are typically held annually.

The American Alliance for Health, Physical Education, Recreation, and Dance, for example, holds an annual convention each spring in a major city in the United States. This five- to six-day convention attracts thousands of professionals and students from all over the country. Similar conventions are held annually by the various state and district associations of the AAHPERD.

Conventions such as these provide many opportunities for professional development (see fig. 6.1). For example, meetings or workshops directed by experienced physical educators who are interested in communicating to other physical educators are typically presented at conferences. Often included are seminars where several individuals are asked to present their views of a particular issue or experiences in such a way to permit interaction between themselves and the audience. Presentations of research findings are often presented, enabling you to see and hear firsthand from the researcher. Each of these formal meeting-oriented formats is designed to provide physical educators an opportunity to gain information that can be valuable to enhancing their skills.

A typical AAHPERD national convention offers a variety of workshops that appeals to a wide range of interests. These may range from "Games and rhythmic activities for learning disabled children" to "Computer applications for physical educators." Seminars may relate to such topics as children in sports, women in sports, or evaluating physical fitness. Also, each of the scientific disciplines within physical education (as discussed in chapter 3) will be represented in research meetings where researchers present short reports of studies they have conducted.

While these types of organized meetings are the predominant method of formalized information gathering at a conference or convention, there are other means of gaining valuable information. One of these is by viewing the exhibits that are typically a part of any conference or convention. These exhibits usually consist of book publishers, sporting goods and athletic equipment manufacturers, and various other agencies that have a product or service to offer the physical educator. The advantage of exhibits is that you can see a wide range of products and services firsthand, as well as talk with representatives of the various companies. Exhibits can save you much time and energy in addition to making you aware of new products or services that may be useful to you in your work.

Another attractive advantage of a conference or convention is the opportunity they provide you to meet and interact with other physical educators. It is always edifying to meet others who are facing problems similar to yours and who have found workable solutions. It is also helpful to swap experiences with others. You may find new ideas to include in your program or you may get some needed reinforcement from people who are interested in incorporating some of your ideas into their programs. The value of interacting with colleagues should never be underestimated as a source of professional development.

One further point should be made about conferences and conventions. Take the time to find out something about them before you consider going. Most publish a program before the conference or convention begins. Obtain one and look through the list of meetings that are scheduled. Determine from the topics to be discussed whether the conference or convention is of interest to you. Some involve a wide range of topics, while others are designed to consider a specific topic.

The conference or convention has become a very popular form of information exchange and socializing for professionals. Most organizations make it a point to encourage students to attend their conference or convention and offer students a reduced registration fee. As an undergraduate, take advantage of attending conventions and get an early start at meeting and conversing with other students and physical educators. You will find that this will be an opportunity to give and receive information and ideas that might otherwise be unobtainable for years. If you belong to a professional association, find out if they have an annual meeting. Then, find out as much about the meeting as you can and take advantage of this interesting means of professional development.

Journals and Periodicals

The forms of in-service training we have been discussing thus far have typically been based on a group meeting format. Enhancement and development of knowledge and skills was through attending formal meetings or interacting with other individuals. This final type of in-service training is a sharp departure from that approach and, as such, is often overlooked as a valuable means of in-service training.

Journals and periodicals that will help you develop as a professional are typically oriented toward a specific topic. Some are published by academically-oriented organizations while others are published by commercial publishing companies. In this section, we will consider some different types of journals and periodicals and suggest what each type can provide the professional physical educator.

1. *Teaching-oriented journals and periodicals.* There are several journals and periodicals that provide information directed specifically at the physical education teacher. Prevalent among these is the *Journal of Physical Education, Recreation and Dance,* published monthly by the American Alliance for Health, Physical Education, Recreation, and Dance. The journal is comprised of articles that provide the physical education teacher with readily usable ideas, suggestions, and information. This "applied" journal, with articles written by physical education teachers and academics, is an excellent resource for the physical educator.
2. *Research-oriented journals.* Each of the scientific disciplines underlying physical education discussed in chapter 3 is represented by one or more journals where researchers in these disciplines present their work. Research journals are valuable because they provide the physical educator an opportunity to discover current research findings firsthand, without having to wait several years for them to be reviewed in a textbook in a secondhand fashion. Reading journals is an excellent way for the physical educator to keep up-to-date in the profession.

Some examples of research journals related to the various disciplines within physical education are presented in table 6.1. Look for these journals in your library and read the table of contents in several issues of each. This will give you a general idea of the kinds of topics covered in each journal. Also, notice how you can subscribe to each of these journals. That information, along with how much a subscription costs, is usually contained in the very early part of the journal. For your purposes right now, you would do well to take advantage of your college or university library. Journals are usually expensive and are directed toward specific types of professionals; you should become familiar with the journals in areas of study that most interest you before subscribing.

Reading the Research Journals

Many times, people shy away from reading research journals because of a feeling of lack of knowledge about research methods or statistics. Do not let this deter you. Many research articles contain useful and valuable information that can be determined without even reading the statistical sections of the article. While understanding statistics would be helpful to you to understand the articles, it is not a necessity.

Before reading an article, read the *abstract.* This brief summary of the article is usually presented at the very beginning of the article. Reading the abstract helps in at least two ways. First, it helps you determine whether the article contains information that would be useful to you without reading the entire article. Titles of articles can be misleading. The abstract helps you know whether the topic you are interested in, as suggested by the title, is presented in a way that will be useful to you. Second, reading the abstract first will help you as you read the article. Since the abstract summarizes, or overviews, the article, it provides you a useful orientation to understanding the article. We will discuss the various parts of a research article in the final section of this chapter, when we consider publishing in physical education.

Table 6.1

Examples of Research Journals Related to Disciplines within Physical Education*

General

Research Quarterly for Exercise and Sport

Biomechanics

Journal of Biomechanics

Exercise Physiology

Medicine and Science in Sports and Exercise

Journal of Applied Physiology

Ergonomics

Motor Development, Learning, and Control

Journal of Motor Behavior

Journal of Experimental Psychology: Human Perception and Performance

Perceptual and Motor Skills

Sport History

Journal of Sport History

Sport Psychology

International Journal of Sport Psychology

Journal of Sport Psychology

Journal of Personality and Social Psychology

Sport Sociology

American Sociological Review

International Review of Sport Sociology

Teacher Education

American Educational Research Journal

Journal of Teaching Physical Education

*Note that this listing is not exhaustive; many additional journals include articles on these topics. Also, some of these journals include research articles on topics that are in other areas; for example, it is common to find biomechanics research in *Medicine and Science in Sports*.

Graduate Education

In-service training gives you an opportunity to develop specific areas of knowledge and skill. It does not provide an opportunity, however, for concentrated study in a planned program of studies. Getting involved in a graduate degree program does allow you this kind of opportunity (see fig 6.2). It enables you to develop your knowledge and skills more fully and in a more organized, structured way. While graduate education is not for everyone, it is certainly strongly recommended for those in the teaching profession. Some states, in fact, require the completion of a master's degree before full teacher certification will be granted.

In this section, we will take a brief look at what graduate education has to offer. We will consider such questions as, What is the difference between a master's and doctor's degree? How long does it take to get these degrees? What kinds of things must I do to get these degrees? Where can I get these degrees? If you are interested in a more in-depth discussion of graduate education in physical education, consult Walter Kroll's book, *Graduate Study and Research in Physical Education*. It contains several chapters that are important reading for any individual who will be selecting a graduate program.

Master's Degree

The master's degree is the first level of graduate degrees. In physical education, most programs offer a master of science (M.S.), master of education (M.Ed.), or master of arts (M.A.) degree. The differences between these are oftentimes subtle, if they exist at all. However, the degrees should represent different course concentrations in the programs. The M.S. is more specific in its orientation. It connotes a program with a solid core of discipline-oriented courses. The M.Ed. is a professional degree, as indicated by the requirement that a certain number of credits be taken in professional education courses. The M.A. typically connotes a more liberal arts-oriented program that is not as discipline-oriented as the M.S. or as profession-oriented as the M.Ed.

Most universities require thirty to thirty-six semester hours of credit for a master's degree. Programs vary in terms of whether or not a thesis is required. Some give you an option of doing a thesis or taking a certain number of courses instead, others require a thesis, while still others do not require one. A thesis is a research project that the student does on a topic of interest. It represents independent scholarship capability and allows the student the opportunity to explore a topic of interest in more depth than would be the case in a regular course. The thesis, while done by the student, is usually supervised or directed by a faculty advisor and a small committee of faculty, usually two or three, in addition to the advisor.

The content of master's programs varies widely from university to university. Some are oriented toward specific areas of study while others are geared to more general approaches. In either case, graduate courses usually permit a more in-depth and critical view of issues important to the physical educator than do the undergraduate courses.

Doctoral Degrees

In physical education, the highest graduate degree awarded is the doctorate. The doctoral degree is designed to equip an individual with knowledge and skills that will enable him or her to become an independent scholar in a particular area of study. There are two types of doctoral degrees typically available in physical education, the Ph.D. and the Ed.D. The Ph.D. (doctor of philosophy) generally is considered to be a research degree; that is, the person holding the Ph.D. has taken courses and conducted research during graduate experience that indicates he or she is capable of being a research-oriented scholar. The Ed.D. (doctor of education), on the other hand, is a professional degree. As such, it is generally designed to enhance an individual's skills and knowledge in the physical education profession. This degree, over the years, has become somewhat of an enigma. Many graduate programs grant Ed.D. degrees that are very research-oriented, while others stay with the more traditional, profession-oriented program. As you advance in your career and consider going into a doctoral program, determine the program you want on the basis of the program content, not on the basis of whether it grants a Ph.D. or Ed.D.

The doctoral degree usually requires two to four years or more of graduate work, depending on the institution. Most programs have a minimum number of semester hours required. A typical number is at least sixty semester hours beyond the master's. Included in these hours is a dissertation or independent project. As with the master's thesis, this requirement is included to allow you to show your ability to conduct independent, in-depth, scholarly work. An advisor and a faculty committee supervise this work.

Doctoral programs vary greatly. Some are highly specialized, while others are rather general. Some are very research-oriented, while others are oriented more toward preparing educators who will be training teachers. Some are very rigid in terms of what and how many courses you must take, while others are more flexible in this regard. Before enrolling in any doctoral program, investigate several thoroughly. Write for information. Visit the institutions if possible. Ask your professors about their recommendations. Be certain that you are enrolling in a program that will offer you what you need to pursue your professional goals.

Specialist Degree

In many universities, an education specialist degree is offered in the graduate program. This degree is a post-master's degree and is generally considered to be for teachers who want education more advanced than their master's program provided but do not want to go into a doctoral program. It is usually thirty or fifty semester hours beyond the master's and includes courses oriented toward professional education. This degree is not widely available, although many states recognize it as part of their teacher pay scale systems.

Professional Organizations

The last part of this section on the educational development of the physical educator will be devoted to identifying and describing some of the professional organizations available to the physical educator. These organizations, while having a wide range of orientations, have in common an interest in providing a service to the physical educator. Some organizations are very general in their goals and interests. Others have very specific, narrowly defined goals. As you read through the various organizations, note their primary goal, who they seek to serve, what they provide their membership, and how they seek to accomplish their goals. For more detailed information, write to the organization itself.

Before discussing some specific professional organizations, let us consider why you would want to join a professional organization in the first place. There are several reasons. High among these is that membership in a professional organization indicates to others your commitment to your profession. You show that, as a professional, you are interested in what happens in your profession. With this type of commitment, you are able to partake of several benefits that membership in the organization can offer. These benefits include an opportunity to voice your concerns about the profession to a group that can take some action. Other benefits include an opportunity to participate in organization functions such as conferences, conventions, or workshops. You will also be entitled to receive literature from the profession that may only be available to organization members. Additionally, most professional organizations offer job placement services to their membership.

For the remainder of this section, we will look at professional organizations in two ways. First we will take a brief look at the American Alliance for Health, Physical Education, Recreation, and Dance, the primary professional organization serving physical educators in general. Second, we will consider some of what we will call *discipline-related* organizations. These will include professional organizations designed to serve individuals in a specific discipline within physical education.

AAHPERD

The primary, umbrella-type organization that seeks to serve all physical educators is AAHPERD, which is organized in such a way as to provide something for everyone in physical education. As an educational organization, AAHPERD states that it is "structured for the purposes of supporting, encouraging, and providing assistance to member groups and their personnel throughout the nation as they seek to initiate, develop, and conduct programs in health, leisure, and movement-related activities for the enrichment of human life." The objectives of the Alliance are presented in the first exhibit in this chapter.

AAHPERD consists of seven associations that are organized around general areas of interest in the health, physical education, recreation, and dance professions. These associations are listed in table 6.2. Membership in any of these is part of membership in the Alliance, as each member is given the opportunity to designate up to two associations with which he or she wishes to affiliate.

Regional and state associations are also sponsored by AAHPERD. Each state in the United States has its own organization. These state associations are, in turn, organized into six geographically arranged regional groups called *districts*. For example, the Southern District Association of Health, Physical Education, and Recreation consists of the states of Alabama, Arkansas, Florida, Georgia, Kentucky, Louisiana, Mississippi, North Carolina, Oklahoma, South Carolina, Tennessee, Texas, and Virginia. In addition to the Southern District, there are the Central, Eastern, Midwest, Northwest, and Southwest Districts. Each of these districts, as well as all the state associations, hold annual conventions. Membership in AAHPERD also allows you to attend these conventions.

Student membership is encouraged in AAHPERD, and annual membership dues are offered to undergraduate students at reduced rates. As a member, you receive *Update,* a monthly newsletter related to current events in physical education; your choice of several research journals, for an additional cost; membership in two of the seven Alliance associations listed in table 6.2; and the opportunity to attend the Alliance's annual convention. Take advantage of becoming a member of AAHPERD as well as of your state association. Your undergraduate training will be enhanced by the opportunities provided for professional growth in these organizations.

exhibit 6.1

The American Alliance for Health, Physical Education, Recreation, and Dance

What Is the American Alliance?

The American Alliance for Health, Physical Education, Recreation and Dance (AAHPERD) is a nonprofit association representing professionals in

- physical education
- sports and athletics
- health and safety education
- recreation and leisure
- dance

More than 42,000 teachers, administrators, researchers, coaches, students, and others belong to the American Alliance. Founded in 1885, the American Alliance continues its mission to improve our country's programs in these fields . . . in schools and communities nationwide . . . to improve the American quality of life.

From its national headquarters near Washington, DC, the American Alliance provides a strong national voice for its members on legislative issues . . . and keeps its members and the public aware of legislative development at the local, state, and federal level.

What Are the Objectives of the American Alliance?

- To provide members with opportunities and materials for professional growth and keep them current on the latest issues, trends, technologies, and legislative developments.
- To improve professional standards and performance.
- To support and disseminate outstanding research.
- To speak with a stronger, unified voice on common issues.
- To increase public understanding of the contributions to American life made by our professions.

When You Join the American Alliance

You'll become a member of your national professional organization and

- keep abreast of the latest developments and trends in your specialized area
- demonstrate your professionalism to prospective employers

You'll get involved with the people of the future, too, top notch professionals already in the field and other students from around the country with the same career goals as you.

You'll get your choice of membership in one or two national associations of the Alliance that serve your particular interests. You may choose from Student Action Council (SAC), the only structure in AAHPERD governed by and designed specifically for students. As a student, SAC is your channel to service and representation within the Alliance.

Special Student Member Benefits for You . . .

SAC News PAC—Two times each year, this newsletter brings you the latest in developments at headquarters and news from the field. Written for and by student members of the Alliance, the SAC News PAC also keeps you posted on upcoming events and projects.

Job Placement—A year-round service, providing you with valuable employment information. A placement booth at the national convention and the "Job Exchange" column in UPDATE help you find the job you want.

Conventions and Conferences—When you attend your state, district, or national AAHPERD convention, you'll participate in workshops and demonstrations and meet the leaders in your field. A hands on experience that provides worthwhile insight into your profession.

Internships—As an HPERD major, you are eligible to apply for valuable nonpaid internships at AAHPERD national headquarters. As an intern, you would receive important experience and meet contacts in your field.

Leadership Opportunities—You'll have a voice in shaping your future, as you serve in leadership roles representing students on various AAHPERD standing committees, Association Boards, and in the Alliance Assembly.

Source: Selected excerpts from American Alliance for Health, Physical Education and Dance publications.

Table 6.2
National Associations within AAHPERD

American Association for Leisure and Recreation (AALR)

This association promotes school, community, and national programs of leisure services and recreation education.

American School and Community Safety Association (ASCSA)

This association represents safety educators and emphasizes sports safety, traffic safety, first aid and injury control, and emergency care in schools and communities.

Association for Research, Administration, Professional Councils and Societies (ARAPCS)

This association coordinates the activities for the following special interest groups: Aquatics, College/University Administrators, City and County Directors, Outdoor Education, Facilities, Equipment and Supplies, International Relations, Measurement and Evaluation, Physical Fitness, Therapeutics, and Student Members.

National Association for Girls and Women in Sport (NAGWS)

This association seeks to foster quality and equality in sports for women by serving those involved in teaching, coaching, officiating, administering, training, club sports, and intramurals at all educational levels.

National Association for Sport and Physical Education (NASPE)

This association is for teachers, coaches, athletic administrators, athletic trainers, intramural directors, and scholars at all educational levels and works to provide leadership and opportunities to influence policy and direction in physical education and sports programs.

National Dance Association (NDA)

This association promotes the development of sound policies for dance education.

Association for the Advancement of Health Education (AAHE)

This association represents the interests of professional health educators working in schools, the community, and clinical settings.

Discipline-Related Organizations

Many organizations have developed to serve the needs of individuals whose professional interests and research are in the scientific disciplines within physical education. These organizations are typically considered academic or scholarly societies in that they exist to promote and encourage the communication of research. These groups vary in terms of the amount of special services they provide.

AAHPERD has incorporated several discipline-related organizations, called *academies,* within its National Association for Sport and Physical Education. These include the Adapted Physical Education Academy; Curriculum and Instruction

Academy; Exercise Physiology Academy; History of Sport and Physical Education Academy; Kinesiology Academy; Motor Development Academy; Philosophy of Sport and Physical Education Academy; Sport Psychology Academy; and Sport Sociology Academy. These academies organize research-based programs for researchers and practitioners at the annual AAHPERD convention.

In addition to these AAHPERD-sponsored organizations, several other independent academic societies serve the needs of the research community in a variety of disciplines. In the United States, these societies include

1. **The American College of Sports Medicine** (ACSM). This is a multidisciplinary, professional, and scientific society that seeks to meet the needs of researchers and professionals in sports medicine and the exercise sciences. In addition to hosting an annual conference, ACSM publishes *Medicine and Science in Sports and Exercise,* a research journal published five times a year.

2. **North American Society for the Psychology of Sport and Physical Activity** (NASPSPA). This organization is comprised of researchers and professionals in the areas of motor development, motor learning and control, and sport psychology. NASPSPA hosts an annual conference and, while it does not publish a research journal, offers members discounted subscriptions to the *Journal of Motor Behavior* and the *Journal of Sport Psychology.*

3. **North American Society for the Sociology of Sport** (NASSS). This society was organized to focus on the special needs of researchers and professionals involved in the study of the sociology of sport. It conducts an annual meeting that is typically organized around a designated theme, although research papers are presented on a variety of sport sociology topics.

4. **North American Society of Sport History** (NASSH). As its title suggests, this organization is oriented to those whose interests relate to sport history. In addition to hosting an annual conference, NASSH publishes the *Journal of Sport History.*

While there are other professional and scholarly organizations that include research interests represented in physical education both in the United States and internationally, the presentation of these few should introduce you to the availability of these groups. As you progress in your professional training and career and develop more specialized interests, take full advantage of what these organizations can offer you. If you wish to know more about these groups, ask the faculty members in your department who teach courses related to the disciplines these societies represent. They will undoubtedly be able to provide you with information or can indicate how to obtain information.

RESEARCH IN PHYSICAL EDUCATION

In chapter 3, you were introduced to the scientific disciplines related to physical education. In that discussion, many examples of research were presented to illustrate the relevance of those disciplines to physical education. In this section, we will consider research in physical education a little more closely to enable you to see even more clearly how research is vital to the physical educator as well as to physical education. To do this, we will first define research. Then, we will discuss what role research can play as a means of professional development for the physical educator. Finally, we will consider the question of what kinds of research can be done in physical education.

Defining Research

In its simplest form, *research* is a means of inquiry. It involves searching for answers to questions. We must be aware that research is not limited to work that is done only in a laboratory. For example, a historian interested in the causes of the American Revolution gets involved in research by digging through libraries, museums, and similar places. A sociologist interested in the socioeconomic characteristics of college freshmen may research the topic by conducting surveys of a number of colleges and universities. Research, then, is not defined by the place where it is done. Research is a process, a means of obtaining information to enable a person to satisfactorily answer a question or solve a problem. It is a means of increasing knowledge about a particular topic or issue.

Kerlinger, in his introductory text about behavioral research, presented four methods of obtaining knowledge. These are relevant to our discussion as they help put our understanding of research into a more appropriate perspective. The first method of obtaining knowledge is the **method of tenacity.** Here, knowledge is based on holding true the beliefs of tradition. This approach is often seen in the comment, "I know this is the best way to do this because it has always been done this way." Even in the face of conflicting evidence, these traditions are typically held to and even form the basis for obtaining new knowledge.

The second method of knowing is the **method of authority.** Here, knowledge is based on what an authority says. Professors, parents, or ministers may be regarded as authorities; therefore, what they say is accepted as being accurate. In physical education teaching, for example, it is not uncommon to hear, "I teach it this way because Professor Smith said that this is the best way."

Third is the **method of intuition.** Knowledge is obtained and accepted on the basis of what "stands to reason." How often do we choose a particular teaching method because it just "feels" right? We often act on this type of intuition, or "gut feeling."

Finally, there is the **method of science,** which we discussed in chapter 3. This method is different from the others in that it incorporates "built-in checks" along the way to obtaining and verifying information.[1]

The method of science is the cornerstone of research for the physical educator. It involves the methodological and objective testing of hypotheses, those "intelligent guesses that offer possible solutions to the problems."[2] Physical educators who base teaching decisions on this method of obtaining knowledge would look to research to support their decisions to choose one teaching method over another. Even if specific research evidence does not exist to directly answer the problem at hand, the physical educator who approaches decisions on the basis of this method of obtaining knowledge will be better equipped to find appropriate support for the choice made.

The scientific method was presented by Kroll as a series of three steps: (1) suitable observation of pertinent information that leads to a summarizing statement or hypothesis; (2) the guided collection and analysis of data to test the hypothesis; and (3) the interpretation of the collected and analyzed data as related to the original research objectives.[3]

Research as a Means of Professional Development

Research should be considered an important and viable means of professional development. One of the benefits of involvement in research activity is that it aids in the development of an inquisitive or questioning mind; that is, you find that you are not altogether willing to accept a point of view simply because someone says something is so. More than this, you also develop an ability to do something about the questions that you raise. You become better equipped to investigate questions or problems as well as to discern possible solutions.

For example, suppose you read that teaching tumbling should be done by letting students work individually at their own pace and in their own area or space in the gym. Your role as the teacher should be to move from child to child to help as each one requires. This approach, you realize, is quite different from what you were taught in your tumbling methods class in college. That instructor taught you tumbling by having you get into a line with the other students in the class. Then, as you moved to the front of the line, you took your turn and performed the stunt. The teacher corrected you as you took your turn. Now, you are faced with the decision of which of these two methods is better for teaching tumbling. Which one will you choose? More importantly, how will you decide which one to choose? You could apply the method of authority and use the approach your college instructor used. Or you could apply the method of intuition and go with the approach that you "feel" is better. Or, you could research the question by looking into various research or education journals and attempt to find articles that would shed some light on your decision by discussing empirical evidence supporting one method over the other. You could even go one step farther. You could set up an experiment of your own by teaching half of your classes using one method while teaching the other half with the other method. In this way, you could determine for yourself which method yielded better results.

Physical educators who do not read research articles or attempt research projects have limited themselves to obtaining knowledge by methods that yield information that is difficult to support. On the other hand, physical educators who are capable of either reading research for themselves or conducting their own research have opened a whole new world of obtaining and verifying knowledge. Do not be mistaken, however, and assume that we are suggesting that this process of applying the method of science takes little effort. It requires both time and work.

You might be thinking, however, that research in physical education is done only by college or university professors. While it is true that professors do much of the research, they are not an exclusive group for conducting this activity. Much of the research published in journals or presented at professional meetings is done by students, both graduate and undergraduate, as well as by elementary and secondary teachers.

exhibit 6.2

Why this research?

"Why This Research?" is answered in the analogy of woodchopping. Woodchopping produces both useful wood and a better woodchopper. Research must give to our fields the building materials of accurate facts and principles with which to construct sound practice and wise philosophy. It must supply ideas to kindle enthusiasm in our professional ranks and, in the public mind, a warm reception for our programs.

Research must also create for us a professional personnel that is expert in its attack on new problems, keenly alert to new opportunities, wisely guided in the efficient application of its energies, and disciplined with a fine humility that is fathered by confidence in one's power and mothered by an appreciation of one's limitations.

The Researcher
In the last analysis no work is better than the worker and the quality of research depends entirely on the knowledge, wisdom, and personal integrity of the investigator.

If you are well informed of advances in your field, and yet endowed with a curiosity that breeds dissatisfaction with the present state of this knowledge,

If you can ask significant questions and also formulate crucial methods for discovering honest answers,

If you have imagination to conceive a dozen hunches, and at once the industry to explore each until disciplined wisdom points to the one of choice,

If you can concentrate on an issue, and yet be alert to happenings on the periphery,

If you stick tenaciously to the rightness of your best hunch, yet possess the objectivity to treat it with detachment as though it were another's and stand ready to give it up when it becomes untenable,

Too often, undergraduates are not given the opportunity to get involved in research. They often develop the feeling that research is something that is beyond them. Do not let this become the situation for you. Experiences in research activity are a desirable part of your undergraduate education. These experiences can influence your attitude about doing research and about reading and applying research in helping you make decisions throughout your teaching career.

If you want to get involved in research activity, talk with any of your professors who you know are actively involved in research. Ask him or her if you could assist in some way. You may find that you could help collect some data or gather some needed information. You might even get an opportunity to carry out an experiment on your own. The experience will be well worth the extra time and effort that it will demand.

If you are possessed of a fantastic memory for facts yet are willing to record them systematically as though you could not trust your memory,

If your mind works with speed and accuracy, and yet you double check your calculations,

If you are justly proud of your theory, yet humble enough to be led by facts,

If you are "hell-bent" on proving your theory, and yet satisfied that disproving it is just as great a contribution to knowledge,

If you have the courage to persist in the face of disagreement, and at once the patience to listen to the opposition,

If you are endowed with energy for long hours of searching and have enough left to organize, tabulate, analyze, and publish your findings,

If your mind is capable of holding the profoundest ideas and you have the understanding and restraint to express them in simple words even though you also know the big words,

If you are eager to forge a reputation for yourself, and at once willing to acknowledge generously your indebtedness to the labors of others,

If you are really capable of research, and your activity persists beyond your doctorate to the time when you must yourself supply both the time and motivation,

If to all of the above you can give honest affirmation, you are better than most of your contemporaries and predecessors but you are none too good for service to health, physical education, and recreation.

Source: A. H. Steinhaus, in *Research Methods in Health, Physical Education, and Recreation,* 3d ed. (Washington, DC: AAHPERD Publications, 1973), 3–20. Excerpted, with permission, from *Research Methods in Health, Physical Education, Recreation, and Dance.*

Types of Research in Physical Education

Application of the method of science in physical education can take several forms. Three general types of research seem to predominate. These have been termed descriptive, experimental, and historical research. These three forms of research are differentiated on the basis of what question is asked and what approach is taken to answering that question. This basis for differentiation is clearly distinct from differentiating the types on the basis of where the research is done; that is, in a laboratory, gymnasium, library, and the like.

Figure 6.3 Historical research involves inquiry into past events.

Table 6.3
Examples of Historical Research Articles

The following articles have appeared in the *Research Quarterly for Exercise and Sport* and are examples of historical research that has been done in physical education.

"Three Specially Selected Athletes" and a recapitulation of the Pennsylvania Walking Purchase of 1737 (Lucas 1983, 41–47)

"Girolamo Cardano and *De Sanitate Tuenda:* A Renaissance Physician's Perspective on Exercise" (English 1982, 282–90)

"The *Research Quarterly* and Its Antecedents" (Park 1980, 1–22)

"The Emergence and Development of the Sociology of Sport as an Academic Specialty" (Loy 1980, 91–109)

"Kinesiology/Biomechanics: Perspectives and Trends" (Atwater 1980, 193–218)

"Strong Bodies, Healthful Regimens, and Playful Recreation as Viewed by Utopian Authors of the Sixteenth and Seventeenth Centuries" (Park 1978, 498–511)

Historical Research

D. B. Van Dalen, a well-respected historical researcher in physical education, states "Historical inquiry begins when some event, development, or experience of the past is questioned."[4] In physical education, this form of inquiry may begin to describe some historical event, such as the nature of the games played by Native Americans (see fig. 6.3). Historical inquiry could also investigate a question related to the influence of an event. For example, what was the influence of the United States hockey team's gold medal in the 1980 Winter Olympics on the development of hockey in the United States? While other approaches are possible in historical research, we must realize that this form of scientific inquiry involves typically more than developing a chronology of events. Historical researchers probe more deeply than that in an attempt to add to our knowledge and understanding of the influence of history on our lives.

The methods of historical research are diverse. These include obtaining primary and secondary sources of information. Primary sources are firsthand evidence, an eyewitness or a genuine object or manuscript. If the historian cannot obtain these types of sources, he or she turns to secondary sources, information from sources that are not firsthand. These include such things as encyclopedias, journals, newspapers, and the like. Records and remains form the backbone of a historian's research tools. Such things as official documents, personal records, oral traditions, pictures, published materials, tape recordings, and films, for example, are critical to providing the information the historian requires.

Read the list of titles of recent articles from *Research Quarterly for Exercise and Sport* in table 6.3. Look at these titles and try to determine what question the researcher was asking and how the information was obtained to develop the article. It will become quickly apparent to you that the historical researcher's task can be an arduous and frustrating one; however, it is an important form of research that physical education must continue to encourage and promote.

Descriptive Research

An AAHPERD text on research methods states that descriptive research is "essentially a fact-finding procedure with an interpretation of how the facts relate to the problem under investigation."[5] Descriptive research is concerned with presenting evidence about how things are: it describes conditions or situations. For example, if the physical educator is interested in how teachers approach the teaching of volleyball, descriptive research is a good tool to use to investigate. The researcher would develop a means of finding out how a variety of teachers teach volleyball and then use an appropriate means of analyzing and interpreting the information.

Descriptive methods of research are commonly used for investigating problems in the areas of teacher behavior, motor development, biomechanics, exercise physiology, sport psychology, and many others. Researchers interested in teacher behavior may wish to determine what effective teachers do that other teachers omit. Motor development researchers may be interested in knowing the differences between five- and ten-year-old boys and girls in their ball-throwing patterns. Researchers in biomechanics may want to know characteristics of the running styles of world-class distance runners. Exercise physiologists may be interested in the possible benefits or problems related to some particular strength training method. Sport psychologists might be concerned with describing the psychological characteristics of a winning basketball team. Each of these problems, while uniquely different, would each be addressed by employing descriptive methods of research.

The examples just presented provide for an interesting array of approaches to solving a variety of problems. For example, teacher behavior researchers might compare different teachers and determine which ones are more effective and what characterizes them. Biomechanists will also be doing some comparing; however, their first problem in studying the question about running styles will be to determine what to observe in running style. Then, runners who will be the most likely candidates for observation and testing must be identified. The sport psychologist is taking a similar approach, but is not comparing the team of interest to any other team, at least not as a means of research. That comparison may come later, but the primary concern is to describe what characterizes the winning team. The exercise physiologist will have to develop valid measures to describe the effects of a strength training program. The motor development researcher will be comparing and identifying both common and distinct characteristics of the children while they are throwing a ball.

These are just a few of the many approaches to the use of descriptive research in physical education. Others can be seen in table 6.4, which lists recent descriptive articles published in the *Research Quarterly for Exercise and Sport.* Try to determine from the titles what the researcher was posing as the question or problem of interest and how the research was carried out to determine an answer.

Experimental Research

Research that involves more than just describing conditions as they now exist—research that actually controls and manipulates conditions—is considered experimental research. Typically, experimental research is concerned with determining cause and

Table 6.4
Examples of Descriptive Research Articles

The following articles have appeared in the *Research Quarterly for Exercise and Sport* and are examples of descriptive research that has been done in physical education.

"Academic Learning Time in Elementary and Secondary Physical Education Classes" (Goudbout, Brunelle, and Tousignant 1983, vol. 54, 11–19)

"A Kinematic Analysis of the Baseball Swings Involved in Opposite-Field and Same-Field Hitting" (McIntyre and Pfautsch 1982, vol. 53, 206–13)

"Body Composition of Olympic Speed Skating Candidates" (Pollock, Foster, Anholm, Hare, Farrell, Maksud, and Jackson 1982, 150–55)

"Children-Adult Comparisons of VO_2 and HR Kinetics during Submaximum Exercise" (Sady, Katch, Villanacci, and Gilliam 1983, 55–59)

"Development of the Overarm Throw: Movement and Ball Velocity Changes by the Seventh Grade" (Halverson, Robertson, and Langendorfer 1982, 198–205)

"Differences in Attitude toward the Concepts 'Male,' 'Female,' 'Male Athlete,' 'Female Athlete' " (Vickers, Lashuk, and Taerum 1980, 407–16)

"Socialization via Interscholastic Athletics: Its Effects on Educational Attainment" (Landers, Feltz, Obermeier, and Brouse 1978, 475–83)

"The Frequency with which the Mentally Retarded Participate in Recreation Activities" (Matthews 1979, 71–79)

effect; that is, what caused the condition that is being observed. The descriptive research approach is generally limited in its ability to determine cause and effect, since nothing is really controlled in such a way as to permit a conclusion that one thing more than some other caused the effect that was observed. For example, the sport psychologist cannot validly say that the psychological characteristics observed on the winning basketball team actually caused the team to win. There may have been other possible reasons for the team's winning record. Experimental research would be needed so that a definitive answer could be obtained.

Experimental research, then, involves controlled and systematic observation. The researcher establishes a hypothesis and then attempts to control and manipulate conditions in order to observe the different effects of these conditions. For example, the researcher in motor learning may want to know what the effects of different practice conditions will be on learning a tennis serve. To investigate this problem, the researcher will manipulate and control practice conditions so that when the results of the different conditions are compared, the only possible explanation for why the students learned better in one situation than in another would be that the practice condition yielding the best results was most conducive to learning.

A list of research articles (table 6.5) that are examples of experimental research published in the *Research Quarterly for Exercise and Sport* is provided. As you read through this list, try to determine what the problem was that was the basis for the study and try to consider how the researcher conducted the experiment.

Table 6.5
Examples of Experimental Research Articles

The following articles have appeared in the *Research Quarterly for Exercise and Sport* and are examples of experimental research that has been done in physical education.

"The Effects of Age and Number of Demonstrations on Modeling of Form and Performance" (Feltz 1982, 291–96)

"The Effects of Contextual Interference on Females with Varied Experience in Open Sport Skills" (Del Ray, Wughalter, and Whitehurst 1982, 108–15)

"Effects of Three Resistance Training Programs on Muscular Strength and Absolute and Relative Endurance" (Anderson and Kearney 1982, 1–7)

"Muscle Fiber Type Composition and Knee Extension Isometric Strength Fatigue Patterns in Power- and Endurance-Trained Males" (Kroll, Clarkson, Kamen, and Lambert 1980, 323–33)

"Comparison of Postperformance State Anxiety of Internals and Externals Following Failure or Success on a Simple Motor Task" (Hall 1980, 306–7)

"The Effects of Muscular Fatigue on the Kinetics of Sprint Running" (Sprague and Mann 1983, 60–66)

This discussion of types of research that can be done in physical education has been brief and not very elaborative. But, remember that our intent here is to simply introduce you to this topic rather than give you an in-depth study of it. You will have ample opportunity for more involved study of research methods later in your educational career. For now, we trust that this brief introduction has made you aware of the importance of research in physical education and that you will approach this subject with an attitude of interest rather than one of fear.

SUMMARY

In this chapter, you have been presented with information that may appear to be premature for you right now, given your stage of experience in the field of physical education. However, an awareness of what will be expected of you after you graduate and become a full-time physical education professional will benefit you as you plan your undergraduate experiences. Professional development is the dynamic pursuit of excellence as a physical educator. Opportunities are available for you to develop your knowledge and skills. Some of these opportunities are provided in the form of in-service training, while others take the form of formal graduate education experiences. Conferences and conventions as well as periodicals and journals should become important and regular parts of your professional life.

Research is a critical part of physical education. Without ongoing research activity, physical education runs the risk of becoming a stagnant and out-of-touch profession. As a physical educator, you too can expand your knowledge and skills by either reading and being aware of research information in the field or by getting directly involved in research activity. Research is not something to fear: it is an important part of the development of both physical education and the professional physical educator.

STUDY QUESTIONS

1. What are some examples of how you can be involved in in-service training as a physical educator?
2. What is AAHPERD and how does it seek to serve physical educators?
3. What are some advantages of being a member of AAHPERD?
4. Why is research important to the profession of physical education?
5. How are historical, descriptive, and experimental types of research different from each other?

STUDENT ACTIVITIES

1. Attend a state, regional, or national AAHPERD convention. Write a report on what was available to the physical educator there and how those things would benefit the physical educator.
2. Review recent issues of the *Journal of Physical Education, Recreation and Dance (JOPERD)* and summarize six articles that you think would be of interest to physical educators in an occupation in which you are interested.
3. Read an assigned article in the *Research Quarterly for Exercise and Sport*. Write a one-page summary of the article's purpose, including a description of the experiment and the author's conclusions.
4. Volunteer to be a subject in an experiment being conducted in your department or college. Write a brief report on what you did, what the experiment was about, and what your thoughts were about being a human subject.

NOTES

1. Fred N. Kerlinger, *Foundations of Behavioral Research,* 2d ed. (New York: Holt, Rhinehart, and Winston, Inc., 1973).
2. D. B. Van Dalen, *Understanding Educational Research,* 3d ed. (New York: McGraw-Hill Company, 1973), 130.
3. Walter Kroll, *Graduate Study and Research in Physical Education.*
4. Van Dalen, *Understanding Educational Research,* 161.
5. Anna S. Espenschade and G. Lawrence Rarick, "Descriptive Research," in *Research Methods in Health, Physical Education, and Recreation,* 3d ed., Alfred W. Hubbard, ed. (Washington, DC: AAHPERD Publications, 1973).

RELATED READINGS

Baker, John A., and Harry A. King. "Leading Physical Education Doctoral Programs: What Characteristics Do They Have in Common?" *Journal of Physical Education, Recreation and Dance* 54 (February 1983): 51–54.

Earls, Neal F. "How Teachers Avoid Burnout." *Journal of Physical Education, Recreation and Dance* 52 (November/December 1981): 41–43.

Karper, William B., and Thomas J. Martinek. "Learning About Physical Education Instruction: Laboratory vs. Field Research." *Journal of Physical Education, Recreation and Dance* 53 (April 1982): 75–77.

Kroll, Walter. *Graduate Study and Research in Physical Education.* Champaign, IL: Human Kinetics Publishers, 1982.

Sol, Neil. "Graduate Preparation for Exercise Program Professionals." *Journal of Physical Education, Recreation and Dance* 52 (September 1981): 76–77.

Personal Fitness

7

Chapter outline

Total Fitness
    The Concept of Total Fitness
Physical Fitness
    Defining Physical Fitness
Health-Related Fitness
    The Components
Skill-Related Fitness
    The Components
Lifetime Sports
Achieving Fitness through Sports
 Participation
Personal Fitness
    Developing a Health and Fitness
        Lifestyle

*Exhibit 7.1 Physical Fitness Begins
    with Physical Educators*
The Physical Education Major: An
    Example to the Nation
Your Responsibility to the Profession
Youth Fitness
Adult Fitness
Misuse of Physical Activity as a Means of
    Punishment or Discipline
Summary
Study Questions
Student Activities
Notes
Related Readings

Student objectives

As a result of the study of this chapter, the student should be able to

1. State the concept of total fitness.
2. Write a working definition of physical fitness.
3. Differentiate between the components of health-related and skill-related fitness.
4. Explain the importance of cardiovascular fitness, especially in adult life.
5. Define wellness and discuss the development of a health and fitness lifestyle.
6. Discuss the physical educator's responsibilities to the profession.
7. Develop guidelines for a health and fitness lifestyle to fit individual needs.
8. Discuss the reasons why youth fitness is a major concern in our profession.
9. List why adult fitness programs, corporate or private, should be monitored by the physical education profession.
10. State why physical activity should not be used as a means of discipline in the physical education classroom.

Our nation is becoming more and more fitness oriented. Why? The answer is that physical fitness will make one's life more enjoyable and last longer, and people want to be healthy and possess vigor in their lives. How important is being fit and living a healthy lifestyle? Ask anyone who has temporarily or permanently lost the opportunity to be fit and you will have the answer: it is the *quality* of each day that we live that is most important. One cannot buy health and fitness: they can be obtained only through a vigorous exercise program throughout life.

While the adult population of our nation is becoming more concerned with fitness and the quality of their lives, we still must face a hard fact. Scores on the national youth fitness test have not improved at all in the last fifteen years.[1] Most American children are not involved as much as they should be in physical fitness and are not receiving the proper education to motivate them to do so. Fitness is not just for the gifted athlete, it is for everyone. Athletic participation during the school years in no way ensures fitness throughout life; therefore, fitness must be taught and practiced from the elementary school years right through high school and college. A total education, both in activity and knowledge is essential. People should not wait until they turn 30, become overweight, and develop health problems before they develop a concern for their personal fitness. This becomes the major challenge awaiting the new physical educator: to educate the nation's population about fitness and develop practices for their fitness during the school years.

Before teachers can educate others about fitness, they must be examples and practitioners themselves. It is difficult to imagine youngsters being motivated to be fit if their teacher or coach is in poor physical condition, overweight, smokes cigarettes, and in general is unfit. Your personal fitness is something you should not take lightly either in the cognitive realm or in activity participation. For most aspiring physical educators, this will not be the first exposure to fitness. However, your personal fitness is a bit more comprehensive than activity alone. The remainder of this chapter will examine briefly the various aspects of fitness, discuss personal fitness, and address the responsibility regarding physical fitness and other fitness concerns for which the future physical educator will be held accountable.

TOTAL FITNESS

The concept of total fitness is not new. There are differing viewpoints on what constitutes total fitness. In the definitive sense of the terminology, *total* means complete in degree or detail.

The physical educator looks upon total fitness in regard to the development of the entire human organism. This includes aspects in addition to the physical aspect. Perhaps this has provided the basis for the general educational tenet that soundness of the body and activity of the mind are very closely related.

The Concept of Total Fitness

Total fitness is a combination of four factors: physiological fitness, psychological fitness, cognitive fitness, and social fitness. These four factors are referred to as the absolute levels of fitness. Within each factor are non-absolute levels of fitness. In physical education, the most concern is with the absolute levels of physiological fitness. The non-absolute levels within physiological fitness are health, cardiovascular fitness, strength, power, muscular endurance, flexibility, and motor ability skills such as agility, coordination, speed, balance, and reaction time. The assessment of these non-absolute levels basically determines the state of physical fitness of the individual. Health is an important factor because, without the possession of good health or the presence of pathological conditions, physical fitness is practically impossible to maintain. A question often asked is, "Is there a difference between physiological fitness and physical fitness?" The answer is affirmative and lies in the fact that to be considered physiologically fit, one has to possess an optimum level of all the non-absolute levels. In order for physical fitness to be reached and maintained, only the health-related components (cardiovascular fitness, strength, muscular endurance, flexibility, and body composition) must be accounted for. Levels such as power and motor ability skills are not essential to health-related fitness but do contribute to the concept of total fitness (see fig. 7.1).

Physical educators can employ the concept of total fitness to themselves and to the people they instruct. Selection of physical activities that meet physiological needs as well as psychological, social, and cognitive needs is essential. Psychological and social patterns or behavior are learned and become somewhat fixed as one approaches adult life. Cognition is knowledge that is learned or understood from perception and experience; therefore, psychosocial and cognitive considerations are very important in their contribution toward total fitness. Physical activity itself cannot produce optimum levels for these three absolute levels (psychological, social, cognitive) of total fitness. However, physical activity is definitely a contributing factor, whereas it is the essential element for physiological fitness.

PHYSICAL FITNESS

First **physical fitness** means being in a state of good health. From this point on, physical fitness is not the same for everyone, even though the variable components of physical fitness are the same. A person's age, occupation, and recreational and play interests are important parts in determining fitness. Physical fitness is further influenced by nutritional habits, body composition, and daily living habits such as physical activity, smoking, stress, use of medications, and sleep. Obviously, defining physical fitness for everyone is an impossible task. For example, the professional football player has different needs from the professional golfer. The accountant has different needs from the construction worker. However, all will still utilize the same basic components. What must be done is to examine the total aspects that are possible within the scope of fitness and to delineate the essential variables to form a core for physical fitness.

One point, however, must be emphasized. In adult life, the most important component of physical fitness is cardiovascular fitness. Without the possession of an efficient cardiovascular system, one cannot really be considered "fit" in the true sense of its meaning. Often in our school systems, this concept is not taught or practiced, usually as a result of an overemphasis on athletics and the skills necessary for many team sports. While athletes themselves may be fit during their sports participation, they often lack the knowledge relating to cardiovascular fitness to maintain this fitness once

Figure 7.1 The concept of total fitness as it relates to physical fitness.

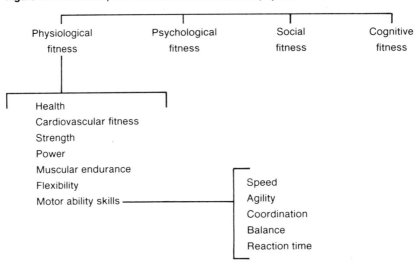

sports participation ceases. What about the nonathlete whose only source of physical education is in the class? These people may be the real losers in a system where fitness, especially cardiovascular fitness, is not taught and practiced. Many people, including athletes, leave our public school systems without the benefit of really being educated to maintain fitness for a lifetime.

Defining Physical Fitness

Although defining physical fitness for all may be an impossible task, a definition is needed for the profession in general to use as a guide. However, even a general definition will have some variation among professionals, depending upon how they view fitness and its components.

In 1979, a definition presented by H. Harrison Clarke was adopted by the President's Council on Physical Fitness and, with slight modifications, was approved by the American Academy of Physical Education. The definition as endorsed by the Academy is, "Physical fitness is the ability to carry out daily tasks with vigor and alertness, without undue fatigue and with ample energy to engage in leisure time pursuits and to meet the above average physical stresses encountered in emergency situations."[2] The problem with such a definition is that no components or parameters are mentioned for one to follow. This includes the health of an individual, also. A sedate individual with a sedate job and sedate leisure time pursuits could theoretically be considered fit without any moderate to strenuous physical activity. Thus, because of its generalities and unexplained theoretical base, this definition can be misleading, especially to the layperson who is unfamiliar with the components of physical education.

Some professionals even avoid putting a definition to the term due to its complexity, but try to explain it by its components. Others assign a narrow description such as **physical working capacity,** or they broaden its scope by using such phrases as **dynamic health, optimal health,** and **wellness.** None of these approaches are incorrect, but neither are they definitive in nature unless an explanation of the underlying theory is also given.

It also becomes apparent that to define physical fitness and to explain it are different; therefore, a reasonable definition of **physical fitness** may be, "A combination of several components, each specific in nature, to improve and maintain health and the physical state of the body." The components would be the ones that pertain to health-related and skill-related fitness. Keep in mind that the combination of such components and their importance in one's present fitness needs will vary. A high school athlete, for example, is probably more concerned with speed, strength, and power, while a middle-age adult emphasizes body composition and cardiovascular fitness.

Explanations of fitness and fitness components are also variable. To illustrate a comparison and another viewpoint, Gutin's Model of Physical Fitness and Dynamic Health (fig. 7.2) is shown with a brief explanation of its components. The theory is that physical fitness is used synonymously with the term dynamic health.

In the end, how physical fitness is taught and learned may be more important than how it is defined. Professional physical educators should comprehend that fitness is a broad term with many and somewhat variable components, each of which will require varying degrees for the state of fitness desired by the individual. This is not to say that a model or several models cannot be constructed to fit the optimum levels for a number of fitness needs. The truly effective physical educator will be the one who can analyze the components of fitness and decide which of these components are important or necessary to the persons being educated and who can select and design appropriate training programs and testing procedures that will adequately improve, maintain, and measure physical fitness.

HEALTH-RELATED FITNESS

The separation of the components of physical fitness into two categories, **health-related** and **skill-related,** is beneficial to understanding what fitness needs are most important to a healthy lifestyle and leisure time pursuits. The average person past high school age needs to be more concerned with health-related components than skill-related components. Possibly as important is the fact that youngsters from elementary through high school age need to be educated and made aware of the importance of health-related fitness for the future quality of their lives. Many factors pertaining to a healthy lifestyle cannot be completely reversed once a person reaches adult life and decides then that fitness is necessary. An example of such is the fact that the number of fat cells cannot be effectively decreased by exercise or diet once adulthood is reached; therefore, exercise and weight control need to be introduced in early childhood in order to lead to a reduction of both the number and size of fat cells during the adult years.[3]

The interest in health-related fitness has surfaced in recent years. Perhaps the most significant event was the AAHPERD Health-Related Physical Fitness Test Program, introduced in 1980. This test evaluates cardiorespiratory function (nine minute or one-mile run), body composition (skinfold measurements), abdominal muscular

Figure 7.2 Components of physical fitness (dynamic health). Although some components are related, each makes some independent contribution to physical fitness. Various diseases can reduce physical fitness directly and indirectly by their influence on other components. Appropriate exercise training can enhance all of the components and can also enhance health by its influence on certain metabolic and degenerative diseases. Components above the dashed line are important to overall health, but do not affect the physical work capacity greatly except in the case of extreme deviations from normality. Components below the dashed line are more directly related to physical work capacity.

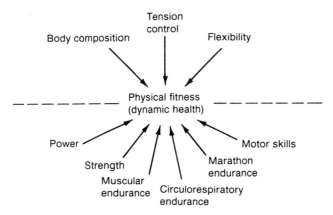

strength and endurance (bent knee sit-ups for one minute), and low back-posterior thigh and joint flexibility (sit and reach test).[4] While the test has a conspicuous lack of evaluation for muscular strength and endurance of the upper body, it is a step in the right direction. Perhaps the most significant part of the test is the philosophy or rationale which emphasizes that one does not have to be an athlete to be fit; that fitness is a continuum; that no definition of physical fitness is the same for everyone; that fitness is different at various stages in life; and that fitness is necessary for optimal health and a healthy lifestyle. Further, an education in health-related fitness should include the guidelines for development, training, and maintenance of that fitness. Such an evaluation throughout the school years can become an effective part in planning exercise needs and fitness for a lifetime.

The Components

Health-related fitness consists of cardiovascular fitness, strength, muscular endurance, flexibility, and body composition. Each of these components has a specific contribution to the health and fitness of the human body. To be considered fit, one would need to possess at least minimal standards on each component and basically be in good health or free from illness and disease. An analysis of each component and its role in health-related fitness follows.

Cardiovascular Fitness

Cardiovascular fitness (CVF), which pertains to the effectiveness of the heart, lungs, and circulatory system, also is termed **cardiovascular endurance, cardiorespiratory endurance** or **function,** and **circulorespiratory endurance.** Regardless of the term, the meaning is generally the same. A common definition is "the ability of the heart, lungs, and circulatory system to provide the cells of the body with the necessary substances to perform work for extended periods of time."[5]

The four major activities leading to CVF are running, bicycling, cross country skiing, and swimming. In general, any activity using large muscle groups continuously for a period of time can produce a similar effect; therefore, other activities can also be utilized for CVF. The key to training for CVF is the **frequency, duration,** and **intensity** of the activity. Cardiovascular activity must be performed at least three to five times per week for approximately fifteen to sixty minutes of activity at sixty percent to ninety percent of maximum heart rate reserve or fifty percent to eighty-five percent of maximum oxygen uptake.[6] These recommendations are based on existing scientific research and expert opinion. The importance of cardiovascular fitness, especially in adult life, cannot be overemphasized. It is the most important component of health-related fitness and will be of assistance in attaining other components.

Strength

Strength is a very important component of health-related fitness. It is important to one's structure, posture, movement, and injury potential. Strength is basic to athletic skill and also affects any performance involving motor skills. Tasks including daily functions, become easier to perform and are more efficiently performed with strength. There are various types of strength; dynamic, enduring, and relative strength are three types that require definition. **Strength** is a measure of external force exerted by a muscle or group of muscles. **Dynamic** refers to the amount of external force that can be exerted maximally during a single contraction. **Enduring** refers to repetition of high or low intensity work and is synonymous with muscular endurance. **Relative strength** is the amount of strength in relation to one's body weight. The importance of relative strength in regard to health-related fitness lies not in how much you can "lift," but rather in how efficiently you can move the body weight you are carrying.

Training for strength improvement or maintenance is accomplished by weight resistance exercises, free body exercises, and developmental activities such as gymnastics or dance. Weight resistance exercises are probably the most efficient way to train as far as time and development are concerned.

Strength training should be performed at least two to three times weekly on alternate days. Weight resistance exercises require more recovery time, while free body exercises and developmental activities can be performed on a daily basis. Free body exercises should be performed to near exhaustion for any strength development and maintenance of muscular endurance.

Three principles, **overload, progressive resistance,** and **specificity** must be applied to any type of strength training in order to produce a training effect. These three principles state that you must overload the muscles, progressively increase the overload, and exercise the specific muscle or muscle group you want to develop in order to increase strength. Strength will aid in improving motor skills, but will not automatically transfer improvements from one activity to another. Strength training will not effectively produce or maintain a high level of cardiovascular fitness and should not be considered a substitute for such.[7] However, strength training is very compatible with cardiovascular fitness training modes and can easily be integrated to offer a well-rounded fitness program.

Muscular Endurance

To totally separate strength and muscular endurance is difficult. They are closely related and should be approached in that manner. **Muscular endurance,** previously defined as enduring strength, is the repetition of high or low intensity work that further involves the capacity of a muscle to continue contracting over a period of time (see fig. 7.3). Muscular endurance is involved in the repetition of aerobic activities such as running or bicycling. Without muscular endurance of the legs, it would not be possible to sustain these activities for any length of time. Training for muscular endurance with weight resistance or free body exercises involves high repetition. In fact, these exercises, like developmental activities, must be sustained to near exhaustion for improvement to occur.

Flexibility

Flexibility is recognized as a trait of successful athletes and skilled performers, as well as being important for daily living. **Flexibility** is defined as the range of motion available at a joint or group of joints. Further, flexibility is the capacity of the joint to move through a normal range of motion. The different types of flexibility, for general purposes, are passive and dynamic flexibility. There is also static and ballistic stretch, which are ways in which flexibility can be obtained. **Passive flexibility** involves a full range of movement without regard to speed. **Static stretch,** which occurs when a muscle is held at a greater than resting length for a period of time, is essential to improving passive flexibility. **Dynamic flexibility** involves a full range of movement with speed or in resistance or opposition of a joint to a particular joint motion. A dancer using a high, flowing kick, and a wrestler trying to resist or get free from a hold uses dynamic flexibility. Passive flexibility and static stretch are the keys to improving dynamic flexibility, because they provide the potential or capacity to move. Dynamic flexibility however, must be practiced specifically for best utilization. **Ballistic stretch** is not recommended as the best way to obtain flexibility. It is defined as the bouncing or jerking of a muscle held at greater than resting length. The injury potential is much greater and the developmental potential is less than with static stretch.

Flexibility benefits are built into many activities, such as basketball and handball, but are absent in activities such as long distance running and bicycling. Here, a program of flexibility exercises will counter the effects of an activity that decreases certain areas of flexibility.

Flexibility training procedures vary also. While static stretch is commonly accepted as the safer and more efficient way to develop flexibility, how long one should hold the static stretch position is not commonly agreed upon. Variations range from five to sixty seconds in the static hold position. The point of agreement is that some discomfort, but not pain, must be experienced. Flexibility training can be performed on a daily basis and, in fact, can be done several times per day if needed. Some experts advocate up to three performances per day for maximum flexibility and believe the interval approach is better than repeating the performance several times in one session.

Figure 7.3 Bent-knee sit-ups are being used to evaluate muscular endurance in this class of college freshmen.

Body Composition

In recent years, the measurement of body composition has received a good deal of attention. **Body composition** refers to the amount of lean body weight that a person possesses including the skeleton, muscles, organs and other tissues, and the amount of body fat, which is the amount of tissue contained or stored in the body as fat. People who are too fat (overfat) have a higher death rate than do lean people and are subject to more health problems such as heart disease, hypertension, and diabetes.[8]

The main purpose of measuring body composition is to determine body fat content for health and fitness purposes; however, measurement also makes it possible to determine what one's ideal body weight should be and to estimate caloric needs to gain or lose weight.

A point of clarification should be the differences between the terms overfat, overweight, and obesity. **Overfat** is having an excessive amount of body weight as fatty tissue. The amount of fat considered excessive varies slightly, according to different experts, with the age of the individual being assessed. Generally, the average college male should be between twelve percent and sixteen percent bodyfat and the average college female between eighteen percent and twenty-four percent bodyfat.

Overweight is an excessive amount of body weight as compared to standards or norms. These standards are usually specified in tables often compiled and issued by insurance companies that state desirable body weight and various frame sizes for males and females. Being overweight is not necessarily harmful if the bodyfat content is not excessive. This is often the case in weight-trained athletes who may have excessive body weight but possess a low bodyfat content.

Obesity is a combination of overfat and overweight accompanied by a lack of functional movement in many cases. Obese persons may not be able to perform many functional movement skills such as bending, squatting, and the like because of inability to support themselves or because excessive fat impedes various movements.

Eliminating overfat and overweight conditions is a function of weight control and physical activity. The key to overweight is nutrition or the amount of calories consumed along with increased activity for caloric expenditure. The key to overfat is physical activity. A combination of aerobic activity plus strength training offers the best results to improve one's body composition.

The most practical method for assessment of body composition is **skinfold measurements.** A skinfold caliper is used to measure the amount of a pinch of skin in various selected sites on the body. About fifty percent of bodyfat is just below the skin, which is why the skinfold offers a reasonable assessment.

SKILL-RELATED FITNESS

Skill-related fitness is not essential to be physically fit nor will it necessarily make a person more healthy. However, the components of skill-related fitness do enable one to move and perform more efficiently, whether it be in work-related activities, daily movement functions, or in sports performance. Further, health-related fitness may also benefit from skill-related fitness, since persons who possess skill-related fitness are more likely to be active throughout life.

Skill-related fitness is compatible with health-related fitness. Many activities promote both types. Individuals who possess both will find participation in either type of activities more enjoyable and beneficial to their health and physical well-being. A person who is physically active cannot help but improve some aspects of skill-related fitness, depending upon the activities performed.

The Components

The skill-related components are agility, balance, coordination, power, speed, and reaction time. Many of these components work closely together and can be trained for by similar modes. However, specificity does exist, and such skills cannot be categorized in general. A combination of these skills or abilities usually determines a skilled performance in a particular sport. Note also that a high level of health-related components may make skill acquisition easier. One cannot improve skill if one is fatigued and lacking strength or flexibility. Since general motor ability may have no relation to the acquisition of skills, we must look at each skill-related component and see how it may be acquired.

Agility, Balance, and Coordination
Agility is the ability to change body positions quickly and accurately to the indicated response or situation. **Balance** refers to the ability of a person to maintain a specific

body position while still or in motion. **Coordination** is the speed and accuracy of correct muscle response to produce a desired movement. The ABCs of skill-related fitness are commonly referred to as the ability to change direction quickly and to move as efficiently as possible with minimal energy expenditure. These three components can be improved or developed by the use of developmental training programs, specific exercises or drills, and sports participation.

Power

Power is the application of strength and speed during a muscular movement. Power equals force times velocity and has to do with the speed of the contraction against less than maximal resistance. Power is closely related to dynamic strength, with speed or quickness of movement as the added dimension. Although strength, speed, and power are related, strength alone will not develop power. Power is displayed in many activities in different ways. Driving a golf ball, hitting a baseball, putting the shot, an explosive start in football, and a gymnast performing a giant swing on the high bar are all examples of power. Some persons may generate power more through strength, while others rely more on the speed factor. Biomechanics teaches us that speed will generate power and can equalize force. However, if two forces are equal, the one that generates more speed or velocity will produce the greater power.

Speed

Speed is the ability to move the body or a region of the body as rapidly as possible from one point to another point. Speed is the rate of movement, or the amount of time it takes for a body or object to travel between two points. Speed usually refers to running speed, as in the sprints in track or football. However, speed can be performed as leg speed in soccer kicking, arm speed in throwing a baseball, and body speed (acceleration) necessary in gymnastics. Speed is related to strength and power. In fact, all skill-related components contribute to speed. Speed requires the expenditure of a large amount of energy in a short time period. Age is a factor in attaining speed. One's peak is usually reached at about 20 years of age and can be maintained for up to 10 years or so depending upon the type of training one practices. Without practice, speed diminishes quickly by the late twenties. Faster running and other movements, unless practiced, may cause more injuries in adults and are not required for health-related fitness.

Reaction Time

Reaction time refers to the time lapse between the presentation of the stimulus (sound-sight-touch) and the first muscular movement of the performer. Reaction time enables the performer to begin movement faster, which can affect other skill components such as speed and power. Reaction time can be improved through the use of many developmental programs, such as strength and speed improvement. There are also many drills involving sight, sound, and touch that will improve reaction time on a general basis. However, whether the drills actually measure the present reaction time or improve it may be questionable. Since there is a relatively high degree of specificity in reaction time response, most physical educators feel that the best method for improving upon a specific activity or sport is to practice the starting stimulus for that activity.

LIFETIME SPORTS

By definition, **lifetime sports** are sports, games, or activities that can be participated in by adults throughout their lives. The scope of such sports includes bowling, badminton, golf, tennis, basketball, soccer, and racquetball, to name a few. Obviously, for some sports, the availability of facilities and equipment may play a role in one's choice. The emphasis on lifetime sports in most instructional programs has led to a better physically educated adult. Many lifetime sports depend on the components of skill-related fitness for performance and enjoyment. The lifetime sports concept does not overemphasize competition, although most sports are competitive in nature. Participating with others of similar ability levels is important. Enjoyment and activity will be lacking if one's partner is overskilled or underskilled by comparison. Participation in lifetime sports can contribute to physical fitness, but does not ensure health-related fitness. In fact, participants in lifetime sports will benefit from a high level of health-related fitness. A fit person will perform with less fatigue and less chance of injury in lifetime sports and will also improve the quality of performance.

ACHIEVING FITNESS THROUGH SPORTS PARTICIPATION

To become physically fit through lifetime sports participation is possible, but it is not likely in adult life without supplemental activity. A term compatible with lifetime sports is **lifetime physical activity,** which denotes those activities not generally considered as sports, such as walking, running, bicycling, and exercises.[9] Rather than just teach lifetime sports, possibly the addition of specific lifetime physical activities to improve the performance of that sport and to maintain fitness should be taught at the same time. As an example, a weekend tennis player who is inactive all week long could prepare for the weekend tennis by jogging two or three times during the week and performing strength, muscular endurance, and flexibility exercises on alternate days. This would help maintain fitness and also improve upon the tennis game.

Very few sports alone will contribute to overall fitness. With the knowledge we possess today regarding health and fitness, to be physically fit in adult life with sports participation alone would be difficult. This is not to negate such participation, since other benefits can be gained; however, adults need to be made aware of this fact and of the need for supplemental activity to ensure health-related benefits.

PERSONAL FITNESS

Your **personal fitness** depends on more than activity alone. In our contemporary society, life is often very complex. It would be a great world if physical activity could solve all of our health problems. Unfortunately, this is not the case. However, on the brighter side, the knowledge that is present about our health and well-being is greater than ever before in history and offers us both quantity and quality in life. From such research and study, some new terms have evolved that offer a more descriptive analysis towards attaining personal fitness.

Lifestyle has to do with the way one lives and the things you do that affect your health. A health and fitness lifestyle is one that includes sound physical and mental health practices. The factors involved in the health and fitness lifestyle are wellness, nutrition, physical fitness, and stress management. This lifestyle can be applied to persons of all ages. However, in our society, an unhealthy lifestyle is the rule rather than the exception for many people. Health problems such as obesity, stress, inactivity, stroke, heart attack, hypertension, drug and alcohol abuse, smoking, poor nutrition habits, excessive eating, depression, frequent minor illness, and general unhappiness all can be directly related to an unhealthy lifestyle.

The responsibility for your health and fitness lifestyle is yours. Most people must be educated to the facts and be given instruction, motivation, and guidance until they can regulate their own lifestyles independently. After all, is that not the major role for physical education in our society? No one can be forced to change lifestyles. The decisions must be internal. As changes are made, the improvement in one's quality of life should be sufficient motivation to continue. Achieving this lifestyle should be an enjoyable process, but keep in mind that any changes may be painful initially, until the body regulates itself and the change becomes part of your lifestyle. Many school age children are innocent victims of unhealthful lifestyles simply because that is what their parents practice. A sad fact is that probably the majority of people in our society have never known the feeling of being physically fit and in excellent health as a result of physical activity and other lifestyle practices. It is a feeling or dimension of life that once you have experienced it, you will never want to lose it!

Developing a Health and Fitness Lifestyle

The first step is to "assess or evaluate" yourself as to your present lifestyle, regardless of your age. As one gets older, some changes will become harder and some effects will be less reversible. Remember also, that your lifestyle must be practiced for a lifetime; it is not a seasonal sport!

The next step is to "analyze the factors" contributing to a health and fitness lifestyle; namely, wellness, nutrition, physical fitness, and stress management. A brief explanation and guidelines for each follows.

Wellness

Wellness is a term that can be used to denote a combination of physical health, physical fitness, and mental health, which are usually reached and maintained by following good health practices. Regardless of how much you exercise or how well you eat, you must recognize that certain health practices must be maintained at specified intervals throughout life to keep you aware of any possible conditions that may affect your state of wellness. Some specific health practices are as follows:

1. Have a complete medical or physical examination by a physician at least every two to five years. This time interval is often determined by symptoms, results of previous examinations, and your age. The older one becomes, the more frequently the exam should be conducted.

2. Have a dental examination (including x-rays) by a dentist and a thorough cleaning of teeth by a dental hygienist every six months, regardless of your age.

3. Have an eye examination by an optometrist once every two years to note any changes in vision or prescription for those who wear corrective lenses.

4. If any unknown symptoms develop, have them checked by the proper medical professional.

5. Do not use drugs or over-medicate. Take prescription drugs only when necessary and as prescribed by your physician.

6. Do not smoke cigarettes.

7. Do not abuse alcohol.

8. Be sure to get enough sleep to satisfy your needs.

9. Keep a current check of your resting heart rate, blood pressure, body weight, and bodyfat content percentage.

Nutrition

"You are what you eat." This cliché is old, but true. Every part of your body is affected by what you eat. Overweight and obesity are both controlled by nutrition. Humans were meant to eat to sustain life, but now, eating is a pleasure and is centered more on taste than on nutritional value. Our eating habits have changed through time to include more sugar and fat in the diet. Many people are misinformed about calories and food values. We rely on many empty calorie sources such as candies, soda, fatty meats, and even alcoholic beverages for our so-called energy supply. Most people lack an intake of starch and fiber (unrefined or complex carbohydrates), which are essential to body function and may play a role in the prevention of certain chronic diseases. Excessive salt in foods, used for taste, may lead to high blood pressure. Saturated fat from fatty meats and other products increases one type of blood cholesterol (low-density lipoprotein) that has shown to be a risk factor for heart disease. However, the major problem from poor nutrition is obesity. A large percentage of the population is affected by some degree of obesity; thus, we can note the extreme importance of food selection for a health and fitness lifestyle. Specific guidelines for nutrition are as follows:

1. Eat a variety of foods to maintain a balanced diet.

2. Emphasize fresh, unprocessed foods over processed foods.

3. Avoid excessive amounts of unrefined sugar, saturated fats, and high sodium products.

4. Avoid excessive eating. One should eat only enough to maintain ideal body weight or less.

5. If weight loss is desired, decrease the amount of calories consumed and participate in physical activities.

6. If weight gain is desired, slightly increase caloric consumption and use intensified physical activity such as strength training in order to avoid gaining bodyfat.

7. Become knowledgeable about caloric content of various foods and caloric expenditures of various physical activities in order to assist in caloric balance.

8. Keep in mind that diet and exercise are the key factors in preventing obesity and decreasing bodyfat or body weight.

9. Beware of "creeping obesity," which usually develops over a period of years, due to a change in one's metabolism.

10. Fat children become fat adults. Be cautious in overfeeding youngsters, as they may develop fat cells (both in number and size) that may make them prime candidates for obesity in adult life. The lack of physical activity also contributes to obesity in children.

11. Breakfast is a very important meal. About twenty-five percent of the daily caloric needs should be eaten at breakfast.

12. Athletes and physically active people do not need excessive amounts of protein. Carbohydrate is the necessary element received preferably through the consumption of unrefined starches (complex carbohydrates).

13. Remember, you are what you eat! The type and amount of food you eat will affect your health and fitness.

Physical Fitness

Since this chapter is mainly about the various aspects of physical fitness and physical activity, we do not need to repeat much of the same information in this section. Let us, however, reemphasize a few important points.

1. Physical activity leading to a high level of health-related fitness is essential for a health and fitness lifestyle.

2. Cardiovascular fitness is the most important component of physical fitness in adult life.

3. Physical activity is important to one's appearance as well as one's health.

4. Physical activity is compatible to maintaining ideal body weight and preventing obesity.

5. Physical fitness is the key to a healthy body and optimal health.

6. Physical fitness contributes to mental and emotional health as well.

7. Physical fitness is not the same for everyone. Individual needs must be accounted for.

8. Physical fitness components must be specifically trained for. Intensity, duration, and frequency of an exercise or activity determine training effect on any fitness component.

9. Health-related fitness generally consists of cardiovascular fitness, strength, muscular endurance, flexibility, and body composition.

10. Skill-related fitness consists of agility, balance, coordination, power, speed, and reaction time.

Stress Management

In our complex society, stress and stress management have become important factors in health and fitness. Stress is encountered by everyone and is a necessary part of life. However, unwanted stress in high doses can cause the body to break down and become prone to disease. Many times, this unwanted or negative stress cannot be eliminated until we learn how to manage stress effectively.

Stress is a state of the body. It is the response of the body to any demands placed upon it. Stress is a major health problem in our society. Stressors, which are anything that produces tension and stress, can be positive or negative, although the effects to the body are about the same. Stress is not the same for everyone; thus, when we study stress, we must look at the individual reaction to stress. Stress situations are necessary to enhance maturity and adaptation. Stress stimulates psychological growth. Just as physical activity is the conditioning process in physiological fitness, stress is the conditioning process for psychological fitness (total fitness concept). One's attitude and experiences toward stressors are also important. Some people thrive on stress situations, others abhor them. The key to handling stress is moderation. The middle-of-the-road individual theoretically adapts best. There is an old saying that can be readily applied to some negative stress situations: "Worry is like paying interest on money you never borrowed."

The following guidelines are for the successful management of stress to promote the health and fitness lifestyle:

1. Identify your stressors and see which of them you can reduce, avoid, or eliminate.
2. Become a positive person. Goal-oriented persons who maintain reasonable goals tend to be more successful and happier than those who are not goal oriented.
3. Do not allow decision making to become a chore. Weigh the facts and be decisive. Indecision is the worst decision!
4. Life has many negative stressors. Do not allow them to accumulate, otherwise your health could be damaged.
5. Do not abuse alcohol to relieve stress.
6. Do not use drugs to relieve stress.
7. If possible, avoid standard medications, unless prescribed by your physician.
8. Do not smoke cigarettes to relieve stress.
9. Do not overeat as a reaction to stress.
10. Positive stress can also be abused. Remember the response of the body is the same regardless of the cause. Do not overdo positive stress situations.
11. Regular physical activity, especially aerobic activity sustained for a sufficient period of time, will alleviate stress. There is scientific basis for the existence of the "runner's or exercise high," which can be obtained through other sustained activities as well.
12. Relaxation techniques can minimize the effects of stress.

13. To avoid negative stressors, seek tasks of work or pleasure that you are capable of doing, that you enjoy, that may give you self-esteem, and that may esteem you in the opinions of others. Negative stress often occurs when you are pressured into doing something you do not want to do or are incapable of doing.

14. Other ways to manage stress:
    A. Talk about your worries or stressors with someone you respect.
    B. Learn to accept what you cannot change.
    C. Get enough sleep and rest.
    D. Balance work and recreation.
    E. Do something for others.
    F. Take one thing at a time.
    G. Give in once in awhile.
    H. Make yourself available to counter boredom.[10]

15. While physical activity is an excellent means of alleviating stress, keep in mind that it is not a "cure" for stress. In fact, overexercise or excessive stressful situations in varsity athletics may cause negative stress.

16. Stress can be managed in various acceptable ways, but to find a way to prevent the stress of life would be better than finding simply a means to help us fight a hostile world. The problem lies in the lack of a proper code of motivation that gives our lives a purpose which we can respect.[11]

Putting Personal Fitness Together

Now that the factors of personal fitness have been basically analyzed and you have assessed or evaluated your present lifestyle, the next step is to compare what you are doing now with the projected changes and new practices regarding wellness, nutrition, physical fitness, and stress management. A word of caution is due so that you do not make this an awesome task that has no chance of success: make your changes and additions with moderation. Take one step at a time and be realistic as to what you can accomplish at one time. Short-term goals lead to long-term goals. Motivation probably will not be maintained if your goals are not attainable. Your final step is to "formulate your plan" and set "reasonable goals" that you will utilize to reach a health and fitness lifestyle.

Maintaining a health and fitness lifestyle is a lifelong job. There is really no vacation or retirement from it. If you become bored with various aspects of a health and fitness routine, then make some changes to alleviate the boredom. Get into seasonal activities if you find the change helps. The human being is a creature of habit; thus, once you establish good habits in your lifestyle, you will not be likely to change. The real reward of your lifestyle will be how good you feel! Once you realize the great feelings in body and mind from being fit and healthy, you are not going to want to change: you will want only to improve upon the feelings. Health and fitness are possible for almost everyone. Accept the challenge! The gratification you experience will leave you smiling, inside and out! Good luck!

exhibit 7.1

Physical fitness begins with physical educators

Health benefits associated with regular physical fitness and exercise have not yet been fully defined. Yet based on what is now known it appears that substantial direct and indirect physical and emotional benefits are possible. It remains that most Americans do not engage in appropriate physical activity, either during recreation or in their work. The objectives for the nation speak for physical education professionals. We have a job to do—now. First and foremost, each of us in the profession must make a personal commitment to achieve or maintain a good level of physical fitness. How can we be effective in promoting health and fitness if our bodies are not living testimonies of our commitment? What we are communicates so much more than what we say!

Source: Dr. Jack H. Wilmore, ''Objectives for the Nation—Physical Fitness and Exercise,'' in *Journal of Physical Education, Recreation and Dance,* 53 (March 1982). © 1982 American Alliance for Health, Physical Education, Recreation, and Dance.

THE PHYSICAL EDUCATION MAJOR: AN EXAMPLE TO THE NATION

How can people effectively teach physical fitness when they are not fit themselves? This is the dilemma in which our profession often finds itself. We must face the fact that many of our physical educators are not fit! Have we become so consumed with our "body of knowledge" that we have forgotten that the body in which that knowledge resides needs to be fit also? What a disappointment to many school youngsters who are taught to be fit when they find their coach is not an example of fitness.

The physical educator should be an example of physical fitness to the nation! Nothing conveys a message like personal example. Unfortunately, our profession is somewhat guilty of a cover-up in this matter. Only recently has this responsibility been discussed in professional literature. Wilmore addresses this matter in his article "Objectives for One Nation," which is the exhibit in this chapter. Goodrich and Iammarino, in "Teaching Aerobic Lifestyle," further add, "It is also essential that the instructor provide a role model for his/her students; he/she should maintain aerobic fitness, communicate personal experience of the benefits of exercise, and pay individual attention to each student to ensure a proper exercise progression and results."[12]

In our early years, physical educators were noted for being fit and for possessing athletic prowess. Physical educators were expected to display physical talent: "We led by example!" Where and why have we slipped today? Possibly, we are not holding the physical education majors accountable for their state of fitness.

Two intangibles provide our motivation to be fit physical educators. The first is pride! You should take pride in everything you do. Your title as physical educator or coach should denote pride—pride that shows in your appearance, fitness, knowledge, and ability to teach others to be fit. The second is responsibility. You are responsible for the education of others in regard to fitness. To educate people, first set a personal example that others can follow and then teach them as best you can. Remember, their lives and health may depend on it . . . and so may yours.

YOUR RESPONSIBILITY TO THE PROFESSION

You have four basic responsibilities to the physical education profession. The first, which has been previously discussed, is that of serving as a personal example of fitness yourself. The other three are the responsibilities for youth fitness, adult fitness, and to avoid using physical activity as a means of discipline or punishment. These last three factors are of importance in the physical education process. A more in-depth look at each of the factors follows.

Youth Fitness

Youth fitness, for purposes of this writing, pertains to physical education from grades K through 12. Since the 1950s, when the results of the Kraus-Weber test shocked the American public, youth fitness has been a major concern. The problem of inadequate fitness in youth has not disappeared and is still a major concern. Some of the reasons are as follows:

1. Fitness activities are not included in the elementary curriculum.
2. The knowledge factor about physical fitness is not being taught at all levels.
3. Physical fitness testing is performed without regard to results and without follow-up programs for those who have low scores.
4. Athletics are a more important part of physical education.
5. Elective curriculums that do not control a student's course selections.
6. Lack of motivation to teach fitness by some physical educators.
7. Coaching duties take preference over teaching duties.
8. The lack of vigorous physical exercise programs in the schools.
9. Lack of motivation on the part of some students.

Despite the many controversial reasons for problems in youth fitness, good youth fitness programs do exist! Good programs start with objectives and the knowledge to carry out those objectives. Physical fitness concepts and activities should be taught in the elementary schools and then continued throughout the high school years (see fig. 7.4). The goal or aim of educating people for a lifetime of physical fitness begins when physical education starts. Too often, the goal is put off until later, and later never comes. At least fifty percent of the physical education programs should be spent in strenuous activities that promote fitness. Most youngsters will support physical fitness once they are fit. Athletics should not be a substitute for physical education. Physical fitness testing should be meaningful and some follow-up should take place. Testing should not be administered once or twice per year without preparation or follow-up; otherwise, the student does not learn anything from the testing. Hayes suggests that physical fitness scores be printed in the newspaper along with the football scores.[13]

Figure 7.4 Fitness concepts should be presented in the elementary school physical education curriculum.

The youth of our country are being introduced to more sedentary living habits every day. Never has a society been able to live in the ease and comfort that our society enjoys. The only problem is that the human body cannot cope with sedentary living habits: it needs strenuous exercise to remain healthy. Reiff and Hayes state, "We have more physical education programs, more gyms, and more swimming pools than any other country in the world. We also lead the world in degenerative diseases. The United States is dedicated to physical fitness and to parking as close as possible to the stadium."[14]

Adult Fitness

If the physical education program in the schools successfully did the job for which it was intended, adults of all ages would not have fitness problems. According to a 1979 Harris poll, only about ten to twenty percent of the American population regularly exercises above a minimal aerobic exercise level.[15] This figure lends itself to the theory that the average adult American is not educated regarding physical fitness.

Regardless of the reasons or causes for this lack of education in adults, (some reasons and causes appear in the section on youth fitness), the result is that many adults become alarmed with their lack of fitness. This alarm is the main reason why the corporate world of fitness, including health clubs, spas, and gymnasiums, is creating a successful business trend. For the physical educator who is interested in the fitness business, this has opened a new dimension for career opportunities. However, the same rules apply; personal example, knowledge, and teaching ability are requirements of the successful fitness counselor or instructor. The fitness industry is becoming aware of the need for qualified personnel, and, in the near future, some certification will be required by fitness corporations because the corporations' success will depend on qualified personnel. In some of the higher quality organizations, a physical education degree may become the minimal requirement.

Most adults who seek help will have some motivation to improve their fitness, whether it be for health problems, weight loss, or just lack of vitality. However, many problems may not be completely reversible and progress in becoming fit may be slow. To give perspective to a person feeling discouraged by slow progress, you might ask, "How long did it take to get into your present condition?" One cannot expect overnight results after twenty years of sedentary living, and one must learn that in order to stay fit exercise must be maintained.

Keep in mind that the adult who seeks fitness is the same one who was improperly physically educated, lacked the motivation to learn in school, or did not build lasting fitness habits. Even in a good physical education program, some people are going to resist learning for various reasons. The adult physical educator must also be aware of fads and fallacies in becoming fit. The unfit adult is very susceptible to "fitness quackery" such as body wraps, electric shocks, and other gimmickry. The knowledge you impart to adults should include information needed for health and fitness lifestyles; that is, wellness, nutrition, fitness, and stress management. In the area of fitness, there is no known substitute for vigorous physical activity in order to keep the human body functioning properly.

Adult fitness is a growing trend. Some of the differences in adult fitness are due to age levels and physical capabilities. Adult fitness should be monitored by the physical education profession, who should be prepared for this task (see fig. 7.5). By 1990, projects Wilmore, the proportion of adults from age 18 to 65 participating regularly in vigorous physical exercise should be greater than sixty percent.[16] If this prediction materializes, physical education professionals should be able to provide the education, motivation, and body of knowledge through research and application to meet the needs of adult fitness in our society.

Misuse of Physical Activity as a Means of Punishment or Discipline

Many physical educators rely upon physical activity, usually exercises or running, as their primary method of maintaining discipline. Is this method successful? Externally, the student may seem to respond to this punishment because it hurts. However, how does this work when one tries to teach physical fitness through the same or similar activities? Are there two types of push-ups, one good and one bad? Is running for punishment different than running for fitness? How does the physical education teacher promote and motivate for physical fitness when the same activities are used as a means of discipline? Punishments are something we try to avoid. Does the student equate the good side with the bad side of physical activity? Further, the types of punishment usually involved are those that relate to cardiovascular fitness or muscular endurance, two

Figure 7.5 The careful monitoring of the body's responses to exercise is important in adult fitness programs.

important components of fitness. How many times are sports skills, for example, kicking the soccer ball, throwing the football, or dribbling the basketball used in the same manner? These would not be considered as punishment by either the teacher or the student. Yet running laps, sprints, and performing push-ups or sit-ups are readily used in a punishment capacity. To synthesize such teacher behavior must cause confusion in the student's mind. "Perform well on the physical fitness test because it shows you are fit" is one side of the issue, while the opposite side states, "Do this activity because you have shown bad behavior or have not performed well." Many high school students and adults have negative attitudes toward physical education because of this practice. In many cases, a complete physical "re-education" is necessary before the adult becomes responsive to physical fitness activities.

The belief that some students respond only to punishment of this nature really means that the teacher has not been exposed to other methods. To monitor and detect all rule violations and disruptive behavior is impossible; therefore, what we are saying by punishing with physical activity is, "What I do (behavior) is not as bad as getting caught for what I do." The teaching of discipline requires discipline. The word itself has multiple meanings. There is a distinction between discipline and deviant behavior. The school's role in the development of discipline is to be responsible for the pattern of behavior that contributes to mental, moral, emotional, and physical growth of normal people. It is doubtful that using physical activity as punishment will contribute to that development. (For a follow-up to this discussion, see chapter 14, "Contemporary Issues and Trends." Alternatives to Physical Activity as a Means of Discipline.)

SUMMARY

The physical education profession is responsible for the physical fitness of the nation. A physical educator should be fit and set the example for others. Our nation is becoming more concerned with physical fitness, and projections indicate that this trend will continue. People want quality in life, and adults, especially, are becoming more concerned about their health and fitness lifestyles.

Fitness is a very broad term and has various concepts. Total fitness looks at the overall individual, combining the absolute levels of physiological, psychological, social, and cognitive fitness. In physical education, physiological fitness is of most concern. Physical fitness is not the same for everyone; thus, it is very hard to define except in general terms. A reasonable definition is, "A combination of several components each specific in nature to improve and maintain health and the physical state of the body."

Physical fitness consists of health-related and skill-related fitness. The health-related components are cardiovascular fitness, strength, muscular endurance, flexibility, and body composition. Cardiovascular fitness is the most important component, especially in adult life. Skill-related fitness includes agility, balance, coordination, power, speed, and reaction time. Skill-related components are not essential for a person to be fit and healthy, but do contribute to performance in sports and games. Health-related components are essential to a health and fitness lifestyle.

Personal fitness is the concern of all persons. Through the physical education process, a person learns the knowledge and activity necessary to become physically fit. A health and fitness lifestyle consists of wellness, proper nutrition, physical fitness, and stress management. In our society, an unhealthy lifestyle is practiced by many and often is passed unknowingly to children from their parents. One must plan and manage these four factors for quality of life and vitality in living. The responsibility for one's lifestyle is ultimately one's own, but physical education should provide the knowledge and experiences to enable people to choose and practice a health and fitness lifestyle.

The physical education major is the main source of fitness knowledge in our society. The educators have a responsibility to serve as an example of fitness for our nation. Other responsibilities include youth fitness, adult fitness, and to avoid using physical activity as a means of discipline or punishment. Youth fitness should begin in kindergarten and continue through high school. Adult fitness has become a lucrative business under the title of corporate fitness and is offering the physical education major another career opportunity. Physical educators have the knowledge and skills to become the controlling force in corporate fitness. The misuse of physical activity, especially fitness activities, as punishment has long been a standard practice in many schools. However, it may be self-defeating in regard to developing positive attitudes toward physical fitness in youngsters, which results in negative attitudes as adults.

Physical or personal fitness is the primary responsibility of all physical educators, both for themselves and for the people they instruct. Physical fitness is an essential element of a healthy lifestyle. Physical educators should be held accountable for their own personal fitness and the knowledge and skills necessary to impart these practices to others.

STUDY QUESTIONS

1. Write a position paper (500 words maximum) on why you are fit and how you became fit. If you do not consider yourself fit, do the same on why you are not fit and what has contributed to a poor state of fitness. Discuss your paper with your course instructor or other physical education faculty of your choice.
2. Write your definition of physical fitness. Be sure to include the necessary components for such. Discuss this definition with your course instructor and classmates.
3. Take the components of health-related fitness and, by using additional readings, determine the intensity, frequency, and duration necessary to maintain and/or improve the fitness level for each.
4. Design a model, using Gutin's model (fig. 7.2) as an example, for physical fitness that you feel you could effectively use to explain fitness to others.
5. Analyze your personal fitness needs and construct a plan to develop a health and fitness lifestyle. Before you implement such a plan, discuss it with someone you would consider a fitness expert.
6. What steps would you take to improve the fitness levels of our nation's youth?

STUDENT ACTIVITIES

1. Make arrangements to have your body composition taken. Also, determine what your ideal body weight should be, based on the percentage of bodyfat you would like to maintain.

2. Visit an adult fitness center or health club and observe or discuss what is taking place in the realm of corporate fitness.

3. Visit an elementary, middle school, and senior high school and observe or discuss the ways in which fitness for a lifetime is being presented and practiced in the physical education program.

NOTES

1. Frank W. Bearden, "First National Conference on Physical Fitness and Sports for All, Texas Association," *Journal of Health, Physical Education and Recreation* 47 (1980): 3, 14, 34.

2. H. Harrison Clarke, "Definition of Physical Fitness," *Journal of Physical Education and Recreation* 50 (1979): 8, 28.

3. Bernard Gutin, "A Model of Physical Fitness and Dynamic Health," *Journal of Physical Education and Recreation* 51 (1980): 5, 48–51.

4. American Alliance for Health, Physical Education, Recreation, and Dance, *Health-Related Physical Fitness Test* (Washington, DC: AAHPERD Publications, 1980).

5. Phillip E. Allsen, "Circulorespiratory Endurance," *Journal of Physical Education, Recreation and Dance* 52 (1981): 7, 36–37.

6. American College of Sports Medicine, "Position Statement on the Recommended Quantity and Quality of Exercise for Developing and Maintaining Fitness in Healthy Adults," *Medicine and Science in Sports* (1977): 9, 31–36.

7. Michael Pollack and Steven Blair, "Exercise Prescription," *Journal of Physical Education and Recreation* 52 (1981): 1, 30–35.

8. C. Corbin, L. Dowell, R. Linsey, and H. Tolson, *Concepts in Physical Education* (Dubuque, IA: Wm. C. Brown Publishers, 1982), 17.

9. Corbin et al., *Concepts in Physical Education* 79.

10. National Institute of Mental Health, *Plain Talk About Stress* (Rockville, MD: Department of Health, Education, and Welfare, 1979).

11. Hans Selye, "Stress," *The Rotarian* (1978): 70–74.

12. Jack H. Wilmore, "Objectives for the Nation: Physical Fitness and Exercise," *Journal of Physical Education, Recreation and Dance* 53 (1982): 3, 41–43.

13. Reiff and Hayes, "Physical Fitness: A Downhill Race," *Education USA* (February 18, 1980): 189.

14. Reiff and Hayes, "Physical Fitness," 189.

15. Louis Harris and Associates, *The Perrier Study: Fitness in America* (New York: Great Waters of France, 1979).

16. Wilmore, "Objectives for the Nation," 41–43.

RELATED READINGS

Allsen, Phillip et al. *Fitness for Life*. Dubuque, IA: Wm. C. Brown Publishers, 1984.

Berger, Richard A. *Introduction to Weight Training*. Englewood Cliffs, NJ: Prentice-Hall, 1984.

Colfer, George, and John M. Chevrette. *Running for Fun and Fitness*. Dubuque, IA: Kendall-Hunt Publishing Co., 1980.

DiGennaro, Joseph. *The New Physical Fitness: Exercise for Everybody*. Englewood, CO: Morton Publishing Co., 1983.

Dintiman, George B. et al. *Discovering Lifetime Fitness*. St. Paul, MN: West Publishing Co., 1984.

Dusek, Dorothy E. *Thin and Fit: Your Personal Lifestyle*. Belmont, CA: Wadsworth Publishing Co., 1982.

Falls, Harold et al. *Essentials of Fitness*. Philadelphia: Saunders Publishing Co., 1980.

Getchell, Bud. *Physical Fitness: A Way of Life*. NY: John Wiley and Sons, 1983.

Heyward, Vivian H. *Designs for Fitness*. Minneapolis, MN: Burgess Publishing Co., 1984.

Marley, William P. *Health and Physical Fitness*. Philadelphia: Saunders Publishing Co., 1982.

Miller, David K., and Earl Allen. *Fitness: A Lifetime Commitment*. Minneapolis, MN: Burgess Publishing Co., 1980.

Stokes, Roberta et al. *Fitness: The New Wave*. Winston-Salem, NC: Hunter Textbooks, Inc., 1984.

Westcott, Wayne L. *Strength Fitness*. Boston: Allyn and Bacon, 1982.

Williams, Melvin H. *Nutrition for Fitness and Sport*. Dubuque, IA: Wm. C. Brown Publishers, 1983.

Teaching Physical Education **3**

A highly visible career option in physical education is teaching in schools, and teaching is the focus of part 3. As part of the total education offered by our nation's schools, physical education has felt the harsh criticism directed at education during the past several decades. It, too, has been forced to respond in formulating plans that are designed to improve the teaching and learning of physical education.

A contemporary approach to teaching occurs in chapter 8. The emphasis in this chapter is on the skills necessary to be an effective teacher of physical education. It also emphasizes additional duties and responsibilities that teachers assume and begins helping students make a career decision as to whether or not teaching is appealing.

Chapter 9 focuses on the subject matter of physical education, including rationales for selecting certain activities that are intended to comprise the school curriculum. Chapter 10 presents an overview of the teaching styles and strategies needed to effectively achieve the goals of the curriculum. Determining whether or not curricular goals are achieved is done through evaluation, the subject of chapter 11.

We hope that your study of part 3 will make you more aware of the components and challenges of teaching physical education.

The Teacher

8

Chapter outline

Student objectives

As a result of the study of this chapter, the student should be able to

1. Differentiate between the traditional view of teaching and the view associated with *teacher accountability.*
2. List the factors that led to the criticisms of the American educational system and the subsequent era of teacher accountability.
3. Discuss the impact of the era of teacher accountability on physical education.
4. Define, according to your text, a *teaching skill.*
5. Define, according to your text, a *learning environment.*
6. List and explain the teaching skills necessary for the establishment of a learning environment.
7. List and explain the teaching skills necessary to effectively teach motor activities.
8. Discuss additional duties and responsibilities expected of teachers in each of the following categories:
   a. civic responsibilities
   b. school responsibilities
   c. class-related responsibilities
   d. professional responsibilities
9. Contrast teaching at the elementary, middle, and high school levels and higher education.

Although the teacher is only one of a number of variables that affect student learning, few would argue that the role of the teacher is considered unimportant. Traditionally, this role has been thought to be assumed by persons who are "born" into the profession, naturally possessing the characteristics that would enable them to teach effectively. *Teaching* has been regarded as intents to transmit knowledge, develop attitudes deemed acceptable by society, and change overt behavior. Whether or not students actually "learned" these things, teaching occurred if the "intent" was apparent.

Another, more recent view holds that teaching occurs only when the learner is affected. This view evolved because of the intense criticism directed at shortcomings in the American educational system and its agents, the teachers, beginning in the 1960s and continuing to today. These accusations prompted educators to focus on specific goals and outcomes that students master as a result of their exposure to educational settings designed to enable them to attain these goals. Contrary to the traditional view that held to "intents" to foster learning by disseminating information to the student who, failing to repeat it properly, was labeled "lazy," "dull," or "incorrigible," the responsibility for student failure shifted to the school and the teacher. In other words, if there was no learning, there was no teaching. The subsequent era of **teacher accountability** took on philosophical overtones about the way teaching ought to be done. Despite the many workshops, in-service training sessions, and professional meetings dedicated to teacher accountability, little was actually accomplished in the way of change for the American system of education. Later, however, the nation began feeling the impact of rampant inflation, and teacher accountability began to be viewed from the business perspective of cost effectiveness. Education was, and is, a costly proposition. Evidence began to accumulate that students were not learning, that they were being graduated unable to read, do simple math, or communicate effectively. The taxpaying public rebelled against continuing to pour vast sums of money into an educational system that failed to produce an educated child.

Physical education has not remained untouched in the era of teacher accountability. A gymnasium, related facilities, equipment, and teacher salaries encompass a sizeable portion of the budget of a school system. Where the goals of physical education are not met (if fitness is not developed or motor skills are not demonstrated), the public is quick to conclude that physical education has not been cost efficient. Eventually, such an attitude could jeopardize physical education programs.

One aspect of physical education is probably the most closely scrutinized in the public demand for teacher accountability. Coaches are often regarded as teachers who work with a specific population of students. Despite their effectiveness in the classroom or gymnasium, these teachers are quickly removed if the public deems their won-loss record unacceptable. Accountability for coaches is demanded, and if the learners (players on the team) are inept at demonstrating what the teacher (athletic coach) taught them, the search begins for a coach who is more effective in this process of accountability.

The era of teacher accountability has prompted educators to view teaching as a process that produces desired behaviors in students. In chapter 1, we briefly mentioned pedagogy as the science or study of teaching. By studying teaching, it has become possible to identify certain behaviors that teachers exhibit to bring about desirable behaviors on the parts of their students.

The act of teaching implies that communication, as the mechanism of teaching, must be established between a teacher and a learner. Talking is the foundation of communication in this relationship and provides one avenue for analysis of the teacher behaviors. Teachers also communicate nonverbally to their students, expressing dissatisfaction with a cocked eyebrow or pleasure by scruffing the hair of a student. Nonverbal communication provides another channel for the analysis of teaching. Through analysis, teaching behaviors have furnished for us some valuable insights that have been traditionally lacking into the complex teacher-learner relationship. This movement has led to the development of **competency-based teacher education programs,** which will be examined in chapter 5. This movement has also caused educators to focus directly on specific teaching skills that affect learning, as opposed to the traditional generalizations about what good teaching entails.

TEACHING SKILLS

By adapting one of Dr. Richard Magill's definitions of skill, we can state that a **teaching skill** is an expression of performance based on a teacher's productivity or on certain characteristics of performance.[1] This definition makes necessary the identification of areas where high levels of a teacher's performance and productivity are needed to accomplish successful teaching.[2]

In order to give form to these areas demanding teaching skills, the *play education* model of Dr. Daryl Siedentop (fig. 8.1) is offered. As mentioned in chapter 1, the play education framework presents a contemporary philosophy of physical education where identifiable teaching skills are needed to realize explicit objectives for physical education in working towards an ultimate aim of physical education.

Siedentop's model has been slightly modified to reflect the teaching skills needed to meet objectives for physical education. The *aim* and *level 1* objectives are the foundation for the two compartments established by the *levels 2 and 3* objectives and the skill areas that are identified to foster the attainment of the objectives and the aim. As you examine the model in figure 8.1, you will notice that the categories to the right of the vertical hashline denote skills necessary to create a **successful learning environment.** Those to the left represent areas of teaching skills necessary to be a **successful teacher of motor activities.** These activities are defined as "acts or tasks that require movement and must be learned in order to be properly performed."[3]

The Aim of Physical Education

A number of aims exist for physical education. Where viable objectives are in evidence in efforts to attain an aim, certain teaching skills must exist for the objectives to be met. Siedentop's play education model provides such an example for us. According to Siedentop, the aim of the teacher of physical education is to increase a student's tendencies and abilities to play competitive and expressive motor activities (see fig. 8.2). (See chapter 1 for a detailed examination of this aim which, in that chapter, takes the form of Siedentop's definition of physical education.) The primary objective in meeting

Figure 8.1 Adaptation of Siedentop's physical education as play education model showing some of the skills needed by a physical educator.

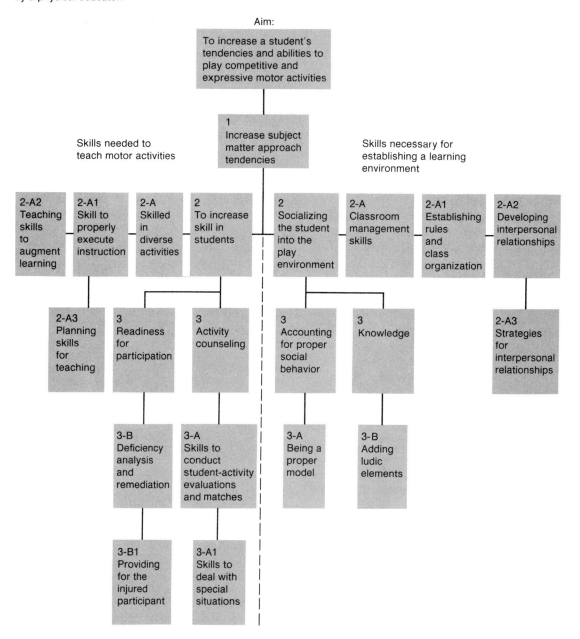

Figure 8.2 Physical education includes the teaching of skills for expressive motor activities.

this aim is for the teacher to increase subject matter approach tendencies. To make this possible, the teacher must promote the desire of a student to enter into and persist in a play environment.

Subject matter makes reference to the motor activities that comprise physical education. Subject matter can take the form of volleyball, archery, square dancing, or any other activity included in curricular offerings. The goal of the teacher is to create an attractive learning environment where skills in the subject matter can be learned through effective teaching. Variables that detract from the creation of a sound learning environment and ineffective teaching are to be avoided to prevent students from disliking situations where the subject matter of physical education is presented.

A Successful Learning Environment Defined

Teachers are responsible for creating an environment that will promote the teaching-learning process. Actually, this entails setting the stage for the teaching of motor activities by promoting variables that enhance teaching-learning and eliminating variables that detract from it. It is imperative that the *environment,* the gymnasium or playfield, be one into which the student willingly and enthusiastically enters (see fig. 8.3). An atmosphere of anticipation is apparent among the students because the teacher-student relationship is sound. The students enjoy being in the presence of the teacher. The successful learning environment is organized to eliminate waste time because rules are established and maintained in such a manner as to provide ample opportunities for the students to be *players.* The students learn how to conduct themselves in the physical education learning environment, since certain behaviors they exhibit add to the opportunities they have to become skilled. The students are *teachable* in the process of becoming more skilled because the demeanor of the teacher provides a model for acceptable behavior where players play. For the student, the skill to be taught becomes more meaningful as they inquire about the ludic elements—rules, strategies, customs, and courtesies—of their play.

Obviously, a successful learning environment does not just happen. It must be extensively planned and implemented through requisite skills that are necessary for its establishment.

SKILLS NECESSARY FOR ESTABLISHING
A SUCCESSFUL LEARNING ENVIRONMENT

Level 2 Objective: Socializing the Student into the Play Environment

Key statement: Subject matter approach tendencies are enhanced by the teacher's ability to present rules, customs, courtesies, and strategies in such a way as to help define the environment where play is to occur.

One does not pull a golf cart onto a green to putt. A courteous player does not make noise while another in the group is swinging the club. Cutting a dog-leg on a par five hole may well be a strategy one employs only after some degree of mastery of hitting a golf ball is attained and circumstances warrant such a gamble. Playing with a golfer who angrily throws clubs and exhibits other forms of temper tantrums is unpleasant. The teacher must account for these aspects of the play environment where golf is to occur in order to make playing golf satisfying to the participant.

Level 3 Objective: Accounting for Proper Social Behavior

Key statement: A successful learning environment requires behavior that is socially acceptable and consistent with the subject matter.

Historically, good sportsmanship and concepts of fair play have been considered characteristics that are derived naturally from being a player. Actually, behaviors that are representative of these traits must be taught in the context in which they are expected to occur. A player's reaction to making a game-winning shot in basketball might be inappropriate if such behavior occurred on a putting green after a long putt was made. Players who sulk after a loss often do so because they believe they are expected to behave in this manner. Teachers of physical education need to formulate strategies that teach desired social behavior in the play environment.

Level 3-A Objective: Being a Proper Model

Key statement: The teacher can best teach proper social behavior by modeling the desired behavior in the context where it is expected to occur.

Teachers who show anger in play, who harass officials, or who cheat can expect the same behavior in their students. An advantage to being a teacher who can actively participate in games with students is that the teacher can exhibit the desired social behavior in its proper context. If teacher participation is impossible, a wise strategy is the complimenting of a player observed exhibiting the desired behavior in the presence of other players. On occasions when improper social behavior occurs, the behavior should be pointed out as unacceptable and a thorough explanation of what is acceptable should follow.

Level 3 Objective: Knowledge

Key statement: Players who are taught proper conduct, rules, customs, and strategies have socialized into an effective learning environment.

As enthusiasm for the subject matter of physical education grows, so does the desire to know and apply more complex aspects of motor activities (see fig. 8.4). The grip size and weight of a tennis racket assume importance to the player who becomes more involved. Securing proper running shoes and studying different training methods

Figure 8.4 Scoring procedures are part of the knowledge teachers impart to students in motor activities.

add to the novice jogger's attraction to running. To establish a proper learning environment, the teacher must communicate the "knowledge" aspects of activities after recognizing the student's desire to know more. In this context, the teacher is a resource person at times when additional knowledge about an activity is sought by the player. Teaching the knowledge parts of activities before socialization into the play environment occurs can detract from the attractiveness of the learning environment.

Level 3-A Objective: Adding the Ludic Elements

Key statement: The addition of ever-increasing complexity to motor activities provides additional meaningfulness for the player.

Skilled players would soon become bored with the same practice routine day after day. By continuing to challenge players with new skills and skill techniques, teachers expose needed variety of players and increase the attractiveness that the activity holds for the players. More complex drills and training methods and the addition of better equipment to augment skills are variables that furnish complexity to the learning environment. Teachers need the skills necessary to implement additional ludic elements at a time when the additional elements can most benefit the player and make him or her more competitive.

Level 2-A Objective: Classroom Management Skills

Key statement: The learning environment is enhanced by teachers capable of managing their classes in order to optimize actual learning time.

Classroom management skills utilized by the teacher influence the amount of learning that takes place in the class. If students are allowed to spend large amounts of time getting organized for and changing activities, they are spending less time participating in and practicing motor skills. Also, a reduction of management time allows more time for actual teaching to occur. Good management skills are contingent upon good planning. In order to learn motor skills, the students must be actively involved in practice. Little is learned by students who are forced to stand in line or watch from the sidelines. Good classroom management skills make skill learning possible.

Level 2-A1 Objective: Establishing Rules and Class Organization

Key statement: Classroom management is dependent upon organizational strategies and rules that are established by the teacher to improve the attractiveness of the learning environment.

Rules governing behavior in the physical education learning environment are important if a proper classroom climate is to be maintained. Rules should be stated in such a manner that they are clear to all students. It is important for the teacher to maintain consistency in enforcing these rules. By rewarding the ability of the class to organize itself and follow the rules, the teacher has added a dimension to his or her repertoire of teaching skills that will enhance the learning environment.

Level 2-A2 Objective: Developing Interpersonal Relationships

Key statement: The relationship between teachers and students that is founded upon mutual respect and admiration provides for a learning environment that is freely entered into by the students.

All of us tend to seek experiences that please us. The learning environment for physical education should be made as pleasant as possible by the teacher. Teachers often take for granted that students are properly motivated to participate in activities and are irritated by students who do not show a high interest level. The cause of this lack of motivation may well stem from poor interpersonal relationships between the students and the teacher. Teachers who fail to take an interest in each student create a learning environment that might be unattractive for some students.

Level 2-A3 Objective: Strategies for Interpersonal Relationships

Key statement: Addressing students by name, initiating interactions with students, and emphasizing positive interactions develop desirable interpersonal relationships.

Inherent "good feelings" have been experienced by all of us when the teacher knew us by our first names. When we consider the number of students seen each day in physical education by the teacher, this task seems impossible. Skills that can assist the teacher in mastery of this task will help create sound interpersonal relationships.

The manner in which teachers interact with students is important. Most interactions occur only when the teacher is cued to respond to a student by an example of misbehavior on the part of the student. "Be quiet and get in line" is an interaction cued by students who are talking excessively and are disorganized. A teacher who is continually critical of students and interacts only in a negative context does little to enhance the attractiveness of the learning environment. Initiating congenial interactions with students and complimenting them for the things they are doing well establishes a sound climate for learning and makes it possible for the teacher to utilize the skills needed to teach motor activities successfully.

SKILLS NEEDED TO TEACH MOTOR ACTIVITIES

The essence of teaching physical education is the conveyance of information designed to improve the motor performance of students. Once a learning environment is established, certain other considerations are necessary if teaching is to be successful. What activities should be taught? What information must be obtained from students and what is the preparedness level they bring to each activity? How do teachers cope with special situations like the disparity of skill levels, coeducational classes, and handicapped students? What are the legal ramifications if a student is injured in the physical education class? Finally, does the teacher know enough about intricate movements in a variety of motor activities to provide appropriate information to the student about the quality of his or her performance (see fig. 8.5)? These questions face all teachers, and dealing with each question demands certain teaching skills if students are to learn motor activities. Again using Siedentop's play education framework, let us examine these areas of teaching skills more closely.

Level 2 Objective: To Increase Skill in Students
Key statement: Subject matter approach tendencies are greatest in players who have a high degree of skill in the selected activity.

As mentioned earlier, all of us gravitate to activities at which we excel. Golf is an attractive activity if the ball can be kept in play, if shots can be reasonably executed, and if an occasional par or birdie can be made. People who have enough skill to accomplish these things persist in playing the game. Anticipation to play is very high; the golfer is attracted to the environment where the subject matter, golf, is to be played.

Conversely, losing golf balls, hitting "fat" shots repeatedly, three-putting greens, and consistently losing to an opponent makes the game of golf much less attractive to the nonskilled player. These players may dread a round of golf and avoid playing, thus deviating from an aim of physical education, which is to increase tendencies to play. The tendency to play is contingent upon the ability to play, and teachers of golf or any other motor activity must have the ability to increase the skill level of the students with whom they come in contact.

Figure 8.5 A skilled teacher/coach presents an excellent model for students.

Level 3 Objective: Activity Counseling

Key statement: Students will be most attracted to and will desire to learn skills in activities that are most meaningful to them.

Closely tied to the development of interpersonal relationships are counselor skills, which are necessary if a desirable selection of activities is included in the curriculum.

Level 3-A Objective: Counseling Skills to Conduct Student-Activity Evaluations and Student-Activity Matches

Key statement: Skill can best be developed in students in activities for which they are suited.

The teacher must be skilled in data collection processes to determine "student abilities, present interests, and anticipated future interests and vocational aspirations"[4] in order to use student input to select activities. Also, by knowing the students, the teacher is more able to offer activities for which the students are best suited "in an attempt to help maximize the meaning that they obtain from participation in the activities of physical education."[5] Not forcing the overweight student into cross-country running or the nonaggressive, underweight student into wrestling are examples of the awareness needed by teachers to more properly match students and activities. The desire of the students to persist in the physical education environment is augmented if they are not forced to perform in activities aversive to them.

Level 3-A1 Objective: Skills to Deal with Special Situations

Key statement: Diverse skill levels, coeducational classes, and handicapped students create special situations that, when planned for, make the subject matter of physical education attractive to all students.

The most common special situation a teacher encounters is the disparity among students regarding their levels of skill. Traditionally, teachers have directed their attention toward teaching the "average" student, omitting the special needs of the poorly skilled and highly skilled. This is not a sound educational practice. Teachers must possess planning and administrative skills to provide adequate instruction and feedback for all students, regardless of their skill levels. (Strategies for teaching are discussed in chapter 10.)

The recent emphasis on coeducational classes, prompted by the Title IX mandate, demands a sensitive teacher with adaptive skills necessary for the modification of certain activities to accommodate both sexes. At the elementary level, this is not a significant situation with which to cope, since girls and boys are more similar at that age in physical and motor development. Later, however, boys tend to become stronger and more aggressive, and they tend to try to dominate in many teacher-oriented activities. Adjustments are necessary in tactics and rules for team games to be attractive to both sexes. In individual activities, teaching strategies can be more uniformly applied, since the raising of the skill level of the individual student is of importance here.

Mainstreaming the handicapped student into the regular physical education class requires additional skills. In most instances, other students in the class eagerly respond to the handicapped student and are cooperative in adjustments that have to be made for the sake of the special student. This kind of learning environment makes entering into play easier for the handicapped student. Knowledgeable application of teaching strategies and minor adaptations of regular games and sports make it possible for the special student to have a personally meaningful physical education experience. In these situations, teachers need special training relative to the kinds of handicaps encountered, limitations of movement that could be injurious, movement that could be physically beneficial, counseling skills to deal with the emotional state of the handicapped student, and strategies that can, as nearly as possible, normalize play for the student.

Level 3 Objective: Skills to Make the Student Ready to Participate

Key statement: In order for skill to develop in motor activities, certain prerequisites of fitness must be met (see fig. 8.6).

Without the necessary grip strength to hold a tennis racket, flexibility to jump a hurdle, or cardiovascular endurance to sustain play in any activity for a reasonable length of time, skill learning is impeded. Teachers need the analytical skill to recognize situations where student progress is not taking place due, for the most part, to a lack of prerequisite fitness.

Level 3-B Objective: Skills for Deficiency Analysis and Remediation

Key statement: Students who have their fitness deficiencies recognized and corrected by a skilled teacher are prepared to develop the skills necessary to enjoy being at play.

Fitness development can be, for some, a desired end that physical education programs are expected to achieve. In this context, however, fitness is a means to an end.

Figure 8.6 Readiness for participation in motor activities may require the development of fitness components.

It provides the player the foundation that makes possible the learning of motor skills. Lack of fitness is a hindrance to a player. It is imperative that teachers have the cognitive skills to recognize fitness deficiencies and have the planning and teaching skills to design and implement programs of a remedial or corrective nature.

Level 3-B1 Objective: Skills to Provide for the Injured Participant

Key statement: Returning the injured player to the play environment as quickly as possible is often contingent upon the first-aid skills and rehabilitation practices of the teacher.

Teachers of physical education who have taught for any length of time can usually document the twists, sprains, strains, and bruises that have occurred over the years. Naturally, safety precautions must always be in effect. These precautions are the first rule if the teacher is to avoid legal responsibilities for injuries that might occur. The courts of law stand behind teachers who have been prudent in eliminating factors from the learning environment that could cause injury and, where injuries have happened, have backed teachers who practiced prudent first-aid skills. Because of the dynamic nature of physical education, injuries will occur. Skills that will enhance the player's readiness to re-participate involve first-aid, proper procedural steps compatible with school policies, and follow-up in conjunction with the school nurse or physician in properly rehabilitating the injury. Prudent first-aid measures are those which authorities agree are logical steps taken pertinent to a specific injury. Teachers need these skills as part of their repertoire of teaching skills.

Level 2-A Objective: A Skilled Teacher in Diverse Activities

Key statement: In order to recognize skill deficiencies and provide appropriate information for their remediation, the teacher should be skilled in the activity being taught.

Although the need for "expert" levels of skill in activities being taught is controversial, it is mentioned here as a desired competency. In eastern and western Europe, teachers of physical education are usually highly skilled former athletes. Naturally, not all skilled performers have the capabilities to be teachers, but a high skill level is an advantage for a teacher in prescribing a correction in a complex motor pattern to make the pattern more efficient.

The teacher of motor skills should at least be a student of an activity and the complex movements comprising that activity in order to improve the skills of the students in the activity. Cognitive skills obtained from biomechanics and motor learning are essential for the teacher.

Level 2-A1 Objective: Skills to Properly Execute Instruction

Key statement: A knowledge of how people learn motor skills and the employment of strategies to augment their learning are requisite skills for a teacher.

Communication skills, mentioned at the beginning of this chapter, are extremely important to the conveyance of necessary information from a teacher to the students. Instruction given to students must be loud enough, clear enough, and concise enough to set the stage for effective practice to commence. The teacher must be aware as to how much information intended as instruction the students can assimilate. Too often, teachers instruct for too long a period of time. Instructional time should be minimized by focusing on key points the class will practice. The modeling effect teachers can use is important during communication with students. Using spoken language that is grammatically correct and free from distracting mannerisms can set a desirable example for the students to follow.

Information about attempts at skill performance, **feedback,** facilitates learning. Knowledgeable and skillful teachers are adept at providing information to students that can be used to improve subsequent attempts at a motor skill.

Level 2-A2 Objective: Teaching Skills to Augment Learning

Key statement: Certain qualities in the repertoire of the skills of a teacher can make the teaching-learning process of motor skill development more effective.

Teachers desire to motivate students to repeat certain skill attempts that are judged acceptable. By pointing these aspects of skill attempts out to students in a positive manner, students are encouraged to repeat these desirable attempts. In addition, feedback designed to correct a faulty skill attempt is important to the student. Ideally, the teacher should possess the teaching skills necessary for a balance to be established between feedback that is corrective and feedback that focuses on correct aspects of the skill attempt.

Modeling is another important method in teaching motor skills. The teacher of skills who is skilled in the activity being taught can easily use modeling to demonstrate the proper way of performing. Sequence pictures, loop films, and video cassettes are other ways to effect modeling for the students.

Because of the importance of feedback to the learning process, the skilled teacher will emit high rates of quality feedback during practice attempts by the students. Quality feedback means that information that is specific to a feature of the skill attempt is included, since this is much more effective than general information. In other words, information about the position of the arms during the swinging of a golf club is more valuable than a general statement like, "That's terrible" or "You're not doing it the way I told you!"

Level 2-A3 Objective: Planning Skills for Teaching

Key statement: In order to make the most efficient use of the time allotted for the teaching of motor skills, the teacher must plan extensively.

Preparation for effective teaching is an aspect of the educational process that goes unrewarded but is very important if learning is to take place in an orderly fashion. At one time or another, many of us have had teachers who seemed disorganized and ill-prepared to teach. A lesson presented without planning is easily perceived by the students as disorganized and is a pitfall an effective teacher avoids. Lesson plans provide a guide the teacher will follow from the start of a class until its completion, while unit plans do the same from the beginning of a new activity to its completion. Planning should occur for class organization, for controlling the behavior of the class, for motivating the class to attempt new skills, and for the evaluation of a daily lesson. Unit plans ensure that no component skill of any activity is omitted, thereby enhancing the performance of the player.

The framework and adaptation of Siedentop's play education model have provided insight for the reader concerning the skills necessary to prepare for and carry out successful teaching. As we shall see, however, expectations of the role of teachers extend beyond the school's play areas.

TEACHING AND . . .

Figure 8.7 illustrates that school administrators, the teaching profession, and the community expect the teacher to assume a variety of additional duties and responsibilities.

Civic Responsibilities

The involvement of a teacher in community affairs might be thought of as a public relations venture between the school and the community. Joint attempts to solve community problems by teachers, parents, and other concerned citizens establish a cooperative bond that can serve to motivate parents and other citizens to help solve many of the problems existing in the schools. Physical educators can "sell" their programs through presentations at parent-teacher meetings and various other civic affairs. In addition, physical education teachers can lend their expertise to organizations sponsoring charity fun runs or similar events involving fitness activities. Because a school is a reflection of community values, teachers should make concerted efforts to participate in the upgrading of the welfare of the community.

Figure 8.7 Teachers' duties and responsibilities extend beyond the actual teaching.

Level of teaching	Civic responsibilities			Class-related responsibilities									School responsibilities							Professional responsibilities				
	PTA programs	Community service	Charity events	Coaching	Locker room supervision	Intramurals	Equipment ordering	Record keeping	Maintenance	Facility design	Budget preparation	Inventorying	Teacher's meetings	Bus driving	Student advising	Committee service	Club advising	Chaperoning	Event attendance	Conference attendance	Reading literature	Curriculum revision	Presenting papers	Research/publish
Elementary	F	O	O	O	O	O	F	F	F	O	O	F	F	F	O	O	O	O	F	O	O	O	X	X
Middle school	O	O	O	F	F	O	F	F	F	O	O	F	F	F	O	O	F	O	F	O	O	O	X	X
High school	O	O	O	F	F	O	F	F	F	O	O	F	F	F	O	O	F	O	F	O	O	O	X	X
Higher education	X	F	O	O	X	O	F	F	O	O	O	O	F	X	F	F	F	O	F	F	F	F	F	F

F = Frequently expected of teachers
O = Occasionally expected of teachers
X = Rarely expected of teachers

School Responsibilities

Too often, physical education teachers, especially those involved in athletic coaching, confine themselves to activities specifically related to their programs. In an effort to establish good interpersonal relationships with other faculty members, physical educators should involve themselves in all aspects of school life. Showing an interest in school plays, musical productions, and committee work, along with regular attendance at teachers' meetings, presents an image that is greatly respected and appreciated by other teachers.

The more mundane tasks of proper school supervision are additional duties expected of teachers. Bus, playground, and cafeteria supervision is essential for the school to function efficiently.

An additional responsibility, that of student advisement, is expected of teachers in higher education, but may occur at any level. Higher education advisement is usually related to guidance in selecting proper courses for the study in the physical education major's program, although advisement of graduate students might be included.

Class-Related Responsibilities

Obviously, teachers expect students to behave properly when preparing for or leaving the play environment. The presence of the teacher can deter misbehavior, thus the duty of supervision of the locker room and play areas. Ideally, intramural competition stemming from activities learned in class occurs, along with competition between or among grades or homerooms. These activities, too, need directing and supervising, and these responsibilities are often expected of physical education teachers.

While physical educators may often serve as consultants to architectural firms that design play areas, just as often this responsibility is delegated to the teachers. Preparing budgets, ordering equipment, maintaining existing facilities and equipment with an eye toward safety aspects, and conducting periodic inventories are all class-related responsibilities within the purview of the physical education teacher.

Keeping accurate records of student achievement can be an awesome task, considering the number of students with which the physical education teacher comes in contact. Devising an efficient evaluation system is an expectation of all teachers.

Professional Responsibilities

Physical education teachers, particularly those in higher education, are expected to present papers, conduct research, and publish articles and books. Whether revising the physical education curriculum or attending a coaching clinic, the expectation is that teachers must constantly strive to better themselves, their programs, and their profession. Louis E. Raths states, "Every teacher is expected to enter wholly into professional life and to make his contribution to the improvement of the profession. He is expected to belong to professional societies, attend conferences, act in accord with professional ethics, keep up to date in the reading of literature, and make some attempts with his colleagues in the community to share new pertinent research results."[6]

TEACHING AT DIFFERENT LEVELS

As a supervisor of student teachers, Dr. Keith Hamilton has had many opportunities to visit elementary, middle, and high schools and to contrast, often on a daily basis, the differences in the physical education programs found at these three levels. Do you know what to expect from physical education students in these traditional levels? What are their attitudes toward physical education and how do they behave in their classes? Could you successfully cope with a class of high school sophomores the same way you might successfully cope with a class of third graders? The following are hypothetical, anecdotal observations designed to illustrate student behavior in physical education classes. These examples are portrayed as fairly typical of student behavior at the three levels that a teacher of physical education may encounter.

At the elementary school, the children were learning the skills of throwing, catching, and bouncing playground balls. Rates of feedback emitted by the teacher were high, and first names were used in conjunction with feedback. The children continuously practiced the skills, and behavior that detracted from the class was nonexistent. Obviously, the children were enjoying their physical education experience, as evidenced by the smiles, laughter, and shouts of glee over their performances. The principal of the school stated that the worst punishment a child could receive was to be forced to miss his or her physical education class. The children, when asked, agreed with the principal's assessment.

At the middle school, interactions between the teacher and the students were negative reactions to student misbehavior. Approximately twenty-five percent of the total class were seated in street clothes in the bleachers. The boys and girls in the squads were reluctant to perform the "forearm pass" in volleyball. The girls remained in the back of the lines, while the boys persisted in "hand-fighting" each other, "wise-cracking" responses to corrective feedback by the teacher, and kicking the volleyballs. A loud cheer went up from the class when the teacher announced that the class period was over.

Although the rates of misbehavior were not as high in the high school as those in the middle school, time spent practicing basketball passing skills was minimal. The drill intended for passing practice became three-on-three games. Rarely was the ball passed to a girl; thus, the girls quickly lost interest and congregated in a corner of the gymnasium. Only half the class was dressed for activity, with the remaining class members seated in the bleachers. The teacher stood idly by, "supervising" the proceedings.

In no way are these examples intended to portray all elementary physical education classes as ideal and all middle and high school classes as chaotic. What is intended is to illustrate that varying attitudes and behavior do exist in physical education and that the prospective teacher of physical education must examine these differences before deciding the level at which to teach. Obviously, the zeal with which formal physical education is approached is different among the three levels. Obvious, too, are the differences in class discipline. Someone oriented toward team sports and desiring to work with highly skilled players would find elementary school physical education teaching undesirable. A teacher at ease with small children but uncomfortable around older students might be a great success as an elementary level teacher. In considering the level at which you might desire to teach, the most important item is that you know yourself. Are you naturally outgoing and at ease with elementary-age children? Do you possess the patience to motivate middle school children whose values might include personal appearance over physical activity? Can you easily accept the misbehavior intended to generate attention or do you have a "short fuse" with students who "step out of line"?

By knowing how your personality relates to the three levels of teaching and by devising a philosophy about teaching that relates to your strengths and weaknesses, you can arrive at a decision about the level you would find most rewarding.

Teaching Physical Education in Higher Education

As Janet Parks points out, "The most obvious difference between elementary or secondary school students and students in college is that college students usually are in school by virtue of their own choices."[7] The advantage this furnishes teachers in junior colleges, colleges, and universities lies in the inherent motivation college students possess in courses in which they enroll. Students in basic physical education programs, programs designed for students majoring in physical education, and programs for graduate students usually strive to excel, which sets the stage for a desirable teaching situation. Discipline problems are practically nonexistent. Facilities and equipment are among the best available, and class sizes are usually manageable. Because teachers in higher education are expected to advise, publish and present papers, and conduct research, teaching loads may, in some instances, be reduced.

The college or university teacher is expected to have an advanced degree and possess expertise in one of the disciplines comprising physical education. The teaching load for one involved in professional and graduate courses may well be entirely in this area of expertise, particulary in large universities. In small institutions, teachers may teach graduate courses, undergraduate professional courses of some diversity, and activity classes. Coaching, directing intramurals, and advising sports clubs are additional responsibilities of teachers in higher education.

The motivations and quality of students make teaching in higher education a highly desirable choice of levels.

DECISION: SHOULD I TEACH?

Your interest in physical education may be in areas other than teaching. Still, teacher education remains a primary thrust for many departments of physical education in colleges and universities, and teaching is an area where many seek a career.

The following sections are intended to present realistic advantages and disadvantages inherent in the teaching profession. These sections are not intended to bias such an important a decision as one's career choice; a decision of such magnitude should not be based on the interpretations of others. Perhaps this presentation of the pros and cons of teaching will assist you in thinking through whether or not a career in teaching physical education is attractive to you.

Advantages of Teaching

It has been said that the three best things about teaching are June, July, and August. Although stated facetiously, there is merit in having one's summer free to recover from the intensity of the nine-month school year. Such recovery can be passive or active. Rest obtained through travel or by relaxing during the summer months is an advantage. This can be a time for families to become reacquainted, for working mothers and fathers to spend valuable extra time with children, and for seeking diversions that bring enjoyment. For economic reasons, however, the months off in the summer often necessitate summer employment, perhaps teaching summer school or in related positions in recreation. Summers also provide the opportunity to advance oneself professionally by taking additional course work toward recertification requirements or an advanced degree. Salary raises are often contingent upon hours accumulated beyond the bachelor's degree, and summers provide an ideal time for study away from the responsibilities associated with teaching and coaching.

The environment where one teaches is usually attractive. You have the opportunity to "be your own boss" in your learning environment, and your teaching success is limited only by your shortcomings. Most teachers are committed to their work, and this common bond, coupled with other similar interests and values, creates excellent working relationships among a teaching faculty. Those who enjoy being around young people will find the working conditions excellent and far from monotonous. The very nature of the diversity of characteristics of young people will provide constant challenges and new experiences. Generally, the teaching day is relatively short, with actual teaching time amounting to about six hours daily. In physical education, it is possible to attain and maintain personal fitness through one's own participation in class activities. (The importance of this modeling effect has been mentioned earlier in this chapter.)

Much of the reinforcement from teaching comes from observing the progress students make and from vicariously sharing in the excitement students show when they realize progress. The subject matter of physical education assumes immediate relevance for school children in the way it enhances their play lives. It is quite possible to see the lifestyles of students positively affected as the result of their physical education experiences. This permits teachers to know that they are actively involved in the welfare of each student, the school, and the community. Teachers do have an impact!

The rewards of teaching must include the opportunity to make a decent living. Many progressive school districts have made salary and fringe benefit packages extremely attractive. As a teacher gains in experience and pursues additional education, salaries do become reasonable. Since many districts are using merit pay incentives for teaching excellence, teachers can be recognized and rewarded for exemplary performance. Retirement systems supported by the school districts, coupled with medical and dental insurance benefits, contribute to the welfare of teachers. Maternity and sick-leave policies ensure that teachers are treated fairly, and professional days are granted for use by the teacher to upgrade his or her qualifications.

The leadership capabilities needed for successful teaching often lead to positions in school administration. An uncommonly high number of successful school principals and superintendents have backgrounds in physical education.

Disadvantages of Teaching

The disadvantage of the low beginning salary for teachers is the one most readily identified. A single beginning teacher can barely "get by" on a first- or second-year teacher's salary, while teachers attempting to support a family during these years will find it nearly impossible. The beginning teacher's salary can often be supplemented by assuming coaching duties, but the long hours involved are rarely compensated fairly.

Administrative expectations, as mentioned in chapter 1, encourage physical education teachers to coach. Although many enjoy the dual roles of teaching and coaching, some desire to teach physical education without the addition of coaching responsibilities. From the viewpoint of some administrators, coaching duties are implicit in the teaching position, making this situation a disadvantage for some physical educators.

Teachers of physical education on elementary, middle, and high school levels are often faced with inadequate budgets, facilities, and equipment. These factors, when combined with large classes and heavy teaching schedules each day, create a sense of frustration for many teachers. Developing interpersonal relationships with students becomes nearly impossible when large classes prohibit getting to know the student as an individual. Equally frustrating are attempts to organize classes without the space or equipment to make the organization process efficient and having classes cancelled because the play area is needed to serve another school function.

The lack of public awareness about the role of physical education is an additional disadvantage. The public cannot distinguish between physical education and athletic programs and are often unable to perceive any worth coming from participation in physical education. Physical educators are commonly called upon to justify the place of physical education in the schools, since it is often accorded status inferior to other subjects by the public.

Many would contend that the general breakdown of respect for authority and the lack of discipline in the schools make teaching an undesirable career choice. A teacher is highly respected in nearly every country of the world, owing to the fact that the teaching profession itself is held in high esteem. In the United States, however, teaching is viewed by the public as a poor choice of vocations. Respect for teachers evolves out of situations where it is earned, as opposed to respecting the position of a teacher, as other countries do. Needless to say, some school systems in this country are out of control, making the teaching position nearly intolerable.

Naturally, no firm decision about a physical education career should be forthcoming at this time. You should continue your study of physical education and more thoroughly investigate the complex role of a teacher, then you should make your decision as a result of the sum of your experiences and the strength of the commitment you feel about teaching. Teaching is not easy; it requires "a well-educated, mature person who has the insight and energy for this demanding job."[8]

SUMMARY

Teaching, traditionally, has been considered an "art," with *intents* to teach justifying the teaching process. In the past several decades, however, public criticism has altered this view of teaching into one where teaching is accomplished only when demonstrable learning has occurred.

Just as good athletes need certain skills to perform well, so, too, do teachers. Certain teaching skills are necessary to create a learning environment that students find attractive and enter into willingly. Being a teacher of motor activities also demands skills to help players become more adept at their activities. Play enriched by good teaching becomes more meaningful for students and helps them to be motivated to play.

The role of the teacher extends beyond the gymnasium or playfield. Teachers are expected to take on additional responsibilities in the school, in the community, and in the profession.

A career decision on whether or not to teach must include the understanding of a number of factors that make teaching attractive for some and unattractive for others. Student needs and values are different among elementary and secondary young people. One's personality may determine success in teaching at these different levels, since personality should be compatible with the level of teaching. The fact that students are highly motivated to do well in higher education makes that level a desirable one in which to teach. At any level, however, the most important ingredient is a strong commitment to teaching.

STUDY QUESTIONS

1. What are some major differences between the traditionally held view of teaching and the view that prompted the development of competency-based teacher education?
2. What is a teaching skill? Can you make a comparison between some skills needed to be a good teacher with some needed to be a good basketball player?

3. What are some characteristics of a learning environment? What are the skills a teacher needs to establish a learning environment?

4. Why is it desirable for a teacher of motor activities to be highly skilled in diverse activities? How are students short-changed if the teacher is good in only two or three activities?

5. What are some expectations of teachers outside of their classrooms when they are actively engaged in teaching?

6. What characteristics of students at the elementary, middle, and high school levels should a teacher be aware of that could attract or deter a person from teaching at those levels?

STUDENT ACTIVITIES

1. Visit a physical education class at a level in which you might be interested. Simply count the number of interactions directed at the students by the teacher. Indicate whether you believe the interaction should be placed in a "negative" or "positive" category. From the results, would you conclude that the teacher is establishing good interpersonal relationships through interaction skills? Why or why not?

2. Who has been your favorite physical education teacher to now? Can you list the teaching skills that have caused him or her to rate as your favorite?

3. The section in this chapter on teaching at different levels details middle and high school physical education classes that are apparently "out of control." Write a paragraph on some strategies you might employ to bring those situations under control. Do you think your personality would enable you to teach at these levels effectively? To implement your strategies effectively?

4. One point of contention in this chapter is the level of skill a teacher should possess to effectively teach particular skills. In this chapter, an expert level of skill is advocated. Do you agree? Why or why not?

5. Write a paragraph explaining why you would or would not choose a career in teaching physical education at this point. If you think you would like to teach, explain why you think you would prefer elementary, middle, or high school teaching. Does teaching in college appeal to you? What steps do you think you would have to take in order to obtain a teaching position in a college?

NOTES

1. Richard A. Magill, *Motor Learning: Concepts and Applications* Dubuque, IA: Wm. C. Brown Publishers, (1980), 11.
2. Ibid., 12.
3. Daryl Siedentop, *Physical Education: Introductory Analysis* Dubuque, IA: Wm. C. Brown Publishers, (1980), 270–71.
4. Ibid., 270.
5. Ibid., 270–71.

6. Louis E. Raths, "What is a Good Teacher," in *Studying Teaching* Englewood Cliffs, NJ: Prentice-Hall, Inc., (1971), 9.

7. Janet Parks, *Physical Education: The Profession* St. Louis: C. V. Mosby Co., (1980), 122.

8. Marie Hughes and Associates, "The Model of Good Teaching," in *Studying Teaching* Englewood Cliffs, NJ: Prentice-Hall, Inc., (1971), 24.

RELATED READINGS

Caruso, Virginia. "Enthusiastic Teaching." *Journal of Physical Education, Recreation and Dance* 53, no. 2 (February 1982).

Caskey, Sheila R. "A Task Analysis Approach to Teaching." *Journal of Physical Education, Recreation and Dance* 53, no. 1 (January 1982).

"Excellence in Physical Education." *Journal of Physical Education, Recreation and Dance* 54, no. 7 (September 1983).

Graham, George. "Acquiring Teaching Skills in Physical Education." *Journal of Physical Education and Recreation* 52, no. 4 (April 1981).

Lewis, Clifford Gray. "Joys of Teaching." *The Physical Educator* 37, no. 1 (March 1980).

Metzler, Michael. "Developing Teaching Skills: A Systematic Sequence." *Journal of Physical Education, Recreation and Dance* 55, no. 1 (January 1984).

Mosston, Muska. *Teaching Physical Education.* Columbus, OH: Charles E. Merrill Publishing Co., 1966.

Olsen, Janice K. "Recycling the Three T's: Teaching, Talking and Terminating." *Journal of Physical Education, Recreation and Dance* 53, no. 2 (February 1982).

Siedentop, Daryl. *Developing Teaching Skills in Physical Education.* Palo Alto, CA: Mayfield Publishing Co., 1983.

Urmansky, Warren, and Nan Carle. "Teacher Contributions to Educational Relevance." *The Physical Educator* 37, no. 4 (December 1980).

The Curriculum

9

Chapter outline

Considerations for the Traditional
Curriculum
  Hetherington's Step 1
  Hetherington's Step 2
  Exhibit 9.1 Hetherington on Curriculum
  Hetherington's Step 3
  Hetherington's Step 4
Purposes of Curricular Activities
  The Domains of Behavior
Nontraditional Organizational Approaches
to Curriculum
  The Conceptual Approach
  The Systems Approach

Factors Affecting the Curriculum
  The Student
  Teacher Expertise
  Geographical Location, Facilities, and
    Equipment
  Legislation
  Professional Input
Evaluation of the Curriculum
Summary
Study Questions
Student Activities
Notes
Related Readings

Student objectives

As a result of the study of this chapter, the student should be able to

1. List and explain Hetherington's four steps for the construction of the school curriculum in physical education.
2. Explain the acronym NOISE as descriptive of the traditional objectives of physical education.
3. Explain the importance of level, scope, and sequence and the role of the teacher in formulating a school program in physical education.
4. List and describe the programs and activities associated with or found within the school programs of physical education for all levels.
5. Compare the *conceptual approach* to the *systems approach* as organizational approaches to curriculum in physical education.
6. Explain the *domains of behavior* at which educational objectives should be directed and give an example for each domain that relates to physical education.
7. List and explain the obvious factors that affect curriculum in physical education.

During the 1920s, Clark W. Hetherington, one of our early leaders in physical education, stated that a broad function of schools is to "formulate a curriculum of activities with educational objectives."[1] Since we recognize that this has been and will continue to be an obligation of educational institutions, let us turn our attention to exactly what is meant by this term **curriculum.**

Broadly speaking, curriculum has been defined as "the life and program of the school."[2] More specifically, curriculum is "a series of rich and guided experiences with some order of priority (progression) and directed toward the achievement of certain objectives."[3] In considering these definitions, we must recognize school factors that ultimately affect the curriculum: the philosophy of education from which desired objectives for students are drawn and the person most responsible for meeting these objectives, the teacher. Willgoose explains that "curriculum is a body of experiences that lies between objectives and teaching methods. It commands a central position [see fig. 9.1]. It is a full program of things to do that will realize the original aims and objectives."[4]

CONSIDERATIONS FOR THE TRADITIONAL CURRICULUM

In recognizing the contemporary value of the insights of Clark W. Hetherington into curriculum, let us examine some of his considerations that are pertinent today. Hetherington explained that "the construction of the school curriculum in physical education requires four steps: (1) an analysis of the influences of social changes upon the activities of children and the status of physical education in the community as a whole, (2) a formulation of the special aims or objectives of physical education, (3) the formulation of a school program in physical education, and (4) the formulation of detailed courses of activities, with a specification of materials and an outline of procedures for the convenience of teachers and students."[5] Using Hetherington's four steps as an outline, let us consider each step in light of the many considerations influencing the traditional curriculum in physical education.

Hetherington's Step 1

Step 1: An analysis of the influences of social changes upon the activities of children and the status of physical education in the community as a whole

Physical education has, historically, been greatly influenced by social changes and the needs of society, a point illustrated in chapter 1. The emphasis on sports and games and the relationship of physical education to athletics was generated by the abilities of early leaders to perceive what was popular in our society at the beginning of the twentieth century. Where Americans have felt their security threatened during the wars of the twentieth century, society placed emphasis on fitness for militarism for the protection of our ideals of a democratic life. The concept of good health has long been an educational goal, and the contemporary influence of personal fitness for good health has had a great impact on the curriculum of our schools and colleges. The current emphasis on protecting our natural environment has influenced physical education curricula, particularly by the selection of activities that can be enjoyed in the outdoors.

Figure 9.1 The central position of the curriculum.

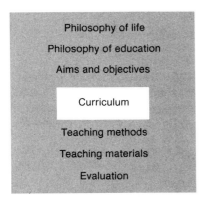

Philosophy of life

Philosophy of education

Aims and objectives

Curriculum

Teaching methods

Teaching materials

Evaluation

Backpacking, rock climbing, spelunking, skiing, and others that have become popular in communing with nature have become part of the curriculum of physical education. Physical education has also been sensitive to criticism directed at it. In the 1960s, the movement of physical education to an academic discipline was spurred by the belief by some segments of society that physical education had no place in institutions stressing academics: this led physical educators to seek and promote a body of knowledge unique to physical education, and thus it became an academic discipline.

Where physical education has been considered a "frill," or "nonessential," ingredient in the education of children, physical educators have responded by showing critics the benefits that can accrue from physical education. The Physical Education Public Information (PEPI) project (see chapter 1) has evolved out of the defensive posture physical education has been forced, at times, to assume. Community-based pressure for physical educators to justify their programs has had a positive effect in helping us clarify the aims and objectives of physical education. Physical education has been able and must continue to perceive societal needs and to respond appropriately to community demands for justification of its programs.

Hetherington's Step 2

Step 2: A formulation of the special aims or objectives of physical education

In chapter 1, we examined six influences that have shaped contemporary physical education. Each of these influences has provided philosophies that determined specific aims and objectives that physical education ought to attain. Because physical education today is the sum of these influences, most statements concerning the aims and objectives include philosophies from each of the influences. These traditional objectives, which are to be met through exposure to the curriculum, are stated in this chapter in the form of an *acronym*. An acronym is a word formed by the first letter of other words. The acronym used here, NOISE, summarizes the traditional aims and objectives that have been most widely accepted for physical education.

exhibit 9.1

Hetherington on curriculum

The school as an institution performs two broad functions in dealing with children: (*1*) It formulates a curriculum of activities with educational objectives, and it organizes and leads the activities; and (*2*) it formulates a program in physical welfare (i.e., the protection of children from mechanical injury, fire, and health handicaps), and it controls these injurious and handicapping influences. These are the old functions of parents, organized as school functions. The relationships and distinctions between these two functions as school functions and as responsibilities of the teacher are of fundamental importance in building a program in physical education.

Physical education began its evolution in the school primarily as a program of activities. It has been centered in a program of physical-training activities. If it were not for this historic fact and the influence of the old distinction between the mind and the body, the term "physical training," and then, later, the term "physical education" (with the confusing use of the word "physical") would not have arisen. Physical education has been, and of necessity must be, in control of one of the great major divisions of educative activities, the big-muscle or physical-training activities. Thus physical education is apt to be interpreted by adults *from an adult standpoint* merely *as exercise*. But the *meaning of physical education* is not confined to the organization and leadership of the activities *as exercises in the adult sense. The* program *in physical education is determined by the inherent and essential values of the activities for the normal growth and development of children, and by the functions of the school and teachers in the leadership of children.* Therefore, the formulation of the program must be based on preliminary studies of the sociological status and the educative and protective functions of physical education. Further, the formulation of the detailed course of activities for the use of teachers must be based on a clear understanding of the principles involved in the program with its background of social demands and of objectives.

Source: Clark W. Hetherington, *The School Program in Physical Education* (Yonkers-on-Hudson, NY: World Book Co., 1922), 2–3. © 1922 World Book Co., Yonkers-on-Hudson, New York.

Noise

The acronym *NOISE* probably originated with students who, when preparing for an examination over the aims and objectives of physical education, arranged this acronym to aid them in responding to a question. An explanation of the five components of our acronym follows:

Neuromuscular development: the efficient and skillful coordination of the nervous and muscular systems that, when applied to movement, produces intrinsically successful experiences to be repeated.

Organic development: the promotion of the attributes contributing to good health for an efficiently functioning life, including satisfactory muscular strength, flexibility, cardiovascular endurance, muscular endurance, and body compositon.

Interpretive development: the cognitive abilities that enable a person to encounter challenges, design strategies for meeting those challenges, and exercise sound judgment in the seeking of solutions, including solutions to problems related to the total self. Included is the ability of a person to fully function in activity by having a knowledge of and ability to apply rules, strategies, and etiquette.

Self-expression: providing for the learner experiences that prove to be inherently meaningful to the practitioner, allowing him or her to explore movement parameters to the ultimate and most satisfying limits.

Emotional/social development: the promotion of movement experiences designed to enable students to have the opportunity to participate, to be successful, and to feel extremely good about themselves and their relationships with others as a result. Important is the belief of each student that he or she is a valuable and fully-functioning member of society and that he or she is perceived by society in a like manner.

The challenge for physical educators is to ensure that these five objectives are met. Criticism of physical education stems from the fact that teaching methodology has failed to attain these desired objectives. As Willgoose states, ". . . The human factor—the teacher—has much to do with the achievement of curriculum objectives. It is quite possible, therefore, to think out and develop a fine course of study, only to find that it only partially does the job for which it was intended because teachers failed to grasp its significance or were indifferent to its content."[6]

Hetherington's Step 3

Step 3: The formulation of a school program in physical education

Level, Scope, and Sequence

Early in this century, Dr. E. L. Thorndike devised what he termed his *laws of learning*. One of these was his *law of readiness*. Simply stated, Thorndike attempted to convey the need for the preparedness of a child physically and psychologically for the learning of certain tasks. Despite what we may have observed in a peewee football encounter, most eight- or nine-year-old quarterbacks are not ready to learn and apply the intricacies of a triple option offense imposed by the coach. Siedentop addresses this point by including his *readiness for participation* objective as part of his play education theory for physical education, which is detailed in chapter 9. He calls upon teachers to prepare a student for the learning of motor skills. Curriculum must reflect the maturation **level** of the students for whom it is designed in order to provide desirable learner outcomes.

In order to illustrate **scope** and **sequence,** let us examine your college catalog as it details the traditional curriculum for the professional preparation of a physical educator. Professional preparation institutions have determined that exposure to specific subject matter is necessary to develop professional expertise. Consequently, liberal studies, the sciences, and foundations and methods courses of a general and specific nature provide what is thought to be the *scope* of study needed to meet the objective of the best preparation of a professional in physical education. Scope refers to the spectrum of exposures to the subject matter deemed important for the attainment of a goal. For the school physical education program, the scope would include every activity that is thought to contribute to the attainment of a developmental objective.

Some degree of logic is necessary in the structure of prerequisite educational experiences necessary before more difficult subject matter is undertaken. As a result, courses in the curriculum are arranged in order to *sequence* the subject matter into a hierarchical arrangement. You may take courses in your professional curriculum that are designed to ensure that you understand basic anatomy and physiology before you begin the study of exercise physiology. You may be required to learn physics before tackling biomechanics, just as you studied grammar and structure before studying literature. A curriculum building upon itself in order to gain insight into more complex subject matter is termed the *sequence of curriculum construction*. An example of this in the school physical education program is using movement education to learn fundamental movement patterns before undertaking the learning of sport skills.

Level, scope, and sequence have, for years, been the foundations for curriculum designs. Understanding the nature and characteristics of learners prior to exposing them to subject matter has always been necessary. Determining the kinds of subject matter that will promote the attainment of desired outcomes is equally necessary. If learning is to be maximized, the order of the presentation of the subject matter, the sequence, must be a consideration.

The Role of the Teacher in the Formulation Process

The school program in physical education is the result of the arrangement and presentation of specific **subject matter** designed to achieve a desired outcome or objective. Subject matter can be as broad as a complete program for developing health-related fitness components or as specific as strategies for effecting a successful free-throw in basketball. As physical educators, we need to know how health-related fitness is attained in order to construct the program through which the objective is to be accomplished. As athletic coaches, we must know enough about the mechanics of shooting a basketball so that our program for skill development will ensure a high success rate when our players attempt a free-throw. As professional physical educators, we must have, as part of our backgrounds, the knowledge and skills of application of the subject matter of physical education to formulate a program that will bring about desired results.

The term *subject matter* might, at first, appear intimidating or mysterious. Quite simply, the subject matter of physical education is what physical education is all about; fitness, sport sociology, basketball, golf, tennis, kinesiology, and sailing represent just a few of the many activities and areas of study that comprise the subject matter of physical education. The teacher's primary function in the design of the curriculum that will make up the school program in physical education is to ensure that all subject matter presented has, as Hetherington says "a developmental purpose."[7]

Hetherington's Step 4

Step 4: The formulation of detailed courses of activities, with a specification of materials and an outline of procedures for the convenience of teachers and students

Teaching styles and instructional strategies are the subject of chapter 10; thus, that aspect of Hetherington's fourth step, procedures for conducting the curriculum, is left for study there. Chapter 1 provided some insight as to how, historically, physical education became comprised of diverse activities reflecting diverse philosophies. For now, let us turn our attention to a description of the *courses of activities* that make up the curriculum which forms the programs of physical education today. An attempt is made here to classify activities by levels, but this attempt is not intended to be absolute. *Lead-up* activities, for example, are usually taught at the elementary level, but can also be presented at the secondary or college levels as preparations for certain sports. Outdoor education usually occurs at the secondary level after concepts about the environment have been learned, but this education is certainly not limited to this level. Some programs and activities are not intended to be primarily directed at any level; they are important to all.

Common Activities and Programs for All Levels

Physical Fitness Activities   In chapter 7, we studied the characteristics of a fit person and the rationale for fitness for good health. Activities vary greatly for the development of cardiovascular endurance, muscular strength and endurance, flexibility, and body composition. Each must include the features of intensity, frequency, and duration in order to provide desired results.

Cardiovascular endurance is developed through jogging, cycling, swimming, and aerobic dancing, primarily, and must be of such a nature that the activity elevates the heart rate to a target *training threshold* (see fig. 9.2). The exercise must continue long enough at that threshold to be beneficial and must occur often enough (such as on an alternate-day basis) for desired results to be attained.

Muscular strength and endurance are best effected by weight training and developmental exercises that cause specific muscle groups to be *overloaded*, or taxed beyond normal.

Flexibility is produced by programs of static and dynamic stretching of a specific muscle, *overloading* that muscle by extending it to a point of mild discomfort beyond normal. Flexibility permits more efficient movement by increasing the range of motion a joint is capable of attaining and it protects the muscles against injuries.

Body composition changes can result from any activity that produces the utilization of calories for energy. Desirable body composition usually means an increase in lean body mass (achieved through muscular development) and/or a decrease in the amount of fat a person has. Popular programs to improve the status of body composition stem from programs used for cardiovascular development, coupled with a reduction in the amount of food ingested.

Figure 9.2 Running develops an essential component of physical fitness, cardiovascular endurance, in people of all ages.

Dance   Dance, as a form of expression, is as old as any activity known to humans. Today, dance is not only a popular activity, but it has also formed the foundation for movement education, which is discussed later in this section (see fig. 9.3). Dance, in the school physical education program, usually consists of modern dance, folk dance, square dance, and ballroom or contemporary dance.

Modern dance, as self-expression through movement, is the most basic form. Comparing the following explanation of modern dance to the vocabulary of movement education is illustrative of its foundation for movement education:

> This contemporary dance form is a vital and expressive type of communication. Thoughts, ideas, and emotions are expressed through the dancer's manipulation of time, space, and energy factors. The individual's creative potential is motivated and challenged in composing dance movement. The student is permitted extreme freedom, which is conducive to the development of individual creativity.[8]

Folk and square dancing are taught in the school program for enjoyment and for fostering the learning of the customs of other countries. Square dancing evolved from folk dancing that is unique to the United States. Both forms are intended to promote social grace and cooperation.

Figure 9.3 The development of flexibility is very important for improving expressive motor abilities.

Ballroom dancing provides the learning of techniques in dancing that are a part of many social occasions. Ability to perform a waltz, fox-trot, tango, and others allows a person to be comfortable in such social settings.

Contemporary dancing often becomes a part of the physical education dance program, with students sharing their knowledge and abilities to perform the "latest" dances done to pop music. Disco dancing was a recent fad that became part of some school dance programs, and other popular dance fads will follow.

Aquatics   Although fewer than five percent of our nation's schools have swimming pools, the schools are still the most viable aspect of society for teaching people to swim and to enjoy the activities to be found in and around water. Gabrielsen, Spears, and Gabrielsen suggest the following as components of the school aquatic program in physical education: swimming (instructional and competitive); synchronized swimming; diving; skin and scuba diving; surfboard riding; canoeing and boating; water skiing; sailing; and bait and fly casting.[9]

Gynmnastics   Miller and Massey say that "a gymnastic program includes a wide variety of activities, among which are calisthenics, tumbling, balancing, free exercise, and apparatus."[10]

Calisthenics are light or developmental exercises that are important unto themselves or of use in warming up for more vigorous activity.

Tumbling incorporates balance and is found in free exercise. "It includes such motor skills as rolling, turning, springing, and twisting."[11] **Free exercise** in women's programs combines tumbling, balance, and dance movements set to music. Men's competitive free exercise does not include music.

Apparatus work in gymnastics includes the use of specific equipment, including the side and long horses, horizontal bars, still rings, uneven and parallel bars, springboards, and balance beams. The trampoline is not included here, since the latest recommendations are that it not be used in school physical education programs, owing to the danger involved with its use.

Basic Stuff Series   Early in the 1980s, a project of the National Association for Sport and Physical Education (NASPE), an association of AAHPERD, brought together some of the contemporary leaders, teachers, and scholars in physical education to formulate the *Basic Stuff* series. These series form "a collection of booklets presenting concepts, principles, and developmental ideas extracted from the body of knowledge for physical education and sport. Each booklet is intended for use by undergraduate majors and practitioners in physical education."[12]

The purpose of this project was to edit the tremendous amounts of information generated by researchers in some of the disciplines of physical education to make the information applicable to teachers and relevant to students. Student motives were identified, from which concepts were selected for the dissemination of information directed at these motives.

Basic Stuff, Series I, includes information gathered from the disciplines of exercise physiology, kinesiology, motor development and motor learning, social/psychological aspects of movement, and movement in the humanities (art, history, and philosophy). Each is directed at the student motives of health, appearance, achievement, psychosocial aspects, aesthetics, and coping, with appropriate concepts to direct learning. *Basic Stuff, Series II,* is written for teachers to assist in their teaching of appropriate concepts at three different levels: early childhood, childhood, and adolescence.

The Basic Stuff project has provided a much-needed step forward in utilizing the accumulated knowledge about physical education for the upgrading of its programs.

Activities and Programs for the Elementary Level

Movement Education   Two opposing schools of thought pertain to **movement education.** The first is that movement education replaces physical education as a totally unique approach to helping children discover what their bodies are capable of attaining as they move. The second regards movement education as a program for elementary school children within the scope of physical education curricula and, as such, provides a way for children to be prepared for more complex movement skills that follow.

As you progress in your educational experiences in physical education and begin developing your personal philosophy about what you believe physical education to be, you may align yourself with one of these two schools of thought about movement education. Movement education has had a significant impact on school programs and has a legitimate theoretical and intellectual base for its existence.

Kruger and Kruger define movement education as education which "embraces the content, methods, and objective of a creatively oriented learning experience that seeks to develop learner awareness of where and how the body moves to fulfill some expressive or functional purpose."[13]

Once children have learned the **basic locomotor skills** (walking, running, jumping, hopping, leaping, skipping, and galloping) and nonlocomotor movements (bending and stretching, twisting, shaking, pushing and pulling, swinging, and striking) the child is exposed to the concepts of **space, force, time, and flow.** The child, using the movement of which he or she is capable, experiments with his or her movements within this framework of concepts. Space, where the body moves, can be personal or general, and the body can assume **levels** in space that are high, medium, and low. Force, light or heavy and hard or soft, is the concept that enables children to discover muscle movements needed to perform tasks. Time, slow or sudden, allows the child to conceptualize the rate at which a movement must occur to perform a task successfully. Flow, smooth or jerky, is the concept for understanding the need for movement to be coordinated as the body is exposed to different variables.

A problem-solving approach, **movement exploration,** is used as the method in movement education. Movement exploration "connotes method rather than content of a movement program. It is a process used by a learner that involves experimentation with possibilities for movement within restraints imposed by the teacher's statement of the task. Obviously, movement exploration is not taught; it is used to promote learning by discovery."[14] Typical questions that the teacher uses to verbalize a movement task include, "How can you balance on three body parts?" or "Can you change levels while catching the ball?"

Kirchner, Cunningham, and Warrell list the purposes of movement education as follows:

1. To assist children to become physically fit and skillful in a variety of situations. This requires the teacher to help the children increase their coordination and flexibility of mind as well as body.
2. To teach children to understand movement so they can build movement sequences from their ever-increasing understanding of what, where, and how the body can move.
3. To encourage self-discipline and self-reliance so children can work on their own ideas individually, in pairs, or in a group.
4. To provide maximum enjoyment and opportunities for creative expression.[15]

Rhythmics   Whether as a child at play or a professional athlete driving the length of a basketball floor for a lay-up, a body in motion that is moving efficiently has a natural rhythm. The importance of rhythm to all forms of movement is illustrated by the number of professional and collegiate teams that encourage their athletes to participate in dance. Rhythmics, at the elementary level, is designed to use the natural rhythm found in children moving and enhance it by having them "learn to gain body control, to change directions gracefully, or to suddenly stop when moving rapidly through space."[16] Rhythmics set the stage for later dance activities and enhance all forms of movement.

Games of Low Organization   "The term *low organized games* is used to denote game activities that are easy to play, have few and simple rules, require little or no equipment, and may be varied in many ways. Low organized game activities may be easily modified to suit the objective of the lesson, the size of the room, and the number of students in the group. They are easy to learn and can be enjoyed by both children and adults, but are used as an educational tool primarily during grades one through three."[17]

Lead-Up Activities   Beginning with the simple skills of throwing and catching, lead-up activities are designed to gradually increase the proficiency needed for sport skills (see fig. 9.4). These kinds of activities are modified to eliminate complex rules and strategies while maintaining the essence of the sport. The amount of time spent in utilizing lead-up activities to develop the skills necessary to play complex sports is directly related to successful participation later: this should be a slow and gradual process to ensure that optimal skill is developed by the child as he or she matures.

Activities and Programs for the Secondary/College Level

Competitive Sports   Sports that pit person against person, small group against small group, or large team against large team for the purpose of matching skills and strategies are deemed competitive. Such sports are intended to establish the superiority of one team or individual over another, generating the positives and negatives associated with winning and losing. In chapter 1, we saw that certain benefits supposedly accrue from sports participation. We studied how competitive sports became the essence of physical education early in the twentieth century and how they became a part of the total educational programs in this country. Due to the popularity of competitive sports and the fact that not all students in the schools have the ability to play on teams in interscholastic competition, physical education programs have included sports as an integral part. Sport in physical education programs enable all students to be exposed to the benefits of sport competition.

Lifetime Sports   William E. Straub calls the Lifetime Sports education projects "the best grass roots project ever sponsored by AAHPERD."[18] Originally, this project promoted the sports of bowling, badminton, archery, tennis (see fig. 9.5), and golf, but has now been expanded, definitionally, to include "physical activities in which students may participate throughout most of their life span."[19] Fox and Syster list the ways that lifetime sports can improve one's quality of life:

1. Release from occupational pressure
2. Diversion from personal troubles
3. Development of friendships
4. Acquiring a general feeling of well-being[20]

Outdoor Education   A movement rapidly gaining in popularity is outdoor education. Outdoor education is defined as "the process of teaching by direct contact and experience with native materials and life situations."[21] Students are taught how to use the environment for their enjoyment without spoiling it for future generations. Backpacking and camping skills are developed, and the program of outdoor education may include methods of survival in the outdoors for extended periods of time. Such experiences have been designed to promote group cooperation and individual initiative and have been successful with youngsters who are socially maladaptive.

Combatives   Part of our heritage in physical education are the skills of combat used by the ancient Greeks in their training for militarism and in their athletic contests. Militarism has long been a rationale for fitness, and activities often associated with militarism such as wrestling, boxing, and the martial arts, continue to be part of modern physical education programs. Boxing is experiencing a rebirth in educational programs, particularly at the college level. Although a popular collegiate sport several decades ago, boxing was eliminated from most programs due to the excessive number of injuries that were occurring. Advances in equipment and conditioning programs and a careful monitoring of matches has led the NCAA to reestablish boxing as an intercollegiate sport with a national championship.

High-Risk Activities   Attention to safety standards and thorough preparation of participants has led to high-risk activities (although they are of questionable merit in most

Figure 9.5 Tennis is an increasingly popular lifetime sport.

Teaching physical education

physical education programs in our schools) becoming a part of some programs, particularly at the college level. The sense of danger in activities such as skydiving, rock-climbing, spelunking, and hang-gliding provides meaningful and exciting experiences for some. Obviously, the question of liability when accidents do occur will probably negate widespread acceptance of these activities in school physical education programs.

PURPOSES OF CURRICULAR ACTIVITIES

The curriculum is comprised of activities that are designed to bring about certain desirable learning outcomes in the form of desirable changes in student behavior. If actual learning occurs, objectives facilitate change in a student's knowledge of the activity, the *value* he or she holds for the activity, and the way he or she improves in the performance of the activity. We know, for example, that exercise produces beneficial results. Because of this knowledge, we may develop a favorable attitude toward strenuous exercise and value it as an important aspect of our lives (see fig. 9.6). The application of knowledge and a favorable attitude may result in our inclusion of thirty minutes per day of jogging. These three areas, or **domains,** *knowledge, attitude,* and *performance,* have been identified in order to give direction to educational objectives.

The Domains of Behavior

Benjamin Bloom, David Krathwohl, and their associates published their *Taxonomies of Educational Objectives* in 1956. *Taxonomy* refers to the classification they used for educational objectives that were directed at the *domains,* termed *cognitive, affective, and psychomotor.* Today, these behavioral domains are often referred to as ***Bloom's Taxonomy.***

The **cognitive domain** is concerned with the intellectual development of the learner, with its focus on the accumulation and comprehension of knowledge. The cognitive domain is usually assessed by written tests, although in physical education, observations of occurrences in a learning environment (application of the knowledge of rules, customs, strategies, and etiquette in a game) may also be used to assess a student's cognitive abilities.

The **affective domain** is characterized by feelings, attitudes, and values about a particular subject that a student has at a given time. The affective domain deals with objectives that are designed to create a positive *internalization* within the mind of the student, so that overt behavior that follows will reflect the formulation of a desirable attitude. "I hate gym class" is a statement that reflects the speaker's attitude or feelings toward physical education. This attitude is often caused by experiences in the physical education class that were not pleasant. Subsequently, overt behavior that reflects such an attitude would be withdrawing from or "cutting" the class. Singer and Dick suggest that objectives in the affective domain "may be among the most relevant educational objectives for the physical education class."[22] Observations by the teacher are the primary assessment tool for the affective domain in determining if, for example, "the acquisition of skill and momentary fluctuations in performance can be partly attributed to interest, motivation, and attitude."[23]

Figure 9.6 The study of Olympism may positively affect students' behaviors.

Obviously, the way we feel about somebody or something is very important. One of the perennial difficulties with the affective domain is in observing that which we cannot see—attitudes, values, or feelings. Such feelings, until they manifest themselves in a student's performance in a particular setting, are difficult to determine without the help of carefully constructed attitude surveys and questionnaires. Often, students

Table 9.1

The Physically Educated Elementary Student

| THE DOMAINS OF BEHAVIOR | | PROGRAM: MOVEMENT EDUCATION | |
Cognitive	Affective	Psychomotor	Objective Attained
The student knows that the amount of force he/she applies to an object will dictate the proximity of the object to him/her	The student wants to become better at dribbling a soccer ball	The student practices dribbling a soccer ball while applying a light force to it	Neuromuscular development
The student understands that movement gives him/her a greater capacity for enjoying a healthy life	The student values the effects that movement provides	The student eagerly runs two laps of the field before class begins	Organic development
The student knows that levels of movement can help one perform movement tasks more efficiently	The student wants to run an agility course in a faster time	The student performs the agility course by lowering his/her body position to assist in changing directions	Interpretive development
The student knows that he/she is permitted to explore, in his/her own way, the possibilities movement provides	The student appreciates all that his/her body is capable of doing	The student readily attempts to determine the capabilities of his/her body as it moves	Self-expression development
The student knows that attempts to solve movement problems posed by the teacher will not be corrected or ridiculed	The student feels good about his/her movement and freely moves in the presence of others	The student participates, at every opportunity, in movement activities, both singularly and in the company of others	Emotional/social development

respond to questions about feelings in the way they think the teacher wants them to respond. For the sake of student involvement in program planning, student attitudes need to be discovered, making a valid evaluative tool extremely useful for the teacher.

The focus of the objectives within the **psychomotor domain** is action. In this domain, the students are called upon to do something, to perform. This domain is highly relevant to physical education, since movement connotes "doing something." Students who hit a drop shot effectively and consistently in badminton, make eighty percent of their free throws in basketball, or create gymnastic routines are examples of those who have attained proficiency in the psychomotor domain. Skills tests, written to include a specific criterion of acceptable performance in a selected activity, provide a means for evaluation of this domain.

Tables 9.1, 9.2, and 9.3 illustrate activities in physical education that are being utilized to attain the desired objectives represented by our acronym, NOISE.

Table 9.2

Physical Education for the Secondary Student

THE DOMAINS OF BEHAVIOR		PROGRAM: BASKETBALL	
Cognitive	Affective	Psychomotor	Objective Attained
The student knows that high levels of skills in shooting, passing and dribbling will make him/her a better offensive player	The student develops drills he/she believes will help him develop these skills	The student practices shooting, dribbling, and passing on a daily basis	Neuromuscular development
The student knows that cardiovascular fitness, strength, and flexibility are attributes a basketball player needs	The student appreciates how being in good condition can make him/her a better player	The student runs, lifts weights, and stretches on a regular basis	Organic development
The student knows the rules, customs, and strategies for basketball	The student feels he can be successful playing within the context of the rules	The student plays fairly and exercises the principles of good sportsmanship.	Interpretive development
The student knows that his/her driving lay-up will probably be blocked by the opponent's big center	The student believes that he/she can beat their big center with his/her drive	The student performs a successful "double-pump" lay-up	Self-expression development
The student knows that proper placement of personnel is important for the team to be successful	The student accepts the team's decision about the position he/she will play	The student plays forward on the basketball team	Emotional/social development

NONTRADITIONAL ORGANIZATIONAL APPROACHES TO CURRICULUM

The Conceptual Approach

In the previous section of this chapter, we examined the domains of behavior at which curricular objectives are directed. Assuming that knowledge about a central idea will shape an attitude favorable to the well-being of the student, which, in turn, will elicit a desirable course of action, the **conceptual approach** has become a major framework for the organization of curriculum. A concept represents a central idea that is meaningful to the learner to the point of effecting a change in the behavior of the one holding the concept. The conceptual approach has evolved from a dissatisfaction with traditional models that impart subject matter in a haphazard manner. Some believe that without the unifying concept what is learned becomes practically irrelevant as one matures; this is thought to be the reason why what is learned in schools is often not applied to adult living.

Table 9.3
The Physically Educated College Student

THE DOMAINS OF BEHAVIOR		PROGRAM: FOUNDATIONS OF EXERCISE AND FITNESS	
Cognitive	**Affective**	**Psychomotor**	**Objective Attained**
The student knows that jogging, cycling, swimming, and aerobic dancing are good programs for developing cardiovascular endurance and for weight reduction	The student dislikes jogging, cycling, and swimming, but realizes the need to control one's weight	The student does thirty minutes of aerobic dancing on alternate days	Neuromuscular development
The student is aware of a family history of cardiovascular disease and knows that regular exercise can strengthen the heart	The student desires to do all he/she can to prohibit the onset of cardiovascular disease	The student exercises regularly, does not smoke, controls the diet, and seeks positive ways to reduce stress	Organic development
The student realizes that thirty-five percent body fat is excessive	The student wants to wear fashionable clothes and feel better about him/herself	The student under a physician's guidance, restricts the daily caloric intake and begins exercising.	Interpretive development
The student knows that a program of static and dynamic stretching will improve movement efficiency by increasing the range of motion at a joint	The student wants to add more difficulty to his/her "free exercise" routine	The student creates stretching exercises for specific muscle groups involved in the more difficult routine	Self-expression development
The student knows that body size and strength can be developed by weight training	The student feels embarrassed when going to the beach because of being self-conscious	The student, with the help of a program that is scientifically designed, lifts weights on an alternate day basis	Emotional/social development

Although the conceptual approach is applicable to all areas of the curriculum in physical education, it has proved to be most successful in the health-related concept of *wellness*. Originating from the well-known School Health Education Study in 1967, the conceptual approach has been especially relevant to the contribution physical education makes to healthful living. Utilizing such unifying concepts as, "Regular exercise is one important factor in reducing the risk of coronary disease as well as other hypokinetic diseases," and "Obesity is a significant health problem that can be controlled, in most cases, with a proper balance between caloric consumption (diet) and

Figure 9.7 Wellness wheel and its relationship to the health continuum.

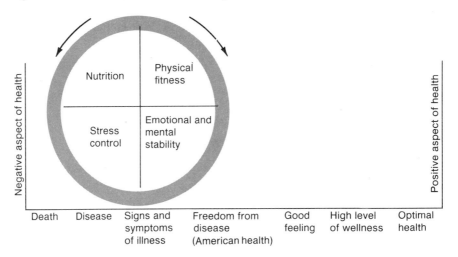

caloric expenditure (physical activity)," Charles Corbin and his colleagues author a text for college and high school that follows the conceptual approach.[24] Using supportive facts and laboratory procedures to reinforce the information related to each of the concepts, the authors want adults to make physical activity an integral part of life.

The purposes of the conceptual approach to physical activity are as follows:

1. To familiarize students with the basic values of physical activities and physical fitness as they relate to preventive health
2. To help students develop a positive mental attitude toward physical activity in their daily lives
3. To provide an opportunity for students to evaluate their own physical fitness status
4. To expose students to various programs of exercise that could apply to their particular needs relative to their body type and their self concept[25]

The conceptual approach is designed to move the learner to a more desirable position on a health continuum, based on the key ideas and supportive information that are presented and internalized by the learner. This is illustrated by figure 9.7, the *Wellness Wheel,* where student understanding of the concept of wellness motivates him or her to move beyond the status of simply "freedom from disease."

The Systems Approach

For a long time in physical education, teachers assumed that desired objectives and ultimate goals were attained automatically through participation by the learners in selected activities. As has been the case for all aspects of education, physical education has been subjected to intense scrutiny during recent decades and has been hard-pressed

Figure 9.8 The systems approach model as an organizational approach.

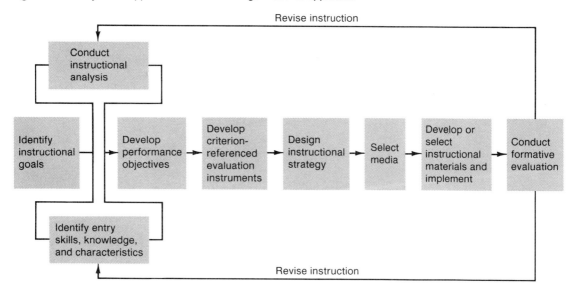

to document the attainment of intended objectives and goals. The missing ingredient appears to have been an evaluation component to determine if objectives and goals were met. Physical educators took for granted that exposure to the subject matter of physical education was of value "somewhere down the road" in the life of the learner. The era of accountability, discussed in chapter 8, demanded something more. One approach to curriculum design intending to eliminate the failure to attain objectives is the **systems approach.**

Robert Singer and Walter Dick author the definitive work in this area, *Teaching Physical Education: A Systems Approach.* Using the behavioral approach to the design of educational objectives (see chapter 10), Singer and Dick present an analytical procedure for teachers to ensure that what teachers set out to accomplish is, indeed, accomplished.

Arguing that the traditional majestic aims and objectives of past rationales for physical education are practically unattainable, Singer and Dick believe that objectives should be developed only from teaching styles that are designed to foster attainment for objectives whose occurrence can be readily documented. Their approach is one where "the teacher is encouraged to proceed systematically, to formulate and sequence instruction in a manner designed to fulfill student objectives that have been clearly specified at the onset of the program and to develop evaluative techniques."[26] By definition, "the term *system* implies that there is a predetermined relationship among the components of the instructional process; each component has its own function, and it also has an effect on the other components."[27] This is illustrated by the model for instruction of the systems approach found in figure 9.8.

By asking the question, "What does the learner have to do to perform a task?" the teacher is guided through the establishment of prerequisite knowledges and skills that would enable the student to perform a new, desired task. These entry level abilities, identified following the formulation of exactly what is to be accomplished, lead to the systematic procedure for the instructional goal to be met. If evaluation procedures show that the goal was not attained, the system requires change in the strategy or instructional procedures as part of the remediation of the student's inability to meet the instructional goal.

The systems approach to objective attainment in the activities included in the curriculum of physical education is a relatively recent one, and its promise for actually helping to attain desired objectives is welcome.

FACTORS AFFECTING THE CURRICULUM

The single most important factor in determining the nature of the curriculum is the student in physical education. The expertise of the teacher is a factor that will determine the effectiveness of selected activities in attaining desired objectives. Geographical locales and the equipment and facilities provided by the schools also affect curriculum. Legislation and professional input are additional factors that determine the activities that are to comprise the curriculum in physical education.

The Student

It has been suggested that three ingredients comprise a learning situation: the teacher, the subject matter, and the student. "As the teacher realizes the vital importance of having a solid mastery of the subject matter and a good opinion of his or her teaching abilities, so should that person have a thorough knowledge of the student."[28]

Each of us is born with certain strengths and limitations. We are affected by naturally occurring factors like heredity and we become products of the factors within our environment that will influence us. The student in physical education will tend to succeed or fail based on his or her strengths and limitations; these strengths or limitations relate to a variety of factors such as genetics, rates at which he or she grows, likes and dislikes, the influence of the home and school, and the way he or she feels about self and relationships with others. If you are planning a career in teaching, part of your course of study in professional preparation will be devoted to studies of the development of children and adolescents. No developmental objective in physical education can be achieved without considering the factors that will have the greatest impact on the progress a student makes toward *self-actualization*.

A great disparity exists among students relating to growth and skill levels. This disparity becomes even greater when special students become part of the learning environment.

The Special Student

In chapter 1, we encountered the major influences that have shaped the current status of physical education. In the section dealing with the influence of medicine and the sciences, we looked at the historical relationship between exercise and the positive effects it has on one's well-being. We learned that Per Ling, the founder of the Swedish system of gymnastics, had a withered arm that became more useful after he engaged in an exercise program. Physical education's contributions to persons afflicted with physical and psychological problems have a long and rich heritage. Even before the federally mandated law (PL 94–142) guaranteed physical education and other opportunities to handicapped persons, programs in physical education for the handicapped were already in place.

In education, a significant amount of attention has been directed at the need to deal with each student as an individual. Physical education has attempted, at least in theory, to adapt its programs to self-actualize the student. In dealing with handicapped students, individual attention has no alternative. As mentioned earlier, adapted physical education programs to meet the needs of the handicapped student can provide a model for individual attention to all students.

Sherrill defines adapted physical education as "a comprehensive service delivery system designed to identify and ameliorate problems within the psychomotor domain."[29] Such a definition connotes that the handicapped student served in an adapted program is one who has, due to many reasons, problems with movement. As mandated by PL 94–142, each special child must be provided with an individualized educational program (IEP) that must be constructed in accord with governmental guidelines, carried out and evaluated in terms of benefit to the student, and filed with federal authorities. The IEP outlines the intention of the program to *ameliorate,* or make less of a burden, those problems the student has with movement. Such a prescriptive venture by a physical educator requires a total understanding of the nature of various handicaps and expertise in designing and implementing appropriate remedial programs. Notice, too, the *accountability factor* that has been built into the federal law that ensures, or at least enhances, the possibility that the program used by the teacher brings about desired results.

Another feature of the federal law is the mandate to place the handicapped student in the *least restrictive environment*. Past policies of placing all handicapped children in self-contained "special" classes proved to be dehumanizing. The least restrictive environment is the regular class situation, and the nearer the handicapped student can get into this situation the better. The regular class is the mainstream of activity for most students. The concept of *mainstreaming* for handicapped students is their placement in the regular class, with allowances granted depending upon the nature and severity of the handicap. Two other, more restrictive environments for handicapped students in schools are the segregated and combined environments. Depending upon which environment could prove most beneficial to the special student, part of the school day might be spent in a segregated environment, while other parts may be spent in the mainstream.

The objectives for physical education for handicapped students are no different than those sought for any student. The educational goal of self-actualization is pertinent to all; we must do all within our means to assist each student to become the best that he or she is capable of becoming. Physical education should ensure that handicapped students receive the same opportunities and benefits that other students receive: special training for the teacher is required in order to make this equality of opportunity possible.

Teacher Expertise

A point that was emphasized in chapter 8 dealt with the need for the teacher to be skilled in a wide variety of activities. Diverse skill enables a teacher to teach each activity more thoroughly and allows for a great variety within the curriculum of physical education. The greater the number of expertly taught activities, the greater the possibility for the student to discover activities that are personally satisfying. This enhances the possibility that, for students, participation in an activity of choice will be a lifelong endeavor.

Can a learner discover the inherent fun associated with square dancing if subjected solely to a regimen of team sports in the physical education program? If the teacher is reluctant to present square dancing as an activity in the curriculum or feels uncomfortable doing so, the possibility of student discovery greatly diminishes. Another learning experience outside the realm of the school physical education program will have to provide exposure to square dancing, and a learning opportunity has been lost. "I'm weak in gymnastics," or "My background in track and field is limited" are reasons teachers fail to present these activities and limit, due to a lack of teacher expertise, the curriculum.

Geographical Location, Facilities, and Equipment

Those who live near large bodies of water can delight in activities such as open-water scuba diving, sailing, surfing, and water skiing within the curriculum of physical education (see fig. 9.9). Yet, they may envy those whose curriculum includes snow skiing, rock climbing, and hang-gliding in more mountainous locales. Activities such as track and field, tennis, baseball, and golf can take place year-round in some areas, while the climate in other regions may make participation in such activities short-term. The success of commercial indoor racketball and tennis complexes is directly attributable to the desirable climates they provide, enhancing and extending participation in these activities. The choices of outdoor activities are limited by factors over which there is no control, the weather and climate in which we live.

Two additional factors affecting the curriculum can be (but often are not) controlled: facilities and equipment. Attempts to teach various activities are limited due to inadequate facilities and equipment. Schools in urban areas may have few outdoor play areas, negating or causing modifications of many activities. Indoor areas in most schools usually consist of a single gymnasium, making for difficult situations if several classes must share it at the same time. Complicating the lack of indoor play space are exceedingly large classes, which can detract from the potential of the curriculum.

An important principle involved in teaching activity skills is that skill acquisition occurs in direct proportion to the amount of quality practice time spent by the student. Consequently, the sharing of a single basketball among thirty-five students attempting to learn the jump shot does not contribute to skill acquisition, nor does any situation where limited equipment inhibits practice time. This factor stresses the importance of obtaining the equipment necessary for the objectives of the curriculum to be met and illustrates that a lack of equipment is a liability to the goals of the curriculum.

Figure 9.9 Geographical location greatly impacts the curriculum in terms of activities that may be offered.

Legislation

In chapter 1, we studied the impact of specific federal laws on physical education. Title IX and Public Law 94–142 are two recent laws that ensure equal opportunity for participation in sport and physical education for both sexes and for handicapped persons, respectively. Coeducational activities have become commonplace at all levels, but still require additional planning in order for each student, male and female, to benefit from the experience.

Just as state departments of education direct colleges and universities in the professional preparation of a teacher (see chapter 5), so, too, do they impact on the curriculum of physical education. Rare is the state that has not developed a curriculum guide for use by its public school districts. State boards of education also influence the curriculum by determining how much physical education is to be offered, the graduation units of credit that must be taken in physical education, the amount of minutes that elementary and secondary physical education must have, and the attendance requirements for students. Directives are given to school administrators to assist them in providing a successful physical education program by

1. Developing understanding of the physical education program's purposes, scope, and content
2. Cooperating with teachers of physical education in formulating policies for the entire physical education program, including intra- and interschool athletics
3. Assisting physical education teachers in planning and conducting the program
4. Scheduling physical education classes so as to group grade and reasonable class size to facilitate instruction
5. Providing certified teachers of physical education
6. Encouraging the teachers to evaluate their programs in a manner consistent with general school policies and practices
7. Providing adequate facilities, equipment, and supplies for a well-balanced program
8. Consulting and assisting with physical education teachers in preparing a budget adequate to provide sufficient material resources for conducting a broad and varied program
9. Helping to interpret physical education to school trustees, parents, and the community in general[30]

Professional Input

Most state departments of education have, as their directors of physical education, persons qualified as physical educators. Generally, state curriculum guides for physical education are devised by these persons and a number of professional physical educators within each state. This helps to ensure that the best contributions of physical education to the well-being of the students are included. This illustrates one way that professionals in physical education contribute to curriculum development. Similar input comes at the district or county level and may augment the input of state departments in the preparation of curriculum guides.

Another area of input from the profession occurs at the national level. AAHPERD has sponsored a number of conferences and workshops that permit an interchange of ideas about curriculum and its development (see fig. 9.10). AAHPERD publications are available from the national headquarters in Reston, VA, that focus on curriculum ideas and improvements, including the latest that relevant research offers.

EVALUATION OF THE CURRICULUM

In chapter 11, the need for and the techniques to conduct evaluation procedures in physical education are examined, including specifics for curriculum evaluation. The purpose of curriculum evaluation is to determine if the programs and processes for

Figure 9.10 The highly successful "Jump Rope for Heart" program is one of AAHPERD's curriculum suggestions.

carrying out the programs can be credited with helping the student in physical education attain desired objectives. Since this is the purpose of the curriculum in physical education, such evaluations are necessary and expected.

SUMMARY

The curriculum of physical education is comprised of activities designed to enable a student to attain desirable outcomes. Physical education activities are considered the medium through which traditional objectives are met, each of which has been shaped by historical and societal influences.

If the curriculum is to be considered valid in fostering objective attainment, it must be appropriate to the level of the student's ability, broad enough to include all contributing activities, and structured from the simple to the complex. Teachers play a vital role in ensuring that curriculum objectives are met by the methods they use to present the subject matter. Planning must be done to ensure that the subject matter and the processes by which it is presented lead to desired outcomes.

Activities designed to meet objectives can be generally applied to all ages and levels or can be specific to certain ages and levels. Each should be structured to positively affect the domains of behavior of the student.

To be effective, curriculum requires organization. Two contemporary organizational approaches are the conceptual approach and the systems approach.

Factors affecting the curriculum include the student, the expertise of the teacher, climate, equipment and facilities, mandates by state departments of education, and input from professionals in physical education.

Curriculum that effectively brings about desirable educational objectives must stand the test of rigorous curriculum evaluation.

STUDY QUESTIONS

1. How would you define *curriculum?* How does curriculum differ from *programs* of physical education? From activities?
2. What are the traditional objectives for physical education? What are some of the influences that brought these objectives about? Why have these objectives been difficult to prove as actually occurring?
3. What is meant by the level, scope, and sequence of the curriculum? How does the teacher affect the impact of the curriculum?
4. What are the two schools of thought regarding movement education? How does movement education differ from movement exploration?
5. What are the domains of behavior specified by *Bloom's Taxonomy?* What is the relationship between educational objectives and the domains of behavior?
6. What are the features of the conceptual approach to curriculum? The systems approach?

STUDENT ACTIVITIES

1. Examples of physically educated students are represented by tables 9.1, 9.2, and 9.3. Using your favorite activity or sport, see if you can develop the desired characteristics in each of the three domains of behavior that will lead to the development of the desired objective represented by our acronym NOISE.
2. Examine your college catalog and identify the level, scope, and sequence of courses that you are to take in your professional development.
3. Arrange a visit to an elementary or secondary school. During your visit, determine if mainstreaming is occurring. If you observe a handicapped student in the program, ask the teacher if you could see the IEP that has been written for the student. Was the IEP carried out? See if you can find out how handicapped students in the school are grouped. Do segregated classes exist? Are combined classes that are segregated and mainstreamed used in the school?
4. List the programs and activities for all levels found in physical education programs. Next to each program or activity, place the letters representing the traditional objectives for physical education, represented by our acronym

NOISE. Decide on a primary and secondary objective that can be derived from participation in these programs or activities.

5. From the list of activities offered in your college's or university's required or elective physical education program, identify those that are unique to your geographical location.

6. Construct three concepts from your favorite activity that you might convey to another person in trying to convince him or her that your choice of a physical activity is the "best." State the supportive information for one of your concepts.

NOTES

1. Clark W. Hetherington, *The School Program in Physical Education* (Yonkers-on-Hudson, NY: World Book Co., 1922), 2.
2. Charles Cowell and Wellman France, *Philosophy and Principles of Physical Education* (Englewood Cliffs, NJ: Prentice-Hall, 1963), 146.
3. Ibid., 46.
4. Carl E. Willgoose, *The Curriculum in Physical Education,* 2d ed. (Englewood Cliffs, NJ: Prentice-Hall, 1974), 78.
5. Hetherington, *The School Program,* 1.
6. Carl E. Willgoose, *The Curriculum in Physical Education,* 3d ed. (Englewood Cliffs, NJ: Prentice-Hall, 1979), 94.
7. Hetherington, *The School Program,* 47.
8. Arthur G. Miller and Dorothy M. Massey, *A Dynamic Concept of Physical Education for Secondary Schools* (Englewood Cliffs, NJ: Prentice-Hall, 1963), 179.
9. Gabrielsen, Spears, and Gabrielsen, *Aquatics Handbook* (Englewood Cliffs, NJ: Prentice-Hall, 1968), 6.
10. Miller and Massey, *A Dynamic Concept of Physical Education,* 183.
11. Ibid.
12. Maida Riggs, Patt Dodds, and David Zuccalo, *Basic Stuff Series II* (Reston, VA: AAHPERD Publications, 1981).
13. Hayes Kruger and Jane Kruger, *Movement Education in Physical Education* (Dubuque IA: Wm. C. Brown Publishers, 1982), 13.
14. Ibid.
15. Glenn Kirchner, Jean Cunningham, and Eileen Warrell, *Introduction to Movement Education* (Dubuque, IA: Wm. C. Brown Publishers, 1970), 5.
16. Maryhelen Vannier and David Gallahue, *Teaching Physical Education in Elementary Schools* (Philadelphia: W. B. Saunders Co., 1978), 407.
17. Ibid., 335.
18. William E. Straub, *The Lifetime Sports-Oriented Physical Education Program* (Englewood Cliffs, NJ: Prentice-Hall, 1976), 3.
19. Ibid., 4.
20. Eugene R. Fox and Barry L. Syster, *Lifetime Sports for the College Student* (Dubuque, IA: Kendall-Hunt Publishing Co., 1972), x.
21. Harold Meyer and Charles Brighthill, *Community Recreation* (Englewood Cliffs, NJ: Prentice-Hall, 1956), 333.

22. Robert Singer and Walter Dick, *Teaching Physical Education: A Systems Approach* (Boston: Houghton Mifflin Co., 1974), 104.

23. Ibid.

24. Charles Corbin et al., *Concepts in Physical Education* (Dubuque, IA: Wm. C. Brown Publishers, 1978).

25. James W. Terry et al., *Physical Activity for All Ages: The Concepts Approach* (Dubuque IA: Kendall-Hunt Publishing Co., 1979), ix.

26. Singer and Dick, *Teaching Physical Education,* 23.

27. Ibid., 57.

28. Franklin A. Lindeburg, *Teaching Physical Education in the Secondary Schools* (NY: John Wiley and Sons, Inc., 1978), 16.

29. Claudine Sherrill, *Adapted Physical Education and Recreation* (Dubuque, IA: Wm. C. Brown Publishers, 1982), 10.

30. South Carolina Department of Education, *Guide for Teaching Physical Education* (Columbia, SC: SCDE, 1980), 4.

RELATED READINGS

Annarino, Anthony. "The Teaching-Learning Process: A Systematic Instructional Strategy." *Journal of Physical Education, Recreation and Dance* 54, no. 3 (March 1983).

Annarino, Anthony, Charles Cowell, and Helen Hazelton. *Curriculum Theory and Design in Physical Education.* St. Louis: C. V. Mosby Co., 1980.

Jewett, Ann, et al. "Proceedings of the Curriculum Theory Conferences." University of Georgia, 1979, 1981, 1983.

Pate, Russell, and Charles Corbin, "Health-Related Fitness: Implications for the Curriculum." *Journal of Physical Education, Recreation and Dance* 52, no. 1 (January, 1981).

"Program Development." *The Physical Educator* 39, no. 2 (May 1982).

"Physical Education Curriculum for the 1980's." *Journal of Physical Education, Recreation and Dance* 51, no. 7 (September 1980).

Salz, Arthur E. "Sports—A School Curriculum Focus." *Journal of Physical Education, Recreation and Dance* 53, no. 7 (September, 1982).

Singer, Robert, and Walter Dick. *Teaching Physical Education: A Systems Approach.* Boston: Houghton Mifflin Co., 1974.

Ward, Diane, and Pete Werner. "Two Curriculum Approaches: An Analysis." *Journal of Physical Education, Recreation and Dance* 52, no. 4 (April 1981).

Teaching Styles and Instructional Strategies

10

Chapter outline

Student objectives

As a result of the study of this chapter, the student should be able to

1. Define and differentiate the terms *teaching style* and *instructional strategy.*
2. Identify the relationship between the performance objectives of a lesson and the selection of a teaching style.
3. Describe the characteristics of what seems to be the "typical" physical education class in terms of what the teachers and students do during the class.
4. Describe several different teaching styles and illustrate how each style would be implemented in teaching physical education.
5. Effectively answer the question, "Which teaching style is best?"
6. Discuss two instructional strategies related to lesson planning.
7. Discuss two instructional strategies related to lesson teaching.
8. Discuss how learning theory principles provide a base for the effective use of instructional strategies and give at least two examples.

One of the most important duties performed by a physical educator is teaching. Teaching is an important link between what the students want to or should learn and the achievement of their goal. Skill improvement is an objective for students in a physical education class in a public school, private school, or college, or for people enrolled in physical fitness programs or in instructional programs at a sports club, for example. How well and how quickly they achieve skill improvement will be largely dependent on the instruction they receive. If you are the teacher or professional involved with these individuals, then you are the one with the responsibility of providing satisfactory instruction. You become an important key to the success these people will experience as they work toward achieving their goals.

In chapter 9, you were introduced to the skills that are needed to become a successful teacher and to the advantages and disadvantages of being a teacher. In this chapter, we will proceed an additional step by considering some of the styles and strategies teachers can use to effectively achieve their own goals of instruction as well as the objectives of the physical education curriculum.

DEFINING TEACHING STYLES AND INSTRUCTIONAL STRATEGIES

When you see the terms *teaching styles* and *instructional strategies,* your first thought probably is that the terms must be synonymous with *teaching methods.* In many ways, you are right. However, we want to consider these terms as including much more than teaching methods; as you will see, teaching methods comprise only a part of what will be included here.

First, let us consider what is meant by the term *instructional strategies.* Instructional strategies are the plans and actions involved in implementing instruction so that the student goals of a curriculum guide, unit plan, or lesson plan might be accomplished. In their book related to the teaching of physical education, Robert Singer and Walter Dick state that an instructional strategy is "like a prescription—it describes the events that must occur, their sequence, the means by which they take place, and their size."[1]

Teaching styles can be best considered as a term that is broader than *instructional strategies.* We will use *teaching styles* to indicate the general approach taken by the teacher when confronted with a teaching-learning situation. As you will find later in this chapter, some instructional strategies may be similar across a variety of teaching styles, while others may be unique to a particular teaching style. Instructional strategies, then, relate more to implementing specific procedures and techniques in carrying out effective instruction. Teaching styles, on the other hand, relate to how you will approach teaching a particular class.

Further insight into these two terms comes from Muska Mosston, a highly regarded scholar concerned with teacher behavior.[2] In his book entitled *Teaching Physical Education,* he states that teaching is actually a **chain of decisions** that must be made before, during, and after the teaching-learning situation (or *transaction,* as he calls it) takes place. Mosston places the various decisions that must be made into three categories, or sets. These categories, **pre-impact, impact,** and **post-impact,** include the decisions made before, during, and after the teaching situation. Table 10.1 presents

Table 10.1

Mosston's Anatomy of Any Teaching Style

Sets of Decisions	Decisions that MUST be made about

Pre-impact
(content:
preparation)
	1. Objective of an episode
	2. Selection of a teaching style
	3. Anticipated learning style
	4. Whom to teach
	5. Subject matter (SM)
	6. Where to teach (location)
	7. When to teach:
	   a. Starting time
	   b. Rhythm and pace
	   c. Duration
	   d. Stopping time
	   e. Interval
	   f. Termination
	8. Posture
	9. Attire and appearance
	10. Communication
	11. Treatment of questions
	12. Organizational arrangements
	13. Parameters
	14. Class Climate
	15. Evaluative procedures and materials
	16. Other

Impact (content: execution and performance)	1. Implementing and adhering to the Pre-Impact decisions (3–13) 2. Adjustment decisions 3. Other

Post-impact
(content: evaluation)
	1. Gathering information about the performance in the
	   Impact Set
	   (By observing, listening, touching, smelling, etc.)
	2. Assessing the information against criteria
	   (Instrumentation, procedures, materials, norms, values,
	   etc.)
	3. Feedback:

About SM   About roles

a. Corrective statements
b. Value statements
c. Neutral statements

Immediate   Delayed

4. Assessing the selected teaching style
5. Assessing the anticipated learning style
6. Other

Source: Courtesy of Dr. Muska Mosston.

some of the specific decisions that are included in each category. While we will consider some of these decisions in more detail later, we present them here to help you identify what is involved in differentiating teaching styles.

According to Mosston, the person making the decisions in each of these categories, that is, teacher or student, is a factor in determining the teaching style being used. Read these decisions and consider how the teacher or student could make the decision and how the respective decisions would influence your general approach to teaching a class. From this beginning, then, we can consider more specifically what is involved in the selection and implementation of teaching styles and instructional strategies.

Performance Objectives

Teaching styles and instructional strategies should be viewed as critical means to important ends. The primary end is the achievement of specific performance objectives by your students. Performance objectives are descriptions of goals that you want your students to reach as a result of a unit of instruction or a particular lesson. Since you will undoubtedly become further acquainted with performance objectives in other courses in your curriculum, we will not go into detail about them here. However, since they are related to the selection of appropriate teaching styles and instructional strategies, a brief discussion of them will be helpful.

Robert Mager presents the most comprehensive discussion of performance objectives and how they should be used. Mager indicates that all performance objectives should possess three characteristics: (1) a performance statement that indicates what the student should be able to do; (2) a conditions statement that indicates the conditions under which the students should perform; and (3) a criterion statement that states how well the students' performances must be done.[3]

You will find that how specific a performance objective statement must be varies from one school district to another or from one education professor to another. However, all performance objectives have in common the three characteristics presented by Mager. Let us consider an example of a performance objective that could be found in a volleyball unit. This objective relates to the skill of setting and is stated as, "The student, standing at the right front position, will set a tossed volleyball over a crossbar twelve feet high, so that the ball will land in a circle on the other side of the bar, four out of five times." In this objective, setting is the desired performance. The conditions include the manner in which the ball is to be received by the setter (a tossed ball) and the height and location of the set (over a twelve-foot-high crossbar and into a circle). The performance criterion statement indicates that the student must perform this set four of five times before acceptable performance is achieved. This example is a very specifically stated objective that provides you with an idea of what performance objectives are. Performance objectives are used, obviously, to establish exact performance standards for students and, thus, greatly assist in the evaluation of a student's skill.

For the teacher, helping students achieve performance objectives is heavily dependent on the teaching styles and instructional strategies that are selected and implemented. As a result, these objectives become important links between the teacher, the lesson plans, and the achievement of the instructional goals by students. All of this suggests that what you *do* as a teacher is an especially critical concern. As a teacher, you are responsible for planning the lesson, organizing the class, presenting the information, evaluating the students, and the like. The implementation of these responsibilities becomes a vital component in your success as a teacher.

How Teaching Styles and Instructional Strategies Are Selected

Choosing *what* will be taught in a unit or lesson is an important part of the teacher's job. However, determining *how* those lessons will be taught is an equally important responsibility. This is where the selection of teaching styles and instructional strategies becomes critical. You should note that many of the steps and decisions you go through to decide what to teach are also involved in the steps and decisions you go through to determine how you will act as a teacher when you meet your class face-to-face.

A very helpful perspective in the selection process can be gained once again from Mosston. His point is that regardless of what you are teaching, important decisions must be made. From his point of view, *who* makes the various decisions, teacher or student, is a critical determinant of the teaching style that will be implemented.[4] We can add to that by stating that *what* the decisions are and *how* they are implemented become critical determinants for the selection of both teaching styles and instructional strategies.

To enable you to more readily see what is involved in this selection process, we will consider a few of the specific decisions that Mosston indicates must be made in any teaching-learning situation. The foremost decision that must be made concerns the **objective of the lesson.** As you may recall, this was the first decision in table 10.1 of the pre-impact set of decisions. If you are not clear about why selecting or developing a performance objective is important here, you should go back to the "Performance Objective" part of this chapter.

The second pre-impact decision is the **selection of a teaching style.** We have already discussed how the teaching style is closely related to the instructional strategies that will be implemented. The fact that Mosston indicates that selecting the teaching style is such an early decision helps to support this point. Before deciding how you will handle the various procedures and techniques to implement your lesson, you must first determine what your overall teaching "style" will be for the lesson. We will elaborate on this point later in this chapter.

Other pre-impact decisions important to the selection of appropriate teaching styles and instructional strategies include the **consideration of who you are teaching** (number 4 in table 10.1). While certain teaching styles and instructional strategies may be appropriate for all grade levels, some lend themselves more specifically to certain ages. For example, the way you organize your class, the way you present the instructions about what to do, and how you provide information to help the student improve should all be directly related to the grade level you are teaching. Notice that in providing these examples, decisions from all three sets of decisions in table 10.1 have been included. This demonstrates the interrelatedness of many of the decisions you must make as a teacher. Your response to many decisions will be dependent on previous decisions you have made.

Rather than discuss Mosston's list of decisions any further here, try something on your own! Read each decision in table 10.1 and, depending on your response to that decision, try to determine how different decision responses could lead to different approaches to teaching the same skill. For instance, how would number 6, "Where to teach," influence the different ways you would teach a particular activity?

TYPES OF TEACHING STYLES

Now that you have seen some of the factors involved in the selection process, let us turn to the task of identifying teaching styles. This discussion will become a foundation on which we can build our later discussion about instructional strategies. As you will see, this foundation will be important because many instructional strategy decisions will be guided by the teaching style implemented by the teacher.

A "Typical" Physical Education Class

Before considering some specific teaching styles, you should have in mind some idea of what the "typical" approach to teaching a physical education class is (see fig. 10.1). You can think about your own personal experiences, but you cannot be certain that

Table 10.2

Duration of Functions for 193 Elementary School Physical Education Students and 20 Classes

FUNCTION	STUDENTS			CLASSES			
	Duration in Seconds	Percent of Total Duration	Mean Duration (Secs) per Occurrence	Percent of Total Duration			
				Range	Median	Mean	Standard Deviation
Practice	25.762	15.3	17.4	0.0–17.5	7.3	13.6	15.8
Game-playing	17.427	10.3	40.4	0.0–56.1	2.1	11.1	16.8
Exercise	6.141	3.6	18.7	0.0–20.2	2.6	3.8	4.8
Explore	253	0.2	18.1	0.0– 3.4	0.0	0.2	0.8
Express/ Communicate	904	0.5	8.5	0.0– 2.2	0.2	0.5	0.7
Position	6.874	4.1	7.0	0.6–15.6	3.1	4.3	3.7
Equip	5.808	3.4	11.8	0.0–14.2	2.1	3.1	3.6
Assist	1.678	1.0	18.6	0.0– 8.0	0.1	1.0	2.0
Diverge	956	0.7	15.9	0.0– 5.6	0.2	0.6	1.3
Receive information	42.798	25.4	21.1	2.8–58.5	20.6	25.8	14.8
Give information	150	0.1	6.5	0.0– 0.6	0.0	0.1	0.2
Await	59.703	35.4	26.1	7.8–65.1	35.5	36.0	20.5

Source: Costello, J. and Laubach, S., "Student Behavior" in W. Anderson and G. Barrette (eds.) *What's Going on in Gym: Descriptive Studies of Physical Education Classes.* Newtown, CT: Motor Skills: Theory into Practice, 1978, Table 2.3, p. 16.

your experiences are unique or if they are shared by many others. To get a more objective view, we can look at an extensive research study that investigated this issue. In a monograph entitled "What's Going On In Gym," William Anderson and Gary Barrette presented results from a series of descriptive studies concerned with describing the characteristics of a typical physical education class. To do this, they and several graduate students at Columbia University videotaped and analyzed eighty-three physical education classes from sixty different schools in three states. Forty of these classes were at the elementary school level; the rest were high school classes. In the series of articles in this monograph, results of this extensive project are described in terms of *student behavior, teacher behavior, teacher-student interaction,* and the various communication methods and maneuvers used by teachers and students in the classes.[5]

Table 10.2 and figure 10.2 provide you with examples of some of the results of this study. Table 10.2 shows various student behavior functions and how long each lasted for 193 elementary students in twenty different classes.

Interestingly, almost 62% of the time, students were either waiting or were receiving information of some kind. Compare these results to figure 10.1, where various teacher behaviors are also presented in terms of the percentage of class time taken by each. Teachers spent over one-third (35.3%) of class time either giving instructions before an activity began or observing an activity without giving any instructions.

Figure 10.2 Teacher time devoted to various functions during twenty elementary school physical education classes.

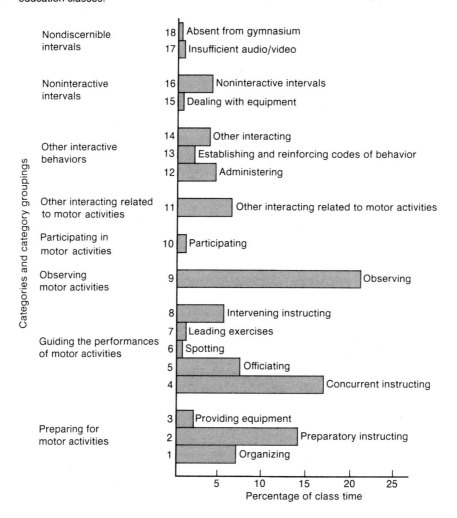

Note that this study made no attempt to express a value judgment on these teaching behaviors. The intent was simply to present a view of what seems to be the current status of behaviors in today's physical education classes. The monograph by Anderson and Barrette represents an objective view of what appears to be typical across the country. Keep the results of this study in mind as we discuss various teaching styles. The results of this study will be especially interesting if you consider how often the variety of available styles are actually implemented by physical education teachers and why one particular style might be preferable to another in certain situations. You may also want to refer back to this study as you read about different teaching styles and try to speculate about what the various teaching behavior percentages might be with a particular teaching style.

Four Views of Teaching Styles

What, then, are some teaching styles available to the physical education teacher? To address this question, we will consider some different views of teaching styles. Some of these views will present a variety of styles, while others will provide a look at a specific style. Keep in mind, here, that the goal of this discussion is to introduce you to various teaching styles. No attempt will be made to present an exhaustive list of teaching styles; instead, we will let this discussion of a few different views of teaching styles serve as a basis for the in-depth consideration you will give this topic in other courses in your curriculum.

Four views will be considered. The first will be a view of only one teaching style, the traditional teaching model. Second, we will consider the broad view of teaching styles presented by Daryl Siedentop. Then we will look at a list of different teaching styles presented by Robert Singer and Walter Dick. Finally, we will consider what is probably the most extensive list of teaching styles, called a "spectrum of teaching styles", which is presented by Muska Mosston. You will notice that each of these viewpoints has unique characteristics as well as some points that overlap. Do not try to evaluate which of these presentations is the "right" one. Consider each one in terms of what it can add to your understanding of the range and types of teaching styles available to the physical education teacher.

The "Traditional" Teaching Style

In a 1971 article in *Quest,* Hoffman discussed what he viewed as the fundamental components of the traditional teaching model. This article was published several years ago, yet it has not lost its timeliness or its accuracy in describing the model that has characterized the teaching of physical education for many years. Although this article is directed toward encouraging a change by teachers in their use of this model, Hoffman's description of the fundamental components provides a useful explanation of this traditional model.

Hoffman presents five *fundamental components* of the traditional teaching model. You should consider each of these components in terms of the decisions presented in table 10.1; by doing this, you will be able to see more specifically how the nature of a teaching style and the decisions made concerning the teaching-learning situation are so closely affiliated. According to Hoffman, the five fundamental components of the traditional teaching model are

1. **Direct mode of delivery.** Here, the teacher tells and shows the students how the skill is to be performed and asks the students to essentially mime the demonstration.
2. **Efficient organization of class set-up.** The class is usually organized in some geometric pattern, such as one straight line, several ranks of lines, a circle, or some other configuration. These patterns are considered "efficient" in that the teacher is easily seen and can readily see and speak to all members of the class.

3. **Neatness and order.** Uniforms are typically required. (Note, however, that this aspect of traditional teaching seems to be rapidly changing.) In addition, the geometric pattern formations that are used for class organization are usually required to be rigidly precise.

4. **Discipline and control.** Students are typically expected to follow very narrowly defined patterns of behavior, as defined by the teacher. Deviations from these are generally responded to with disciplinary measures. Control of what the students are to do and how they are to act in the class is determined by the teacher.

5. **Lack of emphasis on skill analysis.** The teacher typically spends more concern and time involved in matters related to administrative or organizational concerns of the class rather than in matters related to assessing and aiding individual skill level.[6]

Does this style of teaching seem familiar to you? We are considering it here because it seems to describe a vast majority of physical education classes. This style also seems to describe the typical class we saw in the Anderson and Barrette study. As such, then, this discussion provides an excellent beginning point in the presentation of various teaching styles. We will not spend time here evaluating the many reasons for adopting this teaching style: while this traditional model describes the approach many physical education teachers use in their classes, it is but one of many teaching styles available to teachers.

Siedentop's Categories of Teaching Styles

In his book, *Developing Teaching Skills in Physical Education,* Daryl Siedentop states that the variety of teaching methods available to the physical education teacher can be classified into three categories. Each of these *methods* can be considered a teaching *style* in the way we are using this term. These categories are useful for our discussion because they present a broad overview of different teaching styles. We will encounter more specific categories in lists of styles that we will discuss later.

The three categories presented by Siedentop are (1) **direct instruction;** (2) **task teaching;** and (3) **inquiry.** Notice that each category is defined by *who* is primarily involved in directing the activity. In the first category, the teacher is directing the activity; thus, this category shares similarities with the traditional teaching method. In the second category, the focus of activity changes to the student. Here, the teacher still plays an important role, but it is less direct in terms of determining and directing the instructional activities. In this category, a common approach is to use *station teaching,* where different stations are set up for the students to move through at their own pace. Thus, the emphasis is on tasks or skills and each student developing his or her own skill level in these. The student directs his or her own learning or practice activity. In the inquiry style, both the teacher and student are actively involved in directing activity. Typical teaching approaches here involve problem solving and guided discovery experiences. For example, in problem solving, the teacher poses a problem such as "How many ways can you jump over this rope?" The student then actively directs his or her own activity to try different ways of solving this problem.[7]

Singer's and Dick's Classification of Teaching Styles

In their textbook concerning the teaching of physical education, Robert Singer and Walter Dick describe what they consider to be four "families of general teaching models."[8] Note that they use the term *teaching models.* You can consider this term to be interchangeable with what we have been referring to as *teaching styles.* As others have done, Singer and Dick argue that the teacher must first determine the goals for teaching before selecting a teaching model or style.

The first family of teaching models is called **the skill and knowledge approach.** This label is used because the primary goal of instruction in teaching methods found in this family is the precise acquisition of skills and knowledge, that is, these methods are concerned almost exclusively with imparting information to the students. Methods in this family tend to be teacher-oriented in that the teacher is the principle director of activity and information giving. Singer and Dick list two teaching methods as belonging to the skill and knowledge approach family: (1) the **lecture method,** where information is presented formally and directly by the teacher, and (2)the **drill method,** where students are organized to perform activities together in the same way according to specific directions by the teacher.

The socialization approach is the label given by Singer and Dick to the second family of teaching models. Methods of teaching in this family consider the need for educational experiences to provide opportunities for the students to see how to live more effectively as individuals and within society. As a result, instruction is not only directed toward teaching specific movement or sport skills, but it is also concerned with teaching social skills.

The third family is called the **personalization approach.** This grouping includes individualized and programmed instructional methods. Strong emphasis is placed on the development of *self-understanding* in the methods in this family. In physical education, *movement education,* popular in elementary grades, is an example of this approach. Here children are given opportunities to become aware of what their bodies can and cannot do as well as experience and explore a wide range of gross movement patterns in a variety of situations. Problem-solving techniques like the one we considered in the discussion of Siedentop's categories are also strongly favored in this teaching method.

The fourth family, the **learning approach** includes such teaching methods as programmed instruction and problem-solving and creativity methods. These are designed to encourage the "development of students' learning processes rather than their acquisition of specific skill and content." Self-paced instruction, that is, the student is permitted to progress at his or her own rate, is encouraged in this teaching model.

Interestingly, in the Singer and Dick classification system, teaching models are categorized on the basis of both *who* is primarily directing the learning activities as well as *what* is being taught to the student. Methods in the skill and knowledge approach are oriented to teacher-directed activities. On the other hand, methods in the personalization and learning approaches emphasize student-directed activity. The socialization approach does not seem to suggest one or the other type of emphasis.

In terms of what is being taught, that is, the general goal of the instructional process, the four families are quite distinct (see fig. 10.3). Specific skill-related information and skills are the focus of instruction in the skill and knowledge approach.

exhibit 10.1

Problem solving and creativity

A series of questions and problems in the activity unit challenges the learner to think about alternatives and best responses. The emphasis is on the intellectual side of physical education—intellectual in the sense that the learner is not told what to do but resolves the problem and performs accordingly. Once again an individualized approach is vital: people can solve similar problems in different ways. Often there is more than one correct response, although some are better than others. Look at the accompanying figure. The person can go around the obstacle to the goal, remove the obstacle on the way to the goal, or select an entirely new goal. Traditional teaching methods in physical education emphasize the skilled execution of an activity as the wanted outcome; here, the learner is encouraged to think about the activity and to execute it in a generally acceptable way.

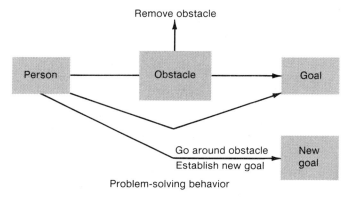

Problem-solving behavior

Source: Singer, Richard N. and W. Dick, *Teaching Physical Education: A Systems Approach*, 2d ed. © 1980 Houghton Mifflin Company. Reprinted by permission of Richard N. Singer.

Social skills are important instruction products in the socialization approach. The personalization approach emphasizes self-understanding, while the learning approach places emphasis on the learning process.

Mosston's Spectrum of Teaching Styles

When the question of *who* makes the specific decisions about the instructional situation is considered, one should look to the elaborate and detailed classification system presented by Muska Mosston. Mosston presents a series of seven categories of teaching styles that he arranges along a continuum, or spectrum. At one end, the teacher makes all the instructional decisions and then gets progressively less directly involved in the decision making as we move along the spectrum to the opposite end. The important

Figure 10.3 Regardless of the teaching style, students should be actively engaged for a large percentage of class time.

point here is *who* makes the decisions in the three categories of decisions that we considered in table 10.1. Mosston's seven teaching styles and their locations on the spectrum are presented in figure 10.4. Also in this figure is a summary of *who* is primarily responsible for making each of the decisions in the three instruction-related decision categories.

Since Mosston's spectrum represents such a detailed account of the variety of teaching styles available to the physical educator, we will consider this system of teaching style classification more closely than we have the others in this chapter. The first teaching style, the **command style,** is very teacher oriented. This style is characteristic of what we considered earlier as the traditional style of teaching physical education. In this style, the teacher usually demonstrates the skill being taught; the students practice the skills, usually together and in an organized, geometric pattern; and the teacher evaluates the students' progress. For example, the teacher may be teaching the golf swing. The class may be organized in a circle around the teacher, who begins by demonstrating and talking about the correct golf swing. The teacher then directs the class to practice the swing together by following the teacher's count for each part of the swing.

The **practice style** is again characterized by teacher domination. However, in this style, the teacher does not command every movement or activity. The primary difference between this and the command style is in the impact decisions. The teacher takes a less direct role in certain of these decisions, such as where to perform, the order of

Figure 10.4 Mosston's spectrum of teaching styles, with the relative roles of teacher and learner on either end of the spectrum and the decision maker(s) during the impact components of a lesson. (T = Teacher; L = Learner; O = Observer; D = Doer)

	A	B	C	D	E	F	G	H	
Pre-impact	(T)	(T)	(T)	(T)	(T)	(T)	(T)	(L)	
Impact	(T)	(L)	(D)	(L)	(L)	(T L)	(LE)	(L)	
Post-impact	(T)	(T)	(O)	(L)	(L)	(L T)	(L)	(L)	

| Teacher Maximum / Learner Minimum | | | | | | | | | Teacher Minimum / Learner Maximum |

Styles: A Command style, B Practice style, C Reciprocal style, D Self-check style, E Inclusion style, F Guided discovery style, G Divergent style, H Learner-designed program

tasks to do, when to begin practicing tasks and the like. A good example of a practice style method is the use of stations to teach different gymnastics stunts or to teach different basketball skills or drills.

The **reciprocal style** is unique in that students work in pairs. Each member of the pair assumes the role of either the *doer* or the *observer*. Students alternate these roles during the class period. For example, in an archery lesson, one student in the pair, the doer, shoots several arrows at the target while the other student, the observer, watches and provides feedback to the doer partner. Figure 10.5 is a good example of how the reciprocal style is put into practice. Notice in figure 10.5 how specific "things to look for" are provided to help the observer direct the feedback to the doer partner. The teacher plays an important role here in ascertaining whether the observer is satisfactorily performing his or her role.

The **self-check style** provides an opportunity for the student to give himself or herself feedback. This style seems especially applicable to activities where students can see the results of their own actions. For example, if shooting a basketball is being taught, the students can be provided with a checklist to use to evaluate their own performances of the stunt.

All of these first four teaching styles have required the achievement of a single standard for performance that has been set by the teacher. As we move along the spectrum through the remaining teaching styles, this important characteristic will change. As you will see, we move from a single to a multiple-level basis for evaluating performance.

Figure 10.5 Instruction sheet for the observer partner in the reciprocal style for archery.

Style   A   B   Ⓒ   D

Name _____
Class _____
Date _____
Partner _____

Archery Task and Criteria Sheet

Instructions for the observer:

Communicate to the doer about how he or she is performing the task (use the ''Things to look for'' column).

Make positive statements to doer first.

Examples of feedback statements:

   ''You are gripping the bow correctly, but remember not to grip it too tightly.''
   ''You are nocking the arrow exactly as the criteria describe.''
   ''The elbow of your drawing arm is in line with the arrow.''
   ''Now I will check to see if you are using the same anchor point.''

Task 1: Each doer shoots six arrows.
          Switch roles after each round of six arrows.

	Things to look for	Yes	No
Stance	Stand astride shooting line, feet apart at shoulder width, body in comfortable position with straight posture.		
Grip	Fit handle in *V* formed by thumb and index finger, bow felt in upper part of hand. Grip should not be tight.		
Nocking	Nock arrow with cock feather facing away from bow, arrow between first and second fingers, string resting along first joint of all three fingers that grip string.		
Draw	Keep bow arm and wrist straight without being rigid; drawing arm, shoulder, and upper back muscles do the drawing. Keep elbow of drawing arm in line with arrow.		
Anchor	Draw until string touches another point on face (check to ensure that anchor point is the same each draw).		
Release	Release by relaxing fingers, allowing string to roll off the fingers. Hold bow hand relaxed but steady during release and follow-through.		

Figure 10.6 Three performance levels of the push-up, based on different types of push-ups.

Task description	Factor	Level 1	Level 2	Level 3
Perform the push-up from the described starting position. Do it three times.	Angle between the arms and the body.	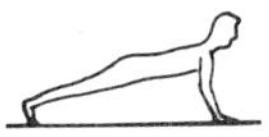	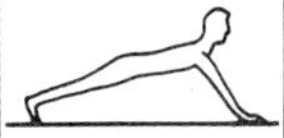	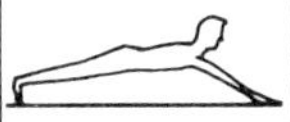

Figure 10.7 Three performance levels of the push-up, based on the number of repetitions accomplished.

Task	Factor	Level 1	Level 2	Level 3	Level 4
Perform the push-up, keeping your body straight throughout, and placing your hands under your shoulders	Number of repetitions	1, 2, 3, 4, 5	6, 7, 8, 9, 10	11, 12, 13, 14, 15	16, 17, 18, 19, 20

In the **inclusion style,** evaluation based on multiple levels of performance of the same skill is introduced. Students are free to set their own goals of performance and will be evaluated accordingly. For example, if the skill being taught is the push-up, different levels of performance can be established on the basis of the angle between the arms and body, as shown in figure 10.6. Levels of performance for evaluation can also be established on the basis of quantity, that is, how many can be performed, as seen in figure 10.7.

The **guided discovery style** is designed to help students discover such things as ideas, concepts, relationships, principles, rules, and limits, among others. For example, Mosston presents nine different topics in swimming that can be taught by the guided discovery style (these topics are presented in table 10.3). This style is the beginning point on the spectrum where the student gets directly involved in the *discovery process.* Rather than being told or shown these things, the student is given the opportunity to find out for himself or herself.

The **divergent style** completes Mosston's spectrum. Sometimes called the problem-solving style, this style requires the student to find solutions to specific problems. The same problem may have many solutions; thus, this style is appropriately called the divergent style. For example, the teacher presents the problems, "What can be done on the parallel bars?" or "How many ways can you jump over these two ropes?" or "What are some things you can do in soccer when an opponent is standing in front of you and you have the ball?" Each of these problems requires the students to design possible solutions and test the solutions accuracy.[9]

While these seven styles represent the spectrum of teaching styles, one additional style is presented by Mosston that requires the successful experiencing of the other seven. In all seven styles, the teacher has handled the decision of what to learn. An eighth style is labelled simply **going beyond** by Mosston, and more formally is considered as the **learner designed program** by Goldberger, Gerney, and Chamberlain.[10] In

Table 10.3
Examples of Guided Discovery Principles for Teaching Swimming

Swimming
1. The buoyancy principles
2. Specific postures for specific purposes (dead man's posture for best floating, for example)
3. The principle of propulsion in the water
4. The role of breathing during propulsion
5. The role of each specific part of the body in propulsion
6. The role of each specific part of the body in propulsion in a specific direction
7. The relationship between a particular phase in a stroke and the physical attribute needed
8. Can you teach other technical aspects of swimming by guided discovery?
9. Can you discover which are the preferred aspects of swimming to be taught by this style?

Source: Mosston, M., Teaching Physical Education. © 1981 Charles E. Merrill Publishing Co., Columbus, Ohio. Reprinted by permission of the publisher.

this style the student initiates the problem and carries out the tasks required to solve the problem. Some task examples are to have students choreograph a two-minute dance routine; design a game using bean bags; or develop an offensive play in football. Each of these tasks in this style requires the student to get more directly involved in the three instructional design categories than do any of the other teaching styles.

Which Teaching Style Is Best?

We have considered several different ways to classify and label teaching styles. The primary difference between all the classification systems has been how extensive or detailed the system is and the labels that are used. Recall that Siedentop uses three *teaching methods;* Singer and Dick have four *families of teaching models;* and Mosston lists seven *teaching styles.* The distinction about the various teaching styles is very similar from one system to another. Teaching styles are typically distinguished on the basis of *who* decides what should be done or who directs the learning activities and/ or *what* the primary goal of instruction is. From this discussion, we can see that physical education teachers are not limited in *how* they can teach a class; the menu of teaching styles from which to choose is large.

With this generous number of styles available, you undoubtedly have considered a very troublesome question about which style in this variety of styles is best. To address this question, we can look at the comments of some of the people who developed these classification schemes.

Siedentop points out that no one method should be considered "best". In fact, he states that the "choice of style is often a personal one for the individual teacher; most teachers feel that they operate best within one particular style." He further emphasizes that all three categories involve and require teacher planning. Selecting the appropriate method is but one part of the teacher's job. How that method is implemented is also important and involves the selection of instructional strategies appropriate to the teaching style or method chosen.[11]

Table 10.4

Means and Standard Deviations of the Hockey Accuracy Test for Three Testing Times for Three Different Teaching Styles

	STYLE B*			TREATMENT STYLE C*			STYLE E*		
	N	Mean	SD	N	Mean	SD	N	Mean	SD
Pretest	32	21.32	5.00	32	20.60	5.18	32	19.99	4.70
Midtest	32	24.57	3.04	32	24.16	3.50	32	23.13	3.94
Posttest	32	25.77	2.47	32	25.06	2.72	32	23.74	3.41

*style B = practice style; style C = reciprocal style; style E = inclusion style

Source: Goldberger, Michael, et al., "The Effects of Three Styles of Teaching on the Psychomotor Performance and Social Skill Development of Fifth Grade Children," in *Research Quarterly for Exercise and Sport* 53, 117, 1982. © 1982 American Alliance for Health, Physical Education, Recreation and Dance. Reprinted by permission.

Singer and Dick argue that their different teaching models give the teacher some options in the teaching situation. They further state that "certain models are better suited than others to the realization of certain objectives, and often styles are combined. But all can and do produce learning."[12]

Mosston stresses that his spectrum is "conceptually anchored in the notion of the non-versus, that is, the realization that *each* style, when used during a given period of time, can accomplish a particular set of objectives. When another set of objectives is sought, a different style ought to be selected. . . . No one style is better or superior to another."[13]

To illustrate the common point made by all these authors—that each teaching style is important and can be useful—we can consider a research study that actually compared the effects of different teaching styles for a specific physical education activity. The study was done by Goldberger, Gerney, and Chamberlain. Fifth grade children were taught a floor hockey shooting skill using either the practice, reciprocal, or inclusion style. Thirty-two children were in each of the teaching style groups. The skill they learned was to shoot a puck into a target area. Each student received sixty practice trials after receiving a pretest to ensure that all groups were similar at the beginning of practice and to serve as a baseline for judging the amount of improvement. Note that each of the students in the reciprocal style group spent thirty trials as the doer partner and thirty trials as the observer partner. Results of the accuracy tests are presented in table 10.4. Notice that all of the groups improved and that all improved about the same amount.

One additional test was administered to all the groups. Each student was rated on a social interaction rating scale. The results of this test showed that students in the reciprocal style group showed more positive social development than those in the other groups.[14]

The conclusion that can be drawn from all of these results is that if the goal of the learning situation is skill learning, then any of the three teaching styles seem similarly appropriate. However, if social development is also an important goal, then the reciprocal style is the best of the three. The point to keep in mind here is that this study very nicely supports what we have been saying throughout this chapter, that is, the most appropriate teaching style is heavily dependent on the objectives of your lesson.

SOME EFFECTIVE INSTRUCTIONAL STRATEGIES

Selecting an appropriate teaching style is only a part of what the teacher must do to prepare for teaching a class. An important and necessary step, the selection of a teaching style, serves primarily to point the teacher in a general direction for developing and implementing a lesson plan. A specific plan of action must still be developed that indicates what the teacher will do while teaching the lesson. This is where instructional strategies come into the picture. As we emphasized earlier in this chapter, instructional strategies are the specific plans and actions the teacher employs to enhance the learning environment for the students.

In this section, we will consider various instructional strategy concerns that will provide you with a foundation for the implementation of appropriate instructional strategies in your own teaching situations. At the outset of this discussion, you should understand that the implementation of instructional strategies involves more than a consideration of what you do or how you act when actually teaching a class. Also involved is the planning that must go on before you ever meet your class. This includes planning the content and organization of your lesson as well as how you will actually teach the class. Thus, both the planning and the implementation of your lesson are important components of what we will consider to be instructional strategies.

These two components, **lesson planning** and **lesson teaching,** should be considered as different phases of the teaching situation. (Please note that while evaluation is also an important phase of teaching, it will not be considered here, but will be studied separately, in chapter 11.) For this discussion, we will use these two phases as the basis for considering some effective instructional strategies. To do this, we will present two elements of each phase and suggest certain principles or guidelines that can be used to employ effective instructional strategies in each. For the lesson planning phase, we will consider the elements of organizing the lesson and the use of instructional aids. For the lesson teaching phase, we will consider the elements of giving instructions and providing feedback.

For the discussions of each of these elements, keep several things in mind. *First,* the two elements discussed under each heading (component) are not involved in that component only. For instance, both lesson organization and the use of instructional aids are involved in the lesson teaching component; however, both should be specifically planned before the lesson begins. Giving instructions and feedback, on the other hand, can only be more generally planned in advance of teaching the lesson: the specific use of these occurs during the lesson itself and will require the teacher to adapt to the demands of each teaching situation.

Second, realize that this discussion does not constitute an exhaustive consideration of instructional strategies. This discussion is an introduction that will serve as a foundation on which you can build through the various courses and experiences in your curriculum.

Finally, putting effective instructional strategies to use is heavily dependent on an understanding of how people learn and what influences learning. To illustrate and to emphasize this learning relationship, we will consider various learning theory principles that substantiate the specific actions taken by the teacher to implement effective instructional strategies during each phase of the teaching situation.

Instructional Strategies Related to Lesson Planning

Success in teaching requires effective planning. The teacher must not only plan what to teach, but also how that lesson content will be taught. This need for adequate planning is important regardless of the teaching style selected. A primary benefit of careful planning, in addition to keeping teachers on course in attaining their objectives, is that careful planning helps to eliminate many potential problems before they occur during the actual teaching of the lesson. Planning not only helps the teacher to be well organized and to accomplish as much as possible in the time available, but also helps the teacher to better deal with the unexpected events that may occur in any class.

The two elements discussed here as related to lesson planning are important parts of teaching an effective lesson. These elements must be considered and included in your planning regardless of your teaching style or your lesson objectives. However, the specific actions you plan in order to implement these lesson plan elements will be directed by both the teaching style you select and objectives you have for your lesson.

Organizing the Lesson

Any lesson you teach will have to fit into specific time limitations. Your class may be scheduled to meet for thirty, forty-five, fifty, or more minutes. Because of this time limit, you must effectively organize your lesson to maximize the potential of achieving the objectives you have specified. *What* you want to accomplish will be determined by your objectives. *How* you go about accomplishing these objectives will, in large part, be dependent on how you organize or structure your students' activities during class.

Examples of the ways different teaching styles will influence your planning in terms of lesson organization follow. If you choose to follow a command style, you must include time for organizing your class into appropriate formations, presenting demonstrations, and group practice drills, among others. The lesson plan is a very structured schedule of events. On the other hand, if you select a style oriented around problem solving, your schedule of events may not be so strictly structured. However, you must still plan very carefully because you must present appropriate problem solving activities, provide adequate opportunities for the students to participate in these activities and determine the physical organization of your class for participation in these activities. Thus, regardless of your teaching style and how structured or unstructured your lesson may be, the need remains to have an efficiently organized lesson.

Here we will consider a few principles that will help direct the teacher's organization efforts. These principles represent important instructional strategies that can guide your planning of a lesson. For each principle, we will consider what it means, give an example of its implementation in planning a lesson, and examine the learning theory base on which the principle rests. Again, this list represents just a sample of the principles or strategies related to planning an effective lesson. You will add more to these throughout your curriculum.

1. **Sequence events in a progressive order.** The lesson you teach should follow a logical progression of events. As much as possible, make certain that students in any activity or event in the lesson benefit from having been in the preceding activity. For example, a logical progression of events for a lesson teaching the tennis serve would be practice the toss; practice the backswing; practice the toss and backswing together without a ball; practice with a ball; and practice serving the ball against a fence. Another example would be to arrange a lesson on basketball passing by having students move from station to station, with each station representing a different passing skill. Have an order established for movement through the stations, for example, simple to more complex passing drills.

   At the base of this instructional strategy is an important learning theory principle known as **transfer of learning.** This principle states that previous learning experiences or practice influence how well we learn a new skill; that is, the previous experience or activity aids or facilitates the learning of the next activity. When teaching a lesson, make the influence be a positive one for students.

2. **Plan an optimum amount of time for each part of the lesson.** This guideline has two important implications for teachers. First, too much or too little time spent in any activity can have equally negative effects on learning. Second, the teacher must be ready to be flexible with the planned time specifications. You may have planned an activity to last twenty minutes, but the students are bored in ten minutes. Be prepared to adapt to this situation and modify your plans by moving on to another activity in the lesson.

   Underlying this strategy is a learning theory tenet known as **attention.** A part of the study of attention concerns how long we can stay attentive or can concentrate in an activity and maintain a consistent level of performing. Research evidence shows that this time (or *attention span*, as it is popularly called) will be short when the person does not make many responses even though alot of activity is going on. The more actively engaged in an activity a person is, the longer he or she will stay attentive and involved in the activity.

   The use of a batting practice drill is a good example here. If the drill is set so that the fielders only field balls hit by the batter, chances are that the fielders will not be engaged in much activity and they will soon be bored. The result will be that when a ball is hit to the fielders, they will not respond as well to it as they would if they were constantly involved in fielding balls. One way to avoid this problem is to have other students hit balls to the fielders in between pitches to the batter.

3. **Provide a variety of activities.** Sometimes a lesson will include only one activity. However, this should be the exception rather than the rule if the function of a physical education class is to enhance the student's learning. While you may be

exhibit 10.2

The importance of learning environment

The Glendale-Feilbach School and its elementary-physical education program are a teacher educator's dream. One could be assured that on any given day undergraduate students would leave their observation at the school with the thought, "I didn't think elementary students could do that." College students would be referred not only to the level of motor skills in which the children were engaged, but also to the manner in which the students conducted themselves during the lesson.

During a recent visit, students were engaged in educational gymnastics. They were given the first task at the gymnasium door. Their teacher, Luann Alleman, indicated the lesson content, the apparatus on which they could work, and asked students to begin working after their apparatus had been arranged. Within minutes, the students grouped themselves, arranged their apparatus, and began to work. From the beginning the teacher's role was to focus on developing content and to refine responses rather than to manage. She began working with individuals and as the class progressed, she stopped children to further develop their tasks.

Except to positively reinforce on-task behavior and occasionally to refocus students' work when the task was not clear, the teacher spent little time on management. Because students worked productively, the teacher was free to devote long periods of time with individuals while using comments on what was being done to benefit the entire class. The teacher increased children's awareness of the potential of the task and continuously refined both the performance and the quality of movement responses by extending individual class tasks.

In May 1976, the Toledo, Ohio Board of Education opened a special school, the first of its kind in the United States, built especially for mainstreaming orthopedically limited children in normal classroom settings. Orthopedically limited children who are mainstreamed into physical education classes at least once a week comprise about twenty percent of the school population. Students in grades four, five, and six have physical education twice a week, while the first through third grades meet three times a week. The school has excellent facilities and equipment and the physical education program is well supported by both the administration and the faculty.

Asked what she is most proud of in her program, Luann points to the students' positive attitude toward learning and their ability to be self-directed. She has designed her program to help all children become independent learners capable of making decisions as they become skillful and versatile movers. The educational approach of her program emphasizes developing the child affectively, cognitively, and motorically through instructional areas equally divided among educational dance, educational games, and educational gymnastics. It is difficult to get people to realize that neither Luann's program nor the learning environment that appears so natural in this setting was not developed quickly or by magic. It took study, commitment, and a lot of hard work on the part of the teacher. It took the opportunity to provide physical education more than once a week. It took good facilities and a supportive school faculty and administration. However, what actually happens in each physical education lesson clearly reflects both the philosophy of the physical education teacher and the intent of the program.

An analysis of a lesson at Glendale-Feilbach reveals the teacher's clear intent to develop both skillful and versatile movement and independent learning skills. Tasks directed toward quality through reinforcement and corrective feedback refine and develop content to high levels. The framework of the tasks permits students to enter the task at an appropriate level. Tasks which continuously ask the students to increase the variety and skillfullness of their responses and which gradually add complexity and refinement to their work extend the initial entry level. The tasks not only reflect a strong psychomotor intent but also seek to involve the students both cognitively and affectively.

The learning environment supports the development of purposeful psychomotor objectives. Because students have learned to make decisions appropriate to them and because they have learned to do productive, independent work, the teacher is able to focus her attention on content. Independent learning skills and a supportive, productive environment have been developed through the same methods used in teaching the movement content. Expectations for behavior are apparent to the children and are reinforced through corrective and evaluative feedback. Students work on independent learning skills in much the same way that they work on movement tasks—with the intent to improve. The degree of student decision making and independence with a management task is expanded very gradually as students are ready for increased responsibility.

Luann is not only a competent teacher, she is a wife and a mother of two teenage boys, chairperson of the Elementary Physical Education Department of the City of Toledo and vice-president of the Physical Education Division of the OAHPERD. As an intern-consultant for the city schools selected by the teachers' union and the administration, Luann works to monitor and assist first-year teachers' development of teaching skills.

Luann has looked beyond Glendale-Feilbach and has participated actively at local, state, and national levels to help other professionals move from the more traditional to the educational approach and to increase their understanding and insight for mainstreaming the orthopedically limited child in physical education. She received an Ohio Dean's Task Force Grant, which financed in part the production of an 8mm film on *Mainstreaming the Orthopedically Handicapped Child in Elementary School Physical Education*. She admits that providing educational experiences for the severely handicapped child is one of her biggest challenges.

Luann went back to school eight years ago and became caught up in the challenges of implementing a new philosophy, methodology, and program. Luann's students, the Toledo Public Schools, and the profession have been well served by her efforts.

As a teacher educator, I personally sleep better at night knowing that what I say *can* and *should* be done is being done *every day*.

Source: Rink, J. E. "The Key is the Learning Environment," in *Journal of Physical Education, Recreation and Dance* 53, pp. 44, 46, Sept. 1982. © 1982 American Alliance for Health, Physical Education, Recreation and Dance. Reprinted by permission.

focusing a lesson on teaching only one skill, such as throwing, shooting a free throw, or balance beam activity, for example, you can and should provide a variety of experiences during the class period. Station teaching is one example of how this variety can be accomplished. Other ways of accomplishing variety in a lesson include devoting a certain amount of time in the lesson for practicing different kinds of throwing in a lesson on throwing. If teaching free throws is the focus of the lesson, students could practice free throws with a partner in a reciprocal style for awhile and then participate in a group drill involving free throws. Another example is to devote time to working on specific balance beam skills, followed by each student spending time devoted to working on a routine on the beam.

While several learning theory principles support this instructional strategy guideline, we will consider only two here. First, our understanding of maintaining attention supports this guideline, just as it did the previous guideline. Giving full concentration to one activity is a difficult task and cannot be maintained for very long. The capacity for concentration time varies between individuals, age groups, and activities, yet for all, the teacher needs to consider this guideline in planning a lesson.

A second, related learning theory suggests that a variety of experiences with a skill increases the amount of learning that can be expected for that skill. The suggestion here is to provide opportunities for students to practice the skill in a wide range of different situations.

Using Instructional Aids

The second element we will consider in the lesson planning phase of teaching concerns the use of aids, devices, or media in the teaching situation. This aspect of teaching is being examined here to emphasize that the implementation of these tools is very dependent on effective planning.

Before considering some instructional strategy guidelines, let us consider the question. What are instructional aids? If we consider this term very broadly, instructional aids include a wide range of devices, machines, or implements that are designed to help present information to the student or to control an activity. As information, these aids could be used to help present instructions or feedback. Such aids as film strips, loop films, slides, movies, videotape, chalkboards, written handouts, records, tapes, overhead transparencies, and the like all help the teacher present information to the students (see fig. 10.8). Other types of instructional aids help control activity to aid the student's practice of a skill. These types of aids include such devices as pitching machines, batting tees, rebounders, and harnesses, for example. Through the use of these types of aids, the teacher is able to set up a practice situation that allows the student to focus on specific parts of the skill.

An important part of implementing effective instructional strategies is the appropriate use of these instructional aids. When properly used, the aids can be a tremendous asset for the teacher; however, without proper planning for their use in a lesson, instructional aids can be more of a hindrance than a help.

Figure 10.8 Feedback through videotape analysis can aid learning.

The following three guidelines should help you see how to plan to effectively incorporate instructional aids in your lessons. Again, support for these guidelines will be provided by considering some related learning theory principles.

1. **Use aids that fit your instructional needs.** This common-sense guideline is important because it emphasizes an aspect critical to the selection of instructional aids, that is, does the aid meet your needs to help provide instructions or feedback or to control a specific part of the activity? You do not want the aid to be a waste of time. For example, videotape replay may be an interesting means of providing students with performance-related feedback, but if the students do not know what to look for in their performances, then the videotape becomes more of a detraction than an aid. Similarly, if a film loop doesn't provide the students with a clear view of the part of the skill you are teaching in the lesson, it cannot be considered to be a very useful aid.

    As we discuss the instruction and feedback phases of the lesson, more should become clear in terms of what is important for evaluating the potential effectiveness of an instructional aid. From our knowledge of characteristics of learners, which was gleaned from research dealing with skill learning, we know exhibit 10.3

Queries for lesson planning

Regardless of the style a teacher chooses, certain questions need to be answered when planning a lesson. These are the basic questions of instructional design, because answers to them go a long way to determine the quality of the learning experience from the learner's viewpoint. These basic instructional design questions are as follows:

1. How will students know what to do and when to do it?
2. How will students know how to do the task?
3. What opportunity will students have to practice the task?
4. How will students get feedback about how they are doing?
5. Why should students want to do the task?
6. How does one task relate to another to form a lesson?

Question 1 refers to instructions about how to organize, when to start, when to stop, when to change, and other such managerial information. Question 2 refers to information about how to do the task itself, what its main features are, what it looks like, what things to avoid, and how best to start practicing it. Question 3 refers to arrangements that maximize student learning time. Question 4 refers to what happens after a student actually practices the task: Does the student get accurate feedback? Does the student know what to look for in his or her own performance? Does the student know when the task has been completed? Question 5 is basically motivational. Many might argue that Question 5 should be answered first, and they may be right. Students will learn nothing unless they engage in practice, and they have to be motivated to do that. Each teacher has a different motivational level in his or her school and often motivational levels differ among classes within a school. Finally, Question 6, "How does one task relate to another?" focuses on the lesson as a coherent series of events leading to lesson goals.

Regardless of whether a teacher uses a direct instruction, a task, or an inquiry style, these six questions need to be attended to in planning the lesson. A task style may require different answers from a direct instruction style, but the *function* each question represents needs to be filled if learning is to occur.

Source: D. Siedentop, *Developing Teaching Skills in Physical Education,* 2nd ed., by permission of Mayfield Publishing Company. Copyright © 1983 Mayfield Publishing Company.

that a critical part of the teacher's role is to focus the students' attention to what should be done. If an instructional aid will help the teacher in this, then the aid should be an effective tool.

2. **Include aids as integral parts of the lesson.** Instructional aids should not be thought of as extras. They should be considered exactly as they are called, aids to instruction. A film can take the place of a demonstration; a pitching machine can eliminate bad pitches from a pitcher; a chalkboard can illustrate a point

being made; or a videotape can provide reality to feedback. As such, use these aids as you would another teacher or teacher's helper. Incorporate them into your lesson in such a way that they become a functional part of your teaching.

Research related to skill learning indicates that people learn better when they have a good model of correct performance of the skill than when they do not have a model. The benefit of this model is that it gives the student something to compare his or her own performance against, thus allowing the student the opportunity to make appropriate judgments about what should be done to improve his or her own skill.

Another learning theory principle related here concerns the use of instructional aids such as a batting tee, which are designed to control an activity. For the beginner, a difficult part of learning a skill is trying to deal with all the different factors that skill learning involves. By using a batting tee, for example, the amount of factors requiring concentration are reduced: the student does not have to think about where the pitch will be, how fast it will be, when it will be time to swing, and similar concerns. Instead, by hitting the ball from a tee, the student is free to concentrate on specific batting techniques without being concerned with all the other attention-demanding aspects of batting.

3. **Aids should show positive transfer to the actual skill.** This guideline is directed specifically to the instructional aids that help control an activity, that is, the mechanical devices or implements used to help a student concentrate on specific parts of a skill, such as the batting tee we just discussed. Use of the device must be to the advantage of the student, that is, the student should be able to more quickly learn to bat a pitched ball because of previous practice with hitting from a batting tee or pitching machine. This is what is meant by *positive transfer*. This learning principle is at the heart of the use of instructional devices to control activities. This principle concerns the facilitating effect of previous practice in some activity on the learning of a new activity. Evaluate any instructional aid on this basis. Will practice using this device be more beneficial to learning the actual skill than if the student spends the time practicing the skill itself? In other words, would the student benefit more by batting against a live pitcher all the time or by having time with the pitching machine incorporated into practice?

Instructional Strategies Related to Teaching the Lesson

After all the planning is completed and the lesson plan is prepared, it is time to face the class and put that lesson into action. You already know what your objectives for the lesson are, what the teaching style will be, and what the content of the lesson will be. Now you must implement those plans.

While many elements of teaching a lesson could be considered, we will focus on only two. The two, giving instructions and providing feedback, are especially important in that they have much to do with the success of your lesson. You, the teacher, are in direct control of these elements while the class is in progress. As was done in the previous section, some helpful guidelines will be provided for each of these elements to direct your implementation of effective instructional strategies in the teaching phase of the lesson.

Giving Instructions

When a teacher gives instructions to a class, he or she is telling the students more than simply what to do; the teacher is also directing the students' thoughts and actions. As such, the giving of instructions can have a great influence on how well a student learns a skill. The following guidelines are a beginning point to enable you to provide effective instructions. Note again how the learning theory principles provide support for these guidelines.

1. **Give instructions that indicate what the student should be concentrating on while practicing.** If you tell a student in a beginning bowling class that you want him or her to practice the approach, what does the student think about while practicing? To a great extent that will depend on what instructions you give the student after that statement. If you say nothing else, you have no control over what the student will concentrate on during practice. However, if you direct the student to "really work on a smooth release" and show what you mean, you will find that the student will concentrate on that aspect of the approach.

   The beginning learner is in a real quandary about what to do to improve his or her performance. Specific instructions that direct that student's attention to what should be done make the learning of that skill better and faster than if the student is left to figure things out alone.

2. **Do not give too little or too much information.** Included in the bowling example we considered in the first guideline was an example of giving the student "too little" information in instructions, which was when the teacher simply directed the student to practice his or her approach. Another problem occurs when the teacher gives "too much" information in the instructions. In the bowling example, this would happen if the teacher pointed out every part of the approach during the instructions, thus giving more information than the student could process. The more optimum situation was when the teacher gave specific instructions concerning only the release phase of the approach.

   An important learning theory principle involved in this guideline concerns how much information a person can handle at one time. Essentially, this principle states that we are limited in how much information we can think about or concentrate on at one time. Given this condition, then, the teacher must be careful to not overload the student's capacity with too much information while the student is practicing.

3. **Make certain that students are paying attention to the instructions.** In the second guideline, we indicated that individuals can concentrate on only a limited amount of information at a time. This is important to consider not only in terms of how much information you give students in your instructions, but

also what they are doing while the instructions are being given. If they are distracted by another student who is conversing with them or by watching something else while you give instructions, that distraction will keep them from being able to concentrate on what you are saying.

Providing Feedback

We will consider *teacher feedback* to be what the teacher tells the student about his or her performance after a practice attempt (see fig. 10.9). Many learning theorists consider this kind of information as being extremely important for the student to experience optimal learning. The reason for this is that teacher feedback information gives the student some direction about measures to be taken for improvement: without this information, the student usually engages in some type of trial-and-error-based strategy to improve. If the teacher makes provision for appropriate feedback information, then the student can save a lot of time and energy in moving toward his or her particular goal.

Teacher feedback can take different forms and be used for various related purposes. As we consider the following three guidelines, you will more readily see what these forms of feedback can be, how they can be used, and how to effectively provide this important information.

1. **Give feedback about one aspect of the skill at a time.** For a beginner, performance of an activity is typically characterized by many mistakes. Since we already know that people can concentrate or think about only a limited amount of information at one time, for a beginner to try to deal with all the mistakes being made is impossible. To help the student with the problem, the teacher should direct the student's attention to the correction of only one mistake at a time. This will help the student to begin an organized, logical progression in improving his or her skill. For the teacher, this means that he or she must be able to determine the most important mistake being made by the student. This requires a good, working knowledge of the skill by the teacher so that the student's performance can be appropriately evaluated and the most useful feedback information given. For example, a student may be having difficulty throwing a ball at a target. The teacher observes that the student is not following through correctly and that the step toward the target is much too long and in the wrong direction. Which of these mistakes should be pointed out to the student first? Since the poor follow-through may be the result of the incorrect step, the step should be corrected first. The follow-through may correct itself when the proper step is made.

2. **Feedback should be specific enough to help the student improve.** Suppose you are in a beginning swimming class and you are trying to learn the crawl stroke. if the teacher tells you, after watching you swim for awhile, that your kick is not right, how helpful is that? It would be somewhat helpful in that it directed your attention to the kick part of the stroke, but it would be limited in its total benefit since the comment did not tell you what part of the kick was *not* correct. For feedback information to be the most effective, what is wrong and what

Figure 10.9 Feedback should help the student perform better in future attempts at a motor skill.

Teaching physical education

should be done for correction should be pointed out. The student can then direct his or her attention to that specific part of the skill and can develop some idea about measures needed for correcting the problem.

The teacher's comments are not the only form of feedback that can help the student improve. Instructional aids such as videotape can be a big help. However, the beginner must be given appropriate direction about what to look for when watching the tape. Other students can also be good sources of feedback. Recall that in the reciprocal style of teaching, the observer partner was provided a checklist to use as the basis for feedback to the doer partner.

3. **Feedback can be a powerful source of motivation.** One important aspect of motivation is that it deals with keeping a person pursuing a goal or objective. In a teacher's lesson or unit, a goal may be to have the student be able to successfully hit a pitched ball. In order to achieve that goal, the student may have to practice for a long time. He or she must be able to deal with making a lot of mistakes and be willing to devote the necessary practice time to achieve the goal. Motivation, then, is important here.

Feedback can serve a critical function in this regard. Up to now we have considered feedback to be primarily mistake-related information, but it can also be information that reinforces correct or improved performance. As such, feedback becomes a form of encouragement for the student to keep on trying and working toward the goal.

A CONCLUSION

In this chapter you have been given a lot of information about different teaching styles and instructional strategies. You undoubtedly wonder if you will be able to remember all of this or do the right thing when you have to teach a class. To help you keep all this information in perspective, we now present two important points to conclude this chapter. First, the experiences and information you will receive as you go through your physical education major curriculum will help you to implement the strategies discussed in this chapter. Remember, this chapter is intended to provide you with a foundation on which you can build. This foundation consists of a solid theoretical understanding of the learning process as well as knowledge important in planning and implementing of instruction.

Second, as you teach, your experiences will be important building blocks on your foundation and in your other curriculum subjects. Your experiences as a teacher will provide you with many answers about which styles or strategies work and which do not work in a given situation. The effective use of teaching styles and instructional strategies, then, depends on the knowledge base you acquire and the experiences you have to build on that base.

SUMMARY

In this chapter, you have been introduced to some of the most critical elements needed to make an effective physical educator. The selecting of appropriate teaching styles and instructional strategies are important for any physical educator involved in teaching. In this chapter, you have seen that a variety of teaching styles exist. These range from teaching styles that are teacher dominated to those that are student dominated. Selecting an appropriate style will depend on several factors, including the performance objectives for the subject you are teaching.

In this chapter, we discussed instructional strategies as related to lesson planning and lesson teaching. For lesson planning, we considered how organizing the lesson and using instructional aids can effectively be planned on the basis of established learning principles. We also considered the same basis for implementing the actual teaching of the lesson by discussing guidelines for giving instructions and providing feedback.

This discussion of teaching styles and instructional strategies has been just a part of what physical education teachers must consider. As you progress through your curriculum, you will be presented with more in-depth discussions of these important matters. This chapter has provided you with a head start for understanding these concerns that relate to all physical educators.

STUDY QUESTIONS

1. What is the difference between teaching styles and instructional strategies?
2. What are performance objectives and how are they related to selecting appropriate teaching styles and instructional strategies?
3. How can teaching styles be categorized according to *who* makes certain teaching decisions? Give some examples.
4. Of the variety of teaching styles that exist, how can we know which one is best?
5. What are three guidelines for organizing a lesson? For using instructional aids? For giving instructions to students? For providing feedback to students?

STUDENT ACTIVITIES

1. Observe three physical education teachers while they are teaching a class. Make detailed notes about what they did during the lesson. Try to classify their teaching styles as closely as you can according to Mosston's spectrum of styles.
2. Write several performance objectives for an activity that you might teach. Specify how you could use different teaching styles to help your students achieve these objectives.
3. Videotape or observe a physical education instructor teaching a class. Write in detail the instructions and feedback you hear the teacher give the students during the class. Compare your observations to the guidelines presented in this chapter.

NOTES

1. Robert N. Singer and Walter Dick, *Teaching Physical Education: A Systems Approach,* 2d ed. (Boston: Houghton Mifflin Co., 1980).

2. Muska Mosston, *Teaching Physical Education,* 2d ed. (Columbus, OH: Charles E. Merrill Publishing Co., 1981), 223.

3. Robert F. Mager, *Preparing Instructional Objectives,* 2d ed. (Belmont, CA: Fearon Publishing Inc., 1975).

4. Mosston, *Teaching Physical Education.*

5. William Anderson and Gary Barrette, eds. "What's Going On In Gym? Descriptive Studies of Physical Education Classes," *Motor Skills: Theory Into Practice,* Monograph 1 (1978).

6. S. J. Hoffman, "Traditional Methodology: Prospects for Change," *Quest* Monograph 15 (1971): 51–57.

7. Daryl Siedentop, *Developing Teaching Skills in Physical Education,* 2d ed. (Boston: Houghton Mifflin Co., 1983).

8. Singer and Dick, *Teaching Physical Education.*

9. Mosston, *Teaching Physical Education.*

10. Michael Goldberger, Phillip Gerney, and James Chamberlain, "The Effects of Three Styles of Teaching on the Psychomotor Performance and Social Skill Development of Fifth Grade Children," *Research Quarterly for Exercise and Sport* 53 (1982): 116–24.

11. Siedentop, *Developing Teaching Skills in Physical Education,* 169.

12. Singer and Dick, *Teaching Physical Education,* 45.

13. Mosston, *Teaching Physical Education,* 12.

14. Goldberger, Gerney, and Chamberlain, "The Effects of Three Styles of Teaching," 116–24.

RELATED READINGS

American Alliance for Health, Physical Education, Recreation, and Dance. *Ideas for Secondary School Physical Education: Innovative Programs from Project Idea.* Washington, DC: AAHPERD Publications, 1976.

Gage, N. L. *Teacher Effectiveness and Teacher Education: The Search for a Scientific Basis.* Palo Alto, CA: Pacific Books, 1972.

Gagné, Robert M. "Behavioral Objectives? Yes!" *Educational Leadership* 29 (February 1972): 394–96.

Harrison, Joyce M. *Instructional Strategies for Physical Education.* Dubuque IA: Wm. C. Brown Publishers, 1983, chapters 10, 14, 15, and 16.

Heitman, Helen M., and Marian E. Kneer. *Physical Education Instructional Techniques: An Individualized Humanistic Approach.* Englewood Cliffs, NJ: Prentice-Hall, Inc., 1976.

O'Donnell, Leo E. "Experience-Based Contracting in Elementary Physical Education." *The Physical Educator* 33 (October 1976): 135–39.

Turner, Robert B., and William W. Purkey. "Teaching Physical Education: An Invitational Approach." *Journal of Physical Education, Recreation and Dance* 54 (September 1983): 13–14, 64.

Evaluation in Physical Education   *11*

Chapter outline

Student objectives

As a result of the study of this chapter, the student should be able to

1. Define the terms *evaluation* and *measurement.*
2. State at least three aspects of physical education where evaluation is important.
3. Distinguish between formative and summative types of evaluation; criterion-referenced and norm-referenced tests; and objective and subjective types of measurements.
4. Define reliability and validity in terms of how they relate to measurement.
5. Identify four different kinds of validity and how each can be determined.
6. Discuss why student, teacher, and curriculum evaluation information is important and how this information can be used.
7. Identify several philosophical issues related to grading.
8. Discuss three ways to evaluate student performance in physical education.
9. Discuss the teacher behavior characteristics that should be evaluated and suggest ways to evaluate them.
10. Discuss how formative and summative curriculum evaluation can be conducted.

An important key to the ongoing success of your role as a teacher or of your physical education program is evaluation. If you want to determine how effective your teaching is or how well your program is accomplishing its goals, you must gather and use information. Without this information, teachers, for example, who have been considered successful may actually be stagnating without evaluation information to allow an adequate assessment of their teaching. For physical educators, evaluation is at the heart of maintaining and improving effective instruction.

In this chapter, you will be introduced to this important aspect of the physical educator's role. You will see what evaluation is and what must be evaluated. You will find that the effective use of evaluation in your teaching will yield benefits in every area of your work. To begin this discussion, then, we will consider what the term *evaluation* actually means. We will also introduce another, closely related term, *measurement,* that will be an important concern in this chapter. Having a good understanding of how these two terms are used in physical education will prepare you to more effectively consider what is involved in the evaluation process in physical education.

THE CONCEPTS OF EVALUATION AND MEASUREMENT

Definitions

While the terms *evaluation* and *measurement* are probably not new to you, you should understand their meanings as they relate to your functions as a physical educator. **Evaluation** is the process of determining how effectively goals or objectives are being achieved. For example, evaluation is important in helping the teacher determine whether students are actually learning. This evaluation, in turn, provides the primary basis for making decisions with regard to continuing, modifying, changing, or stopping the use of certain teaching methods or certain parts of the curriculum.

Measurement is actually a part of the evaluation process because it provides a specific means for collecting information essential for evaluation. As such, **measurement** can be defined as the use of assessment that will provide information for evaluation. We will get more specific about what this means later in this section and chapter.

What Should Be Evaluated?

The answer to the question of what should be evaluated is an important one for physical educators. It is the first step in the evaluation process to enable you to make specific and appropriate judgments about the job you are doing. To introduce you to the evaluation process and its role in physical education, we will consider three different aspects of physical education that are important for evaluation purposes. First is the evaluation of the **student.** Since grades are an integral part of education, student evaluation is a built-in requisite of the teaching profession. The second candidate for evaluation is the **teacher.** Teachers' performances must be evaluated if they are to know how well they are doing their jobs and what they need to maintain, develop, or change. Finally, the **curriculum** must also be evaluated. This is essential if teachers are to know how effectively their programs are meeting the goals of curriculum.

Table 11.1

A Summary of Some Distinctions between Formative and Summative Types of Evaluation

	FORMATIVE	SUMMATIVE
Purpose	Feedback to student and teacher on student progress throughout an instructional unit	Certification or grading at the end of a unit, semester, or course
Time	During instruction	At the end of a unit, semester, or course
Emphasis in Evaluation	Explicitly defined behaviors	Broader categories of behaviors or combinations of several specific behaviors
Standard	Criterion-referenced	Generally norm-referenced, but can be criterion-referenced

Source: Baumgartner, Ted A. and Andrew S. Jackson, *Measurement for Evaluation in Physical Education* 2d ed. © 1982 Wm. C. Brown Publishers, Dubuque, Iowa. All rights reserved. Reprinted by permission.

Before discussing these three areas, we will first establish a foundation of understanding concerning the process of evaluation. To do this, we will consider some basic tenets of the study of both evaluation and measurement. First, what are the general types of measurement and evaluation? Second, what are some of the basic underlying principles of measurement itself? Each of these points are important to the teacher because they establish a base on which all evaluation questions can be founded.

BASIC TENETS OF EVALUATION AND MEASUREMENT

Types of Evaluation

Two primary types of evaluation are typically considered in relation to the needs of physical educators. These are called formative and summative evaluation. Both of these types of evaluation can be conducted by the teacher or students and both are related to the evaluation of students, teacher, or curriculum. Table 11.1, as presented by Baumgartner and Jackson, provides a good summary of the similarities and differences between these two types of evaluation. (See fig. 11.1.)

Formative Evaluation

This type of evaluation occurs *during* the teaching of a unit of instruction, that is, during the *formative* stages of instruction. As you can see in table 11.1, formative evaluation provides a source of feedback for the teacher or student that can be used to judge or assess progress. Note that this type of evaluation is usually based on **criterion-referenced** performance. This term, related to *mastery learning*, indicates that evaluation should be measured against a specific standard or criterion. In this way,

exhibit 11.1

Formative and summative evaluation objectives

Formative Evaluation

Formative evaluation occurs during the progress of a unit of instruction and is intended to improve instruction by providing feedback to both the learner and the teacher. Continual feedback is demanded as students progress through various stages of learning. The teacher becomes a "consumer" of the effectiveness of the quality of instruction as observed through formative evaluation tests.

When the role of evaluation is viewed as an integrated part of instruction and assessment, teachers should formulate specific and desirable behavioral (instructional) objectives for the learner to attain. These objectives, when related to desired behavior or change in learner behavior, are defined in such a way that each is measurable. Many individualized programs of instruction are designed to elicit certain outcomes from students which are easily measured and quantified.

Specific instructional objectives can be written for most behaviors found in the psychomotor domain. . . . First, the teacher must be able to describe completely and clearly the desirable behavior or to identify the action the student should perform. (Example: to execute a short serve in badminton or to jump in a vertical plane.) Second, set the conditions under which the behavior is expected to produce desirable results. (Example: from service court across the net into opposite court landing in bounds.) Third, decide what standard will be used for evaluation of the mastery of the task performance. (Example: with eighty percent accuracy.) Each behavioral objective should be organized in a hierarchy that begins with the simplest level of skill and ends with the most complex level. Mastery of each objective is then dependent upon mastery of all preceding objectives.

Formative Evaluation Objectives For Beginning Badminton

Short Serve

Level 1: The student will successfully execute seven out of ten short serves which pass over the net and land within the boundaries of the opposite singles court.

Level 2: The student will successfully serve seven out of ten serves which pass over the net and land in each designated area of the service court.

Level 3: The student will successfully serve seven out of ten serves which pass between the net and a rope placed one foot above the net and land in a designated area of the opposite service court.

When evaluation is used to improve performance and is approached through behavioral objectives in a formative fashion, the strategies of "learning for mastery" become important. In mastery learning a teacher assumes that students can master a representative or relative portion of the material. The task of instruction then becomes one of finding ways to assist the students to learn the skill in the most accommodating and efficient manner. . . .

Summative Evaluation

Summative evaluation is evaluation that occurs at the end of a unit of instruction. Evaluation of the final outcome usually results in a grade that depicts the total achievement of the student over a specified period of time. Final assessment may include a test that is a valid measure of the student's ability to perform a particular skill. The summative test could be a sample of all the formative tests used during the unit of instruction.

Summative Evaluation Objective For Beginning Badminton

Given ten trials, the student will execute the short serve which will pass between the net and a rope stretched one foot above the net and land in a designated area of the opposite service court. The student will try to score a maximum number of points. (Note: The teacher may decide to set a more precise standard for performance, i.e., with eighty percent mastery.)

The teacher may use the scores obtained from the summative test for determining grades, passing the student for subsequent courses (from beginning to advanced), and comparing results with past students' performance scores to determine what changes might be necessary for future course offerings. . . .

Source: Aten, Rosemary, "Formative and Summative Evaluation in the Instructional Process," in *Journal of Physical Education and Recreation,* 51, 68–69, 1980. © 1980 American Alliance for Health, Physical Education, Recreation and Dance. Reprinted by permission.

Figure 11.1 Skills testing can be formative or summative.

evaluation provides a basis for making a judgment about how effectively progress is being made toward that standard. In other words, the criterion would represent a certain level of *mastery* of a skill, and evaluation would consist of comparing a particular performance to that standard or *criterion* rather than to other students, teachers, or programs. For example, if you wanted to evaluate aerobic fitness, a minimum criterion could be set at running 1.5 miles in twelve minutes. Each student would then be evaluated on the basis of his or her performance as related to that standard.

Summative Evaluation

This is the type of evaluation with which most teachers and students are familiar. It occurs *at the end* of a unit or period of instruction. For example, giving a grade to a student at the end of a grading period is a form of summative evaluation. As stated in table 11.1, this type of evaluation is typically called *norm-referenced,* although it can be criterion-referenced. Norm-referenced means that the evaluation is based on *norms,* that is, scores by all members of a particular group are compared against each other. This group may be a class, school, state, or nation, among others. For example, a norm-referenced grade in tennis might be based on a wall volley test result. A student's grade would be determined by comparing his or her score to others in the class or to some other group, such as a national norm for that particular wall volley test.

We will not get involved in the controversy about which of these types of evaluation is better. Accept for now that both types of evaluation are important and useful. Keep these two types in mind as we consider each of the three specific areas for evaluation in physical education and ways to accomplish both types of evaluations.

Types of Measurements

We have already established that an essential part of the evaluation process is measurement. We must understand some of the basic tenets of measurement if we are to understand evaluation, since measurement provides a means for making evaluation decisions. The first of these tenets is that there are different types of measurement. For our purposes, we will consider two general categories: **objective measurement** and **subjective measurement.** The importance of developing an understanding of these two categories should become more evident as we discuss the evaluation of students, teachers, and the curriculum later in this chapter.

Objective Measurement

If you and one other person time a runner in a race, chances are usually pretty good that those measurements will be similar. When one thing can be measured by more than one person and the results of those measurements are similar, the measurements are considered to be **objective** (see fig. 11.2). The more similar these independent measurements are, the more objective they are. This type of measurement is usually based on a quantifiable standard that requires little personal, or subjective, judgment by the person doing the measuring. For example, How far did he jump? How fast did she run? What was her score in bowling? How many home runs did he hit? Each of these are measurement questions that can be answered by an objective measurement.

Figure 11.2 The stopwatch provides an objective measurement of performance.

Subjective Measurement

When the measurement of a performance depends on the personal judgment of each individual observing the performance, then the measurement becomes more related to the knowledge, skill, and perceptions of those individuals. These types of measurements are known as **subjective** measurements. Typically, questions related to the quality of performance, such as form, style, or technique, are answered by using subjective measurements. This does not imply that a quantifiable measurement cannot be made in these situations; quite the contrary is often true. In sports, for example, measurements of such things as form or technique are usually put into numbers. The important point here is that a subjective measurement, even if the result of that measurement is a number, is heavily based on the subjective evaluation of the observer. Good examples of this can be seen in the scoring of performances in diving, gymnastics, and figure skating. It is not uncommon to find two or more judges who present quite different scores for the same performance.

Objective vs. Subjective Measurements

If you wish to reduce the likelihood of argument or controversy about an evaluation, choose the most objective measure possible. The advantage of objective tests is probably most apparent from your experiences with tests and grades. Multiple-choice tests are more objective than essay tests and, typically, lead to fewer disagreements between student and teacher with regard to the test grade.

Many physical educators have a tendency to argue for the exclusive use of objective measurement in physical education. However, such an argument should be labelled unrealistic. In terms of student performance evaluation, the nature of many physical education skills makes purely objective measurement impossible. A similar problem exists for establishing purely objective measures to judge teaching performance. The skills performed by a teacher are very difficult to identify and, thus, to evaluate objectively.

Because of the nature of the teaching profession and the variety of subjects in physical education, students and teachers alike must come to grips with the reality of the need for both subjective and objective measurement in evaluation. However, an attempt should be made to maximize the objectivity of the measurement, because teachers and students are more satisfied with objective measurements.

Essential Qualities of Measurements

Regardless of how subjective or objective a measurement might be, some essential qualities or characteristics about that measurement must be considered before that measurement is selected for use in the evaluation process. We will consider two of these qualities, validity and reliability. Each quality is an essential part of measurement theory and should not be taken lightly. The effective use of any measurement will be directly related to how it "measures up" in terms of its validity and reliability. As such, these terms become important parts of the foundation needed for the discussion of the remainder of this chapter.

Validity

A concern with any measure or test is how valid it is. When used in this way, the term *validity* refers to how well the test or measure actually measures what it was designed to measure. If a test was designed to measure badminton skill, then the validity question is, To what degree does the test measure badminton skill? If the measurement is to be representative of diving form, then the validity question again is, To what degree does the measurement actually represent diving form?

There are four different types of validity. These types may be related to only one form of test or measurement or to several. These types of validity are worth considering because they provide a means of defining the concept of validity in tests and measurements and they provide a means of indicating how the validity of a test or measurement can be determined.

1. **Face validity.** When a test or measurement *obviously* measures what it is intended to measure, it has face validity. In other words, taken at *face value,* the test or measurement appears valid. For example, a test requiring a person to

stand on one foot on a small block of wood (the Bass stick test) has face validity as a test of static balance, since that is what this test obviously measures.

2. **Content validity.** If you are concerned with the validity of the contents of a test, then content validity becomes important. To have content validity, the test must satisfactorily represent what is being tested. This type of validity check is especially important for such tests as unit exams or skill tests, since these tests are designed to assess the students' progress or levels of success in a particular unit of instruction. For example, the content validity of a tennis skill test would be judged according to how well the test reveals the students' tennis skills, which students should have learned from the tennis unit content. If the tennis unit concerned only certain aspects of tennis, the unit skill test should test only those aspects covered in the unit. For a written test, the content validity again should be determined by comparing the content of the unit test with the actual content of the unit of instruction.

3. **Construct validity.** In terms of tests, a *construct* is a trait or ability that the test says it measures. For example, *serving ability* in racquetball is a construct related to racquetball playing skill. A skills test for racquetball serving has construct validity if the test score adequately discriminates the better servers from the poorer servers. A very common construct of concern to physical educators is "cardiovascular fitness." Construct validity for these tests would be determined according to how well the results of the test reflect a person's level of cardiovascular fitness. Other common constructs tested in physical education include "strength," "agility," "teaching ability," and the like. A common method of determining construct validity is to compare the test results to another test that has already been established as a valid test of the construct. If the results of the two tests are similar, then the new test has construct validity. For most test and measurement situations in physical education, construct validity may be the most important type of validity.

4. **Criterion validity.** Many times, tests in physical education are designed to be an uncomplicated and efficient means of determining certain characteristics about an individual. Skill tests are typically like this. They are designed to be administered simply and quickly and to allow a quick assessment of a person's skill level. A wall volley test in tennis, for example, is a test of tennis playing skill. Criterion validity for this type of test is essential because it is concerned with how well the test actually assesses the criterion skill, the tennis playing skill in our example. A typical way to determine the criterion validity of a skills test is to have an expert or panel of experts observe the players and judge their skill levels. The results of the skills test are then compared to the experts' ratings. The closer the two results are, the better the criterion validity of the skills test. The obvious advantage of having a skills test with criterion validity is that it saves time and cost in comparison to bringing in experts to do the assessment.

Reliability

The second essential quality of a test or measurement concerns how *repeatable* the results are. This repeatability of a test result is called **reliability.** The primary concern here is that if the test were given to the same individuals two or three times, would the results be similar each time? Similarly, if something were measured two or three times, would each measurement be similar? The more similar these repeated test results or measurements are for the same individuals, the more reliable the test or measure.

Reliability is an important part of measurement theory. Its determination is heavily based on statistical procedures and is typically represented by a coefficient of reliability. This coefficient is an estimate of reliability and ranges from 0 to 1.0, with the numbers closer to 1.0 indicating stronger reliability. We will not go into the various methods used to determine reliability. You will become more acquainted with these methods in other courses in your curriculum, such as tests and measurements. However, at this point, be aware that the reliability of a test or measurement is a quantifiable quality and is one of the most important qualities of any test or measurement.

The Relationship between Validity and Reliability

An important criterion for any test or measurement is that it must be reliable to be valid. However, the converse is not true, that is, a test or measure is not valid just because it is reliable. For example, a test of arm strength that does not yield repeatable scores on successive test administrations to the same individual cannot be considered valid. However, if the test does yield repeatable results (and is, therefore, reliable) it may not be a valid test of arm strength. Validity would have to be determined by the various validity tests we considered. Just because a test gives repeatable results does not mean that the test is measuring what it says it measures. Because of this relationship between validity and reliability, you must take each into consideration before selecting a test or measurement for use in any physical education situation.

EVALUATING STUDENT PERFORMANCE

An inherent part of a physical education teacher's job is giving grades or providing some means of student performance assessment. This is often a very controversial part of the teacher's job because of the argument by some that physical education skills should not be graded as classroom skills, like mathematics or reading. Regardless of this philosophical controversy, the fact remains that as a teacher, you must evaluate students' performances. In this section, we will consider various means of accomplishing this evaluation. Please bear in mind that this will not be a comprehensive presentation of these methods nor will it be an attempt to direct you in procedures for grading. We will leave those concerns to more appropriate courses in your curriculum. Instead, the intent here is to introduce you to student evaluation by providing you with a view of some of the evaluation methods and procedures available to you. Some methods and procedures may be new to you, while others are like those you have already experienced as a student.

We will consider three basic concerns related to the student evaluation process. First, why is this evaluation important? Second, what should be evaluated with regard to student performance? Third, how can student performance information for an adequate evaluation be obtained? Answers to these questions should provide you with a sufficient foundation on which you can build your further understanding of student evaluation.

Why Student Evaluation Is Important

The best way to address the importance of the student evaluation is to consider how student evaluation information can be used. From this discussion, the value of student performance evaluation should be more evident. Before beginning this discussion, let us point out that an understanding of how to *use* student evaluation information is equally as important as an understanding of how to *obtain* this information. The latter concern will be considered next.

An excellent list of reasons why tests and measurements should be used in the evaluation process is presented by Johnson and Nelson. Included in this list are several points specifically applied to student evaluation. Consideration of these reasons suggests how the information gathered to allow student evaluation can be used. The uses suggested by Johnson and Nelson include the following:

1. Motivate students when there appears to be a leveling off of interest in the instruction
2. Help the teacher assess students' performances
3. Help students evaluate their own knowledge and/or skills in various physical activities
4. Enable the teacher to objectively measure improvement by testing before and after the unit of instruction
5. Diagnose needs in relation to body mechanics, fitness, and motor skills[1]

These five uses of student performance evaluation information support the contention that gathering this information and evaluating students' performances are important. Questions remain, however, concerning what information should be obtained, how it should be obtained, and how it should be interpreted. Answers to these questions are necessary if the purposes of evaluation are to be fulfilled. As a result of this need we will use these questions as the basis for the remainder of this discussion.

Initial Grading Concerns

The two important questions concerning what evaluation information should be obtained and how it should be gathered cannot satisfactorily be addressed until certain grading-related issues have been confronted. When the teacher has addressed grading-related issues, the answers to the evaluation information questions become almost matter-of-fact. In this section, we will discuss some of these important grading-related issues. Rather than attempting to resolve these issues, this discussion will serve only as an introduction to issues that need to be addressed as you progress through your curriculum and your career. You will find that resolving these issues is a process that can be advanced only by increased knowledge and experience. An important part of resolving these issues will be your own philosophy of education (philosophy of education was discussed in chapter 1). The essential question here is, What should education be accomplishing with students? Your educational experience should include an opportunity to explore this interesting and important issue.

In their discussion of grading, Johnson and Nelson study several different issues that relate nicely to our concerns here. We will consider some of these issues in order to acquaint you with some of the many issues that must be considered in the process of providing adequate student performance evaluation.

Improvement vs. Status

This is a common evaluation issue in physical education. Should students receive grades based on improvement throughout the course of instruction or should grades be given based on the students' status in the class, as determined by actual achievement in the skill? Johnson and Nelson indicate that "while some teachers feel that improvement . . . is of utmost importance, most physical educators support the concept of grading on relative achievement commensurate with grading practices in other subject areas."[2] However, many teachers propose that student evaluation should be based on neither improvement nor relative class status. These educators argue for more criterion-based evaluation. For example, Singer and Dick present an evaluation system based on criterion-referenced testing that requires the teacher to test a student before and after the instructional unit.[3] These results would then be compared against the performance objectives established for the class. Grades would be based on each student's individual performance as related to the performance criteria.

Effort vs. Performance

Another perplexing grading issue concerns whether a student's evaluation should be based on the effort shown by the student or on the student's actual performance in the skills being learned. In any system where achievement of performance objectives is important, evaluation based on actual performance must be included in the evaluation system.

Teaching for Testing vs. Teaching for Learning

Teachers often organize their teaching units around the information that will be requested on the unit test. Students are often influenced by this approach and can be heard asking the teacher, "Will this be on the test?" Depending on the teacher's response, students will or will not include the information in their notes. An important consideration in this issue is the objectives the teacher determines for a teaching unit. These objectives should permit instruction that includes experiences that are for the general good and edification of the student even though related questions may not be on a test.

Grading Based on Status in Single vs. Grouped Classes

If teachers are following a norm-referenced approach to grading, then the composition of the norm group becomes important. Teachers who grade according to a criterion-referenced approach do not have to be concerned with this problem, since a student's

Table 11.2
Principles for Grading in Physical Education

1. Measurement and evaluation for grading purposes must be based on the educational objectives of the course, not trivial or insignificant rules and procedures.

2. Grading in physical education should be commensurate with grading in other subject areas of the school.

3. The awarding of grades should be closely related to experiences occurring in real-life situations where honors, promotions, and rewards result, thereby preparing students for life after graduation.

4. Grades should be assigned on the basis of the number of points accumulated in a course, reflecting the students' relative achievement in meeting the objectives.

5. Grades should be based on a sufficient number of observations. In physical education, grades should be based on more than one objective.

Source: Johnson, Barry L. and Jack K. Nelson, *Practical Measurement for Evaluation in Physical Education.* © 1979 Burgess Publishing Co. Reprinted by permission).

evaluation is not based on performance that is related to other students. Johnson and Nelson offer an interesting comment concerning this problem: "If we were to look at the towns along a highway, we would undoubtedly find in each town successful, average, and less successful people. In each town people will have achieved their status independent of the influence of other towns."[4] Class or section grouping would seem to be reasonable only for grading purposes if all sections received similar experiences and circumstances.

Absolute vs. Curved Grading

This issue is directly related to our discussion earlier of criterion- and norm-referenced evaluation. Grading "on a curve" requires a norm-referenced type of evaluation. The approach you choose to follow will be based on your understanding and adopting of more philosophy of education concepts than we can deal with here. However, this grading issue must be acknowledged because it will directly influence you in what evaluation information you seek to obtain. The norm- vs. criterion-referenced evaluation issue is far from resolved in physical education, as evidenced by the many highly respected physical educators advocating each of these types of evaluation.

Principles of Grading

While there is much about student evaluation that we cannot attempt to resolve in this book, some basic principles related to grading would be helpful guidelines for you at this stage of your career. These guidelines are presented by Johnson and Nelson and are reproduced in table 11.2 to help provide you with some general direction in this complex area of student evaluation.

Methods of Student Evaluation

By now you should be more aware of some of the philosophical issues that are important in the establishment of student evaluation procedures. Since our task in this book is to introduce you to the many facets of physical education, we will let other courses in your curriculum, such as tests and measurements and philosophy of education or physical education, address the specific details of student evaluation. However, before concluding this section on student evaluation, we will introduce you to some of the methods of evaluation available to the physical educator. These methods of evaluation include written knowledge tests, skills tests, tournaments, expert judging or opinion, attitude inventories, social behavior inventories, and a host of others. For our purposes, we will consider only three of these methods: written knowledge tests, skills tests, and social behavior inventories. These three can be considered as representing ways to evaluate objectives related to cognitive, psychomotor, and affective domains of behavior. The intent here is to acquaint you with these evaluation methods so that you will be aware that methods exist for basing grades on more information than can be gained by observing physical performance alone.

Written Knowledge Tests

If a teacher is concerned with the knowledge students in a physical education class gain in such areas as rules, terminology, and etiquette, then two things must be done by the teacher. First, the objectives of the instructional unit must reflect this concern. Second, a way to evaluate achievement of these knowledge-related objectives should exist. One convenient means of evaluating these is the written test.

Written knowledge tests can be given in a variety of forms (see fig. 11.3), which include true-false, multiple choice, matching, fill-in-the-blank, and essay-type tests. Each form of written test has its advantages and disadvantages. Before administering any test, teachers should know these advantages and disadvantages as well as the kinds of information the test results can provide.

Baumgartner and Jackson classify knowledge tests as either mastery or discrimination tests.[5] **Mastery tests** are related to criterion-referenced evaluation and are a type of formative evaluation. They are designed to determine the student's mastery of the subject matter and typically demand a high percentage of correct responses for a passing grade to be given. Mastery tests are pass-fail in nature.

A **discrimination test** is a norm-referenced type of test and is more of a summative than formative form of evaluation. A test of this type is designed to discriminate levels of knowledge among students. Grades on the test are typically related to standards based on percentage of correct answers or on performance as related to other students.

Constructing a test is not an easy task. The test must be both valid and reliable. Because of the complexities that must be dealt with in constructing a good written test, many teachers opt to use **standardized** tests. These are tests that have been developed by educators or professional test makers and have been validated and shown to be reliable. However, in many areas of instruction, standardized tests either are not available to the teacher or are not adequate to meet the teacher's needs. In these cases, which seem to be more the rule than the exception, teachers must construct their own tests. You will discover what is involved in this important process in other courses in your curriculum.

Figure 11.3 Written knowledge tests are given in a variety of forms and help formulate student grades.

Skills Tests

It is often difficult to evaluate skill level in a complex physical activity such as tennis or football by simply observing a student's performance in that activity. Such evaluation is usually too subjective to suit most teachers and students and it is much too time consuming for most teachers. An alternative to this type of evaluation is to evaluate overall performance on the basis of performance of specific skills that make up the whole activity. This type of test is typically called a **skills test.**

In tennis, for example, skills tests could be given for several of the component skills of tennis, such as serving, forehand ground stroke, volleying, and the like. To do this, the teacher could use one or more standardized skills tests available for tennis, such as the Hewitt's Revision of the Dyer Backboard Tennis Test and the Hewitt's Tennis Achievement Test. The advantage of these tests is that they have generally good reliability and validity and have performance norms available.

Skills tests offer an objective and convenient means of evaluating sports skills of students. Teachers must, however, obtain or develop validity and reliability information for any skills test before using it. Teachers should also determine whether or not a skills test will satisfactorily evaluate one or more objectives for their teaching unit. These and other concerns must be taken into account in the implementation of any skills test. You will undoubtedly become acquainted with many skills tests (as well as with the pros and cons of their use) in other courses in your curriculum.

Social Behavior Inventories

Teachers who include objectives related to social behavior should be prepared to evaluate their students in terms of achievement of these social behavior objectives. One means of evaluating social behavior is to use **social behavior inventories.** Again, standardized inventories exist to enable teachers to administer valid and reliable tests of social behavior. One example of this type of test is the Johnson Sportsmanship Scale, presented in table 11.3. By administering this test, teachers can have a quantitative means of assessing their students' attitudes about the social behavior called sportsmanship.

One of the problems with social behavior tests is their history of poor validity. Obviously, acceptable social behavior can be very subjective. Thus, the problem of validating a test of social behavior is one of trying to reach agreement concerning the nature of what is being tested. However, acceptable social behavior tests do exist and should be considered by teachers as a means of assessing this important objective of physical education.

Using Information to Evaluate Students

So far, we have considered a variety of student evaluation issues. Included in these has been a consideration of some basic, philosophically-oriented concerns that must be considered in the evaluation process, some different types of approaches to evaluation, and some examples of different types of tests that can be used to evaluate student achievement. What we have not yet discussed is how all of this evaluation information should be put into a usable form for the student. Without immersing ourselves too deeply in this issue, we will address it by considering the one approach commonly taken by most teachers; giving a grade to represent achievement or performance in a unit of instruction.

The first concern here is the means teachers typically use to determine grades for students. Interestingly, many of the ways to assess student performance that we considered earlier are actually used in determining grades. Some revealing insight into this question is provided by a recent survey of grading practices of teachers in physical education. Jack Nelson, Joyce Moore, and Jeff Dorociak surveyed 383 physical education teachers from elementary and secondary grades throughout the state of Louisiana. In one part of this study, teachers were asked to respond to questions concerning the criteria used for grading purposes. Table 11.4 shows the percentage of teachers who indicated they used a particular criterion in grading either regularly, occasionally, or never. Note that this table does not indicate how much weight the teachers gave to each of these criteria, but it does show what criteria were included in the grades. Interestingly, 61.6 percent of these teachers regularly included "skill," either observed or from a skills test, in their grading. Also, in light of our earlier discussion concerning

Table 11.3

A Sample of Ten Items from the Johnson Sportsmanship Scale

Example: A pitcher in a baseball game threw a fastball at the batter to scare him.

strongly approve   approve   disapprove   strongly disapprove

(If you strongly approve of this action by the pitcher you would circle the first response category as shown.)

SAMPLE OF TEN ITEMS
(Request complete scales from the original author)

1. After a basketball player was called by the official for traveling, he slammed the basketball onto the floor.

   strongly approve   approve   disapprove   strongly disapprove

2. A baseball player was called out as he slid into home plate. He jumped up and down on the plate and screamed at the official.

   strongly approve   approve   disapprove   strongly disapprove

3. After a personal foul was called against a basketball player, he shook his fist in the official's face.

   strongly approve   approve   disapprove   strongly disapprove

4. A basketball coach talked very loudly in order to annoy an opponent who was attempting to make a very important free throw shot.

   strongly approve   approve   disapprove   strongly disapprove

5. After a baseball game, the coach of the losing team went up to the umpire and demanded to know how much money had been paid to "throw" the game.

   strongly approve   approve   disapprove   strongly disapprove

6. A basketball coach led the spectators in jeering at the official who made calls against his team.

   strongly approve   approve   disapprove   strongly disapprove

7. After two men were put out on a double play attempt, a baseball coach told the players in his dugout to boo the umpire's decision.

   strongly approve   approve   disapprove   strongly disapprove

8. As the basketball coach left the gymnasium after the game, he shouted at the officials, "You lost me the game; I never saw such lousy officiating in my life."

   strongly approve   approve   disapprove   strongly disapprove

9. A basketball coach put sand on the gym floor to force the opponents into traveling penalties.

   strongly approve   approve   disapprove   strongly disapprove

10. A football coach left the bench to change the position of a marker dropped by an official to indicate where the ball went out of bounds.

    strongly approve   approve   disapprove   strongly disapprove

Source: Johnson, Barry L. and Jack K. Nelson, *Practical Measurement for Evaluation in Physical Education.* © 1979 Burgess Publishing Co. Reprinted by permission.

Table 11.4

A Summary of Responses from Teachers of Physical Education Concerning the Criteria They Use in Grading Students

CRITERIA	NEVER f*	(%)	OCCASIONALLY f	(%)	REGULARLY f	(%)
Absences	106	(27.7)	106	(27.7)	171	(44.6)
Tardiness	128	(33.4)	110	(28.7)	145	(37.9)
Dressing out	61	(15.9)	13	(3.4)	309	(80.7)
Proper uniform	84	(21.9)	37	(9.7)	262	(68.4)
Showering	304	(79.4)	43	(11.2)	36	(9.4)
Physical fitness	73	(19.0)	152	(39.7)	158	(41.3)
Skill-observed	41	(10.6)	106	(27.8)	236	(61.6)
Skill tests	40	(10.5)	107	(27.9)	236	(61.6)
Written tests	67	(17.5)	108	(28.2)	208	(54.3)
Improvement	49	(12.8)	113	(29.5)	221	(57.7)
Attitude	38	(9.9)	73	(19.1)	272	(71.0)
Participation	2	(0.5)	9	(2.4)	372	(97.1)
Effort	19	(5.0)	58	(15.1)	306	(79.9)
Sportsmanship	17	(4.4)	79	(20.6)	287	(75.0)

*f = frequency; the number of teachers indicating the use of this criterion.

Source: Nelson, Jack, Joyce Moore and Jeff Dorociak, "A Survey of Grading Practices in Physical Education in Louisiana," in *Louisiana Journal for Health, Physical Education, Recreation, and Dance, 28*, 18–21, 1983. Southeastern Louisiana University, Hammond, LA. Reprinted by permission.

the role of improvement in grading, note that 57.7 percent regularly used improvement as a part of their grading criteria. Such things as "participation," "effort," "sportsmanship," and "attitude" were all used regularly by over 75 percent of the teachers.

Another part of this study asked teachers to indicate how they would give a unit grade for a unit in a sports skill such as volleyball, basketball, or flag football. This part of the study gives a view of what percentage of a unit grade would be based on specific criteria. Again, some rather interesting results were obtained. First, the results did not indicate that teachers gave much weight to "skill" and "knowledge." Over 25 percent of the teachers indicated they *would not base any of the grade* on skills, 50 percent said they would give 15 percent or less to skills, and 70 percent would not base over 25 percent of the grade on skills. In fact, only 6 percent of the teachers indicated they would base 40 percent to 60 percent of a unit grade in a sports skill on skill. Written tests were used even less, with almost 20 percent of the teachers indicating that they would not use tests and 40 percent would not base over 15 percent of the grade on written knowledge tests. Interestingly, social behavior found its way into many teachers' grading systems in heavy percentages. For instance, 45 percent indicated they would base 5 percent to 25 percent of the unit grade on "sportsmanship," while 44 percent said they would base 5 percent to 25 percent of the grade on "attitude." Approximately 16 percent of the teachers indicated they would base 100 percent of the unit grade on "participation."[6]

exhibit 11.2

Student records: A case study

Third graders quietly enter the St. Andrew's gym, go to their stations for strength or stretching, and begin sit-ups, pull-ups, or sitting toe-touches. Dolly Lambdin, one of the physical education teachers in this K–6 private school in Austin, Texas, records a P+ on her behavior sheet for Jim, who is practicing hard on his weakest area of fitness. Other children mark the day's scores on individual record cards as they work—some alone, some helping each other. While students spend the next few minutes doing continuous locomotor skills, Dolly creates a record of those who can and cannot sustain skipping, hopping, or jumping for a minimum thirty-foot distance by watching the class and crossing names from a mimeographed list. No formal testing is involved and no scores are recorded.

Because the day's lesson is part of a rope jumping unit, students find their own task sheet and choose the next task to practice. Frowns of concentration and effort, as well as smiles for accomplishing a "checkoff," appear on these third graders' faces while they work to master jumping skills. When the class is completed, Dolly scans the record cards collected after the opening sequence and makes a note to remind herself to invite three youngsters to join the Early Morning Program to improve their fitness levels.

Scenarios like this are played out by Dolly throughout the school year. Her excellence as a teacher stems in large part from the rapid orchestration of many complex decisions. She does not display unusual or elaborate instructional techniques, but rather appears only to have mastered a wide range of familiar and quite simple skills. Dolly's extraordinary power to help children learn rests in her capacity to orchestrate—to do the right thing at the right time for the right student(s).

Fruits of Trial and Evaluation

In six years at St. Andrew's, through deliberate trial and evaluation, Dolly and her teaching colleagues have evolved a record-keeping system which consistently allows them to make decisions which help children learn. Having started with a few simple records, evaluated their utility and economy, and having discarded those which required too much effort or were irregularly used, the physical education staff has gradually built a method for maintaining a continuous picture of each student's progress and achievement in fitness tests, basic motor skills, specific play skills within activity units, and interpersonal behaviors.

Student records help Dolly make accurate and consistent decisions in a number of recurring areas:

• *Planning class activities.* "It's so great to know exactly how many kids in a class can do a particular skill before you plan the lesson."

- *Feedback and motivation.* "For most tests, students carry their cards from station to station. We encourage them to read the card and be aware of their progress, profile of achievement, and skills yet to be mastered. I talk a lot with the kids about two things: specific learning goals and personal improvement through practice. The big question is always, 'What did you learn today?' or 'How much better was today's performance compared to your last test?'"

- *Administrative decisions.* "Students with three or more skill or fitness areas marked low on their card are invited to Early Morning Gym (a prestigious before-school remedial class). The occasional student with a poor behavior record would not be invited. I just check the cards and have a solid reason for either decision."

- *Evaluation.* "Every six weeks we send parents a simple checklist showing specific points of improvement or continuing difficulty. Parents know what we are trying to accomplish and can see precisely how well their child is doing. I add a written note only when there is something important to say. Giving letter grades would be a waste of time, but communicating real information pays off for everybody."

- *Recruiting parent support.* "When our request for action or assistance is based on facts, they pay a lot more attention."

- *Justifying program to administrators.* "Comparing our scores to national norms is very impressive stuff."

More Than an "Ordinary Idea"

Dolly's use of student records shows how an ordinary idea can produce extraordinary results. Her careful consistency pays off in students' (1) high levels of fitness and motor skill, (2) steady progress in movement mastery at all ability levels, (3) strong administrative support in the form of facilties, equipment, class schedule, assignment of students, and school policies, (4) wide parental understanding and approval of program goals, and (5) high prestige among students for before- and after-school learning activities. Nearly all experienced teachers achieve some of these outcomes some of the time. Through consistent orchestration of many small details, exceptional teachers like Dolly maintain most of these conditions *most* of the time.

Source: Locke, L. and P. Dodds, "How One Teacher Uses Student Records," in *Journal of Physical Education, Recreation and Dance* 53, 41–43, Sept. 1982. © 1982 American Alliance for Health, Physical Education, Recreation and Dance. Reprinted by permission.

A study like this one is certainly revealing and makes us take a hard look at the practice of teaching physical education as compared to the theory. Since grades are the primary form of summative evaluation used by teachers, the grades should reflect the relative importance of the objectives of the instructional unit. Without this kind of relationship, student evaluation becomes an instrument that has little significance. As you begin your career as a physical educator, be aware of the importance of student evaluation and begin to develop a philosophy that will give evaluation a proper role in your teaching practices.

EVALUATING TEACHER PERFORMANCE

This section and the one that follows discuss evaluation as directly related to the instructional aspects of teaching. Singer and Dick indicate that "instructional evaluation involves two basic components: an analysis of instructional **content** and an analysis of instructional **procedures**."[7] In this section we will focus on the latter component, instructional procedures. We will consider instructional content in the next section when we discuss evaluating the curriculum. As we did when considering student evaluation, we will approach the topic of teacher evaluation by addressing the issues of why this evaluation is important, what should be evaluated, and how evaluation should be conducted.

Why Teacher Evaluation Is Important

Successful teachers do not become successful automatically. As Siedentop points out, "For teaching skills to improve, there should be goals, feedback on a regular basis, and a chance to improve."[8] Teacher evaluation is one of the primary forms of feedback that will help satisfy Siedentop's formula. Without this information, teachers do not have an objective means for making decisions concerning the effectiveness of their teaching. Teachers who balk at evaluation are inviting potential deterioration of their own teaching skills. The important thing to remember here, however, is that the evaluation must be done properly if it is to be at all useful to the teacher as feedback. Since "proper" evaluation is the key here, we will consider the aspects of teacher behavior that should be evaluated and some of the ways in which teacher evaluation can be carried out (see fig. 11.4).

What Teacher Behavior Should Be Evaluated?

If you were asked the question, "What does a good teacher do?" how would you answer? That, in effect, is what is being asked when we pose the question concerning what teacher behavior should be evaluated. In order to properly evaluate the effectiveness of a product, we must first know what characterizes the product being evaluated. In our case, the "product" is the rather nebulous construct labelled "a good teacher." We want to evaluate a teacher's behavior with respect to how it matches our conceptualization of how a successful teacher acts.

This is a subjective issue that is often the focus of many battles in education circles. However, certain common characteristics are shared by individuals who are readily considered to be "good" or "successful" teachers. These characteristics are generally accepted as a reasonable basis for defining or describing a successful teacher. From this kind of description we can gain insight into what teacher behavior should be evaluated to provide the most useful information for improving the teacher's performance.

Gage presents a list of characteristics that are sufficiently representative of the behavior of successful teachers. Gage describes the classroom conditions that tended to be related to improving student achievement. These conditions were determined on the basis of several research studies summarized by Gage. This list of "teacher-should" statements actually describes characteristics of a successful teacher.

From his list, five conditions are presented here. The teacher should

1. Move around the class a lot, monitoring and checking students' work
2. Be organized (both in the daily schedule and in lesson planning and presentation)
3. Give students an equal opportunity to respond
4. Not be entirely dependent on command style teaching techniques; appropriately use guided-discovery techniques
5. Liberally provide reinforcement and feedback[9]

Bear in mind that this list of characteristics is only representative of many different lists that have been developed to describe the successful teacher. We will use this list as a base on which we can build our study of how to evaluate teacher behavior.

Methods of Evaluating Teachers

The problem of which items should be considered when evaluating teachers' performances is a complex one that, unfortunately, has no universally accepted solution. Among the difficulties in achieving a solution are such problems as the availability of a wide range of evaluation methods and the wide disparity of opinions concerning which technique is best. In this introduction to teacher evaluation, we will not attempt to resolve these issues; rather, we will help you attain a basic understanding of how teacher evaluation can be done. To do this, we will summarize a fairly complete review of teacher evaluation methods as presented by Siedentop.

Siedentop categorizes teacher evaluation techniques into two classifications: traditional methods and systematic observation methods. Traditional methods are presented as having many shortcomings and, thus, they should be abandoned. Systematic observation methods, on the other hand, have been the "foundation on which teaching research has been built" and are presented as valid and reliable means for evaluating teaching performance.

Traditional evaluation methods include

1. **Intuitive judgment.** An experienced supervisor observes and judges the teacher teaching.
2. **Eyeballing.** An observer watches the teacher over a period of time, takes no notes, records no information, and discusses the teaching performance with the teacher.
3. **Anecdotal records.** An observer watches the teaching session and uses notes to record incidents or situations to be used as the basis for a discussion with the teacher.
4. **Checklist and rating scales.** These usually consist of a list of teacher characteristics about which an observer makes a judgment, usually on a point-based scale.

Siedentop argues that these traditional methods are simply unreliable. They depend heavily on the subjective perceptions of the observer and, as a result, have limited value. They can have increased value, however, when used along with one of the systematic observation methods.

The systematic observation methods include

1. **Event recording.** Teacher performance categories are defined and then observed in terms of the number of times that particular behaviors occurred during a teaching session. For example, one category may be "teacher-student positive interactions." Each time the teacher interacts in a postive way with a student, the observer makes a mark under that category. At the end of the session, the observer counts the number of occurrences of each behavior.
2. **Duration recording.** This method is similar to event recording except that the observer notes the amount of time a particular behavior lasts during the teaching session. For example, a teacher may be engaged in providing feedback to a student for ten seconds on one occasion. At the end of the session, the total amount of time the teacher spent providing feedback can be determined by

adding all the time recorded for providing feedback to the students. This total can then be converted to a percentage indicating the percent of total class time devoted to this behavior.

3. **Interval recording.** The observer divides the total class time into intervals (e.g., ten-second intervals). The observer watches the teacher for ten seconds, decides which behavior best characterizes the teacher during that interval, and then records that behavior during the second ten-second interval. Another ten-second interval is observed and the same process is continued.

4. **Group time sampling.** As in the interval recording technique, a specific interval of time for observation is determined (e.g., ten seconds). Rather than observing the teacher, the observer scans the class and counts the number of students engaged in the behavior category of interest for this particular observation interval.

5. **Self-record.** The teacher, rather than an observer, records the number of times a specific behavior occurs within a period of time.[10]

Many formal systematic observation methods have been developed over the past few years. An excellent overview of these is presented by John Cheffers, in an article in *Quest* (see Related Readings). Perhaps the most popular systematic observation method was developed by Ned A. Flanders (see Related Readings). Several have been developed specifically for physical education: of these, the most successful are the Cheffers Adaptation of Flanders Interaction Analysis System (CAFIAS), developed by John Cheffers of Boston University, and the Academic Learning Time in Physical Education (ALT-PE), developed by Siedentop, Birdwell, and Metzler at Ohio State University.

A good example of how the ALT-PE can be used to describe teacher behavior is seen in a recent study by Placek, Silverman, Shite, Dodds, and Rife. The teacher they observed was a male physical education teacher with twenty-two years of teaching experience. The observed classes were first, third, and fifth grade physical education classes experiencing instructional units in manipulative skills (e.g., throwing, kicking), team sports, and movement experiences (i.e., problem-solving activities related to the movement concepts of space, time, force, and flow). A total of fifty-three students were observed, twenty-nine males and twenty-four females.

The ALT-PE requires an observer to watch children for six seconds, record the behavior in an appropriate behavior category for the next six seconds, observe again, record again, and so on. Each observer in this study watched four different children at a time. A total of 153 observations were made. At certain times, all five observers watched the same child as a means of determining how well the observers agreed on their observations. Interestingly, the observers' agreement was very high. Table 11.5 shows the results of the observation in terms of the percentage of class time spent in various ALT-PE categories.

In table 11.5 *setting* indicates the nature of the class interaction between teacher and student. *Direct* indicates the teacher in direct control of the decisions. This is a setting similar to Mosston's command style, which you studied in chapter 10. Note that seventy-seven percent of the total class time was characterized by this style. Of the total class time, eighty-five percent was devoted to physical education content (Content-PE). Game playing and scrimmaging took up the majority of this time, with

Table 11.5

Percentage of Class Time* Spent in Selected ALT-PE Categories for First, Third, and Fifth Grade Students in Physical Education

OBSERVATION CATEGORIES			PERCENTAGE OF CLASS TIME
Setting			**100%**
Direct			77
Task			22
Reciprocal			0
Group			0
Questioning			1
Content-General	**15%**	**or**	**Content-PE**	**85%**

Content-General	15%	Content-PE	85%
Wait	1	Skill practice	12
Transition	11	Scrimmage	31
Management	3	Game	37
Break	0	Fitness	1
Nonacademic instruction	0	Knowledge	3
		Social behavior	1

*Class time: 19–39 minutes

Source: Placek, Judith, et al., "Academic Learning Time (ALT-PE) in a Traditional Elementary Physical Education Setting: A Descriptive Analysis," in *Journal of Classroom Interaction* 17 (1982): 41–47. © 1982 *Journal of Classroom Interaction.* Reprinted by permission.

twelve percent devoted to *skill practice,* that is, "intensive direct skill of isolated motor skills practiced alone or in small groups,"[11] and less than one percent of the time was spent on *fitness* activities. The remaining fifteen percent of the total class time was devoted to general content (Content-General), with moving between activities (Transition) making up most of that time.

While this study was directed toward describing teacher-student interactions for research purposes, the usefulness of an instrument such as the ALT-PE for teacher evaluation purposes can be easily seen. Information can be objectively gathered and given to the teacher to enable him or her to know, from an objective point of view, what went on in the class or classes just taught. The teacher must then use this information to maintain, modify, and/or change his or her teaching practices. Only through this final application step does effective teaching have a reasonable chance for being developed and maintained over an extended period of time.

EVALUATING THE CURRICULUM

An evaluation of the physical education curriculum involves determining the effectiveness of the curriculum content taught to students rather than the methods used for teaching this content. Baumgartner and Jackson stated, with regard to program or curriculum evaluation, that the "most crucial question to ask . . . is, Are students achieving important instructional objectives?"[12] This statement helps us focus our attention on the important need for any curriculum or program to identify goals and objectives. These, in turn, form the basis for the evaluation process that will determine program effectiveness.

Why Curriculum Evaluation Is Important

The need for curriculum evaluation centers on the importance of having information that can be used to make decisions about the curriculum. Student achievement and teacher effectiveness, while they may be crucial concerns, do not represent the only issues that must be addressed concerning program effectiveness; in fact, several issues must be considered. Taken together, the issues indicate the types of decisions that must be made concerning any program. Tom Evaul addresses this in stating that the purpose of curriculum evaluation is to provide the basis for answering five questions: (1) Are the objectives of the program being met? (2) Are there any positive or negative side effects? (3) What are the strengths of the program and how can it be improved? (4) Is the program worth the time, exertion, and money invested? (5) How is the program perceived by others?[13]

Answers to questions such as these can help in determining how a program or curriculum must be modified, changed, or continued. The problem, however, is the same as with any other area where evaluation is essential, that is, how can valid and reliable evaluation procedures that will provide the answers to these pertinent questions be conducted?

Methods of Evaluating the Curriculum

Of all the areas in physical education where evaluation is important, curriculum evaluation seems to suffer the most from a lack of standardized methods for accomplishing the task. While most tests and measurement or curriculum textbooks emphatically state the need for curriculum evaluation, there is, ironically, little information available about how to proceed with such an evaluation. Most texts discuss the need to conduct both formative and summative evaluations, yet finding standardized tools for doing these evaluations is difficult. Since this is the case, what do curriculum evaluation experts in physical education suggest?

A representative suggestion can be found in an article by Helen Heitman. She states that program or curriculum evaluation could be satisfactorily accomplished by comparing program goals to student achievement. Of particular importance in her view is the need to consider "global long-range goals." For example, one of these goals could be, "Students, upon completion of the curriculum, will continue in physical fitness and recreational activities throughout life."[14] Evaluation of the achievement of this goal would be accomplished by surveying graduates of the program. This, then, would be a form of summative evaluation of the overall effectiveness of the curriculum in achieving this major goal.

Formative evaluation in relation to this long-range goal could be carried out by means of assessing student performance on standardized fitness tests, such as the AAHPERD Youth Fitness Test, and in classes designed to teach recreational activities.

Criteria would be established in each of these summative and formative evaluation procedures that would give evaluators an objective basis for determining the effectiveness of the program. For example, in the summative evaluation, if sixty percent of the graduates were engaged in regular recreational or fitness activities, then program effectiveness would be acceptable. In the formative evaluation situation, a criterion could be established, for example, that "at least sixty percent of the students upon graduation will have AAHPERD Youth Fitness Test percentile scores of 50 or better. . . ."[15] Data such as these would provide information that could enable appropriate decisions to be made related to the five questions presented earlier.

As Evaul appropriately states, "Evaluation is the key component of any program. Without it, there is no basis for making decisions about the continuation or modification of the program."[16] This statement should become a standard for you to carry throughout your career as a physical educator because it sums up the need for you to be aware of how effectively you are accomplishing the objectives of your program.

SUMMARY

In this chapter, you have been introduced to one of the essential aspects of your job as a physical educator. The need for evaluation cannot be overemphasized. We have seen that both formative and summative forms of evaluation are important. Each can be carried out to evaluate student performance, teacher performance, and the curriculum. Appropriate evaluation methods for each of these areas must be based on sound evaluation and measurement theory, which means that these methods should be valid and reliable. Without this theoretical foundation, information gathered from any evaluation attempt becomes suspect and meaningless.

Student evaluation involves such concerns as what the basis for grading should be, how grades should be determined, and what forms of evaluation should be used. Teacher behavior must also be evaluated. This can take several forms, all of which can be categorized as being either traditional evaluation methods or systematic observation methods. Curriculum evaluation is important for determining the effectiveness of an instructional program. Evaluation of a curriculum can be done using formative and summative evaluation methods.

As you have studied these different forms of evaluation, you have become more aware of the need for evaluation in physical education and have established a foundation on which you can build as you progress through your curriculum as a physical education major.

STUDY QUESTIONS

1. What is the difference between formative and summative methods of evaluation? How can these methods be applied to evaluation needs in physical education?
2. How do reliability and validity differ? How can a test be reliable and not valid?
3. What are four important principles for grading in physical education? Give an example of how each principle can be implemented in a physical education teaching unit.

4. What would be some arguments for and against the use of absolute grading? Of curved grading?

5. How do systematic observation methods of teacher behavior differ from other teacher evaluation procedures?

6. What would be an example of using a formative means of curriculum evaluation in physical education?

STUDENT ACTIVITIES

1. Organize two debate teams to debate the following resolution: Grades in physical education should be based on student effort rather than student performance.

2. Visit various physical education departments in the schools in your city and inquire how teachers are evaluated. Make a list that compares and contrasts your findings.

3. Interview the physical education supervisor for the schools in your city to learn how the physical education curriculum is evaluated. Write a report presenting the pros and cons of this procedure.

4. Volunteer to help a physical education teacher administer skills tests. Write a report indicating how the test was given and how the test results were used by the teacher.

NOTES

1. Barry Johnson and Jack K. Nelson, *Practical Measurement for Evaluation in Physical Education,* 3d ed. (Minneapolis: Burgess Publishing Co., 1984).

2. Ibid., 61.

3. Robert N. Singer and Walter Dick, *Teaching Physical Education: A Systems Approach,* 2d ed. (Boston: Houghton Mifflin Co., 1980).

4. Johnson and Nelson, *Practical Measurements,* 62.

5. Theodore A. Baumgartner and Andrew S. Jackson, *Measurement for Evaluation in Physical Education* (Boston: Houghton Mifflin Co., 1975).

6. Jack Nelson, Joyce Moore, and Jeff Dorociak, "A Survey of Grading Practices in Physical Education in Louisiana," *Louisiana Association of Health, Physical Education, Recreation, and Dance Journal* 46. (September 1983): 18–21, 28.

7. Singer and Dick, *Teaching Physical Education,* 184.

8. Daryl Siedentop, *Developing Teaching Styles in Physical Education,* 2d ed. (Boston: Houghton Mifflin Co., 1983).

9. N. L. Gage, *The Scientific Basis of the Art of Teaching* (New York: Teachers College Press, 1978).

10. Siedentop, *Developing Teaching Styles,* 252.

11. Judith Placek, Stephen Silverman, Shirley Shite, Pat Dodds, and Frank Rife, "Academic Learning Time (ALT-PE) in a Traditional Elementary Physical Education Setting: A Descriptive Analysis," *Journal of Classroom Interaction* 17 (1982): 41–47.

12. Baumgartner and Jackson, *Measurement for Evaluation,* 339.

13. Tom Evaul, "How Do We Help Others by Structuring Programs in Human Movement?" in *Introduction to Physical Education: Concepts of Human Movement,* ed. John Cheffers and Tom Evaul (Englewood Cliffs, NJ: Prentice-Hall, Inc., 1978), 229–43.

14. Helen Heitman, "Curriculum Evaluation," *Journal of Physical Education, Recreation and Dance* 49 (March 1978): 36–37.

15. Ibid., 36.

16. Evaul, "How Do We Help Others?" 242.

RELATED READINGS

Aten, Rosemary. "Formative and Summative Evaluation in the Instructional Process." *Journal of Physical Education, Recreation and Dance* 51 (September 1980): 68–69.

Cheffers, John. "Observing Teaching Systematically." *Quest* 28 (1977): 17–28.

Cheffers, John, Edmund Amidon, and Ken D. Rogers. *Interaction Analysis: An Application to Nonverbal Activity.* Minneapolis: Association for Productive Teaching, 1974.

Flanders, Ned A. *Analyzing Teaching Behavior.* Boston: Addison Wesley, 1970.

Kneer, Marian E. "Ability Grouping in Physical Education." *Journal of Physical Education, Recreation and Dance* 53 (November/December 1982): 10–14, 68.

Mood, Dale L. "Physical Education Measurement: Past Practices, Present Developments and Future Challenges." *The Physical Educator* 37 (1980): 202.

Safrit, M. J. "Criterion-Referenced Measurement: Applications in Physical Education." *Motor Skills: Theory Into Practice* 2 (1977): 21–35.

Safrit, M. J., Andrew Jackson, and Carol Stamm. "Issues in Setting Motor Performance Standards." *Quest* 32 (1980): 152–62.

Schick, Jacqueline. "Written Tests in Activity Classes." *Journal of Physical Education, Recreation and Dance* 52 (April 1981): 21–22, 83.

Siedentop, Daryl, D. Birdwell, and M. Metzler. "A Process Approach to Measuring Teaching Effectiveness in Physical Education." A paper presented at a Research Symposium at the annual American Association for Health, Physical Education, Recreation and Dance Convention, New Orleans, March 1979.

Thomas, Jerry R. and Katherine T. Thomas. "Strange Kids and Strange Numbers." *Journal of Physical Education, Recreation and Dance* 54 (October 1983): 19–20.

The Nature and Scope of Physical Education

4

Too often, physical education and athletics have been perceived by the general public as being one and the same. Because of the sport emphasis found in both, the confusion may be understandable. Also contributing to this confusion is the fact that many physical educators, particularly in the public schools, assume positions coaching athletic teams, which is the subject of chapter 12.

In chapter 13 we will examine the relationship that exists between physical education and a number of other fields allied with it through historical and philosophical ties.

In chapter 14 we will study the constantly evolving nature and scope of physical education. Because of its complexity, physical education is not free of controversial issues that contribute to its ever-changing nature.

We hope that through your study of part 4, you will better understand the relationship between physical education, athletics, and other allied fields. We hope, too, that you will begin formulating a philosophy of physical education that will enable you to properly deal with trends and issues found in physical education.

Coaching and Athletics

12

Chapter outline

Student objectives

As a result of the study of this chapter, the student should be able to

1. Describe the qualities of a successful coach.
2. Distinguish between the various roles for which a coach may be responsible.
3. List the different coaching positions and the responsibilities that accompany the various positions.
4. Describe the necessity of professional preparation for the coaching experience.
5. Define ethics in coaching and develop a knowledge of how ethics influence coaching.
6. Discuss the effect of the win factor on the coaching profession.
7. Describe the problems in athletics and the coaching profession.
8. Explain the various reasons why coaches leave the profession.
9. Relate the importance of physical education professional preparation to coaching athletics.
10. Stimulate interest and thought pertaining to future decisions about the coaching profession.

WHAT IS A COACH?

A coach is a teacher, a leader, a director of learning, and an evaluator of performance. Parents will allow you, more than any other teacher in the schools, to give direction to their sons and daughters. A coach must be goal oriented, yet must realize that patience is of utmost importance. Frustration will surface many times, yet the coach must still pursue the goals and objectives of physical education without a letdown in enthusiasm. A coach is also very vulnerable—vulnerable to success, criticism, and, especially, to the athletes with whom he or she may work. A coach is an organizer. The responsibility of trying to satisfy the needs of athletes, administration, parents, and the media—all of whom are relatively undisciplined in their knowledge of the working of an inter-scholastic athletic program—is often stressful. A coach is also a friend to athlete and nonathlete, in many cases. Coaches have an excellent opportunity to serve as role models for youngsters. The coach models attitudes, values, and behavior: the task of constantly providing reinforcement for others by one's own behavior is not an easy one. Overall, a coach is a person, like you and me, who likes his or her job and is dedicated to the task. This person, however, takes the same human needs and weaknesses into a most precarious position in our society.

The purpose of this chapter is to examine many aspects of the coaching profession. This examination will prepare you to make a choice about whether or not the coaching of athletics is going to be part of your future as a physical educator.

Qualities of a Coach

The most important quality of a coach is that he or she is first a good teacher. Coaching is teaching! A good teacher can become a good coach if the desire to coach is present and coaching knowledge is learned. Do not underestimate the importance of your teaching preparation in your ambitions to become a successful coach. Most prospective coaches start as assistant coaches at the junior or senior high school levels. One point of agreement in a profession where disagreement is prevalent is that the beginning coach must be a good teacher first.

Coaching Roles

Coaching is a role in itself, but because of the nature of the profession and the amount of emotion and human interaction, the role of the coach demands a large number of adjunct roles. The application of these various roles lends to the excitement and human drama that go with the life of a coach. Preparation for these roles stems from preparation for life itself. Experience as well as expectation makes for more successful fulfillment of roles. This is one of the primary reasons why most persons should begin their careers as assistant coaches. To learn the various roles of the head coach and how to handle them is as important as the skills and strategy of the game (see fig. 12.1).

The role of the teacher has been explained previously. Other expected roles include leader, disciplinarian, organizer, an example for attitudes and values, and director of the game when in competition. These roles are basically taken for granted, but what

about other roles that may be separate from sport itself? Take, for example, the young-ster who may be using the coach as a substitute father or mother. Public relations is an essential part of coaching and must be considered in the application of a successful program. You must sell your program to the various groups involved in school athletics. You will also counsel students and listen to their personal problems. When violations of training rules or school or team policy take place, you may have to weigh the verdict and pass judgment yourself, which is not a pleasant task but, nonetheless, is a role that is expected from the coach. Finally, you may have to play the role of a defense lawyer or prosecutor to gather all of the details in matters affecting your team and athletes. In various situations that are foreign and since the coach must always maintain self-control, the coach must also be an actor of sorts while performing some roles.

The various roles of a coach appear complex, and one may wonder why this complexity occurs. Sport is a **microcosm,** or miniature, of our society. The values and behavior in sport reflect the values and behaviors of society itself. Sociologists are fascinated with sport and its relationship to American social life. Since sport parallels society in many ways, common sense suggests that involvement in sport demands involvement with the various aspects of human behavior and the social order.

COACHING POSITIONS

The variety of coaching positions encompasses a spectrum that ranges from the head coach at a very small high school to the last assistant on a major university team. The responsibilities of the position of head coach and assistant coach have many commonalities, whether the level of the position is in high school or the professional ranks. However, each level of the coaching spectrum also has specific job components that make that position different from another level. Changing positions from one level to another is not always as simple as it may look, even if the opportunity is present. Many a high school coach has left to go into college coaching only to return to the high school profession after a few years. The reason for this change is not always a lack of success in the college field, but the preference for high school coaching.

This section gives an overview of the responsibilities of the head coach and assistant coach as well as the responsibilities that accompany the various coaching levels within the profession.

Head Coach

The responsibility that the head coach incurs bears worthy the subtitle of "the boss." Coaching is basically an *autocratic* profession. Many decisions in coaching situations cannot wait for committee meetings or democratic processes. Also, in most situations, the head coach directly bears the responsibility for the success or failure of the program.

One of the major duties of the head coach is in staff organization. According to at least one sage observer, a head coach is only as good as the assistants on the staff. The selection and assignment of assistant coaches is a critical factor for success in some sports. The head coach also must select a system for play, establish an off-season training and conditioning program, plan and implement practice procedures, be responsible for safety and equipment, evaluate personnel, and become a public relations specialist, as well as performing many other tasks. Coaching is not a seasonal job for the head coach, but one that demands attention during the entire year. The head coach must pay attention to detail, be highly organized, and be able to communicate expectations to others. The first step in doing these is for the head coach to develop and convey a personal philosophy toward coaching and the sport to the assistants and all others directly involved in the program. The head coach can relay personal philosophy by leadership, by example and attitude, and by teaching those involved through various meetings, workshops, or clinics.

A head coach must also be a motivating force for players and coaches. The ability to prepare a team or an individual for a peak performance at the proper time is an intangible coaching quality. On the less pleasant side, the head coach must have the ability to live with criticism and continue with the performance of duties as if nothing has happened. You will take criticism, sarcasm, and, in some cases, be put under extreme pressures that are truly not warranted by your actions. This is part of the nature of the coaching profession. Much of your satisfaction for your efforts will come from the interaction and associations with the young men and women you will coach. A good head coach has a continuing interest in the development and welfare of each individual he or she coaches. Watching and guiding youngsters through a difficult stage of life and teaching them values as well as skills and fitness is what coaching is all about. If you make this your profession in life, be sure that when someone calls you "coach," you have earned this title by your total performance of the role. For many people who have participated in high school and college athletics, the person they call coach has a very special place in their hearts and has been a positive influence in their lives.

Assistant Coach

Many qualities make up a successful assistant coach. While the goal or outcome of coaching is the same in all positions, the role of the assistant coach is somewhat different. Opinion varies regarding the exact qualifications that contribute to becoming a successful assistant coach. One reason for this is the variety of levels, and thus the variety of qualifications, of assistant coach. One's particular skills may be suitable to one or more levels. First assistants or varsity assistants work directly with the head coach. Junior varsity, freshman, or junior high school assistants may actually be in charge of teams or assist those who are in charge. The assistant coach may range from a teacher of beginning skills to a designer of defensive or offensive strategy. Scouting ability, which often has to be learned, is almost always part of an assistant's job. The ability to scout opposing teams and analyze strategy as well as evaluate personnel is of particular importance in team sports.

One major qualification of an assistant coach that every head coach likes to see is loyalty. Sabock defines loyalty as each coach's commitment to the program, to the athletes, and to the decisions affecting the team arrived at through debate and consensus.[1] Loyalty is not defined as blind obedience or total subservience to the head coach. Sabock further states that loyalty among coaches will practically eliminate the possibility of assistant coaches joining the community experts who delight in criticizing the head coach; assistant coaches should react to criticism of the head coach and the program as a criticism of themselves.[2] The head coach needs your loyalty as an assistant coach. Loyalty is necessary for good interaction with the athletes, administration, and the public. Those who find it difficult to be loyal in a given situation should listen to the words of Elbert Hubbard.

Loyalty

If you work for a man, in heaven's name work for him, speak well of him, and stand by the institution he represents. . . . Remember . . . an ounce of loyalty is worth a pound of cleverness. . . .

    If you growl, condemn, and eternally find fault, why not resign your position, and when you are on the outside, damn to your heart's content. . . . But as long as you are a part of the institution, do not condemn it. . . . If you do, the first high wind that comes along will blow you away, and probably you will never know why. . . .

Successful assistant coaches should also have a thorough knowledge of their sport and be willing to continually improve this knowledge through participation in clinics, by reading books and coaching journals, and by becoming a student of the game. Playing experience will provide some physical as well as mental experiences for the beginning assistant coach. Other qualities sought are enthusiasm, initiative, dependability, a willingness to work, and the ability to contribute and share ideas pertaining to the program. The assistant coach also needs to develop the ability to take criticism. This criticism is often different from criticism aimed at the head coach; the assistant may get indirect criticism and must be careful to maintain loyalty.

The assistant's role as a teacher and technician of skills and drills is paramount to his or her on-the-field responsibility. Another area of great importance is the capacity to serve as a liaison between the head coach and the athlete. To be an effective liaison, the assistant coach must first develop a positive rapport with the athletes. In fact, in some situations, the assistant coach's rapport or interaction with students may be stronger than the head coach's interaction with them. As an example, in football, the head coach is in charge of the overall program, while you as defensive line coach have a much closer relationship with the athletes, since you teach them skills and drills and actually supervise their phase of the game. Similar situations occur in track and field between the running coach, the throwing events coach, and the jumping events coach, for example. This interaction is very important in maintaining the morale of a team and keeping dissension to a minimum. A point to keep in mind in this liaison role is to never directly criticize the head coach or disagree with the head coach in front of the athletes. Instead, be a good listener and try to resolve problems without a breach of loyalty to the head coach.

A final quality of a successful assistant coach is one of considerable debate. Should the assistant coach have a desire to be a head coach and be on the lookout to improve his or her coaching status? Many feel that the desire to become a head coach and advance is a positive trait. Most beginning assistants do want to become a head coach some day. Be prepared to exercise patience while you are waiting for your head coach job. Make sure you are well prepared and organized before you step into a head position. Your first head coaching position may make or break you as a successful coach. You may not have a second chance if you perform poorly and are not prepared for the head responsibility; therefore, take your time and develop the skills necessary to advance in the profession. To be a successful head coach, you must first be a successful assistant coach.

Junior High School Coach

The coach of sixth, seventh, or eighth grade athletes must be a good teacher first. Your main purpose is to teach skills and techniques of the game in order to give the young athletes a broad base upon which to develop to their fullest potentials. Values and attitudes toward sport in general and your sport in particular must be taught and practiced. Many times, bad habits in both skills and attitudes from improperly supervised youth sports programs must be unlearned. Junior high school youngsters are vulnerable to their first exposure to a "real coach." Your behavior will make a firm impression upon them. Another point to keep in mind is to make sport fun at this level. Enough pressure is applied in high school and college sport; therefore, make junior high sport a positive learning experience.

The junior high school coach needs a tremendous amount of patience and a thorough understanding of growth and development of the age levels involved. Junior high school is an excellent career entry level for the beginning coach, and it offers many intangible rewards such as the admiration and loyalty from athletes who will always regard this coach as the first who taught them how to play the game.

High School Coach

Philosophically, the high school coach should provide an extension of the skills, attitudes, and values of the junior high coach. However, to be realistic in most situations, the high school coach is expected to win. Most coaches accepting such responsibility are goal oriented and want to be winners. Wanting to win is good, unless it becomes an overriding matter in which ethics and the welfare of athletes are disregarded. High school coaching is a highly motivated situation and can provide an exciting lifestyle. However, make no mistake that a lot of hard work and long hours go into the preparation of a high school team (see fig. 12.2).

The physical education major with college playing experience is a strong candidate for a varsity high school job as a beginning coach. Strategy and knowledge of game situations are important factors. The beginning high school coach must still acknowledge that many of the athletes are in the learning stages of the game and should not be regarded as highly skilled or "pro-type" athletes. Again, a thorough knowledge of the growth and development patterns of high school-age youth is essential. Another factor for which the high school coach must prepare is the recruitment of superior athletes by the colleges and universities.

Finally, for those who have ambitions to be college or professional coaches, successful high school experience is a must. In reality, it is the first step up the ladder of coaching success. However, many high school coaches prefer this level and want no higher pursuits. Truly, the coaching of high school athletes offers many rewards for the dedicated coach. Some of the best coaches in the profession are at the high school level.

Figure 12.2 The coaching profession is being enhanced by an ever-increasing number of qualified female coaches.

Junior College Coach

The junior college athletic program basically serves two purposes. The first is to provide the student athletes with high quality programs for participation and enjoyment and the second is to prepare some student athletes for the four-year college and university programs. Many highly skilled university athletes, both male and female, are products of the junior college system. Junior college coaches thus serve a dual purpose. They recruit and coach athletes for the needs and success of their programs and also must keep in mind that many athletes will desire to participate at higher levels.

The junior college coach depends upon success to aid in recruiting. Most athletes who intend to prepare for college and university programs want to improve their skills and participate in successful programs where they will receive exposure and the opportunity to be recruited. Not all junior colleges operate in this manner; in many schools, athletic participation is organized for the student body and is not just a feeder system for other colleges and universities.

Figure 12.3 Basketball is a sport that places a great deal of stress on the coach.

The typical junior college coach is a successful high school coach who has earned a master's degree. In addition to having the same qualifications as the high school coach, the junior college coach needs to be a successful recruiter even in nonscholarship situations. The junior college coach interacts with young adults living in a community environment away from home, as compared to the high school coach, who interacts with students who live at home and are under their parents' guidance. In some instances, the junior college coach may not be under as much pressure to win as the high school coach is under. This is especially true if the coach is a member of the teaching faculty and has proven to be a competent instructor. The junior college coach may also use this experience as a stepping stone to the college or university coaching level. The main qualifications are success at the junior college level, proven recruiting ability, maturity as a coach, and success in producing quality athletes for the four-year schools.

College/University Coach

College and university coaching take two paths. The first lies in the direction of schools in which athletics are a money-making venture. This includes most of the large and well-known universities. Sports are a business, to put it bluntly, and a very competitive business at that. The coaches at such institutions are under tremendous pressure from the public, the school, the media, and alumni or other special interest groups to produce winners (see fig. 12.3). The jobs are well paid, but are also highly competitive. Most coaches who move into the major college ranks do so with successful high school or junior college backgrounds. Many are known for producing scholarship-quality athletes. A few even go with the superstar they have coached. Most prospective college coaches are also chosen for their potential recruiting ability: the recruitment of superior athletes is the primary job of some college coaches. These jobs offer excitement, glamour, prestige, and an abundance of hard work.

The other path awaits the college coach who is in a situation in which the only pressure is to run a well-organized program. Many of our mid-size and smaller schools fit this category. The selection of the coach depends upon all of the factors previously mentioned, but teaching ability may also be a consideration in obtaining the position. Such schools do not lack the desire to win or to be successful, but they feel that the athletic program is part of the total education process and not an end in itself.

Regardless of the type of college program, the coaches are often similar. Head coaches must be very good at public relations and motivation. They are the planners of overall strategy and coordinators of all other aspects of the entire program. Assistant coaches are mainly involved in implementing the head coach's philosophy and strategy. They are also responsible for the teaching of skills, techniques, and strategy. Assistant coaches' duties also involve scouting and recruiting of future college athletes. The recruiting aspect cannot be underestimated, because the success of almost every college program, regardless of size or the amount of scholarship aid that is given, depends upon a successful recruiting program for high school and junior college athletes.

If college coaching is anticipated in your future, be sure to obtain a master's degree, which is a prerequisite at most institutions, especially those where you are also part of the teaching faculty.

Professional Coach

Most professional coaches enter the ranks in one of two ways. First, many have been highly successful pro players who have turned to coaching in the pros after their playing careers are finished. Second, professional coaches are hired from the college ranks, usually from the major colleges or universities with highly competitive programs. Many such coaches are not only successful, but are well-known personalities. With these two main avenues of entry, it is highly unlikely that at this time you can really prepare to be a professional coach.

Coaching at the professional level is not always coaching in the true sense of the word. Managing, the term used in baseball, or organizing personnel may be just as appropriate. In many cases, the athletes receive higher compensation than the coaches do, and if a conflict erupts between coach and player, often the coach is the one who goes. The professional coach needs to be a specialist in public relations. The salaries are high, but the security is low. Few will make it to the professional coaching ranks and few will remain there throughout a career. Professional sports are an exciting life for one who attains pro status and is successful.

PROFESSIONAL PREPARATION FOR COACHING

All coaches are not physical education majors. This fact often places the school systems in a dilemma as to the certification or requirements a coach must have. School administrators often have difficulty finding teachers to fill school coaching positions. Often these jobs are at the assistant coach level, but sometimes they involve head coaching positions. The physical education major is normally prepared in most curriculums to assume coaching responsibilities. However, not enough physical education teaching jobs are available for all coaches to be physical education majors. A major point to make for the future coach is that by obtaining teaching certification in an area other than physical education, you will open the doors to more opportunities in the coaching of interscholastic sports.

The remainder of this section on professional preparation for coaching will address the additional preparation and knowledge you can acquire to enhance your coaching qualifications.

Development of Your Personal Coaching Philosophy

Even in the training stage of your coaching career, you should develop a personal philosophy of coaching. Harper states, "philosophy is a way of living. In cultivating the philosopher in us, it may be that we may not actually end up thinking differently at all, but what is clearly necessary is that all of us learn to think for ourselves. To philosophize is to accept that we do not know in advance where our thinking may lead us; we rarely even know what we seek in such thought."[3]

A **personal philosophy of coaching,** then, is not a regimented course of action. Actually, it is an openness toward formulating one's actions based upon experiences and knowledge that one encounters. Your philosophy will change as the years go by. Again, your experiences and behaviors will formulate these changes. By developing a personal philosophy of coaching, you will be acknowledging and expressing your beliefs as well as the sources of your beliefs, which is important in knowing why you do what you do.

Knowledge of Your Sport(s)

When you begin your coaching career, you most likely will not know everything about the sport(s) you will coach. As a college athlete or a beginning coach, you can broaden your knowledge in a variety of ways. You can read coaching textbooks, both general and those specific to a sport. You can read some of the several, very informative coaching journals, which provide up-to-date, pertinent information on sports, and can attend various coaching clinics or workshops whenever they are available. Another way to broaden your knowledge base if you are not a participant in sport in college is to associate or affiliate yourself with the college team in some capacity that would allow you to attend practice sessions, develop a relationship with the coach and/or staff, and attend the games; this way you will be able to watch an entire philosophy at work.

Your goal is to become a **student of the game.** To do this, you must be willing to learn. You must read books and journals well beyond those assigned in your professional preparation to attain this goal. While some head coaches may prefer enthusiasm over knowledge, enthusiasm cannot replace a basic knowledge of the sport when it comes to teaching the athletes. When you interview with the athletic director and head coach for a staff position, they will expect you to have a thorough knowledge about the sport(s) you will be coaching.

Participation in Sports

The debate over whether one can be a successful coach without having actual playing experience is ageless. While there are exceptions, the general rule is that playing experiences are helpful. Let us define what **playing experience** means. Obviously, if a person plays sports in college and desires later to be a coach, playing experience will definitely enhance the person's qualifications. What about high school participation, college intramurals, club sports, recreation leagues, and the like? Again, all of these fall into the category of participation, but at what level? Sports participation that is not well organized with coaches, officials, and standards of play may not produce desirable results. High school participation can lead to a successful coaching career even if the participant was not good enough for college sports. But a person without high school or college participation most likely will not develop a sincere interest in coaching organized sports.

The main advantages of playing experience lie in the physical and emotional domains. There is no substitute for the experience of being physically and emotionally involved in play and making mental decisions (see fig. 12.4). Nor can the importance of training and conditioning processes that take place in sport be negated. When a youngster fumbles on the goal line, strikes out with the bases full, finishes last in an important race, or misses an easy lay-up, he or she can relate to the feelings of others "who have worn the shoe" and experienced such a physical and emotional crisis. However, if you are not a college or high school athlete and you desire to become a coach, your best alternative to primary participation is to become a student of the game and obtain as much exposure as possible to those playing the game in order to relate to players' physical and emotional experiences. The best way to pursue this involvement may be to become a team manager or student trainer.

Playing experience does have drawbacks in the coaching profession. Some athletes who are highly skilled have never really learned their basic skills through motor learning processes and really do not know how to teach those skills to others. Also, many highly skilled athletes are not tolerant of those less skilled and become impatient when youngsters cannot learn quickly; thus, such coaches develop a dislike for those who are unskilled. This goes back to competitive playing situations, where the unskilled are cut loose from the team and where there is an emphasis on perfection at all times. Extremely competitive situations tend to degrade individuals who cannot make the team, because some coaches do not want those who do make the team to associate with "losers." Finally, many athletes pride themselves in their skill level, fitness level, pain tolerance, and their coachability. All of the youngsters you coach will not fit this model. You must remember that you are coaching a group of youngsters who have various reasons why they play the game, various ability levels, and various backgrounds.

Figure 12.4 Some athletes have the ability to function as coaches on the field during the heat of intense competition.

Pre-Coaching Experiences

Many coaches in the profession would advise the future coach to obtain some coaching experiences prior to beginning an interscholastic coaching career. Many opportunities exist for such pre-coaching experiences for any interested man or woman. The most frequent opportunity lies in youth sports programs. The sports common to the elementary-age youngster are soccer, baseball, basketball, tee-ball, football, and softball. Many areas may also have youth opportunities in swimming, gymnastics, and track and field. Recreation leagues and summer programs in many communities may provide coaching experiences involving youngsters of junior and senior high-school age.

While these may seem like excellent practice opportunities for future coaches, some caution is advisable. Many coaching practices in the youth league leave much to be desired. One of the major problems with youth sports is the lack of qualified coaches. While the future physical educator and coach would be an asset to such programs, the fact remains that many such programs are organized from an adult point of view and would expose the beginning coach to considerable pressure. Adult examples during the play of youth sports often prove to be a harsh reality both for the young athlete-to-be and the future coach. One should check carefully into the ethics, organization and structure, quality of officiating, and the amount of adult involvement prior to assuming any coaching duties.

Summer camps may provide brief, but organized opportunities to coach. Sports are an important part of camp life. In many urban areas, private schools may be willing to hire part-time coaches to assist with programs. In this position, you should consider working as an assistant so as to learn from someone who has experience in the head coach position.

Some of the best coaching experience can be gained as part of your professional preparation and will also help prepare you more for a coaching career in interscholastic sports. This can be done as part of your student teaching experience. If coaching is a part of your plans, talk with your university supervisor and cooperating teacher and let them know of your desire to work with the athletic program as well as teach physical education. This experience will give a realistic view of the responsibilities of a full-time teacher and coach. As a student teacher, do not expect too much responsibility, but appreciate the opportunity to work with the coaching staff and athletes—an opportunity that will provide you with valuable experience that may enhance your qualifications in obtaining your first teaching and coaching position.

Coaching the Opposite Sex

With the advent of Title IX and the growth of women's sport (see fig. 12.5), coaches of both sexes will be inevitably involved in coaching youngsters of the opposite sex. At this time, the greater number of crossover roles lie in males coaching female athletes. The gender of the coach is not of importance, but how effective he or she is in the coaching profession is very important. Youngsters, regardless of their gender, identify with the coach if he or she is competent, organized, and a good leader.

Figure 12.5 Female athletes now have increasing opportunities for athletic participation beyond the high school level.

Some male coaches contend that they have to change their coaching style and technique for female athletes. Research shows that this change is unnecessary. Regarding strenuous training or physical activity for the female athlete, Colfer concludes,

1. One can be athletically skilled and train rigorously without any loss of femininity.
2. The female is perfectly capable of performing strenuous activity without any physiological impairment.
3. Active females possess a better state of health than those who are inactive.
4. Strength can be improved or developed in the female at a higher ratio than that of the male.
5. In summary, there is no reason to advocate different training techniques for the female athlete.[4]

Some general factors, however, should be considered by the prospective coach of the opposite sex. These pertain both to the male and female coach and should be accounted for prior to the actual crossover coaching role.

1. A coach should acquire knowledge about the physical makeup of the athlete. This should include knowledge pertaining to the anatomy, physiology, and response to physiological stress situations.
2. A coach should acquire knowledge about the psychological, emotional, and social makeup of the athlete.
3. Coaches should not patronize members of the opposite sex.
4. Coaches should keep all relationships with members of the opposite sex strictly on a professional basis.
5. Coaches should plan their teaching of skills, strategy, and conditioning to the present ability levels of the athletes and not base them on the sex of the athletes.
6. It is advisable to have an assistant coach, trainer, or faculty member of the same sex available to relate to problems that are unique to the male or female athlete.
7. Coaches should never enter the dressing areas or toilet areas of athletes of the opposite sex. Team meetings, etc., should be scheduled in appropriate areas regardless of whether the meetings occur in a game or practice session.
8. Coaches should take caution in handling the injury and training needs of athletes of the opposite sex and should have a member of that sex present at all times.

In general, the differences in personalities and psychological characteristics of successful male and female athletes are miniscule. Coaching athletes of the opposite sex should not produce any difficulties if one is prepared and willing to acknowledge the few problems that may arise.

Coed Sports

Coeducational sports participation is not prevalent throughout our society. Title IX states that equal opportunity must be provided, but that separate teams are to be operated when the activity involved is a contact sport or the selection for such teams is based upon competitive skills. For the most part, this creates separate but equal competition and accommodations under this law. Therefore, we may have teams who practice together, but do not compete together. Still, in a coaching sense, such teams could be considered coed. Take, for example, a high school swim team in which both boys and girls train under the guidance of the same coach, but compete on a separate basis. Similar examples could be taken from cross-country, track and field, and gymnastics.

Boys and girls can train successfully together under the tutelage of the same coach. The key word in this statement is *train*. In this context, training means that athletes are training together for similar competition, but not to compete against each other. Some of the physical, psychological, and sociological reasons why the opposite sexes do not compete against each other are discussed in chapter 2, in the section entitled Women in Sport and Physical Activity.

Little difference exists between the male and female regarding strength, skill, and endurance in relation to total body weight, lean body weight, and the same exposure to learning and practice. The training needs of women and men are basically the same. Perhaps the major benefit from having boys and girls train together lies in the social domain, where boys and girls learn about members of the opposite sex, especially during the times of physiological and psychological stress that occur in practice sessions as well as in competition. This type of interaction ultimately will develop realistic, healthier respect and admiration for the opposite sex. In regard to giving preferential or special treatment to either sex, the coach must treat everyone on an entirely equal basis with the exception of handling separate personalities. Any breach of this rule or any special treatment of either sex could result in team dissension.

Conditioning for Athletes

All sports require a certain degree of physical fitness and other conditioning specific to the requirements of the performance. Coaches in today's athletics have to know more than just drills and exercises for their teams. A coach must be familiar with specific conditioning for a sport as well as the various specialty areas of training in order to assist athletes to develop to their fullest potential.

The primary specialty area is strength training. All sports performance can be improved through strength training programs. A well-prepared coach is aware of the various equipment, methods, and techniques for strength training. In response to the question "Why strength training for athletes?" Colfer states that research into the area of strength training has shown without a doubt that it is beneficial in the development of strength, power, flexibility, and muscular endurance.[5] The idea that strength training adds unwanted weight, decreases speed, and is harmful to performance in any sport where running speed, agility, and reaction time are important is outdated and incorrect. As coaches, we are always looking for methods to use that will improve upon the natural ability of the athlete. Strength training is one such method.

Another important aspect of athletic preparation is in the improvement of running speed. Research has established that running speed can be improved.[6] The majority of athletic performances, whether in team or individual sports, have a high value on running speed. As Colfer adds, speed programs are not just designed for sprinters. Every athlete needs speed. Fast or quick legs will benefit all athletes regardless of the sport. Improvement of speed will not only increase performance, but will tend to cause less strain in running. To use speed effectively, speed must be practiced and be specific to the task.[7] Informed coaches will learn and know to what extent speed improvement programs will benefit athletes in their sports.

Coaching Certification

Due to the increased need for coaches in interscholastic sports, the demand for coaches at all levels cannot be filled by the physical education staff alone. Many future educators would like to prepare themselves for coaching careers also, without being physical education majors. The physical educator will likely receive all of the courses of instruction essential to a coaching career and certification as a coach, if applicable. However, what about those not in physical education?

The *South Carolina Journal* (*SCAHPER*), in a study by C. J. Johnson, reports that the number of coaches not certified in physical education exceeds the number who are certified.[8] An AAHPER task force, in 1968, studied coaching certification and came up with the following recommended courses for a coaching minor: Principles and Problems of Coaching; Theory and Techniques of Coaching; Physiological Foundations of Coaching; Kinesiological Foundations of Coaching; and Medical Aspects of Athletic Coaching.[9]

Noble and Corbin report in their study surveying coaching certification throughout the fifty United States, Washington, DC, and Puerto Rico that five states have minimum coaching certification requirements in addition to teachers' certification. Two states have coaching certification available, but it is not required, while forty-five states, the District of Columbia, and Puerto Rico have no specific requirements for coaching; however, most of them require that a coach be a certified teacher in order to coach in the public schools.[10]

Noble and Corbin further add that the support for coaching certification is largely from within the teacher preparation institutions.[11] The opposition to coaching certification is largely from administrators charged with having more and more coach-teachers. Some resistance also comes from high school athletic associations and practicing coaches.

While coaching certification is being studied at various levels, all physical educators, both present and future, are encouraged to support the need and concept of coaching certification.

Evaluation of Coaches

As a coach, you will be evaluated in many ways. Your athletes, parents, community, athletic director, head coach, school administrators, and other teachers will all pass judgment in one way or another about your performance as a coach. Each will pass judgment on the basis of how they perceive your job. For example, a teacher within your school will note your teaching ability; the athlete will look at your knowledge, fairness, and leadership; parents will look at how safely you conduct your program; and the downtown businessperson may judge only on your win-loss record. Unfortunately, the win-loss record usually weighs most heavily in the decision to rehire a coach.

Success in coaching is a result of multiple talents. A coach is evaluated on administrative responsibilities; organizational ability; adherence to school philosophy and policy; skills and knowledge in coaching; interest and enthusiasm; relationships with the athletes; safety and prevention of injuries in the program; and, finally, performance. The measure of performance consists of performance of the team, performance of the individual athlete, performance of the coach, and the outcome of the contest.

How coaching evaluation takes place varies from school to school, but be assured that as a coach you will be evaluated from many sources. In most cases, the athletes will have little to say about your evaluation. Many good coaches are forced to leave a position because of the pressure to win. If this should occur, you must examine yourself and note whether such a dismissal was for lack of winning only or because of your performance in other areas as well.

The Future for Coaches

The future for the coaching profession is strong. Even with cuts in school budgets, athletics continue to flourish and even expand. The same can be said for the future in college and professional sport as well. In most areas of athletics, coaches are in demand. Note, also, that many coaches will leave the profession for a variety of reasons; thus, openings for new coaches occur continuously in the profession.

Some changes, however, within the preparation of the future coach will occur. The new coach is going to have to be better prepared in the areas of physical fitness in order to relate the values of athletics to the needs of adult life. Interpersonal relationships will play an important role, also. The coach may become less autocratic, in some aspects, with the team and individual athletes. Knowledge of the game and coaching skills will need to be at a higher level than ever before. Coaching certification requirements will become a factor in obtaining a coaching position, especially if those aspiring to coaching are not physical education teachers. The future coach will rely more on intellect than ever before; smarter coaches, not just in skills or strategy, will earmark the profession. People will no longer be content to settle for the "old coach" image. The new coach will emerge as a "physiologist of athletics."

In accordance with these statements, the new coach will need to know more than ever about the profession as a whole. Some coaching course concepts may change. As Sabock states, "Rarely do high school coaches ever get into difficulty because they lack knowledge of a "game." Rather, their difficulties stem from unhappy parents, critics in the community, problem athletes, or relationships with other coaches on their own staff. These areas are most often overlooked in the professional preparation of coaches."[12] He further adds, "Somewhere in preparing young people for coaching, emphasis and time must be devoted to teaching them about the profession."[13] A future coach who is more informed about the profession should face fewer adjustments and problems, especially those which may cause the coach to leave the profession prematurely.

COACHING ETHICS

The word *ethics* has many interpretations. Dictionaries often define the word as relating to morals; the discipline whose subject is the nature and grounds of moral obligation; moral philosophy that teaches people their duty and the reasons for it.

We can see two key factors in ethics. One is morals and the other is judgment. First, one's ethics develop from the way one is taught and the experiences that take place in a given area. Ethics also are influenced by one's needs. As an example in coaching, if your job depends upon winning a championship, would you allow the key player, who is injured, to participate at the risk of more serious injury?

Jack Scott wrote about and described the need for an athletic revolution. Although his revolution never materialized and was not successful in a college situation under his own implementation, some major points were valid. He perceived more humane treatment for athletes and the need for more humane behavior on the part of coaches.[14] The downfall of organized athletics that he predicted has not materialized. In fact, athletics have not produced much change in society's values except, possibly, in the professional sports world. Perhaps what Scott really had in mind was a need for an attitude change toward ethical behavior in coaching.

Many sport associations and state governing bodies for interscholastic sport have written codes of ethical behavior. Many of these codes you will probably examine further in your coaching courses. The problem with most written guidelines is that their generality allows for many interpretations, some of which are made by coaches who bend guidelines to fit a need. As a coach, on what are ethics really based? The answer is you—your interpretation of moral standards in the profession and the value judgments that you will make pertaining to loyalty, honesty, courage, honor, and written standards. You will have to decide if the end justifies the means. Of most importance in regard to ethics are the lessons and values you teach others, mainly the athletes you coach. Never forget that the behavior you practice influences them. If you teach or profess standards of ethical behavior to forty people in one year, the standards are no longer just yours, but are also the standards of forty-one people! The lessons of the game will remain long after the scores are forgotten. You should be primarily concerned with teaching ethical behavior and values to your athletes, which is best done by personal example.

THE WIN FACTOR

If your philosophy of coaching is to win at all costs, then forget about any standards of ethical behavior. Yet, the win factor has firmly established itself at all levels in American sport. In many arenas of sport, the coach has to win or else face unpleasant consequences. Even in high school situations, these consequences may be the loss of a high salary, the loss of job security, dismissal, loss of the chance to move to an administrative position, reduced college coaching opportunities, loss of peer group recognition and status, a decline in personal pride, and a fear of failure.

Sport is a microcosm of society: the values in sport are those of society. American society has three highly valued means to achieve: hard work (and talent), continual striving, and deferred gratification. This describes adequately our processes in sport.

exhibit 12.1

Professional code of ethics for coaches

As a professional physical educator and coach I will

Take responsibility for the safety and welfare of my athletes.

Respect each athlete as an individual first.

Promote academic as well as athletic achievement for each athlete.

Teach American social values along with a spirit of cooperation and teamwork.

Practice ethical behavior with players, coaches, other teachers, and school administrators.

Strive to develop further knowledge and expertise in the sports I coach.

Abide by the rules of the game—both written and unwritten.

Serve as a positive example for physical fitness, sportsmanship, moral character, and leadership.

Accept both victory and defeat with dignity.

Strive to teach the athlete how to prepare for fitness in life when athletics are through.

Show respect for the judgment and integrity of all sports officials.

Discourage the "win at all costs" and "me first" attitude prevalent in sport and society.

Discourage unnecessary violence in sport.

Discourage the use of drugs and steroids and educate my athletes about the dangers of such substances.

Take responsibility for the position I have as a coach and use the authority and supervision relegated to me in a wise and prudent manner.

Encourage spectators and the nonparticipants in sports to show respect and sportsmanship.

We ask our athletes to pay the price, have a "never say die" attitude, and to deny immediate pleasures for later rewards. This is the route to success. However, can success, which is often equated with winning, be achieved without compromising ethical standards?

As a coach, you can only answer yes, otherwise your values are not ethical. Coaches who pay attention only to the win factor are not for the best interests of sport.

An article in *Sports Illustrated,* "American Renewal," states that competition cannot serve society if it is antisocial. Winning at any cost and true sportsmanship are incompatible. Winning has become so paramount that other important values are not evident in American sports today.[15]

Figure 12.6 Sharing the elation of winning an important athletic contest is one of the high points of coaching.

You can teach winning and still teach values (see fig. 12.6). Your philosophy of coaching and demonstration of ethical behavior will enable you to do so. In a contest, striving to win and doing one's best regardless of the outcome are more important than just winning. Few individuals, if any, go through life totally undefeated in sports participation as well as in other aspects of life. We learn from losing, and the goal is to improve so as to decrease future losses. However, what is losing? If losing is just the score or outcome of a contest, then it is a temporary setback. If it is an attitude toward life or the result of a lack of effort, then it becomes a problem. A coach has to analyze and rationalize what winning and losing are, and then dispense this philosophy to the athletes. No one should be in the coaching profession to lose, but to have a win-at-all-costs philosophy is destructive to the concept that sport is a valuable educational tool.

PROBLEMS IN ATHLETICS

Most of the major problems in athletics could be considered violations of ethical behavior, also. However, some problems are not caused or initiated by the coach and, therefore, do not result directly from the coach's behavior. In fact, the coach may have positive influence on the prevention of some problems. Many problems in sport are also society's problems and are not particular to sport alone. One should carefully note this factor and not use sport as a scapegoat.

In this section we will discuss existing problems in sport to make you, a future coach, aware of them.

The Teacher vs. The Coach

Should a coach be considered a teacher first in the eyes of the school and community? If a coach is a good teacher in the school system, should he or she be fired for a lack of success in winning games? In many instances, the public's narrow view of the overall role that a coach plays in the development of their children creates this dilemma. However, the system still exists and makes many coaches care little about teaching duties since their jobs do not really depend upon teaching. This has hurt the physical education profession the most in the area of its status in education in general. Perhaps Olcott summarizes the solution best: "For a positive direction in teaching/coaching, the message is simple: a good coach would not give up at the goal line; neither should he/she give up in the classroom. With proper motivation and direction from educational leaders, there need be no teacher/coach conflict."[16] Together, the teacher and coach can be teamed for excellence (see fig. 12.7).

Specialization of Athletes

Have you ever heard a 13-year-old respond, "I'm a kicking specialist" in answer to the question, "What position would you like to play on the seventh grade football team?" Professional sport has crept down to the elementary level. Athletically inclined youngsters used to play all sports. Today, a college athlete in more than one sport or a high school athlete in more than two is a rare sight. Specialization at an early age has robbed

Figure 12.7 The coach should be, above all else, an enthusiastic teacher.

our youth of some very valuable and fun experiences and of character-building benefits derived from participation in a variety of sports. When a high school football athlete starts practice in August, plays through November, begins off-season training in December, has spring practice in April, and has possible uncoached workouts throughout the summer, finding time for participation in any other sports is difficult. True, some players who specialized early in sport became famous players, but this is not true for the majority of young athletes. Most young athletes will, in fact, never become famous players, but in the meantime their focus on a specialty may cause them to forego the learning and training needed to be physically educated in adult life.

Should Athletic Participation Count as Credit for Physical Education?

In many areas, credit is given in physical education for participation in athletics. This can take various forms. Athletes are excused from physical education during the season or do not actively participate in class. Athletes are assigned to an athletic period that is nothing more than additional practice time or they are excused from physical education totally. Physical education, if properly taught, is more than just sports participation, especially in the area of physical fitness. Knowledge of physical fitness and a variety of lifetime sports for use in adult life is part of being a physically educated person. In some respects, an athlete who does not participate in a well-rounded physical education program is not physically educated despite sports participation. Many of our team sport athletes end their athletic involvement when participation is finished. Their sports have little carryover or fitness value in the rest of their lives. The coach, who is also a physical educator, should do his or her best to keep athletics and physical education class separate and to see that the athlete is an active class member.

Cheating in Sports

Cheating in sports is, at this time, a major problem in college athletics. The main areas lie in illegal recruiting practices, payments to athletes, and false records for grades and degrees, for example. One of the common excuses for such cheating is the win factor. Another is that college sport, in some institutions, is a business that expects results at almost any cost. The losers in all of these situations are the college athletes who do not obtain a degree and cannot attain professional status; they come away from a four-year college career empty-handed. Dr. Harry Edwards states that "less than two percent of players on a college athletic team make the pros. The average American male has less than one chance in fifty-five thousand to become a professional football, basketball, or baseball player."[17] As a further example, he adds that over eighty percent of the National Football League players have no college degree.[18]

Dr. Harold Enarson, former president of Ohio State University, defends college sport by stating that cheating, not professionalism, is the problem. "Everyone does not shoplift. Everyone does not forge false records. Everyone does not break the rules in business, the professions, or government, and everyone does not cheat in intercollegiate sport. The great majority of coaches, athletic directors, trustees, presidents, and alumni do want to abide by the rules."[19]

Cheating in interscholastic sports also takes place, but in forms different from cheating in college. Falsifying grades, lying about an athlete's age in order that the athlete may participate, or using an incorrect address in order that the athlete may play for a certain school are some of these forms. Coaches have been known to hold practices before season opening dates, among other various infractions of rules. All of these are usually justified by "It will help the team or the athlete." Perhaps the worst form of cheating in high school athletics is to teach illegal tactics in various sports. In this kind of cheating, the only crime is getting caught. Most rules of the game are for safety and fair play for either side. Such violations purposely taught give the athlete a sense of the coach's poor value judgment.

It is the coach's job to not partake in any form of cheating in sport. Cheaters have no degree of honesty and integrity. If you ever establish yourself as a coach who cheats, chances are you will always rely on such practices if needed. Most coaches do not, and those who do are soon known to their peers and usually at some time in their career will face the consequences for their actions. Again, cheating is a matter of ethics.

Violence in Sports

Violence in sports is prevalent in society today. Violence is assumed by some to be a reflection or outgrowth of society's values. Others contend it is due to the emphasis on winning at all costs in sports. Violence in sports can take many forms: player vs. player, player vs. spectator, player vs. official, coach vs. official, spectator vs. official, and spectator vs. spectator, to name several. Violence begins with the conduct of the coach, player, or spectator and then usually becomes a self-feeding mechanism to the other groups. The coach is the key person responsible for player behavior as well as personal behavior. In interscholastic sport, the coach may also be able to assert more influence on spectator behavior.

Certain sports are violent and aggressive in nature. As long as these sports are played within their rules and regulations, problems should not arise. As the coach, you have a responsibility to serve as a role model for socially acceptable behavior and to maintain the narrow line that separates aggressive play and violent behavior on the part of your athletes.

Recruitment of High School Athletes

The college recruitment process often can be an exciting time both for the player and the coach. As a new coach, your initial recruiting experiences may leave you flattered and in awe, but this usually wears off.

College recruitment of athletes is not an underhanded process—a misunderstanding held by many people. If colleges or universities want an athlete, they will most likely compete in any legal way possible. College coaches who recruit are not bad people. In most cases, they started out in the same position you are in and have to recruit successfully to keep their jobs.

Your first responsibility as a coach is to the athletes. Educate them about the recruiting process and never oversell their abilities. Try to keep their lives as regular as possible and them as levelheaded as possible. Never make decisions or answer for them. Parents may often provide you with more headaches than the recruiters do. Above all else, never deal or accept gifts from college coaches. Do not become indebted in any way. Check the reputation of specific colleges and coaches. A good point to check is the graduation ratio for athletes.

The quickest way to stop the use of illegal tactics or deals is to refuse to be part of them. In many recruiting illegalities, the high school coach is involved in some aspect. Do not compromise your honesty or integrity. There is honor and comradery among coaches, but not for those who violate the rules of fair play.

Drug Abuse in Sports

The use of drugs in athletics has reached an all-time high. Yet, most professional athletes are not involved in illegal drugs. Some athletes may take drugs to kill pain, to psych up, to come down, or to get "high." However, would the majority of our athletes at all levels and in all sports be able to be conditioned and perform at their peaks if addicted to drugs?

Certainly, professional athletes who use drugs will have some influence on the young athletes to whom they are role models. Keep in mind, however, that these same drugs are available probably in your own community and even in the hallways of your school.

Drug abuse is not just a problem in athletics; it is a problem in society. In your career, you will probably encounter athletes who use drugs in some form or another.

As a coach, you have no recourse but to condemn any use of drugs other than use prescribed by a physician and under the doctor's scrutiny. Educate your athletes to the harmful consequences of drugs, especially to the fact that dependency, whether physiological or psychological, can result with experimentation or social use of some categories of drugs. This should also include alcohol and cigarette smoking. Many circumstances involving the use of drugs in professional sport are not pertinent to interscholastic athletics, but unless the athlete is educated about such matters, he or she may tend to associate with the professional stereotype.

Drug abuse is a problem in all cultures and subcultures. It is a problem likely to continue in society for some time. However, athletics are not solely to blame for drug abuse. In many instances, sport itself offers its own "high" to many people, young and old alike, who do not need drugs as a crutch to cope with life.

Youth Sports

Youth sports programs present certain problems for the interscholastic coach. Practices in some programs contribute to improper skill learning and the development of poor attitudes that cause youngsters to shun athletics in general.

The major problem with youth sports is the adult influences upon them. Unqualified coaches with little knowledge of the game and even less knowledge pertaining to development and learning patterns in youth often teach the youngsters. Many such coaches model themselves after big-time college or professional coaches. Adults make the rules, implement the game, and put a lot of pressure on youngsters to win and be the best when what the youngsters want to do most is play. Further, the adults, mainly parents, often show poor sportsmanship at the games, harass the officials, and in general demonstrate poor values to their youngsters.

Competent coaches and as little negative parental influence upon the leagues as possible can help the situation. Also, letting all youngsters play regardless of skill level and the outcomes of the games will lessen the pressure to win. Proof that a youngster will not be a strong competitor in later sport without such pressure in youth sport does not exist.

The junior high coach and, ultimately, the high school coach will obtain the by-products of youth sports programs. In your best interests, you should look into such programs in your community and offer your expertise and influence to set up and monitor youth sports programs. You may be improving the caliber of your future teams, but, more important, you will help a lot of youngsters enjoy sport. A quote from the *AAHPER Youth Sports Guide* sums up the situation: "Each child has the right to play as a child . . . not as an adult."[20]

WHY COACHES LEAVE THE PROFESSION

This is a precarious subject, to say the least. Why coaches leave the profession may depend upon the person with whom one talks. Example: Coach Jones has just been dismissed from his position as basketball coach at Central High School. When asked to comment on the situation, the following people stated,

> Coach: I just did not win enough games. I didn't have the talent to compete in this league.
>
> Principal: Coach Jones did not perform well as a teacher. He spent too much time on his coaching duties and not enough on teaching.
>
> Athletic director: We need to reorganize our program, and Coach Jones did not fit into the plans.
>
> Booster club president: He didn't win us a championship.
>
> Parent: We had the material but didn't have the coaching.
>
> Downtown businessperson: He lacked good public relations. He wasn't "in" with the proper groups.

All of these comments may be correct to some extent, but you can be fairly sure that if Coach Jones had been a "winner," he still would have his job. Regardless of other reasons, the lack of winning is related in many cases to dismissal. School administrators are hesitant to admit that winning is a primary dismissal factor. In one study on this subject, only 6 percent of 100 school administrators stated failure to win as the primary cause for dismissal. In rebuttal, almost 100 percent of 141 coaches felt that failure to win was the leading cause for dismissal.[21]

Lackey surveyed school principals in regard to why coaches were dismissed and why the principals felt coaches left the profession by personal decision. In response to why coaches are dismissed, relationships with players and students ranked first, with personal coaching habits ranking second. Failure to win placed third. In regard to coaches choosing to leave their positions, career changes were a strong first, with personal factors second and pressure third. The principals were then asked to state two main reasons why any coach would leave the profession. The first was failure to properly motivate players and the second was unacceptable personal coaching habits. Failure to win as a reason was a distant eighth.[22] Templin and Washburn disagree with Lackey's findings and cite evidence relating to the win factor: "In one area of the state encompassing twenty-six high schools, fifty-four men have coached basketball in the last six years—an average of two coaches per school. One school has hired and fired four coaches in the last five years. The average tenure of a basketball coach at a school has been only three years, and the average lifetime tenure of a coach has been seven years. Coaches have little time to produce winners."[23]

Coaches often tend to remain quiet about the circumstances of their leaving a position because they want to be hired elsewhere and do not want reputations as gripers or complainers. This attitude is similar to the ones we try to instill in athletes: "When the going gets tough, the tough get going" *and* "A winner never quits and a quitter never wins." This stoic attitude makes pinpointing the actual reasons for coaches leaving the profession difficult. Generally, the following indicate some reasons why coaches leave the profession:

1. Coaches become discouraged or disenchanted with the athletes and students. They have a lack of identity and fail to relate well.
2. The amount of time involved in coaching is not worth the sacrifices some coaches must make. Family demands make coaching difficult.
3. Coaches are forced out due to pressure to win or cannot handle the criticism when they have poor seasons.
4. Coaches become disenchanted with the public relations aspect of the job; that is, dealing with parents, school administrators, booster clubs, community groups, and the media, for example.

Decision: Do You Want to Be a Coach?

The coaching profession is noted for rapid turnovers and for being a nomadic profession. However, this is not unlike other occupations in our society. But we tend to think that teachers and coaches are not part of the so-called "rat race" or "fast lane" in society. Undoubtedly, this is not true of the coaching profession. The life of a coach is, for the most part, in the fast lane, which adds to the excitement and challenge of being a coach and may also be why few persons actually retire as coaches.

Another aspect of dealing with pressures in the coaching profession is termed *coaching burnout*. You have all read or heard about athletes, teachers, doctors, and other professionals experiencing burnout. A basic definition of burnout is the inability to cope with job stress. Malone and Rotella describe coaching burnout as follows: "Coaches who experience burnout may begin to perceive their jobs as impossible. They may start to question their ability to lead and coach athletics effectively, and it may seem as though their athletes no longer appreciate their dedication. Feeling helpless and out of control, coaches nearing burnout find that they may tire easily, feel depressed, and may experience frequent health problems. They may become less patient with their athletes, assistant coaches, and supervisors. Eventually they become closeminded and inflexible. A negative attitude toward coaching soon develops."[24]

There are various ways to prevent burnout. A positive attitude and realistic view of coaching can help, as can a reduction in coaching loads or, in some cases, taking an entire year off from coaching. Having future career goals whether in coaching or not are also important. Be a person who plans for the future, concentrates on the present, and learns from the past. Do not let coaching totally consume your lifestyle. You must have some outside interests that will allow you to relax. Some coaches spend every hour of the day on coaching and, on a social basis, cannot converse or discuss anything outside of coaching or their sport. This leads to the development of a very narrow and boring person. Coaching burnout can be prevented if one monitors strengths and weaknesses in regard to the demands of the coaching profession. Coaching as a career is not for everyone, and excessive stress leading to burnout may be an indicator that one should look for an alternative career or concentrate on other areas in education.

A great deal of material has been discussed in this chapter in a rather condensed version. At this point, you may have questions about the coaching profession that you did not consider before. Some of them may be answered in future coaching courses or may have to wait until experience can answer them. Coaching has always been controversial; still, coaching may afford you a very exciting and rewarding lifestyle. Sport is definitely here to stay in our society, and competent coaches are the essence of sports participation.

Prepare yourself well in all aspects of physical education and coaching areas. If being a coach is what you want most and you are up to the challenge, then go to it. Welcome to the profession, coach.

SUMMARY

Coaching is a noble profession. Various reasons motivate people to enter the profession. A coach is a teacher, leader, and director of learning as well as an evaluator of performance. A coach should be goal oriented, but not to the point of possessing a win-at-all-costs philosophy. The many types of coaches that exist make stereotyping of coaches difficult. However, coaches differ mainly in coaching philosophy, organizational ability, interaction with athletes, motivation of athletes, and ambition. Coaches tend to be somewhat autocratic in nature. The coach also fills various roles that are separate from sport itself. Often these roles fill a void in the athlete's life.

Coaching positions range from junior high school to professional athletics. The responsibilities involved in coaching, even at different levels, have many similarities. A head coach needs to be a highly organized individual with the ability to motivate athletes and assistant coaches alike. Most assistant coaches strive to become head coaches. A major qualification of any assistant coach is loyalty to the head coach and athletic program. All coaches are not physical educators.

Preparation for coaching is complex. It involves development of a coaching philosophy, knowledge of the game, participation in sports, and coaching experiences. As a coach, you will be evaluated in many ways by athletes, parents, school, and community. Success in coaching is a result of multiple talents; however, in some situations, success is equated only with winning.

Ethics in coaching are very important for the development of values in youth. A coach's ethics depend upon moral values and judgment in various situations. Behavior is an excellent means of demonstrating ethics. Ethical standards cannot be part of a win-at-all-costs philosophy.

There are problems in athletics, many of which are violations of ethical behavior. However, many problems in sport are also society's problems and are not particular to sport. Cheating in sport, violence, motivation of athletes, youth sport programs, and drug abuse present some of the current problems facing the coaching profession.

The future of the coaching profession is strong. Athletics continue to flourish and coaches are in demand. The preparation of future coaches is a concern, because the coach of the future will need to be more informed about the profession as a whole in order to have fewer adjustments and problems. The old coach image will disappear and the new coach will emerge as a physiologist of athletics.

STUDY QUESTIONS

1. Discuss various ways in which coaches can earn and maintain respect from the athletes they coach.
2. Discuss the statement "winning is not everything; it is the only thing" versus "it is not whether you win or lose, but how you play the game."
3. Examine and discuss the reasons why you want to become a coach.
4. In groups of four, establish a professional code of ethics for the coaching profession. Compare your code with the codes of other groups in class.
5. Discuss various ways that a coach can become a citizen of the school and maintain good rapport with other teachers.
6. Prepare a list of the various problems in coaching and athletics. Determine which of these problems are violations of ethical behavior, a result of society, particular to a specific sport, or a result of the coach's behavior. Discuss your findings with your classmates and course instructor.

STUDENT ACTIVITIES

1. Obtain permission and attend a week's practice sessions at the junior or senior high school of your choice. Observe carefully all of the procedures and duties that the coach(es) carry out before, during, and after the sessions.
2. Interview a junior or senior high school coach in the sport of your choice. Before the actual interview, prepare a list of ten questions that you will ask that may help to enlighten you to the current situations in public school athletics. Cover various subjects through questions such as what qualities are sought in an assistant coach? What are the major issues? What problems should one be aware of? The written report for this interview should be subjective in nature rather than yes or no responses. If possible, and with permission, use a tape recorder for the session rather than taking notes. Also, some coaches may appreciate having the questions in advance so they may prepare for the interview.
3. There are various types of coaches as well as various coaching roles. Within your class, perform various role playing situations such as a head coach meeting with assistants; a coach trying to motivate an athlete; a coach disciplining athletes; or a coach meeting with parents who think their youngster should be playing more. The situations are endless. Role play the situations that are of most interest to class members.

NOTES

1. Ralph Sabock, "Loyalty and the Assistant Coach," *Journal of Physical Education and Recreation* 52 (1981): 3, 46.
2. Ibid.
3. William Harper, "The Philosopher in Us," *Journal of Physical Education, Recreation and Dance* 53 (1982): 1, 32–34.

4. George R. Colfer, "Coaching the Female Athlete in Track and Cross-Country," *Athletic Journal* 57 (1977): 5, 14, 88–92.

5. George R. Colfer, *Handbook for Coaching Cross-Country and Running Events* (West Nyack, NY: Parker Publishing Co., 1977), 187–89.

6. George B. Dintiman, "How to Run Faster," *Champion Athlete* (1977): 4–8.

7. George R. Colfer, "Improving Performance in Running Speed," *Texas Coach* 24 (1982): 6, 50–51.

8. C. J. Johnson, "A Status Survey of Coaches of Interscholastic Athletics in South Carolina," *South Carolina Journal of Health, Physical Education and Recreation* 12 (1980): 2, 18–19.

9. Arthur A. Esslinger, "Certification for High School Coaches," *Journal of Health, Physical Education and Recreation* 39 (1968): 8, 42–45.

10. L. Noble and C. B. Corbin, "Certification for Coaches," *Journal of Physical Education and Recreation* 49 (1978): 2, 69–73.

11. Ibid.

12. Ralph J. Sabock, "Professional Preparation for Coaching," *Journal of Physical Education, Recreation and Dance* 52 (1981): 8, 10.

13. Ibid.

14. Jack Scott, "Sport and the Radical Ethic," *Quest* (January 1973): 71–77.

15. "American Renewal," *Sports Illustrated* 54 (23 February 1981): 9, 62–80.

16. Suzi Olcott, "The Administrator's Role in Creating a Positive Direction for the Teacher/Coach," *Journal of Physical Education, Recreation and Dance* 52 (1981): 9, 21.

17. Harry Edwards, "Common Myths Hide Flaws in the Athletic System," *The Center Magazine* (January/February 1982): 17–21.

18. Ibid.

19. Harold Enarson, "Cheating, Not Professionalism, Is the Problem," *The Center Magazine* (January/February 1982): 13–15.

20. Jerry Thomas, ed., *Youth Sports Guide for Coaches and Parents* (Washington, DC: AAHPERD Publications, 1977).

21. Donald Lackey, "Why Do High School Coaches Quit?" *Journal of Physical Education and Recreation* 48 (1977): 4, 22–23.

22. Ibid.

23. T. J. Templin and J. Washburn, "Winning Isn't Everything . . . Unless You're the Coach," *Journal of Physical Education, Recreation and Dance* 52 (1981): 9, 16–17.

24. C. J. Malone and R. J. Rotella, "Preventing Coaching Burnout," *Journal of Physical Education, Recreation and Dance* 52 (1981): 9, 22.

RELATED READINGS

Cordas, Michael. "The Venerable and Vulnerable Coach." *Journal of Physical Education, Recreation and Dance* 53 (1982): 6, 41–42.

Eitzen, S. D., and G. H. Sage. *Sociology of American Sport.* Dubuque, IA: Wm. C. Brown Publishers, 1978.

Fuoss, Donald E., and J. Troppmann. *Effective Coaching: A Psychological Approach.* NY: John Wiley and Sons, 1981.

Gallon, Arthur J. *Coaching: Ideas and Ideals.* Boston: Houghton Mifflin, 1980.

Klafs, Carl, and M. Joan Lyon. *The Female Athlete.* St. Louis: C. V. Mosby Co., 1978.

Pate, Russell et al. *Scientific Foundations of Coaching.* Philadelphia, PA: Saunders College Publishing Co., 1984.

Pflug, Jerry. "Evaluating High School Coaches." *Journal of Physical Education and Recreation* 51 (1980): 4, 76–77.

Porter, David T. "Heart Rate of Basketball Coaches." *The Physician and Sports Medicine* 6 (1978): 10.

Robinson, R. J. *Reaching Your Athletic Potential.* Tigard, OR: Quality Publications, 1981.

Sabock, Ralph J. *The Coach.* Philadelphia, PA: Saunders Publishing Co., 1979.

Scott, Jack. *The Athletic Revolution.* NY: The Free Press, 1971.

American Alliance for Health, Physical Education, Recreation, and Dance. *Youth Sports Guide: For Coaches and Parents.* Reston, VA: AAHPERD Publications, 1979.

The Allied Fields

Chapter outline

Health Education
Dance
Recreation and Leisure
Outdoor Education
Intramurals
Safety Education
Athletic Training and Sports Medicine

Exhibit 13.1 The Role of the Athletic Trainer
Summary
Study Questions
Student Activities
Notes
Related Readings

Student objectives

As a result of the study of this chapter, the student should be able to

1. Identify the criteria that makes each field an ally to physical education.
2. Discuss the significance of the allied fields to physical education and the interrelationship with each field.
3. Give a brief description of the professional preparation and qualifications for each allied field.
4. Determine why health education and physical education are considered working partners, yet separate disciplines.
5. State the rationale for the recent separation of dance from physical education and discuss the reasons why dance educators want dance recognized as an allied field.
6. Identify the cooperative role of physical education with the allied field of recreation and leisure.
7. List the various disciplines that contribute to the preparation and administration of outdoor education programs.
8. Identify the importance of intramurals to school physical education programs at all levels.
9. State reasons why safety is an integral part of physical education and the responsibility of all physical educators.
10. Discuss the importance of the certification of athletic trainers.

Many fields, or disciplines, are in one way or another allied or related to physical education. The criteria for this relationship is more than casual. Many of these fields were part of physical education until a period in our history in which they became separate disciplines or they developed directly from the physical education field. The allied fields are more than just career options to physical education. They all have interrelationships with physical education that depend upon skills and knowledge acquired. An example in dance is that physical fitness is a necessary element. Health is concerned with the wellness of the individual, as is physical education. Safety is a built-in consideration in physical education, yet safety education is also part of many other disciplines. Athletic training and sports medicine have developed from the needs in sport and physical education as well as through advances in medical science and technology.

The significance of the allied fields to physical education is important: not only do they give our profession more credibility, they also give physical education the opportunity to broaden its own horizons to meet the ever-changing needs and demands from the allied fields. The interrelationship of physical education with each particular field serves to strengthen both. The relationship is mutual, although some controversy about this mutuality has been present at times. An example of such controversy is the recent separation which has been acknowledged by AAHPERD and many state associations, of dance from physical education.

The purpose of this chapter is to present the backgrounds of allied fields and the relationship of allied fields to physical education to show the role that physical education plays within particular fields. This chapter will look at the effects each field has upon the others and will examine the professional preparation and qualifications for work in the allied fields.

The fields selected for review are health education, dance, recreation and leisure, outdoor education, intramurals, safety education, and athletic training and sports medicine. These fields were chosen because of their close affiliation with our profession and because of the insight they may provide for you, the physical education major.

HEALTH EDUCATION

Health education began as an integral part of the physical education program. Yet, since its beginning, health has been evolving into a separate discipline. In early physical education programs, health was understood to mean that through physical activity, one would achieve health. The concept of **total health** was a primary goal of the physical educator.

In the late 1950s, health began to emerge as a major field of study on the college campus. In some schools, it was a partner to physical education; in others, it was still part of the physical education program. As health emerged as a major field of study, the scope of professional preparation grew also. The major contributing factor to the identification and expansion of health as a field of study has been the enormous growth of knowledge in the areas of health science. Now, a student of health education studies in such areas as community health, public health, sex education, drug education, nutrition, and consumer health, among others. Also, the opportunity for specialization is available in many areas of health education.

The public school health education curriculum has also undergone change. No longer is the study limited to first aid, personal hygiene, and disease prevention. Public school students are given the benefit of the advancements in health sciences, which will help the students live more healthy lives and will assist them in making decisions in various content areas such as nutrition, sexuality, substance use, consumer health practices, emergency medical care, and others. Emphasis is not only on the physical health of the individual, but on emotional and mental aspects as well. The goal of the health educator is to impart knowledge as well as effect behavioral changes and attitudes to enhance the individual's decision making and to guide that individual to complete well-being.

Most colleges and universities today practice the separation of health and physical education within professional preparation. The courses of study required for certification are equal for each area. In most cases, a combined degree with the lesser emphasis on health does not exist. One does not have to be a physical educator to be a health educator, and vice-versa, although each should have some basic knowledge and skills from the other in order to understand that discipline more clearly.

The major relationship of physical education and health education is based on their combined beginnings, a sharing of many goals, and the mutual purpose of developing a healthy individual. Some attempts may be made to discard or minimize health's affiliation with physical education; however, both disciplines would probably benefit as working partners. This may be more practical as well as philosophic. Due to economic and financial restraints in the public schools as well as preconceived ideas held by some administrators and the public, there will likely be persons who will fill combined roles as physical educator, health educator, and coach. However, such an individual will probably be separately certified in both areas and will recognize the importance of each, and yet will be able to synthesize the subject matter of each to benefit the student in both areas. As an example, nutrition learned in health could be applied to physical fitness as part of physical education. The opportunities for the interrelationship of both disciplines are numerous.

Graduate programs at both the master's and doctoral levels exist in health education. Various leadership roles within health, many of which may lie outside of the public schools, are also numerous. Health education degrees normally prepare the graduate for positions in public and community health, health services, and education. A practical consideration for graduate students today is to explore the private sector as well as the public sector. An example is a specialist in nutrition who performs services and counseling for private individuals or groups. In education, one can look to becoming a college instructor or administrator in health or, in the public school domain, to becoming a school health coordinator for a school system or district. This type of position includes the development of the overall school health program for the school or district.

Health education, as it has developed over the years, appears to be aware of its roots in physical education. Health education and physical education are still very close and have common goals and interests. Physical education has helped health education to develop and has nurtured many of its values. However, health education has grown and developed its own identity, with its own goals to achieve. As this development has taken place, so have controversies or, "growing pains." There is some indecision on the goals of health education; there is disagreement as to professional preparation and training; there is concern about the involvement and possible takeover of health by the medical professions; and there are varying views on health being a separate and unique discipline. Finally, there is concern about the limited impact health education has shown in effecting behavioral change, especially in the public schools. Some people feel that a reunification of health with physical education should take place. This is not likely to happen. However, for the benefit of both, the working partnership should be sustained.

DANCE

In 1980, dance was added to the name of the American Alliance for Health, Physical Education, and Recreation, creating AAHPERD. **Dance** is now recognized as a separate discipline and is represented by the National Dance Association. Dance educators and dance professionals have been striving for this recognition for many years. Some state associations have followed suit, but not without controversy. The first time the motion for dance to be added to the Texas association was introduced, it was voted down. South Carolina, in 1979, brought the motion to their state convention, but due to a technicality it did not come to a vote. This prompted two articles in their state journal. Stina Merril states that adding the *D* to HPER gives an equal status to the artistic and scientific sides of physical education.[1] Keith Hamilton counters, "Dance, why not volleyball?" referring to the fact that physical education has several artistic sides, such as gymnastics or volleyball, and that the inclusion of an activity area itself will prompt equal billing from other activity areas.[2] Regardless of one's feeling toward this controversy, dance is, undeniably, an allied field to physical education.

Dance has existed in all cultures throughout history. Dance is an expression of work, play, war, religion, philosophy, and art. Dance development in the United States has evolved from our cultural heritage and definitely has been influenced by our history. **Dance as education** can be attributed to the efforts, which began in the early 1900s, of Margaret H'Doubler of the University of Wisconsin.[3] She is acknowledged as the country's first true dance educator. As physical education was introduced and developed in our schools, dance became part of many curricula.

Dance consists of many aspects in addition to the public school curriculum. Dance is an art form, which is demonstrated by dance in the theater, ballet, and other forms of creative dance. Dance is therapy and self-expression. Dance is recreation, such as folk and square dance, which are also used to transmit our culture. Dance is fitness, as demonstrated by aerobic dance and jazzercise, and is also part of sport. Dance is entertainment: it is a spectator activity. Dancers themselves are athletes. A highly skilled dancer needs the same skills and fitness levels of athletes in other sports.

The requirements for a dance educator or instructor vary in accordance to the type of dance taught. Most physical educators can teach some forms of dance, such as folk or square dance, from professional preparation alone. However, the average physical educator could probably *not* teach skills in ballet or other art forms of dance without advanced training and participation. Since dance is a broad discipline with several forms, a major or dance specialization is essential to acquire skills and be qualified to teach a variety of dance activities. This also leads to the subject of dance certification for purposes of teaching. As of 1981, only eight states offer dance certification. However, several colleges and universities currently offer a major course of study in dance. Dance degrees vary as to whether they are teaching or nonteaching degrees. Dance is undergoing constant change due to its recognition as an allied field and the growing popularity of dance programs. Standards and recommendations regarding professional preparation and certification for dance should most appropriately be developed by the National Dance Association through the American Alliance and the state associations.

Leadership roles in dance are many, including dance educators, dance instructors, choreographers for dance companies, choreographers for dance teams such as the Dallas Cowboy Cheerleaders, certified aerobics and jazzercise instructors, square dance callers, and directors of dance studios and the professional theater (see fig. 13.1). Opportunities in professional dance are very competitive and require many years of training and experience. One can compare professional dance to professional athletics insofar as percentages of those who make it to the pros are concerned. Qualifications for these various leadership positions differ. However, in any aspect of professional dance or commercial studios, the dance professional usually is an experienced, skilled performer.

What is the role of dance in sport? Obviously, dance is present in the performance of cheerleaders, pep squads, drill or dance teams, and even sometimes in the band. However, as previously stated, dancers are athletes. The attributes of dancers are highly desired traits for other athletes as well. Flexibility, agility, cardiovascular fitness, and muscular endurance are just some of the commonalities. Dance can improve athletic skill. Football coaches such as Knute Rockne and Woody Hayes used dance as part of their training procedures for football.[4]

Is the role of dance in physical education clearly defined? As a separate discipline allied to physical education, dance will emerge in a different perspective. Physical education has served as a proving ground for dance, yet in some ways, it may have also hindered dance's progress. Physical education and dance need each other and should continue to be supportive of each other. Dance educators and sport educators strive for the same goals and can synthesize their skills and knowledge to the benefit of each other. Dance will continue to be the essential activity and artistic form of movement it has always been. However, with new dance educators, men and women attentive to the place of dance in the total education process, the diversity of dance will continue to flourish.

RECREATION AND LEISURE

Recreation and leisure services represent a major economic unit in the United States. Statistics show that Americans spent 160 billion dollars on recreation and leisure in 1977, and by 1985, the total climbed to about 300 billion dollars.[5] This expenditure is a clear indication of how avidly Americans pursue "the good life" beyond the limits of work and home.

Physical education and recreation and leisure are separate entities, or disciplines, and the separation is growing as recreation continues to grow. This separation is not detrimental to physical education, since the role of physical education also will expand.

Figure 13.1 Dance educators assume one of the varied leadership roles that dance encompasses.

The nature and scope of physical education

Recreational or leisure time may be the final test of our degree of civilization. Leisure time provides us with the means for either improving the quality of our lives or for destroying ourselves. During the past twenty years, Americans have been besieged by a phenomena of recreation and leisure pursuits. Also, we have had the available time to give in pursuit of leisure activities.

Leisure time is often depicted by advertisements as people enjoying themselves in various tasks. Leisure time may be spent in physical activity, outdoor recreation, art, music, science, and even through the mass media. People who use leisure time for positive experiences should find reward and benefit from their chosen activities. On the other hand, if leisure time is misused, it can contribute to stress, boredom, negative escapes such as drugs and alcohol, and deviant behavior. The difference between the use and misuse of leisure time is skills and knowledge acquired and the opportunities afforded to each individual. This is the task for recreation and leisure: to offer diverse opportunities for all individuals.

The role of physical education is to provide the skills and knowledge that can be used for beneficial leisure-time activity. Obviously, physical education cannot be responsible for all recreational pursuits, but regarding sports, fitness activities, dance, outdoor education, and play activities, physical educators are the providers of skills and knowledge.

Recreation has been described as an activity or experience chosen voluntarily and carried on within one's leisure time for the satisfaction it provides or for values and benefits the participant or society experiences. Recreation should be a balance of work and play. Recreation was once thought of only as means to restore an individual for more work—the purpose of vacations. Today, with more leisure time available, recreation contributes to the total individual throughout the year.

The objectives of physical education and recreation are basically the same. Physical education assists recreation in attaining objectives by the teaching of skills and knowledge involving physical activity. This is especially true pertaining to teaching a variety of lifetime sports so that individuals may have choices.

Recreation, like physical education, is a profession. The recreation field is so diversified that no single standard or mechanism will serve for those who seek a career. Traditionally, many recreation programs were included in the physical education curriculum. However, today the diversity precludes this. Various degrees are offered in recreation. Many colleges and universities have departments of parks and recreation and offer courses of study that are necessary for management positions. A look at career options within recreation makes this point very clear.

Leadership roles are very prominent in recreation. Undergraduate, master's, and doctoral degrees are available in recreation and leisure studies. For the present, students in physical education may need to supplement their education to fit the needs of the various career options in recreation and leisure. Some of these options are

Activity director	Aquatics specialist
Activity outfitter	Armed Forces recreation administrator
Administrator	Camp counselor
Animal handler	Campground attendant

Camping director	Naturalist
Carnival game operator	Outdoor and waterway guide
Church recreation director	Outdoor recreation manager
Circus performer	Park ranger
Community center director	Park superintendent
Community development specialist	Playground leader
Community education worker	Prison recreation specialist
Concert promoter	Professor
Concessionaire	Recreation aide
Condominium social director	Recreation facility manager
Cruise ship activity director	Recreation therapist
Dance instructor	Resort manager
Environmental interpreter	Senior citizen programmer
Fitness specialist	Sightseeing guide
Forester	Ski instructor
Golf pro	Stadium manager
Program planner for the handicapped	Tennis pro
High-risk recreation facilitator	Tour guide
Hotel manager	Theme park manager
Industrial recreation specialist	Travel agency consultant
Interpretive naturalist	Travel planner
Leisure counselor	Volunteer agency supervisor
Leisure education specialist	Youth agency recreator
Municipal recreator	Youth director
Museum guide	Youth sports coach

Recreation has brought a rise to cultural programs. Community, state, and national governments are committed to developing and improving many of our natural resources and provide the funding and support for many public programs. Without such support, many of our leisure-time selections would no longer be available. This is especially true on the community level. However, recreation and leisure have a private sector. The private sector is that which is usually only afforded by the affluent. Obviously, the choice of leisure-time pursuits depends, in many cases, upon the amount of money that can be spent for equipment, travel, facilities, and the like. There also tends to be a sociological factor regarding leisure-time pursuits. Different economic classes tend to have similar pursuits based upon occupation and wealth. In various communities where a single occupation is predominant, there are also similar recreational pursuits. Participants in sports and physical activities are more likely to be younger, more highly educated, and more affluent than nonparticipants.[6] The difference that emerges between the more and less affluent and between the more and less educated is not in how much free time they have, but in what activities they take part.[7]

One problem in the area of leisure arises for the physical educator. Since all recreation and leisure time is not spent in physical activities, physical educators must be aware of physiological needs and strive to educate the public to use some of their leisure time for health and fitness. Outdoor sports and outdoor recreation activities consume less than four percent of our leisure time.[8] In comparison, television has emerged as a primary recreational pursuit, consuming about one-third of our leisure time, and has replaced other recreational pursuits. With the new wave of computers and computer-type video games, we in physical education must be aware that physical activity may be losing the overall battle for leisure time. Our task is imminent. We must work with recreation and leisure studies to provide the skills and knowledge to turn people to more active leisure pursuits.

Recreation has followed the path of health education in its relationship to physical education, except for the fact that recreation and leisure time existed before physical education. Early programs placed recreation as part of physical education. However, this has changed in the face of recreation's increased diversification. The current status of recreation leads to some questions pertaining to survival of both recreation and physical education and their cooperative efforts. Is physical education providing the school-age child the knowledge and skills needed to use leisure time effectively? Is recreation providing the necessary leisure opportunities to meet the public need? Will physical education and recreation survive as separate entities, or is more cooperation needed to meet society's demands? The answers are not easy, but it appears that a definite cooperative effort would be beneficial to cope with society's needs. In physical education, a person is educated about the physical. Recreation provides the opportunity to develop skills during leisure time. This interrelationship calls for more unity in program goals and in the development of programs in conjunction with those goals. In other words, both disciplines must constantly be aware of what the other is doing and strive to assist the other in every way possible. Professionals in both areas must broaden their perspectives about the other discipline and assist each other in coping with change rather than working independently.

OUTDOOR EDUCATION

A basic explanation of **outdoor education** is education in the out-of-doors, education about the out-of-doors, and education for the out-of-doors (see fig. 13.2). Outdoor education is certainly an area that can be termed as multidisciplinary. Physical education lays claim to outdoor education, but some would dispute this point due to the fact that many professional preparation programs do not provide sufficient courses of study for the subject. One study pertaining to Texas colleges shows that only thirty-nine percent of colleges and universities (N = 89) taught at least one outdoor education course in their professional programs. Only four universities teach a graduate course or summer workshop in outdoor education, as reported in the same study.[9] Statistics such as these lead one to believe that other disciplines must contribute to the preparation and administration of outdoor education programs. Some of these disciplines are recreation, leisure studies, forestry, environmental studies, biology, and ecology, to name a few.

Some experts contend that outdoor education should not be considered as a separate discipline or allied field to physical education, stating that outdoor education is included as a part of many national and state associations and is given exposure by writings in the American Alliance journal (*JOPERD*). Others contend that it should be separate because the body of knowledge in the subject is often supplied by other disciplines. In the early stages of outdoor education, two private educational organizations, Outward Bound and the National Outdoor Leadership School (NOLS), provided the necessary qualifications for leadership to be an outdoor educator. In fact, private clubs such as the Sierra Club and the Mountaineers, as well as community organizations such as the YMCA, scouting, and recreation programs, have trained many leaders in the skills and knowledge necessary. At the college and university levels, many of the outdoor leadership programs are contained in such departments as recreation, leisure studies, or parks and recreation. This leads one to question the total role of physical education in training outdoor educators. Obviously, many physical educators receive training and would qualify to teach and lead outdoor education activities. However, many other physical educators would not qualify. Since the approach to outdoor leadership training is at this time multidisciplinary, the inclusion of outdoor education as an allied field seems only reasonable. Outdoor education, at its broadest scope, requires advanced training or training in addition to that offered by most physical education programs.

The skills for outdoor education are numerous. Backpacking, hiking, overnight camping, fishing, hunting, shooting and gun safety, aquatic activities, rappelling, rock climbing, mountaineering, archery, bicycling, outdoor cooking, orienteering, spelunking, adventure activities, and wilderness survival skills are some of the titles for various activity courses. Theory courses that might be included in professional preparation may have titles such as camp counseling, outdoor education, camp leadership, or outdoor recreation. Such courses usually contain skills and knowledge, since most aspects of outdoor education are best taught by doing.

Leadership roles in outdoor education are varied. The opportunities for teaching in public school and at the college level are numerous. Agency and private positions with camps are also plentiful. For the physical educator who wants to teach and coach in other areas as well, outdoor education offers an excellent summer opportunity. Such schools as Outward Bound also employ physical educators who are qualified and have previously completed their programs.

The growth of outdoor education can be attributed to many reasons. People want to get back to nature, explore the environment, and, generally, do things for themselves. A lot of personal satisfaction can be found in learning to cope with the environment. Perhaps the need is created by advanced technology, our push-button society, and urban styles of living. Also, stress is a major factor in society. "Getting away from it all" into the environment has social-psychological payoffs. Leaving the television and the automobile behind often provides an emotional release for distress. Risk and adventure activities are also becoming more popular in our society. Meeting such challenges can provide physical and mental satisfaction for the participant. However, in the school situation, teaching and participating in high-risk or adventure activities must be approached with caution as to the liability and legal responsibilities involved for the teacher and the school.

The relationship of outdoor education to physical education is difficult to define because this relationship is constantly changing with the growth of professional programs and courses. We in physical education must be involved and continue to strive to broaden outdoor education experiences in professional preparation. This should not diminish the purpose and roles of such programs as Outward Bound and NOLS, but should strengthen their ties with physical education. Other disciplines will still provide knowledge and leadership to integrate with physical education. Outdoor education activities will continue to grow in popularity. Whether outdoor education is part of physical education or an allied field is less important than whether we can synthesize all of the disciplines and provide the leadership to meet the present and future needs and challenges of outdoor education.

INTRAMURALS

Intramurals were selected to be included as an allied field because they contain the elements of physical education and the concept of recreation. **Intramurals** utilize the skills and knowledge from physical education in a recreational setting. This is not to say that intramurals are not competitive, nor is it to say they are not sport. The word *intramural* means "within the walls." Other words often associated with intramurals are sports and activities. These words are used to categorize the type of activity taking place.

Intramural sports actually were a beginning to our athletics of today. Colleges formed clubs or teams within their schools and competed against each other. As the concept grew, student control of the teams gradually was taken away; thus the beginning of intercollegiate sports. Intramurals returned as a "sports for all" concept and has expanded today to phenomenal size on many college campuses. Intramurals are included as part of the physical education, recreation, or athletic programs at most colleges, universities, high schools, and junior high schools.

Most intramural personnel have preparation in physical education or recreation. The college or university program normally has faculty positions to organize and administrate the intramural program. High school and junior high school programs are normally supervised by physical education teachers or athletic coaches. Advanced degrees in physical education or recreation usually are required for college and university leadership positions. The **intramural director** must be a very organized individual and have a good working relationship with the student body to effectively administrate the program. Student input is also important, and student control and responsibility are highly desired in most intramural programs.

The program of activities for an intramural program at any level is wide open. Some factors, such as weather, facilities, and equipment, may influence the selection of activities, but, mostly, a program's activities should meet student needs and interests. Some activities are purely recreational while others may be very competitive (see fig. 13.3). Participation, not winning or losing, is the key factor. The National Intramural Sports Council (NISC) has publications on activities and recommendations for those interested in professional preparation with intramurals in mind. The NISC is a substructure of NASPE in the American Alliance for Health, Physical Education, Recreation, and Dance.

Intramurals were once regarded as a poor relative of physical education. Such situations are usually caused by poorly administrated programs, those run by athletic coaches whose primary concerns are their varsity teams, lack of funding, overworked physical education teachers, or a lack of student interest and participation. Intramurals are now recognized as being very important to the skill participation needs of the majority of students.

The innovation and diversity of current intramural programs is phenomenal. The intramural concept is also now becoming more prevalent in the elementary school. This is especially noteworthy since attitudes developed at an early age are likely to be maintained in later life. Coeducational activities of all types are very prominent on the intramural scene. Coeducational intramurals are more conducive than other sports activities to developing social appreciation and understanding of the opposite sex, since intramural participation is chosen by the participant.

Sports clubs are a part of intramurals that are rapidly developing across the nation. A sports club is a collection of students who want to participate in a particular sport that is usually not offered on an extramural basis. Sport clubs are aimed at filling the void between varsity athletics and intramurals.

As previously stated, intramurals are not always run by the physical education department. Who should run the intramural program is a topic of controversy. Various institutions, including public schools, have differing philosophies on this matter. The

best situation would be to have a separate intramural department. However, in many cases, this is not feasible. Student services would be another option, along with physical education, recreation, or athletic departments. Possibly, who runs the program does not matter as long as the program is allowed to function properly in the best interests of the students.

The relationship of intramurals to physical education is twofold. First, the skills and knowledge learned in the physical education classroom need a practice field. Intramurals provide that for the athletically below-average to above-average student. Opportunities for participation are essential. The socialization factor (most people interact in physical activity better in social groups) is another plus for the intramural program. Secondly, intramurals have the same goals and values as physical education. Positive experiences through intramurals from elementary to college can be a laboratory of life experiences and social values such as competition, winning and losing, and teamwork among individuals. If varsity sports participation is educational and teaches values, then intramurals should serve the same purpose with a more equitable participation balance and a broader distribution of activities for all.

SAFETY EDUCATION

Safety education is a unique discipline. It is a multidisciplinary profession drawing from several different areas. The person who works in safety education may have backgrounds in education, engineering, psychology, medicine, and physics, among others.

Safety is often referred to as accident prevention. This is a necessary part of sport, education, business, corporations, and public and private work. Safety on our roads and highways is an ultimate goal in our society, but safety is also stressed in other areas of life, whether at work, home, or play.

The type of training to be a **safety professional** varies depending on the job requirements. This also presents some problems in the professional preparation of those who choose the profession. For example, a safety professional for a factory environment would have to know the type of work performed there before safety procedures could be instituted.

Safety education in physical education is more precise. Safety is an integral part of physical education and sport. It is an ally. We are safety-conscious all of the time in the implementation of our programs in swimming, wrestling, or gymnastics, among many others. We use lifeguards or the "buddy" system in the water, equalize the weight and skill of competitors on the mat, and teach spotting techniques on the apparatus. Even sports or activities with less risk are given safety priority. The relationship of safety education to physical education is indeed a strong one.

Most physical education professional preparation programs offer some course or courses in safety education. These usually deal with first aid, emergency care, and cardiopulmonary resuscitation (CPR). To date, very few programs actually stress safety on the job as to specific situations. Various activity-based courses such as gymnastics and aquatics, due to their high risk, do stress safety, but others do not. Locker room and shower safety, and safety practices used in handling large numbers of people, equipment, and facility are usually not taught. These practices must be acquired by the physical educator usually on an on-the-job basis.

How, then, does the physical educator become a safety educator? First, anyone in our profession must acquire what is termed *risk acceptance*.[10] We must understand that all sport and physical activity initiate some risk. Those of us who are exposed constantly to risk acceptance learn to counter with safety techniques. We then teach others these techniques through participation. Bikers ride with traffic; runners run against traffic. Why? Because they are the safest ways. When one becomes a physical educator, safety is an ever-present concern.

As physical educators, we are responsible for the health, safety, and well-being of those we teach and coach. Accidents and injuries will always occur, but should not happen because of negligence or lack of prudent behavior. If negligence is the cause of an accident, the physical educator can be held liable. Safety education is more than just physically avoiding injury; it is a state of mind toward being safe while performing risk-taking activities that the coach or teacher tries to develop. Students and athletes who adopt this philosophy are less likely to become involved in accidents or injuries.

The school environment is relatively safe. Possibly, sport and physical education produce the greatest risks. Therefore, many school systems appoint a physical educator as the school's safety professional. The safety professional for any school or other facility is responsible for policies, procedures, and accident reporting. A safety committee should also be formed and a safety handbook written.

The physical educator has several concerns for safety. These are supervision of an activity, instruction of an activity, conditioning of participants, and watchfulness for defective or inadequate equipment and unsafe facilities. Most accidents result from carelessness in one of these areas. The physical educator is responsible to identify hazards, reduce or remove hazards, compensate for hazards, and avoid new hazards. Above all, he or she must always act in a prudent manner and not be negligent in the performance of duties.

Another way in which the physical educator can improve safety is through reading professional journals and attending professional meetings. Safety issues are often covered at various state and national conventions. The American School and Community Safety Association (ASCSA) is an individual-membership organization representing the interests of safety educators and other school and community professionals working in programs where safety and accident prevention are critical.

Safety education is a profession within a profession in physical education. In some college and university programs, a person can major in safety education, which can lead to various opportunities in the field of safety. However, every physical educator to some degree also majors in safety education. This responsibility in our profession cannot be taken lightly because it can lead to litigation. In actuality, safe environments enhance and create exciting developmental learning experiences in physical education and sport; however, the possibilities of accidents and injuries threaten the existence of some programs. The relationship of physical education to safety education is in our past, present, and future. It is a unity that we in physical education are greatly dependent upon for the betterment of our programs.

ATHLETIC TRAINING AND SPORTS MEDICINE

Athletic training and sports medicine have seen phenomenal growth in the United States. The main reasons for this growth are the increased participation in physical activity by all segments of the population and the adverse reaction to physicians who advocate "go home and rest" as a cure for sports-related injuries. More attention has been given to sports-related injuries, which has led to a higher level of sophistication on the part of sports medicine practitioners.[11]

Athletic training and sports medicine are separate disciplines, yet are closely allied to physical education. No longer does the coach or physical educator possess adequate skills or knowledge to render judgment on the severity of an injury or to administer appropriate treatment. Athletic training is a specialty area that can be incorporated into the physical education degree, but having a single course in such training does not qualify a person as a trainer.

The National Athletic Trainers Association (NATA) established procedures for prospective athletic trainers to receive certification. The NATA is recognized nationally as the governing body for standards in the athletic training field. Candidates who are seeking to become certified athletic trainers should complete requirements for a valid teaching certificate in another area as well as athletic training. In addition, minimal standards required by the NATA include 1,800 clock hours of laboratory experience. Upon completion of the baccalaureate degree, the student is required to pass an examination given by the Professional Examination Service to become a certified athletic trainer. Graduates of NATA programs are well-qualified professionals. Certification by the NATA currently represents the only national standard available for

exhibit 13.1

The role of the athletic trainer

Over the last four decades the field of athletic training has changed dramatically. Forty years ago a training room would probably have a treatment table, a heat lamp, a jar of hot liniment, and a foot powder bench. Today, we find a room or rooms with tables for taping, tables for treatment, exercise benches, and sophisticated ice, heat, and pressure modalities along with storage cabinets full of just about any type of adhesive tape, elastic braces, and hundreds of other items that make life easier and more pleasant for both the athlete and the trainer. The main thing that hasn't changed over the years is the overall dedication of the person or persons that make up the athletic training staff. The educational level and academic background of the athletic trainer has changed, but they still have the necessary time in their long day for an extra few minutes for that last athlete. Much more emphasis is placed on pre-injury and post-season conditioning today, but the trainer is still always concerned for the athletes. We have gained a lot in knowledge and procedures, but we still have the same dedicated people performing the functions and duties as we did four decades ago. It is with this type of hard work and dedication by the trainer that our athletes of today, as were those of years past, able to perform to their highest capabilities.

Source: Bernie Lareau, Head Athletic Trainer, University of Texas at San Antonio. Former Head Athletic Trainer for the San Antonio Spurs (NBA), Indiana Pacers (NBA), and Chicago Bears (NFL).

evaluating the competency of athletic trainers. Athletic training has the support of higher education, also. By 1970, four collegiate programs were functioning in compliance with the curricular standards required for NATA certification. Today, over fifty approved programs are functioning under these guidelines [12] In addition, several states have adopted a licensing procedure for those who intend to practice athletic training in those states.

While the athletic trainer is part of sports medicine and the sports health care delivery system, several other areas exist in sports medicine that are not as closely related to the physical education degree. All types of physicians would be theoretically qualified. However, physicians considered most qualified are those who limit their practices to sports-related injuries. Many orthopedic specialists follow this route. Also considered are physical therapists, sports podiatrists, nurses, and other allied health professionals. The athletic trainer in the public school situation has the task of bridging the gap between the athletic program and the medical community. A trainer serves to assist both ends of the spectrum.

The emergence of athletic training and sports medicine has its effects upon physical education. The only negative consequence is that physical educators who want to be athletic trainers will have to add courses and laboratory time to their undergraduate preparation. Positive consequences are that coaches will be free to attend to coaching

Figure 13.4 The athletic trainer is responsible for seeing that athletes are ready to participate in competition.

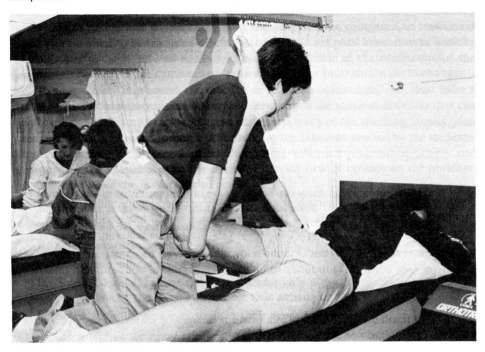

duties and pursue their areas of expertise without medical responsibilities that they may not be trained to handle. Most coaches would favor this system. Studies show that injury rates decrease progressively in years when a qualified athletic trainer is added to the staff. Rehabilitation time is also lessened for those who suffer athletic injuries. Another point to be considered is the liability factor: the chances for a physical educator to be sued for negligence will lessen with a certified athletic trainer handling medical and health care.

The relationship of athletic training to physical education is one of mutual interests. One is dependent to some degree upon the other. Injuries will always occur in physical activity since such activity always involves some risk. The role of physical education is to provide the knowledge, skills, coaching, and conditioning for participation in physical activity. Athletic training takes into consideration prevention, conditioning, (see fig. 13.4), diagnosis, evaluation, treatment, and rehabilitation for injury. We need athletic training and sports medicine to keep physical activity as free from injury as possible, and when injury does occur, to ensure the fastest recovery time possible.

A final point to consider is the significance of the **sport scientist** in sports medicine. Many people believe that sport scientists play an important role in the development of elite athletes in such countries as the Soviet Union and East Germany. To meet this challenge, The Athletic Congress (TAC) and other governing bodies have organized sports medicine committees to give direction to the selection, evaluation, and training of American athletes. Work on this project is being done in the following areas: medical evaluation for athletic potential; biomechanical analysis of performance; nutrition appraisal and guidance; and psychological testing and profiling and the acquisition of data to develop standards for the identification and selection of athletes having elite potential. Sport scientists also are working with training methods, adaptability to stress, and other research about the human mechanism.[13] This relatively new field of endeavor, under the title of sports medicine, will inevitably provide new and exciting opportunities for the physical education professional interested in this discipline.

SUMMARY

Allied fields are an important part of the physical education profession. Two major points are basically established from the content of this chapter. The first is that physical education needs the allied fields to more successfully carry out the goals and objectives for which it stands and, second, that the allied fields need physical education to fulfill various roles and support their endeavors. In many cases, one could not exist without the other. As an example, athletic training or sports medicine would be unnecessary without sport and physical education. The allied fields also give physical education the opportunity to broaden its scientific and academic resources. Finally, there is a mutual benefit that should be sustained: that is, as any allied field broadens its scope, so should physical education, and vice-versa. Despite a trend in our earlier history in physical education to be self-contained, physical education professionals today fully realize that we must reach out and attach ourselves to other disciplines and assist in their development as well as support our own goals.

The allied fields presented in this chapter appear to be the ones most closely related to physical education. Some have been part of physical education for many years, while others have developed from the skills and knowledge acquired from physical education.

Health education is a working partner with physical education to promote the goals of wellness and health in the individual. Dance, the newest of the allied fields, is an important part of sport and fitness. Physical education and dance will continue to be supportive of each other. Recreation and leisure are not only big business, but are also a means of improving individual lifestyles. Physical education provides the skills and knowledge, while recreation provides the opportunities for development. A cooperative effort on the part of both disciplines is essential to meet society's needs. The relationship of outdoor education, a multidisciplinary field, to physical education is more difficult to define. Some contend that outdoor education should be part of physical education only, yet other disciplines provide knowledge and leadership. Perhaps as professional preparation in outdoor education increases, the involvement of both disciplines will be easier to interrelate. Intramurals contain the elements of physical education and recreation and can function under either category. For students of all ability levels, intramurals provide a practice field or proving ground for the knowledge and skills learned in physical education. Safety education is an integral part of physical education, yet is a multidisciplinary field itself. A profession within our profession, safety in sport and physical education is essential to our existence. Athletic training and sports medicine have experienced phenomenal growth. Their relationship to physical education is one of mutual interest and cooperative effort. One would not exist without the other.

The purpose of this chapter is to make the prospective physical educator aware of the allied fields and to help him or her understand physical education's role in and relationship to these particular fields. Physical education is also a multidisciplinary field and one that lends itself very well to a broad range of interrelationships.

STUDY QUESTIONS

1. Should physical education try to maintain total control of the allied fields or support them as separate disciplines? Debate the pros and cons of this issue and discuss which side of the issue is in the best interests of the goals and objectives of physical education.

2. Should health and physical education be separate entitites? State why or why not and reference your response by citing sources such as professional journals and textbooks you researched.

3. Why should dance, among all of the various activity categories in physical education, be selected as a separate discipline? Reference your response.

4. How can physical education prepare and ensure that sufficient leisure time and recreational activities will be spent for the benefit of health and physical fitness? Reference your response.

5. Should outdoor education be part of physical education or be a multidisciplinary field? Reference your reponse.

6. Who is best qualified to administrate the intramural program at the elementary school, middle school, high school, and college or university levels? Reference your response.

STUDENT ACTIVITIES

1. For any allied field, list the possible career opportunities and see what additional training or requirements the professional physical educator would need to qualify for employment in that field. For any allied field, find a college or university professional preparation program in that field and report on its content.

2. Some controversy always exists regarding the separation of some allied fields from physical education. Select one allied field and find at least two references that will debate each side of the issue. Report your findings orally or in written form.

3. Invite a guest speaker in any of the allied fields to discuss his or her discipline with your class.

4. Plan a field trip or visitation in any allied field and report on how the skills and knowledge in physical education contribute or relate to that field.

NOTES

1. Stina Merril, "Adding the 'D' to Our Name," *South Carolina Journal of Physical Education and Recreation* 12 (1980): 2, 5.

2. Keith Hamilton, "Dance—Why Not Volleyball?" *South Carolina Journal of Physical Education and Recreation* 12 (1980): 2, 6.

3. Elizabeth Hayes et al., "History of Dance in the Alliance," *Journal of Physical Education and Recreation* 51 (1980): 5, 32.

4. James Lance, "Practicing for Touchdowns," *Journal of Physical Education, Recreation and Dance* 52 (1981): 5, 38.

5. C. E. Mueller, "Leisure Expenditures," *US News and World Report* 32 (December 1980).

6. Don C. Hilliard and Louis A. Zurchers, Jr., "The Temporal Segregation of Activities and Their Meanings in Leisure Sports Settings," *Journal of Physical Education and Recreation* 49 (1978): 8, 58–60.

7. John Robinson and Geoffrey Godbey, "Work and Leisure in America: How We Spend Our Time," *Journal of Physical Education and Recreation* 49 (1978): 8, 38–39.

8. Ibid.

9. Mildred J. Little, "The Status of Outdoor Education/Outdoor Adventure Offerings in Texas Colleges and Universities," *Texas Association for Health, Physical Education and Recreation Journal* 46 (1977): 1, 60–61, 67.

10. Gerry Maas, "Intramurals: Something for Everyone," *Journal of Physical Education, Recreation and Dance* 52 (1981): 7, 19.

11. Joseph J. Godek, "Sports Health Care: Balancing the Issues," *Journal of Physical Education, Recreation and Dance* 53 (1982): 6, 31.

12. Kenneth S. Clarke, "Health Care Delivery in Athletics," *Journal of Physical Education, Recreation and Dance* 53 (1982): 6, 32–33.

13. "An Overview of Sports Medicine," *The Athletic Congress Record/USA* 3 (1982): 3, 5–6.

RELATED READINGS

Arnow, Mike. "Teaching Dance Through Sport." *Journal of Physical Education, Recreation and Dance* 52 (1981):5, 39.

Balog, J. "The Concept of Health and the Role of Health Education." *Journal of School Health* 51 (1981): 7, 461–64.

Carlton, Phil, and Rob Stinson. "Achieving Educational Goals Through Intramurals." *Journal of Physical Education, Recreation and Dance* 54 (1983):2, 23–24.

Cobb, Robert S. "Health Education: A Separate and Unique Discipline." *Journal of School Health* 51 (1981):9, 603–4.

Cooney, Larry. "Sports Clubs." *Journal of Physical Education and Recreation* 50 (1979):3, 40–41.

Dougherty, Neil J. IV. "Liability." *Journal of Physical Education, Recreation and Dance* 54 (1983):6, 52–54.

Haering, Franklin C. "Safety is Big Business." *Journal of Physical Education and Recreation* 50 (1979): 6,41.

Hamburg, M. V. "Curriculum for Health Coordinators." *Journal of School Health* 48 (1978):4, 241–42.

Kegerreis, Sam. "An Economic Alternative." *Journal of Physical Education and Recreation* 50 (1979):7, 70–71.

"Health Care for Student Athletes." *Journal of Physical Education and Recreation* 50 (1979):6, 78–79.

Kleinnan, Seymour. "The Reunification of Health and Physical Education." *Journal of Physical Education, Recreation and Dance* 53 (1982):4, 19–21.

Landwer, Gerald E. "Where Do You Want To Go?" *Journal of School Health* 51 (1981):8, 529–31.

Loft, Bernard I. "Safety Problems in Physical Education and Athletics." *Journal of Physical Education and Recreation* 52 (1981): 1, 60–61, 76.

Marcum, C. Everett. "Risk Acceptance Among Physical Educators." *Journal of Physical Education and Recreation* 52 (1981):1, 73–75.

McAvoy, Leo. "Outdoor Leadership Training." *Journal of Physical Education and Recreation* 49(1978):4, 42–43.

Means, Louis. *Intramurals*. Englewood Cliffs, NJ: Prentice-Hall, Inc., 1973.

Merki, Don. "The Future of Health Education." *Journal of School Health* 51(1981):10, 632–36.

Reid, Marsha A. "Careers in Leisure and Recreation." *Journal of Physical Education and Recreation* 50 (1979):4, 34.

Schreyer, Richard M. et al. "Common Attributes, Uncommonly Exercised." *Journal of Physical Education and Recreation* 49 (1978):4, 36–38.

Sheltmire, John C., and Kathy Bartlett. "Physical Education and Recreation: Will They Survive as Separate Entities?" *Journal of Physical Education and Recreation* 50(1979):7, 18–19.

Spiker, John C. "Athletic Trainer Education." *Journal of Physical Education and Recreation* 50 (1979):7, 72.

Staley, Frederick A. "Outdoor Education in the Total Curriculum." *Journal of Physical Education, Recreation and Dance* 54 (1983):1, 56–57.

Stone, Donald B. "School Health Education: Some Future Challenges." *Journal of School Health* 49(1979):4, 227–28.

Ulrich, Celeste. "Education for A Dynamic Lifestyle." *Journal of Physical Education and Recreation* 48 (1977):5, 48.

For additional reading materials on any of the allied fields, you should first consult with your course instructor in regard to a specific textbook on the subject that is preferred. Many other resources are available, also. A brief listing of pertinent periodicals and other publications that have specific readings and address the relationship between physical education and the allied field is as follows:

Health Education
Health Education Journal, published by AAHPERD Publications.
American Journal of Public Health, published by the American Public Health Association.
School Health Education, published by the American School Health Association.

Dance
Journal of Physical Education, Recreation and Dance, published by AAHPERD Publications.
Dancing: A Guide for the Dancer You Can Be, published by AAHPERD Publications.
Encores for Dance, published by AAHPERD Publications.

Recreation and Leisure

Journal of Physical Education, Recreation and Dance, published by AAHPERD Publications.
Leisure Today Series, published by AAHPERD Publications.
Parks and Recreation, published by United States Department of Parks and Recreation.

Outdoor Education

Journal of Physical Education, Recreation and Dance, published by AAHPERD Publications.
Information and publications from the National Outdoor Leadership School.
Information and publications from Outward Bound, Inc.

Intramurals

Journal of Physical Education, Recreation and Dance, published by AAHPERD Publications.
NIRSA Journal, published by the National Intramural Recreational Sports Association.
Intramural Portfolio, published by AAHPERD Publications.

Safety Education

Journal of Physical Education, Recreation and Dance, published by AAHPERD Publications.
Various publications from the National Safety Council.
School Safety Handbook, published by the Association of School Business Officials of the United
  States and Canada.

Athletic Training and Sports Medicine

Athletic Training, published by the National Athletic Trainers Association.
Physician and Sports Medicine, published by McGraw-Hill, Inc.
The First Aider, published by Cramer Products, Inc.

Contemporary Issues and Trends 14

Chapter outline

Issues in Physical Education
    Options to Physical Activity as a
      Means of Discipline
    Should Athletic Participation Substitute
      for the Physical Education Class?
    The Role Conflict between Teaching
      and Coaching
    Physical Education and Coaching:
      Separate, but Equal?
    Status of the Profession: A Scholarly
      Discipline?
    Exhibit 14.1 Characteristics of a
      Profession: Does Physical Education
      Meet These Criteria?
    Professional Preparation: Knowledge
      or Skill?
    Objectives for Physical Education
    Teacher Competency
    Teaching and Coaching Salaries
    Teacher Unionism
Trends in Physical Education
    Coeducational Physical Education
    Elective and Selective Physical
      Education

Mainstreaming in Physical Education
Rainy Day Activities
Team Teaching in Physical Education
Teaching Knowledge as Well as Skills
Fun in Physical Education
Assertive Discipline
Computers in Physical Education
Problems in Physical Education
    Discipline and Apathy in the Public
      Schools
    Violence in the Schools
    Class Size in Physical Education
    Motivation of Students
    Individualized Instruction
    Teacher Burnout
    Exhibit 14.2 Problems within Our
      Profession
    Safety and Risk Acceptance
    Legal Liability
Summary
Study Questions
Student Activities
Notes
Related Readings

Student objectives

As a result of the study of this chapter, the student should be able to

1. Develop awareness of the many issues, trends, and problems that are present in the physical education profession.
2. Identify several of the reasons for the changes that are likely to take place in physical education in the future.
3. Differentiate between terms, issues, trends, and problems.
4. Identify other issues, trends, and problems in the physical education profession.
5. Examine and discuss the role conflict between teaching and coaching.
6. Describe how physical education is a profession that demands risk acceptance among its professionals.
7. List options for the use of physical activity as a means of discipline in the physical education classroom.
8. Give several examples why physical education is a scholarly discipline.
9. Discuss why objectives in physical education are prone to change.
10. Describe burnout as an occupational hazard for physical educators and coaches and the reasons for its cause.

When one looks at any discipline or profession, one sees that some form of change constantly takes place. Physical education is no exception. Change normally takes place when the need for change is demonstrated and justified. At the roots of change are issues and problems. The finding of a solution for either results, many times, in a trend. Change in physical education over the past years has been slow. The reasons for this are varied. Some consider physical education a very conservative and traditional discipline. Another factor is that many of the other disciplines within education do not consider physical education a scholarly discipline and in some ways expect less from us as a profession. A final point is that technology, which has caused many changes in society, has been slower to reach physical education, although technology's impact has been greater in recent years.

Regardless of the reasons or the causes, change is normally a slow process that evolves over a period of years. Meanwhile, many issues or problems remain unresolved or in dispute until such change evolves into a trend. For purposes of definition, an **issue** is a question or matter under dispute. A **problem** is a question or matter to be resolved. A **trend** is a move in a general direction or a tendency for a point of resolve. Physical education has many issues, problems, and trends.

The purpose of this chapter is to familiarize physical education majors with some of the issues, problems, and trends that they will encounter upon entering the profession. The questions or matters discussed here do not reflect all of the possibilities under these categories. This chapter must be considered a sampling of the various issues, problems, and trends confronting our profession. The matters discussed here should create positive thinking on your part and expose you to some of the contemporary items that will confront you as you become a professional physical educator.

ISSUES IN PHYSICAL EDUCATION

Options to Physical Activity as a Means of Discipline

The rationale against the misuse of physical activity as a means of discipline was presented to you in chapter 7. **Discipline** is training that is expected to produce a specified character change or pattern of behavior. Does physical activity serve that purpose? The answer is no. Why do so many physical educators use this practice? Some have been taught to use this process, while others have never been taught not to. Again, some physical educators feel it is the only method that works.

We have options to physical activity as a means of discipline, and they must be patiently tried and developed. The first is entitled *teacher behavior modifications*.

Modeling: Teachers need to model, or serve as examples, for the characteristics or desired patterns of behavior that they want the students to copy. *Example:* If punctuality is desired, then the teacher needs to model punctuality.

Teacher enthusiasm: Teachers who express themselves verbally and nonverbally with excitement about teaching their subject matter tend to attract positive student involvement. *Example:* A physical education teacher who practices fitness will likely inspire his or her students while teaching fitness activities.

Instructional clarity: Clarity is what the teacher says or does and the student's perception of those behaviors. Confusion resulting from instruction that is not clear is a leading cause of student misbehavior. *Example:* A teacher who is perceived with clarity by the students will have less time for disruptions because the students will be responding to the instruction with less confusion.

Other applicable methods include instilling self-discipline on the part of the students, establishing rules and regulations that are consistent, and using assertive discipline (see "Trends in Physical Education," in this chapter). Discipline, by any definition, cannot function without strong leadership and support on the part of the school administration.

Should Athletic Participation Substitute for the Physical Education Class?

In many school situations, the participation in athletics substitutes for the physical education class. This practice occurs in many states, although many curriculum guides state rules to the contrary. The practice varies from taking the athlete out of class for the season to having an athletic period in which all of the athletes in that sport meet under the guise of physical education, but in reality the class is an extension of the team practice or off-season training.

This practice is detrimental to the physical education of the athlete and also to the image of the teacher/coach. If an athlete specializes in only one sport, such as football, and it becomes a year-round involvement in the physical education class, the athlete will probably not learn about personal fitness for adult life, a variety of lifetime sports, aquatics, and other activities in the program. Therefore, we may have a skilled football player in high school, but an uneducated person in regard to the broad spectrum of physical education activities and knowledge that are necessary to be a physically educated person in adult life.

The way to stop this practice is by strict enforcement of state laws and curriculum guidelines and by the total involvement of the physical educators and coaches who are in charge of the program and who will not allow athletics to be a substitute for the physical education class.

The Role Conflict between Teaching and Coaching

Most physical education teachers/coaches tend to start their professional careers intending to be equally devoted to both roles. However, once into the mainstream of the profession, this tendency begins to create a role conflict. To not allow one role to dominate the other is very difficult. The role conflict is seldom resolved unless one of the roles disappears. There are various reasons for this. Winning is accepted as the main responsibility and goal of the successful coach. Very few successful coaches get fired for poor teaching ability in any subject area. Yet, many good teachers may be fired if their coaching is not successful. Teaching expertise seldom is a substitute for losing games.

The teacher/coach soon perceives the main responsibility of the job as winning games, which often results in a redefinition of the role in which the teaching part becomes secondary. This may also cause some conflict with other school faculty, since they perceive their roles differently and are critical of the coaching role in education. This also tends to alienate physical education as an equal, or academic, discipline within education. Another point of conflict is that coaches are accustomed to making on-the-spot decisions, while other decisions in the school are made more democratically and take more time. Often, the coach then feels a lack of loyalty or commitment to the school, since the authoritarian or autocratic decision process is seldom used in matters other than coaching.

A new coach soon realizes that the better coaching positions are passed on to coaches who are recommended by their established peers; therefore, the way to move up is to fully adapt to the role of the coach. Dedicated coaches usually do not remain active in the pursuance of educational skills, but instead devote the time to coaching skills and knowledge.

Society, not the profession, has put the teacher/coach in this role conflict. The parents and citizens of the schools and communities who decry the system are often the ones who foster it by their demands for athletic success, that is, to win. Until society changes its attitudes, the resolution of this role conflict is doubtful.

Physical Education and Coaching: Separate, but Equal?

One solution to the teaching/coaching dilemma is to employ separate personnel for teaching physical education and coaching athletics. This solution often has actually become an issue. The reason for this is the fact that by separating the two, education and the schools would have to admit that athletics are a separate entity in total education. Also, the separation would require the hiring of additional faculty, which would increase current costs. Such a solution would resolve the role conflict between teacher and coach and strengthen the status of physical education. Certified teachers and coaches could select the role they want and put all their efforts into that role. Coaches would be more effective and teaching competency in physical education would be strengthened. Unfortunately, this solution is not as feasible as it may sound due to economics and educational philosophy. However, the resolution of the teaching/coaching role conflict may be worth the additional costs and philosophic changes.

STATUS OF THE PROFESSION: A SCHOLARLY DISCIPLINE?

Since the 1960s, a thrust, or trend, toward the recognition of physical education as a more scholarly academic discipline has been taking place. The body of knowledge has accumulated through research and other scholarly activities involving exercise physiology, biomechanics, motor learning, sport sociology and psychology, history, and philosophy. In all aspects, the physical education profession has grown as a scientific body. This may promote the advancement of physical education as a scholarly discipline, but further analysis of what is taking place in education is needed, which is the major point of this issue.

---

exhibit 14.1

Characteristics of a profession: Does physical education meet these criteria?

1. Provides a unique service to its clients.
2. Possesses a body of knowledge that is based upon scientific theory and provides a continuous flow of new facts.
3. Has a unique function to perform in society in what it seeks to accomplish.
4. Provides a rigorous training program for those who enter their chosen profession.
5. Is very selective about whom it admits initially to such a training program.
6. Is capable of self-organization by developing a code of ethics and establishing norms so that satisfactory practices are identified and incompetents are eliminated.
7. Is viewed as a lifelong occupation with persons rarely leaving the field.
8. Is altruistic, with its members having a high regard for and a devotion to the interests and welfare of others.
9. Is autonomous and free from lay evaluation and control.

Source: McBride, Ron, "Characteristics of a profession: Does Education Meet These Criteria?" in *TAHPERD Journal,* May 1984. Texas Association for Health, Physical Education, Recreation and Dance. University of Texas, Austin, TX.

The search for scholarship has been a function of the colleges and universities and has been conducted by their faculty and graduate students. The continuation and application of such scientific endeavors is still in question. The gap between those who perform the research and the practitioners of our profession is often referred to as the **ivory tower concept.** In simpler words, much of the scientific knowledge lies out of reach or is of doubtful value to be applied by the teacher/coach, who is regarded as the practitioner. Further, much of the research does not directly apply to the teaching/ coaching situation. Most teacher/coaches continue to teach as they have been taught, without improving upon their frameworks and experimenting with new models, styles, or designs, for example.

In essence, we are a *scholarly discipline,* but the bridge has not yet been built between the researchers and the practitioners. Until this occurs, we will probably not gain the recognition we deserve for our scientific contributions. Both sides of the issue must build the bridge. The colleges and universities must do research that is applicable to the teacher/coach and implement ways for communication of findings. The practitioners must be encouraged to develop a stronger interest in scholarship and the utility of research to improve their profession. Professional organizations and publications are a start, but these must be integrated so that both sides of the profession can contribute and utilize the body of knowledge upon which our profession is based.

PROFESSIONAL PREPARATION: KNOWLEDGE OR SKILL?

Professional preparation programs in physical education tend to focus on one of two areas: conceptual knowledge of the subject matter necessary to be competent in the profession or skill acquisition necessary for competency. The two philosophies differ mainly in the approach to professional preparation. Is the successful professional a master of knowledge or a technician of skills? The job description one seeks would help answer this question. But, on a broad scale, our professional preparation programs at the undergraduate level are supposed to prepare the candidate for a variety of options within the profession. We can specialize, but the best place for this is in graduate school.

Prior to the mid–1960s, most professional preparation programs were highly technical and skill oriented, with the primary goal of producing teachers and coaches for the public schools. About this time, several colleges and universities began to emphasize knowledge over skills. Some programs went to the extreme where little activity at all was required by the major. This was the "root" for another problem of today: the unfit and unskilled physical educator. With the expansion of career opportunities within our profession, this issue will become harder to resolve, and, possibly, specialization for all at the undergraduate level is imminent. However, at this time we need professionals who are knowledgeable as well as skilled and highly fit to teach and serve as examples for our profession. Professional preparation programs of today need to be aware of and provide the necessary elements for both the conceptual knowledge and skill acquisition to produce a competent professional.

Objectives for Physical Education

How often have you heard objectives mentioned as being organic, neuromuscular, social, emotional, and intellectual? Depending upon which of the early scholars were studied, most objectives fell into these broad categories and were often vague in interpretation or unexplainable. This is not to criticize our early scholars, for the identifying, defining, and promoting of objectives occurs even today.

The primary issue is that objectives do change, and we should not regard them as sacred. Further, objectives must be ordered for the specific aspect that they are trying to define. For example, within physical education we have objectives for our professional preparation programs, objectives for elementary physical education, objectives for secondary physical education, and objectives for college physical education. All the objectives have some similarities, but specific objectives exist, also.

Objectives tend to change as society changes and as educational theories and philosophies change or emerge. Some professionals view changing objectives as harmful to the values and goals of the profession. However, the opposite is more likely to be true, and that is a shifting of importance of various objectives is healthy and stimulates thinking within the professions. Controversy, in this instance, is a positive trait. Since objectives are the basis for changing the knowledge, skills, attitudes, and values of our students, our objectives should also change periodically, as long as our educational goals are not compromised. Also, objectives are reversible. Any time evaluation takes place, we can make the changes necessary to fit the needs of our programs.

The objectives of the past are insufficient to meet the needs of today, just as today's objectives will not meet the needs of tomorrow. The objectives themselves may be similar, but their order of importance or emphasis and their interpretation by the new professionals will be different. A final point to consider is that objectives for our programs will be more effective if they are based on the needs and interests expressed by the students themselves.

Teacher Competency

The competency of teachers in all disciplines has always been one of education's most controversial issues. Physical education is no exception. Some professional preparation programs of the past had entrance exams or entry level tests that were usually skill or fitness oriented. More recently, some programs are requiring exit or comprehensive examinations relating to the major field. Passing such exams is usually a degree requirement. Both of these methods have as their goal the production of qualified professionals in the field of physical education.

History shows that we have progressed through various stages to check the competency of our teachers. First was the requirement to have a college degree. Next came teacher certification programs that were licensed and monitored by the states; these programs were and still are variable enough so that a person certified to teach in one state may not meet certification requirements of another state. Not satisfied that a degree and certification are reliable, some states, cities, and districts are using teacher competency examinations to further cite knowledge and skills for competency of the teachers they hire. The idea of testing teacher competence is not new. In 1876, teachers in Houston, Texas, were required to pass a written examination consisting of several categories. Most teacher competency tests today are also relatively general in nature.

The use of teacher competency examinations has become an issue in education. The advocates state that we need further quality checks on the people who will become our educators. They emphasize that teachers are not prepared adequately and that such a test is necessary. On the other side, the dissenters state that enough is enough. Students must earn a college degree and meet state certification requirements and now they have to take a competency test that will determine if they are qualified to teach. Are our college and university programs that inadequate? Further, some school districts even require a master's degree as the minimum requirement for teachers. This issue cannot be answered here, but is definitely an issue past, present, and future that demands awareness of beginning physical educators in regard to their professional careers.

Teaching and Coaching Salaries

The teaching and coaching professions have never been known as financially lucrative fields. Teachers have always been regarded as middle class citizens economically. Upon analyzing the situation, one would think that the people who have the responsibility of preparing our youth for adulthood should be among the highest paid in our society.

The opposite is basically true. Teaching salaries are barely holding their own among salaries of other professions. In fact, they are on the lower end of the pay scale. Teaching and coaching have always been regarded as service professions, and most people who enter into these fields do not do so in order to get rich quickly. However, should teaching remain at the lower end of the professional economic scale?

This presents various issues. In order to compensate for low pay, many teachers and coaches "moonlight," which often may hinder their duties at the schools. Lower salaries cause discontent, which may affect performance in the classroom. Most important is that many qualified persons leave or never enter the teaching profession. As top students, they are able to find better paying jobs elsewhere. On the other hand, some people contend that teachers are paid fairly for the release time they have and for the job they do. Some people cry for quality in education, but denounce the appeal for more realistic salaries. For the most part, for all of the competency checks that are present in the teacher certification process, poor teachers could be weeded out, and, with a new, higher salary scale, qualified and capable personnel would return to or enter the teaching profession.

Coaching salaries vary, also. Many times, the extra money provides incentive to coach. However, the amount of time the coach spends in the performance of duties usually negates the extra income. Some coaches are paid for their duties as part of their salary and receive no extra income. Usually, a lighter class load or release time serves as compensation. While a teacher/coach tends to have a higher income on paper, the money is hard-earned, pertaining to the time-money ratio.

Teaching still has its positive factors economically. Security in the form of tenure is available to many teachers. Longevity at the same school or district builds equity into the income and tends to equate the salary scale to some degree. Further incentives to do advanced study and receive higher degrees also increase one's income potential. Many public high school teacher/coaches would, in fact, have to take a pay cut to teach at the college level. In summary, although teacher salaries are not the best, they are adequate for a middle income existence, and if the person likes what he or she is doing, then teaching and coaching are still worthwhile professions.

Teacher Unionism

One of the major transitions from the college or university to the public schools is the reality that not all aspects of teaching are completely "professional" in the true sense of the word. One of these factors is **teacher unionism.** More often than not, this topic is avoided or ignored in professional preparation, the reason being that unionism is not considered part of a professional career. Yet, unions do exist, are becoming more prominent in education, and are to some degree compulsory in some districts and states. In fact, teachers who refuse to join may be discriminated against or lose their jobs.

Unions are supposedly for the teacher, and they do help in bargaining for income, better working conditions, support for the teacher, and other factors. Contrary to this, however, unions support a certain ideology from which no member has a right to disagree. The most common situation is that of the right of refusal to go on strike if the union decides to strike. Members have no choice but to go with the union or suffer the consequence as dissenters. Unions are formed by political power and money and render the individual helpless under the union's control, the same situation often rendered by the school of bureaucracy which the unions are supposedly against.

A professional should have a choice and a voice. One of the ideals throughout the history of education is the right we have to teach the way we want and to be individuals within the school setting. Unions take away some of those rights. You no longer have a voice as an individual, since the union makes binding decisions, both good and bad, for you.

As a beginning professional educator, you may have to make a choice or have no choice at all. However, keep in mind that in some states compulsory unionism is illegal and the right to work is protected. Other states have no choice regarding joining and support of a union. Your professional preparation should offer you some information about the union movement in education and the regulations regarding the state(s) in which you plan to teach. Regarding the issue of teacher unionism, you should have enough information for responsible decision making and to recognize the reality that this issue may face you rather quickly in public school education.

TRENDS IN PHYSICAL EDUCATION

Coeducational Physical Education

Coeducational classes in physical education are a reality. According to the program changes mandated by Title IX of the Education Amendments of 1972, the regulations generally prohibit sex-segregated physical education classes while allowing separation by sex during competition in wrestling, boxing, basketball, football, and other body contact sports. Full compliance of the law was to be accomplished by 21 July 1978. Therefore, coeducational physical education classes are a must in many activities and can be utilized in touch or flag football, basketball, and similar sports if properly controlled and supervised.

This trend presents some problems to the beginning physical educator, namely, how do I teach members of the opposite sex? How do I control the class? How do I account for individual differences in abilities? The answers to these and many other questions lie in the realm of professional preparation. Are we teaching our physical education majors to teach coeducational classes?

First, let us examine some of the advantages of coeducational teaching. Social interaction (see fig. 14.1) among the adolescent members of the opposite sex has a strong impact upon socialization and maturity. Class control may be somewhat easier, and the teaching of the opposite sex should be an enjoyable experience for the competent teacher.

Some of the problems that may be experienced lie both with the prospective teacher and professional preparation. Prospective teachers of both sexes must be made aware of the physiological and psychological make-up of the opposite sex. Also, they must be concerned with the ability to teach heterogeneous groups as well as provide motivation for both sexes to participate without fears or inhibitions in the coed setting.

Figure 14.1 Coeducational physical education classes help students learn to interact with members of the opposite sex.

All in all, coeducational classes should provide a rewarding experience for teachers of both sexes. The main factor is to be prepared, and this is the job of your curriculum in professional preparation, that is, to provide you with the necessary skills to effectively manage the coeducational class.

Elective and Selective Physical Education

A positive trend in secondary school physical education is that of the elective and selective curriculums. **Elective** is defined as the physical education subject and activity that are elected by the student. **Selective** is defined as physical education that is required as a subject, and the student selects the activity. Both are being utilized more than ever before in the physical education curriculum and demonstrate several strengths. The selective curriculum seems to be used more widely because of required physical education in most states. The *best teacher concept* is perhaps the major strength: this is where a teacher who has superior knowledge or is a specialist can teach that activity to more students more often. These curriculums also meet individual needs and interests of the students, provide variety in activities, offer increased motivation due to the selection process, offer different activity levels (ability grouping), and provide common interests for both students and teachers. Finally, fewer discipline or control problems will be present in the class due to the previously stated factors.

Weaknesses may be present, also. First, some students may select limited activities; therefore, a definite selection process is required. The teacher who is a specialist may become bored with the repetition of the same activity. Also, more time is necessary for the organization and administration of the programs as compared to traditional curriculums. Finally, restrictions on class or section sizes plus limitation in activity offerings due to facilities and equipment may defeat some of the motivation of the program.

To successfully implement the elective or selective curriculum, one must have a definite plan for implementation. After you decide upon the scope of activities that can be offered and evaluate the interest areas and competency of the teaching faculty, plan your overall curriculum including a procedure for the selection process by the students. Be sure to include guidelines for the process that will meet program objectives and eliminate needless repetition by the students.

Example: For selecting activities in a thirty-six-week curriculum (twelve activities for a three-week duration), students must

A. Select two physical fitness activities.
B. Select two team sport activities.
C. Select two individual sport activities.
D. Select a level II course (advanced course only after the successful completion of the level I course for that activity).
E. Select six other activities to meet their needs and interests.

Through the use of elective or selective curriculums, the student has the opportunity to explore an activity thoroughly, select a variety of activities, and have opportunities for success. The student also gains experience in intelligent decision making and feels more freedom in the program. Finally, fun should also be a final outcome.

Mainstreaming in Physical Education

Public Law 94–142, Education for All Handicapped Children Act of 1975, states that physical education should be a direct instructional service to all handicapped children. The school district responsible for the education of the child shall provide the services within the regular instructional program offered by the physical education instructor (see fig. 14.2). This is known as *mainstreaming.* The law further states that some handicapped students may need specifically designed physical education programs and may need separate classes, in some instances, or even services through the public or private sector. However, the law is primarily focused on mainstreaming for most of the handicapped population. This places the responsibility for handicapped physical education on the physical education classroom teacher. Further, the physical educator should be a participant in the individual student's educational diagnosis, evaluation, and prescription, and to the extent appropriate, handicapped students should be educated with students who are not handicapped.

Figure 14.2 Mainstreaming allows handicapped students to enjoy the same activities that their peers enjoy.

The mainstreaming trend is not without problems. The major problem lies in professional preparation. Is the major student receiving sufficient training to implement mainstreaming? The majority of physical educators view adapted physical education as a specialization with separate training. To some extent, this is reflected in our curriculums, because many of our adapted special programs are at the graduate level. All professional preparation programs contain an adapted course, but how many other courses are taught with mainstreaming in mind?

Many prospective teachers are inhibited from performing an adequate job in mainstreaming their classes because of their general lack of knowledge. Also, many physical educators have an underlying negative attitude toward working with the handicapped in the total classroom situation. To counter this situation, physical education majors must be informed and develop a positive attitude toward mainstreaming. Our professional preparation programs must provide the knowledge factor concerning the handicapped and integrate this into the other aspects of the program so that physical educators will accept mainstreaming as a normal responsibility of the teaching profession.

Rainy Day Activities

One of the weakest areas in many otherwise excellent school physical education programs is the rainy day program. Recently, a trend has developed to strengthen this weakness. Rather than have the physical education program hit the "blahs" or become disorganized, many teachers are preparing for inclement weather situations by planning rainy day schedules that are both challenging and motivating for the students.

Organized and planned activity must take place on rainy days as an alternative to the regular program. Students should be kept active in mind and body in the subject matter for physical education. Socializing in the bleachers or using the physical education period as a study hall are not in the best interests of our profession. Some rainy day options are as follows:

1. Modify the regularly scheduled activity to fit an indoor situation.
2. Change the class activity for rainy days. *Example:* for each unit taught, a built-in rainy day activity is also planned. A four-week unit in flag football has table tennis, indoor bowling, and shuffleboard scheduled for all rainy days during that unit. A four-week unit in soccer has aerobic dance scheduled for all rainy days during that unit.
3. Plan rainy day activities for the school year. *Example:* a three-on-three basketball tournament that lasts throughout the entire year for rainy days. A round robin approach is taken, with no teams eliminated, but all win-loss records kept. Other tournaments, such as table tennis or one-wall handball, could accompany the basketball activity for added participation.
4. Plan lectures, films, and demonstrations to fill the anticipated number of rainy days.
5. Student planning. Take one class period early in the year and let students select and plan what they would like for future rainy days. Choices from the teacher that are feasible may be given as a guide, but student creativity should be allowed.
6. Innovation. There are numerous innovative ways to plan for rainy day activities, even with limited space and facilities. Think of many different or new ideas that you could utilize within your situation to meet student needs and interests.

Some contemporary suggestions are as follows:

Lectures on the components of physical fitness
Lectures on rules, regulations, and strategies for various activities
Physical education and sports films
Demonstrations by skilled teachers or students in various activities
Recreational activities
Outdoor education activities
New games
Aerobic dance
Physical fitness activities (stations)

Career education (in physical education)

Videotape various skills for student analysis

Planning for elective or selective programs

Training techniques: how to tape an ankle, finger, and wrist, for example

Injury prevention and treatment. Example: shin splints, and tennis elbow

Nutrition

Way-out games (inspired by TV program)

Indoor superstars or decathalon competition

Rainy day programs can be interesting and stimulating for the student and the teacher. The *key* is preparation and organization for such programs so that the teacher is not caught unprepared and to ensure that the subject matter meets the needs and interests of the students.

Team Teaching in Physical Education

The idea of team teaching in physical education is not new, but it is now being utilized with various teaching styles to provide more effective instruction. Two very strong factors exist in regard to team teaching. The first is that the best teacher can provide the instruction to the class for that particular activity. The **best teacher** is the one who has the most knowledge and skill in an activity. Second, by having more than one teacher in the classes, homogeneous groupings of students have more supervision, thereby offering the students a better opportunity for success.

Team teaching results when two or more teachers combine their classes within the same activity. The duties of the class should be shared equally and are designated to alleviate any confusion. Team teaching is a cooperative effort to improve instruction. It can fail when either member of the team neglects the duties assigned or if one teacher tries to assert authority over the other. Team teaching is not a strong teacher compensating for a weak teacher, but two teachers interacting in one class for the benefit of the students.

Another form of team teaching occurs with the use of teacher aides. However, the primary function of the teacher aide is to assist the classroom teacher, not to teach the class. Teacher aides can be a great asset in a crowded class situation. The physical education teacher should assist in training the aide so that the class policies and procedures are followed correctly. The use of aides allows the teacher to be mobile and allows for homogeneous grouping. One final point should be made: teacher aides should not serve as a substitute for hiring qualified teachers, but should be a supplement for the purpose of improving instruction and supervision in the physical education classroom.

Teaching Knowledge as Well as Skills

For many years, the teaching of knowledge was nonexistent in the physical education classroom. Skills were the order of the day. Granted, rules and regulations were taught also, but only enough to allow the activity to be played. With the renewed emphasis on physical fitness, lifetime sports, aquatics, outdoor education, and others, conceptual knowledge and theory are becoming equally important. A good example of this is in physical fitness. If fitness is taught without a knowledge base, little understanding results on the part of the student as to why the activities are being performed; why they are necessary; how the body is trained; what benefits will be gained; and the like. Perhaps this is one of the failings of the past in teaching various activities for the carry-over value to adult life. If a youngster is to carry skills into adult life, the necessary knowledge must accompany the skill learning. The teaching of knowledge should begin in the elementary school program and progressively continue through the secondary school program.

Fun in Physical Education

Physical activity is normally fun for children. The concept of **fun** in physical education has long been one of our objectives. However, somewhere along the way, many programs have lost the fun concept. How do we see this? Many secondary school students no longer have any enthusiasm toward performance in physical activities. Adults dislike activity in some cases based upon physical education and athletic experiences from their school days. What is even worse is that elementary school youngsters who come to school full of love and vigor for activity are turned off by their intermediate years. The reason? It is no fun anymore!

This lack of fun has various factors. We often are so zealous as teachers to have everyone be an achiever that we forget that the average-skilled youngster may never be an achiever. We must remember that he or she still can have fun and be fit for activity. Youth sports stress winning from six-year-olds. When they cannot live up to adult expectations, some youngsters withdraw from participation. Many of our teaching strategies are directed toward the skilled youngster, while not meeting the needs of those less skilled. For those who cannot achieve and even face embarrassment, physical education becomes a chore.

A trend today is to put fun and challenge back into our programs. The trend has surfaced as new games, movement education, individualized instruction, lifetime sports, outdoor education activities, and many others. However, we must be cautious. To have people of all ages appreciate and enjoy physical activity, they must have positive experiences. The way we teach or present activities is as important as what we teach. The highly skilled and competitive individuals will not suffer. Plenty of challenges exist for the athletes without making our classes "pressure cookers" and having the average- or below-average skilled youngster develop a dislike for physical activity. For the survival of our profession and for the health and enjoyment of the people we teach, fun must stay an integral part of our school physical education programs.

Assertive Discipline

A new technique in discipline and class control that is proving successful in many situations is assertive discipline. Basically, **assertive discipline** is a commitment to standardizing behavior based upon communication to the students about the desired behavior and the consequences for violations. The teacher must know at all times what he or she expects of the students. **Behaviors** must be communicated both verbally and visually, usually by posting signs and handouts. **Consequences** are also posted and must be used with consistency. **Positive assertiveness** (reinforcement) maximizes the teacher's influence with students, while **negative assertiveness** (consequences) lets students know what punishments will be provided. In other words, good behavior is recognized and rewarded and bad behavior is not tolerated to any degree.

Assertive discipline is really a combination of two techniques: external discipline provided by the teacher and internal student self-discipline. Rules and regulations are set by the teacher, yet because expectations are communicated, the student is encouraged to develop self-discipline and behave willingly with full knowledge of the consequences if he or she does not. Assertive discipline relies upon the responsibility of the student to behave in ways that are mutually beneficial to self and others; it relies on the teacher to enforce the consequences as stated. This method of discipline works best when used consistently in all classrooms in the entire school. However, it can be utilized by the teacher in the physical education classroom independent of the rest of the school. Like any other discipline plan, assertive discipline only works as well as the teacher who enforces it and with the backing and support of the school administration.

Computers in Physical Education

In recent years, we have experienced an explosion of technology in the United States. One of the most visible outgrowths of this tremendous increase in technology is the emergence of computers into almost every facet of American life. Computers are seen by experts as essential to progress in industry, commerce, art, science, and medicine. Even many of our leisure-time activities revolve around home entertainment provided by personal home computers.

Computers crept into education when their value as time-saving instructional aids in the classroom was realized. Today, innovative physical educators have found that the usefulness of computers does not have to be confined to the classroom, physical educators and coaches have found a variety of applications for computers in the gymnasium and on the athletic field.

Several technological advancements in the past two decades have made computers both affordable and available to any person who might wish to explore their uses. First, the size of computers was greatly reduced. The first computers had to be housed in entire rooms, but today, through the advancements of microtechnology, the computer components that used to be housed in entire rooms are now housed in desktop computers called *microprocessors*. Second, storage of information in older computers was cumbersome due to the use of large, round, hard discs filled with tape as storage devices. Today, storage of information is much less a task because soft, "floppy" discs, which can store a tremendous amount of information, are the storage devices of choice. Last, universal computer languages such as BASIC and PASCAL have been developed, which enable any person with limited computer knowledge to easily learn to communicate with the computer and to write his or her own programs to direct the computer to do countless activities.

One of the first publicized practical applications of computers in sport or physical education came a few short years ago, when rumors surfaced that the Dallas Cowboys of the National Football League were using computers to compile game statistics for use in plotting strategy against opponents. This notion was not accepted lightly by the American public, who at that time feared the dehumanizing effects of computers on society. Many felt that if computers and their mysterious powers of artificial intelligence could creep into the great American institution of sport, then computer uses were totally out of control. Those fears have since subsided, and now it would be nearly impossible to find a professional or major intercollegiate sports program that does not utilize computers in some portion of their programs. A few of the applications of computers at this level include preparing scouting reports, compiling and assessing game statistics, evaluating team members' performances, and creating and controlling workout schedules.

Physical educators are further exploring the utility of computers. The use of computers as record keeping devices for tasks such as skill test or written test scores and attendance greatly simplifies the processes and saves time. Computer applications in physical education are innumerable, making computers versatile educational tools. Computer programs can be created or computer software (pre-written programs that direct the computer to carry out a given function) utilized to direct learning of skills, rules, and game strategy for any activity. Another practical educational use is to administer, score, and record written tests.

Computer applications in physical education have been perhaps most useful to those who perform research in physical education. The researcher has found that collection and analysis of data, which, prior to computer use, was tedious and complicated, has greatly enhanced the ability to perform precise and meaningful research. The speed at which computers can collect information is thousands of times faster than the speed at which a human could collect information. Thus, as computer usage continues and is refined by researchers, the amazing tasks computers perform will lead us ever closer to the answers about how we move and what makes us move more efficiently.

PROBLEMS IN PHYSICAL EDUCATION

Discipline and Apathy in the Public Schools

At first glance, the number one problem in public school teaching appears to be a lack of discipline on the part of many students. However, if one looks into the entire school situation, the number one problem facing teachers is the apathy on the part of the students toward school and learning in general. Discipline would not be the problem it is if student apathy was not so prevalent. Regardless of the type of motivation provided by the teachers and schools, some students will resist positive influences without reason. If a person will not accept the education provided, than he or she cannot be educated. Apathetic students usually become discipline problems. If they will not conform and accept the education offered, they become a disruptive influence to the teacher and class, even if they are not unruly: passive disruption and confusion result for the rest of the class, which can lead to further discipline problems. As an example in physical education, nondressed, unexcused students create a problem since they cannot or will not participate in class. Then, while the teacher tries to teach, the nonparticipants of the class must be supervised; otherwise, they many times cause other distractions for the teacher or class. Many of our nondressers fall into the apathy category. Failure of the course means nothing to them. What recourse, then, does the teacher have if the failure to receive an education does not concern the student?

No one answer exists to the cause of apathy among our students. Often, society, as well as the schools and the parents, gets the blame. One point is certain: the apathetic individual lacks values in life and self-esteem. Physical education and athletics cannot always change apathetic attitudes, but they certainly try and, in some instances, meet with success. However, keep in mind the ageless saying: only those who want to be helped can be helped.

Violence in the Schools

In 1978, an estimated 70,000 public school teachers were physically assaulted by students in their classrooms. With violent crimes against teachers ranging from murder and rape to harassment, violence in the schools has become a problem. Further, only an estimated ten percent of the violent crimes are ever reported. In some instances, school officials are to blame for cover-ups designed to mask their lack of control. Teachers are sometimes fearful or too embarrassed to admit that such violence has happened to them.

Another form of violence in schools is property violence, involving property of both the teacher and the school. Theft and arson are serious school problems resulting in higher costs to all taxpayers. Damage to property of teachers, such as homes or cars, also occurs as a form of violence.

Many people think the violence problem is mainly an urban or big-city situation. This is not true. Small towns, rural areas, and wealthy communities are affected as well. The blame for violence appears to be a vicious circle. The community blames the schools; the schools blame the parents and a lack of home discipline and supervision; and society in general receives the blame from all. Juvenile crime has increased over 245 percent in the last thirteen years. Apathy among our youth, the lack of respect for authority, and a breakdown of law and order, especially regarding the consequences for the juvenile offender, contribute greatly to violence in the schools.

The effects on teachers are stressful, to say the least, and cause many competent teachers to leave the profession. Some states and local school districts are getting tough on those who bring violence, drugs, and alcohol on campus by suspending those offenders indefinitely. Yet, the problem continues. Physical education teachers are not exempt from such attacks upon themselves or their possessions. Many schools look upon their coaches and physical educators as the mainstays of discipline, a position which may make them more than other teachers vulnerable to violence. One problem in dealing with violence is that few teachers have ever been prepared to face or react to violence in the schools in their professional preparation.

Class Size in Physical Education

A major complaint from many physical educators has to do with the size of their classes. "How can I use effective teaching strategies and present adequate instruction when my classes are twice the size that they should be?" Many school administrators use the physical education classes at their convenience or as dumping grounds for excess students. Many times, the physical educator is placed in the untenable position of being accused of poor teaching, yet he or she may be in charge of a class of sixty or more students. In some public schools, physical education class sizes range from twelve to one-hundred students.

The Texas Association for Health, Physical Education, and Recreation has published a recommendation for class size in *Statements of Basic Beliefs*:[1] "Class size in physical education should be consistent with the activity being taught. While effective instruction requires both large and small groups, classes with forty or more students are considered to be excessively large." Further, the Texas Education Agency states in their guidelines that "the recommended class size for physical education be consistent with class sizes in other curriculum areas."[2] Most professionals would agree with these statements and conclude that we would have more effective teaching in our classes if class size met these guidelines.

Motivation of Students

Motivation is a key factor in many of the successes one has in life. The motivation a teacher provides is perhaps as important as the methods by which instruction is presented. We are all taught during professional preparation to be motivating teachers or coaches. The challenge lies in the area of how we motivate and the outcomes of the motivation process.

First, our techniques should provide long-term motivation over temporary, immediate results. For motivation to be effective, the student or athlete should accept personal responsibility or be self-motivated. Let us examine the normal pattern of motivation. By providing rewards, reinforcement, or threats of punishment, students and athletes are given constant sources of motivation along with feedback about their performances. Actually, they are being manipulated by an external source—the teacher or coach. This is known as **external motivation,** or **external control.** If we take away this external control, motivation declines. What we really want from motivation is for the youngster to develop **internal control,** or the ability to be responsible for **self-motivation** in many instances. Once self-motivation is realized, youngsters will feel that they have control over their environments and that they can affect what happens to them. Committed with a feeling of personal responsibility, they become eager to learn and improve skills without outside intervention.

The teacher's or coach's role is to provide external control to a point where students or athletes are ready to take responsibility for their own actions. The teacher must be cautious not to overuse external motivation. It must be withdrawn slowly as the personal responsibility or internal control is developed. Overuse of external control will eventually negate internal control. As physical educators, we are often guilty of the overuse of external control. We need to realize that to live in a democratic society successfully, we must educate our students to think and act for themselves with good judgment rather than having to be controlled by external sources of motivation.

Internal control is necessary to be successful in athletics, maintaining physical fitness and other wellness practices, obtaining optimum benefits from education, and in achieving success in one's career. As physical educators and coaches, we can be a major force in the development of responsible individuals for our democratic society.

Individualized Instruction

Individualized instruction, which could be considered an issue or trend, also presents a problem for many physical educators. In the strict interpretation, a very low student-teacher ratio is presumed necessary to accomplish the goal (see fig. 14.3). In physical education, this is not usually possible. The concept of individualized instruction is used quite often in our teaching strategies. It can be accomplished through such teaching styles as stations, small groups, reciprocal teaching with students, and through the setting up of individual programs in weight training and other fitness activities. Movement education activities also utilize the individualized approach.

The difficulty lies in the fact that too often in physical education we tend to group all students together without regard for their capacities to learn. When we do show regard to learning capacity by the use of homogeneous grouping and the proper teaching styles, we are, in fact, providing a form of individualized instruction. Physical fitness activities and other individual activities are, perhaps, easier to implement than team sports or group activities by this approach, but any activity can be individualized to some degree to assist students to learn. Class size and limitations on equipment and facilities can increase the difficulty, but compensation can be made.

While some may disagree that the approach taken here is not true individualized instruction because we do not have a one-to-one or two-to-one student-teacher ratio, the effect we can provide is the same. Perhaps **personalized instruction** would be a better term in physical education, because what we are trying to do with various styles and strategies is to develop a personal approach to our teaching with regard to the student's capacity to learn. In essence, by interacting with the student, whether it be with a personal training program for fitness, homogeneous grouping in a team sport, the use of various teaching stations, or by problem solving as in movement education, we are utilizing the individualized instruction concept.

Teacher Burnout

Burnout in any job occupation is defined as chronic stress. Burnout is an occupational hazard for physical educators. The possibility that we can avoid burnout entirely during our professional careers is small. To suffer from burnout is not a disgrace or a sign of weakness in an individual. We burn out due to overwork, boredom, lack of change, resistance to change, worry about problems that we cannot control in the schools, apathy, attitudes of students, and other contemporary factors.

Figure 14.3 Individualized instruction is more readily facilitated where the student-to-teacher ratio is low.

exhibit 14.2

Problems within our profession

Education, in general, and the allied disciplines of health, physical education, recreation, dance, and athletics share many problems—not the least of which is an eroding public image and, subsequently, declining teacher morale. Our critics are many, our defenders seem to be few. Almost every one is an authority on education, and the more education they have had, the more critical they become. It would not seem unlikely, however, for a profession as visible and universal as "teaching" to receive more than its share of flak. Criticism is as prevalent and sharp from within the profession as it is from without. Illiteracy, declining test scores, unrealistic and unimaginative programs, and insensitivity to the needs of youth are all charges leveled at the profession by its patrons and critics. Low salaries, large classes, intolerable conditions, and nonsupportive parents are the counter charges fired by the profession. This set of circumstances has led to a fairly recent and common phenomenon referred to in the literature as "teacher burnout." A mounting problem in education, teacher burnout is no longer just a problem of the large, comprehensive, metropolitan, inner city school; the condition is becoming more universal and exists at all levels of instruction.

Source: Poteet, John, "Problems within Our Profession," in *TAHPERD Journal*, May 1980. Texas Association for Health, Physical Education, Recreation and Dance. University of Texas, Austin, TX.

We recognize burnout very slowly. The symptoms are as broad as the causes. **Exhaustion** is one of the first symptoms and is usually accompanied by a lack of enjoyment for teaching. Others include feelings of restlessness, fatigue, depression, and insomnia. Some may experience excessive drinking and/or eating problems and even changes in sexual patterns. Build-ups of anxiety, tension, and frustration may lead to high blood pressure, increased heart rate, headaches, and stomach ulcers. Burnout itself is not harmful, but its symptoms and consequences can kill you. The body's ability to manage and combat stress was discussed in chapter 7.

As a consequence of burnout, many teachers quit or withdraw from teaching temporarily. Others fight burnout, but ruin the enjoyment and satisfaction in their lives. We can combat burnout. The first step is to recognize the problem and admit that you may be a victim. Various counseling and self-help groups may help you face the realities of the situation, but in the long run, you must help yourself to alleviate the causes. First, set realistic goals for yourself; stimulate yourself within the profession; reduce pressure situations; allow yourself some time to develop new interests; maximize all, but especially summer vacations; and, if necessary, look for a change in your job. Many people need a new challenge or a change of status or job to offer stimulation. If you are just bored, the best way possible to alleviate burnout is to look for mobility within the profession or look for a change of status. This may require advanced degrees and training, but if it makes life fulfilling once again, it's worth it. Finally, before giving up a present job or career, explore what is new in physical education through professional associations, meetings, and workshops. Burnout may just be the fact that a teacher has done nothing since college days to change or improve upon his or her teaching styles and techniques and has reached a state of boredom or staleness from a lack of professional development.

Safety and Risk Acceptance

Every physical educator must be aware of the many safety hazards present in our profession. Accidents happen when people are involved in a variety of physical activities. The *risk element,* even though guarded against, is, in fact, one of the stimulating factors in physical activity. Therefore, to try and eliminate all of the risk factors from physical activity is not feasible. However, we must strive to control accident-producing factors within our limitations. All physical educators have a legal and moral responsibility to provide for the safety and welfare of all participants they teach or supervise in sport and physical activity. A breach of this responsibility may cause you to be legally liable in regard to accident or injury and may result in a lawsuit against you. This is a fact that you should not fear, but one that should be a concern of all teachers.

Physical educators expose themselves more than most other teachers to greater risks in regard to safety. This requires that we accept these risks as part of our job. Some of the reasons for the need of risk acceptance are that, as previously stated, physical education and sport have many built-in risk factors. Also, in physical education, we work with large groups of people and, in many instances, those people are involved in intense competition, which heightens the risk factor.

Organization and prevention are the key factors in keeping safety problems to a minimum. Each school should have an appointed *safety professional* from the physical education staff. All facilities, equipment, and activities should be checked for possible risks and hazards. Hazards should be removed or reduced if possible. A *safety plan* including procedures to be followed should be established and then presented to the staff as an in-service program. All teachers on the staff should also be committed to safety consciousness and assist the safety professional in all ways that they can. Teachers must learn to recognize potential hazards and be prepared to handle such hazards if they develop. An additional factor to point out in regard to safety is that the teacher must keep the class under control at all times, including locker room situations. A teacher lacking class control and allowing horseplay by the students increases the risk factor and the possibility of being held liable in some instances.

Legal Liability

To avoid being the victim of a lawsuit, physical educators must be aware of their duties regarding **legal liability.** Some terms that need to be defined are as follows:

> **Negligence** The failure to act as a reasonable person guided by ordinary conditions. The failure to conduct oneself in a reasonably prudent manner to avoid exposing others to danger or risk of injury.

Liability Legal responsibilities that are not fulfilled and, therefore, are enforceable by court action.

Tort A wrong or injury that does not result from a crime or breach of contract.

The basis for tort liability is that negligence must take place and be proven, a factor that can only be established by the courts. Some examples of negligence are as follows:

A teacher leaves the physical education class unsupervised and an injury occurs.

A teacher forces students to perform a stunt or skill they are not capable of performing and injury results.

A teacher allows a student to perform without the required protective equipment and injury results.

A teacher allows a mismatch in a competitive activity such as wrestling where body weight is a critical factor and injury results.

However, if the teacher acts in a **prudent manner** (see fig. 14.4) and performs his or her duty to protect others from unreasonable physical or mental harm and to avoid acts of omission, then the chances of negligence are greatly minimized. Some of the primary duties involve the amount of care exercised in high risk activities; a consideration of individual differences among students; to provide adequate instruction, which may include demonstration in some activities; and to provide adequate supervision as required by the activity.

Physical educators also need to be aware of **product liability** because they may be named as a co-defendant if faulty or improper equipment is a cause of injury, especially if injury occurs due to improper sizing, fit, or need of repair. This is another reason why every precaution should be taken to buy the best equipment that a budget will allow and to not compromise for cheaper quality.

In summary, legal liability should be a major concern of every prospective physical educator. It is a topic you will undoubtedly be exposed to during your professional preparation and during your professional career. You do not need to be a lawyer to understand your rights and duties in regard to liability. In order to protect yourself, you should make every effort to learn and understand the responsibilities of the position you are in and to exercise the appropriate behavior to avoid negligence in its various forms.

SUMMARY

Issues, trends, and problems occur as a result of change or a need for change in any discipline. While some items mentioned may appear to represent a certain amount of discontent and frustration for the professional physical educator, they also signal our profession that we cannot remain stagnant. If we do, we will certainly be left behind in our quest for excellence and to be considered an academic or scholarly discipline.

Figure 14.4 A prudent teacher is always conscious of the hazards that exist in physical activity.

Many of the issues addressed in this chapter reflect the need for change or a more definite position and interpretation of the point of dispute causing the issue. An example is the issue of the role conflict between the physical education teacher and coaching. Once an issue is resolved to some point within the profession, a trend usually develops.

The trends presented in this chapter reflect issues that have been resolved to some degree and, by law or by selection, are being utilized more in our physical education programs. Coeducational physical education classes and putting fun back into the physical education program are examples of such trends. Some trends eventually become part of the status quo, while other trends simply decline with time or disappear usually due to a lack of effectiveness in improving our physical education programs.

Problems often present a different situation. Some problems such as discipline in the schools, may never be resolved, because as society changes, the type of discipline problem changes, also. Many problems, such as class size in physical education result from economics and the status quo; we realize how to solve the problem, for the most part, but do not or will not do so. Finally, some problems, such as risk acceptance and safety, are continuous problems that we cannot eliminate completely and must learn to control to some degree.

The issues, trends, and problems presented in this chapter are by no means comprehensive or complete. Many others not reported here are covered in other chapters of this book. Examples of such are the fitness status of physical educators (chapter 7) and sports violence (chapter 12). The purpose of this chapter is to familiarize physical education majors with each category in order to develop interest to some degree about contemporary items that many will be confronted with as they become professional physical educators.

STUDY QUESTIONS

1. What is your opinion on using physical activity as a means of discipline? State the rationale or reason for your present beliefs. What options do you think would replace the use of physical activity?

2. Now that you have read and completed this textbook, go back through each chapter and see how many additional issues, trends, and problems you can identify. Make a listing and compare in class discussion.

3. Select any trend presented in this chapter and, through journal articles and other sources, trace the development of the trend including what issues or problems led to its development.

4. What is your present opinion on teacher unionism?

5. How prepared will you be to teach coeducational physical education? Analyze your strengths and weaknesses in this trend and discuss with your course instructor what additional preparation you will receive in your professional preparation.

6. Is physical education a scholarly discipline? State why and what makes it such. What are the detractors or reasons why some elements of education are in disagreement? What can we, as a profession and as individuals, do to change those opinions?

STUDENT ACTIVITIES

1. Select one problem presented in this chapter. Arrange an interview with a public school physical educator to get his or her view or opinion on the problem and how he or she is working to resolve it.

2. Invite a public school principal to your class to discuss discipline and apathy among students and violence in the schools. It would be helpful if the principal is a former physical educator.

3. Visit a mainstreamed physical education class. Observe how the mainstreamed youngsters function in the class. Make notes about questions you may have and discuss your notes with the instructor after class if possible or with your course instructor.

4. Invite a guest speaker to explain the how and why of assertive discipline and its techniques. Ask the guest speaker to address its use in the physical education class.

NOTES

1. Texas Association for Health, Physical Education, and Recreation, *Statements of Basic Beliefs* (April 1980).
2. Texas Education Agency, *Guidelines for Physical Education in the Secondary Schools* (Austin, TX: TEA, 1978).

RELATED READINGS

Due to the brevity and introductory nature of the topics included, specific reference citations were omitted except for footnotes 1 and 2. A broad spectrum of materials influenced the writing of this chapter, and to encourage you to pursue current information on these and other contemporary topics, the following list of professional resources is recommended:

Journal of Physical Education, Recreation and Dance; Research Quarterly for Exercise and Sport; and *Update,* published by AAHPERD.
State professional journals, published by various state associations for Health, Physical Education, Recreation and Dance.

The *Physical Educator*, published by Phi Epsilon Kappa Fraternity.

Quest, published by National Association for Physical Education in Higher Education (NA-PEHE).

AAHPERD publications and audiovisuals.

Alliance Update, published by AAHPERD.

NASPE News, published by the National Association for Sport and Physical Education (AAH-PERD).

Phi Delta Kappan, published by Phi Delta Kappa, Inc.

Practical Applications of Research, newsletter published by Phi Delta Kappa, Inc.

Proceedings from various conventions and professional meetings.

Handouts and published materials from workshops, professional meetings, and the like.

Other professional publications, including textbooks, journals, manuals, and newsletters, pertaining to physical education and general education.

Open discussion with other professionals while attending conventions, workshops, and meetings. Do not neglect this resource!

Appendix

Planning Your Career

Among the many questions that you may want answered before you actually seek a position are, Where do I find job opportunities? How do I inquire about or apply for a position? What questions will I be asked? How do I present myself and my credentials?

Most colleges and universities have career placement offices to assist you. The first step is to obtain placement services. Placement services vary, but most of them provide

1. Reference forms that the student can give to persons who may serve as prospective references.
2. Placement dossier. The dossier usually contains information such as personal data, professional training, experience, honors and awards, membership in societies and organizations, publications and presentations, records of courses and copies of transcripts, and completed reference forms. The dossier is sent to prospective employers at the student's request.
3. Information about available job opportunities.
4. Arrangements for interviews on campus for prospective employers and students.
5. Counseling services for the student.
6. Similar services after graduation.

There are other various ways in which you may find job opportunities. Other sources of job leads include

1. Professional associations such as your state organization for health, physical education, recreation, and dance.
2. State and local teaching and coaching associations, some of which provide newsletters on employment opportunities.
3. Employment agencies. Make sure you know who is paying the fee, you or the employer, before you sign a contract with an agency.
4. Newspapers and professional publication ads.
5. Recruitment information from organizations, companies, and school districts that assess their employment needs and actively recruit for their affiliate.
6. Inquiry. Most of us have some idea where we would like to begin our employment. Inquire directly to that source for the position.

A well-prepared resume of your professional career and training will greatly enhance your initial chances of consideration by a prospective employer. The resume should include a summation of information that states your qualifications for the position. Be sure to address the resume toward your job interests. Keep the components of the resume brief, but concise. State complete information. The reader should be able to obtain a full description without losing interest. References are an important part of your resume. They should be included on the final page as well as the address of your current placement file. Consider the following information for inclusion on your resume:

Name

Present address/permanent address

Telephone numbers

Age/birthdate

Height, weight, health status

Educational background (including teaching certificates)

Undergraduate activities

Undergraduate honors

Teaching experience (include student teaching)

Coaching experience

Related experience

Other experience (include military, if any)

Professional societies and organizations

Publications

Presentations

Current references

Placement file address

For many people, the interview is the hardest part of the job-search process. Keep three things in mind regarding interviews:

1. Experience and preparation for the interview will help.
2. The interview is a period of professional interaction.
3. The interview is your chance to express and "sell" yourself. A positive and self-assured attitude may be the highest priority for selection if other qualifications are equal.

Preparation for the interview is essential. Know your resume and other pertinent information. Be ready to discuss your teaching philosophy and be prepared to discuss the particular job for which you are applying. The following is a list of questions typically asked during interviews for teaching and coaching positions in public schools.

What is your philosophy of physical education?

Why do you want to become a teacher?

Why do you think you would like to teach in our school district?

How do you relate physical education and athletics to the total school curriculum?

What are your views on student discipline?

How important is winning in athletics?

How do you feel about the personal appearance of youngsters on your team?

What are your views on coeducational physical education classes?

As a coach, how do you view your relationship to other teachers in the school?

How would you develop positive attitudes toward lifetime physical fitness among your students?

What are your plans for future professional advancement and education?

State a general plan on how you would organize the physical education program (specific to grade levels applying for).

Why should we hire you?

You should ask questions to learn as much as possible about the position for which you have applied. The following are general questions that you may want to ask during an interview for a teaching or coaching position in the public schools.

How did this job opening come about?

Could you describe a typical schedule for the school day?

What is the present salary schedule? Benefits?

When can I expect notification about the position?

What is the administration's attitude toward physical education and athletics?

What will be my basic responsibilities and duties?

Are there opportunities for graduate study nearby?

Is any type of summer employment available?

What is the typical physical education class size?

Is there strong pressure to win from the administration or community?

What is the existing philosophy as to physical education and athletics?

What discipline procedures are presently being used?

Will release time be allowed for attending professional meetings and coaching clinics?

The following guidelines should be considered when preparing for your job interviews.

1. Dress appropriately for the area of the country and the type of position for which you have applied. Overdressing is better than "underdressing" for the initial interview.

2. Pay particular attention to your grooming and personal hygiene.

3. Find out as much as you can about the school district prior to the interview.

4. Be on time. You should plan to arrive ten to fifteen minutes early.

5. Be prepared. Know how to pronounce the interviewer's name, school's name, and the like. Write down questions to ask.
6. Bring pen and notepad to interview.
7. Use a firm grip in your handshake. Pronounce the interviewer's name upon greeting.
8. Do not chew gum, smoke, or fidget. Sit up and do not slouch.
9. Look the interviewer in the eye when talking.
10. Be courteous and sincere.
11. Remember, nervous is normal. Be prepared for the interview, and the nervousness should pass.
12. Rehearse your role, anticipated questions, and answers prior to the interview. Use common sense in unanticipated questions.

The interview should be a positive experience and work to your advantage. One point to keep in mind: as you gain experience with interviewing, you will become more proficient in the process. If you are truly interested in a position you have interviewed for and feel that you made a good impression, use the following guidelines to pursue knowledge of your status.

1. Establish a timeline for notification about the position during the interview.
2. Once the interview is completed, send a letter of your interest in the position. Let them know you want the job.
3. Depending upon the type of position, after a reasonable length of time, call the potential employer and check on your status.
4. If you are still being considered for the position, inquire as to any additional information that you could provide to strengthen your status.
5. Make sure that all the necessary information has been received by the prospective employer.

Glossary

affective domain behavior involving feelings, attitudes, and values

agility the ability to change body positions quickly and accurately to the indicated response or situation

anatomy the study of the structure of the human body and its parts

anthropometic measurements the recording of the dimensions of a person's body parts

applied research experiments that can be directly related to practical applications

assertive discipline a commitment to standardizing behavior based upon communication to the students about the desired behavior and the consequences for violations

balance the ability of a person to maintain a specific body position while still or in motion

ballistic stretch the bouncing or jerking of a muscle held at greater than resting length

basic locomotor skills walking, running, jumping, hopping, leaping, skipping, and galloping

basic research experiments investigating theoretical issues

biomechanics the study and analysis of the body in motion and of the effect of forces relating to this motion

block approach an approach to teacher education including input from the various disciplines comprising physical education, providing the cognitive skills the prospective teacher needs to meet specific objectives

body composition the amount of lean body weight that a person possesses including the skeleton, muscles, organs and other tissues, and the amount of body fat, which is the amount of tissue contained or stored in the body as fat

calisthenics systematic rhythmic bodily exercises usually performed without apparatus

cardiovascular fitness the ability of the heart, lungs, and circulatory system to provide the cells of the body with the necessary substances to perform work for extended periods of time

coach a teacher, a leader, and a director of learning and evaluator of performance

coaching burnout the inability to cope with chronic job stress associated with being a coach

cognitive domain behavior involving intellectual activities such as thinking, remembering, and making decisions

competency-based teacher education (CBTE) model that features an inductive approach to deciding what the student is to learn

conceptual approach a central idea that is meaningful to the learner to the point of effecting a change in the behavior of the one holding the concept

contemporary physical education the enhancement of the well-being of humans through movement and the study of physical activity's effects on individuals and society

coordination the speed and accuracy of correct muscle response to produce a desired movement

curriculum   a body of experiences with some order of progression directed toward the achievement of certain objectives

descriptive research   a fact-finding procedure concerned with describing the characteristics of individuals or events in order to answer a problem under investigation

discipline   (1) an organized body of knowledge collectively embraced in a formal course of learning; (2) training that is expected to produce a specified character change or pattern of behavior

discrimination test   a norm-referenced type of test, more summative than formative

dynamic flexibility   a full range of movement with speed or in resistance or opposition of a joint to a particular joint motion

dynamic strength   the amount of external force that can be exerted maximally during a single contraction

elective   the physical education subject and activity that are selected by the student

electromyography (EMG)   the recording of the muscle's electrical activity in response to a stimulation

emotional/social development   the promotion of movement experiences designed to enable students to have the opportunity to participate, to be successful, and to feel extremely good about themselves and their relationships with others as a result

evaluation   the process of determining how effectively goals or objectives are being achieved

exercise physiology   the study of the effect of exercise or training on the cardiorespiratory system

experiment   a controlled and objective method for obtaining reliable information

experimental research   an inquiry that controls and manipulates conditions, usually concerned with determining cause and effect

external control   students are manipulated by an outside source, the teacher or coach for motivation purposes

feedback   what the teacher tells the student about his or her performance after a practice attempt

flexibility   the range of motion available at a joint or group of joints

free-body diagrams   drawing simple sketches of the body and drawing arrows that represent the external forces on the body and/or external torques exerted on the body during movement

group cohesiveness   the degree to which members of a group want to be together

group dynamics   an area of study in the social sciences devoted to advancing knowledge about the nature of groups

health-related fitness   components of strength, muscular endurance, cardiovascular fitness, flexibility, and body composition

historical research   inquiry into an event, development, or experience of the past

human movement   the means by which expression is given to emotion, mood, gesture, and communication in temporal and spatial relationships

in-service training   educational opportunities of which working professionals can take advantage without having to quit their jobs and pursue advanced degrees

instructional strategies   the plans and actions involved in implementing instruction so that the student goals of a curriculum guide, unit plan, or lesson plan might be accomplished

internal control   students have the ability to be responsible for self-motivation

interpretive development   the cognitive abilities that enable a person to encounter challenges, design strategies for meeting those challenges, and exercise sound judgment in the seeking of a solution

intramurals   utilization of the skills and knowledge from physical education in a recreational setting

issue   a question or matter under dispute; a point of controversy

kinematics   the study of motion without reference to the forces causing the motion

kinesiology   the study of human motion

kinetics   the study of the forces that cause motion

knowledge of results (KR)   the information a student receives about a response that will be helpful in improving the response on the next practice attempts

liability   legal responsibilities that are not fulfilled and, therefore, are enforceable by court action

lifetime physical activity   activities not generally considered as sports, such as walking, running, bicycling, and exercising

lifetime sports   sports, games, or activities in which adults can participate throughout their lives

low organized games   activities that are easy to play, have few and simple rules, require little or no equipment, and may be varied in many ways

mainstreaming   placing the handicapped student in the regular class and adapting the situation for the maximum benefit of the student

mastery tests   a type of formative evaluation, related to criterion-referenced evaluation

measurement   the use of assessment that will provide information for evaluation

method of authority   a method of obtaining knowledge based on holding true to beliefs of known authorities

method of intuition   a method of obtaining knowledge based on what stands to reason

method of science   a method of obtaining knowledge based on the methodological and objective testing of hypotheses

method of tenacity   a method of obtaining knowledge based on holding true the beliefs of tradition

modeling   the process of using an individual as an example for teaching characteristics or desired patterns of behavior

motor control   the study of how we control the actions involved in performing a motor skill

motor learning   the study of the learning and acquiring of a motor skill

movement exploration   a method in movement education used by a learner that involves experimentation with possibilities for movement within restraints imposed by the teacher's statement of task

muscular endurance   the repetition of high or low intensity work that further involves the capacity of a muscle to continue contracting over a period of time

negligence   the failure to conduct oneself in a reasonably prudent manner to avoid exposing others to danger or risk of injury

neuromuscular development   the efficient and skillful coordination of the nervous and muscular systems that, when applied to movement, produces intrinsically successful experiences to be repeated

"new" physical education   a concept combining educative aim, recreative aim, and remedial aim that promotes organic growth, efficient motor ability, character, and intellectual ability

NOISE   an acronym for *n*euromuscular development, *o*rganic development, *i*nterpretive development, *s*elf-expression, and *e*motional/social development

obesity   a combination of overfat and overweight accompanied by a lack of functional movement

objective measurement   when one thing can be measured by more than one person and the results of those measurements are similar

olympiad   a calendar designation of the Greeks that specified the four-year period between Olympic games

organic development   the promotion of the attributes contributing to good health for an efficiently functioning life, including satisfactory muscular strength, flexibility, cardiovascular endurance, muscular endurance, and body composition

outdoor education   education in, about, or for the out-of-doors

overfat   having an excessive amount of body weight as fatty tissue

overweight   an excessive amount of body weight as compared to standards or norms

participant   either primary involvement through physical activity or sport, or secondary involvement through consuming or producing sport

passive flexibility   a full range of movement without regard to speed

pedagogy   the science of teaching

peer teaching   the prospective teacher simulates the classroom experience with college or university classmates acting as public school students

personal philosophy of coaching   an openness toward formulating one's actions based upon experiences and knowledge that one encounters

physical education   any process that increases a person's tendencies and abilities to participate in motor activities

physical fitness   a combination of components, each specific in nature, to improve and maintain health and the physical state of the body

physiology   the study of the functions of the human body and its parts

play education   a model of learning that presents a contemporary philosophy of physical education where identifiable teaching skills are needed to realize explicit objectives for physical education

positive self-concept   feeling good about one's individuality

power   the application of strength and speed during a muscular movement; force multiplied by velocity

problem   a question or matter to be resolved

psychomotor domain   behavior characterized by the action or performance of physical movement

Public Law 94–142   guarantees that handicapped children will have their physical education needs met within the structure of free, public education

qualitative analysis   a method of analyzing movement that identifies what is occurring throughout the movement in verbal terms

quantitative analysis   a method of analyzing movement that identifies what is occurring throughout the movement in numerical terms

reaction time   the time lapse between the presentation of the stimulus (sound-sight-touch) and the initiation of a movement response by the performer

reciprocity   the waiver of specific course requirements by a state Board of Education of validating credentials earned by a teacher in another state

recreation   an activity or experience chosen voluntarily and carried on within one's leisure time for the satisfaction it provides or for values and benefits the participant or society experiences

relative strength   the amount of strength in relation to one's body weight

reliability   the repeatability of a test result

research   a means of obtaining information to enable a person to satisfactorily answer a question or solve a problem

safety accident prevention

scholasticism intense intellectual education lacking in physical education

scientific method of inquiry the approach taken to gathering information through objective observation

scope the spectrum of exposures to the subject matter deemed important for the attainment of a goal

selective physical education that is required as a subject, with the student selecting the activity

self-actualization one's development of his or her fullest potential by recognizing that each person is an individual and unique, and that each unique individual is highly valued

self-expression providing for the learner experiences that prove to be inherently meaningful to the practitioner, allowing him or her to explore movement parameters to the ultimate and most satisfying limits

sequence the hierarchical arrangement of the structure of educational experiences

skill-related fitness the components of coordination, agility, power, speed, balance, and reaction time

skill tests performance tests designed to allow an evaluation of performance of specific skills that make up the whole activity

skinfold measurements a caliper is used to measure the amount of a pinch of skin in various selected sites on the body

social loafing when individuals work together on a particular task, the total effort expended is not as great as the sum of all the individual effort possible

sociology the study of the interactions of individuals and groups in their various social environments

sociology of sport the study of sport's influence on society and society's influence on sport

speed the ability to move the body or a region of the body as rapidly as possible from one point to another point; the rate of movement

sport all forms of physical activity, recreational or competitive

sport psychology the study of social- and clinical psychology-related topics to sport as well as to all movement settings

sports clubs a collection of students who want to participate in a particular sport that is usually not offered on an extramural basis

standardized tests tests developed by educators or professional test makers that have been validated and shown to be reliable

static stretch occurs when a muscle is held at a greater than resting length for a period of time

strength a measure of external force exerted by a muscle or group of muscles

stress a state of the body in response to demands placed upon it

student teaching a period of supervised induction into teaching, scheduled usually during the fourth year of college study as part of a bachelor's degree program

subjective measurement when the measurement of a performance depends on the personal judgment of each individual observing the performance, and the measurement becomes more related to the knowledge, skill, and perceptions of those individuals

Swedish gymnastics system a series of exercises developed by Per Henrik Ling, combining military gymnastics, pedagogical gymnastics, aesthetic gymnastics, and medical gymnastics

systems approach the teacher proceeds systematically to formulate and sequence instruction in a manner designed to fulfill student objectives that have been clearly specified and to develop evaluative techniques

taxonomy   the classification used for educational objectives directed at the cognitive, affective, and psychomotor domains

teacher accountability   the responsibility for student failure rests on the school and the teacher

teaching   intents to transmit knowledge, develop attitudes deemed acceptable by society, and change overt behavior

teaching skill   an expression of performance based on a teacher's productivity or on certain characteristics of performance

teaching styles   the general approach taken by a teacher when confronted with a teaching-learning situation

team teaching   two or more teachers combine their classes within the same activity

Title IX   law ensuring that equal opportunity for participation shall be afforded members of both sexes at institutions receiving financial assistance from the federal government

tort   a wrong or injury that does not result from a crime or breach of contract

total fitness   the complete development of the entire human organism combining physiological, psychological, cognitive, and social fitness

transfer of learning   previous learning experiences or practice influences how well one learns a new skill

trend   move in a particular direction or a tendency to be added or included more frequently

turnen   Friedrich Jahn's system, which combined intellectual education and physical education in the eighteenth century

tutoring   a teaching-learning encounter between a single teacher and a single student focusing on a single component skill

validity   the degree to which the test or measure actually measures what it was designed to measure

wellness   a combination of physical health, physical fitness, and mental health, which are usually reached and maintained by following good health practices

Credits

Photos

CHAPTER 1
1.2: The Citadel Department of Physical Education; **1.3:** *SCJOHPERD;* **1.4:** The Citadel Department of Physical Education; **1.5, 1.6:** College of Charleston Athletic Department.

CHAPTER 2
2.1: © Tom Ballard/EKM-Nepenthe; **2.2:** College of Charleston Athletic Department; **2.3:** © Ron Cooper/EKM-Nepenthe; **2.4:** © Steve Takatsuno; **2.6a and b:** © Bohdan Hrynewych/ Southern Light.

CHAPTER 3
3.2: © Jerry Markatos/Southern Light; **3.3:** © Ron Byers; **3.4, 3.7:** The Citadel Department of Physical Education.

CHAPTER 4
4.1: *SCJOHPERD;* **4.2:** © Jill Cannefax/EKM-Nepenthe; **4.3:** © John Maher/EKM-Nepenthe; **4.4:** © Ron Byers.

CHAPTER 5
5.1: *SCJOHPERD;* **5.2:** The Citadel Department of Physical Education; **5.3, 5.4:** *SCJOHPERD;* **5.5:** The Citadel Summer Camp.

CHAPTER 6
6.1: courtesy of AAHPERD; **6.2:** © James Shaffer; **6.3:** EKM-Nepenthe Historical.

CHAPTER 7
7.3: The Citadel Department of Physical Education; **7.4:** © John Keskinen; **7.5:** University of Texas at San Antonio Department of Physical Education.

CHAPTER 8
8.2, 8.3, 8.4: *SCJOHPERD;* **8.5:** The Citadel Athletic Department; **8.6:** University of Texas at San Antonio Department of Physical Education.

CHAPTER 9
9.2: University of Texas at San Antonio Department of Physical Education; **9.3, 9.4:** *SCJOHPERD;* **9.5:** College of Charleston Athletic Department; **9.6:** *SCJOHPERD;* **9.9:** The Citadel Summer Camp; **9.10:** *SCJOHPERD.*

CHAPTER 10
10.1: © Bohdan Hrynewych/Southern Light; **10.3:** © Jill Cannefax/EKM-Nepenthe; **10.8:** © Bohdan Hrynewych/Southern Light; **10.9:** © Ron Byers.

CHAPTER 11
11.1: © Bohdan Hrynewych/Southern Light; **11.2, 11.3:** © Ron Byers; **11.4:** © James Shaffer.

CHAPTER 12
12.1: The Citadel Athletic Department; **12.2:** College of Charleston Athletic Department; **12.3, 12.4:** The Citadel Athletic Department; **12.5:** *SCJOHPERD;* **12.6:** College of Charleston Athletic Department; **12.7:** The Citadel Athletic Department.

CHAPTER 13
13.1: *SCJOHPERD;* **13.2:** The Citadel Summer Camp; **13.3:** The Citadel Department of Physical Education; **13.4:** © Ron Byers.

CHAPTER 14
14.1, 14.2: © Ron Byers; **14.3, 14.4:** *SCJOHPERD.*

Illustrations

CHAPTER 1
1.8: From Siedentop, Daryl, *Physical Education: Introduction Analysis* 3d ed. © 1980 Wm. C. Brown Publishers, Dubuque, Iowa. All Rights Reserved. Reprinted by permission.

CHAPTER 3
3.5: From DeVries, Herbert A., *Physiology of Exercise* 3d ed. © 1966, 1974, 1980 Wm. C. Brown Publishers, Dubuque, Iowa. All Rights Reserved. Reprinted by permission. **3.6:** From Northrip, John W., Gene A. Logan, and Wayne C. McKinney, *Introduction to Biomechanic Analysis of Sport* 2d ed. © 1978, 1982 Wm. C. Brown Publishers, Dubuque, Iowa. All Rights Reserved. Reprinted by permission. **3.8:** From

Magill, Richard A., *Motor Learning* 2d ed.
© 1973, 1980 Wm. C. Brown Publishers,
Dubuque, Iowa. All Rights Reserved. Reprinted
by permission. **3.9:** From Corbin, Charles B., *A
Textbook of Motor Development* 2d ed.
© 1973, 1980 Wm. C. Brown Publishers,
Dubuque, Iowa. All Rights Reserved. Reprinted
by permission. **3.10:** From Cratty, Bryant J.,
*Psychology in Contemporary Sport: Guidelines
for Coaches and Athletes,* © 1973, p. 273.
Reprinted by permission of Prentice-Hall, Inc.,
Englewood Cliffs, NJ. **3.11:** Copyright 1985
National Sporting Goods Association, Mt.
Prospect, IL.

CHAPTER 7

7.1: From Colfer/Cheverette, *Running for Fun
and Fitness* 2d ed. © 1980 Kendall/Hunt
Publishing Co., Dubuque, Iowa. Reprinted by
permission. **7.2:** From Gutin, Bernard, ''A
Model of Physical Fitness and Dynamic
Health,'' in *Journal of Physical Education and
Recreation,* Vol. 51, No. 5, May 1980. © 1980
American Alliance for Health, Physical
Education, Recreation and Dance. Reprinted
by permission.

CHAPTER 8

8.1: From Siedentop, Daryl, *Physical
Education: Introductory Analysis* 3d ed. © 1980
Wm. C. Brown Publishers, Dubuque, Iowa. All
Rights Reserved. Adapted by special
permission.

CHAPTER 9

9.1: From Carl E. Willgoose, *The Curriculum in
Physical Education* 4th ed. © 1984, p. 81.
Reprinted by permission of Prentice-Hall, Inc.,
Englewood Cliffs, NJ. **9.7:** From Terry, James
W., et al., *Physical Activity for All Ages: The
Concepts of High Level Wellness,* 2d ed., 1984.
Reprinted by permission of Kendall/Hunt
Publishing Company. **9.8:** From Singer/Dick:
*Teaching Physical Education: A Systems
Approach.* Copyright © 1974 Houghton Mifflin
Company. Used with permission.

CHAPTER 10

10.2: From Anderson, W. and Barrette, G.,
''Teacher Behavior'' in W. Anderson and G.
Barrette (eds.), *What's Going on in Gym:
Descriptive Studies of Physical Education
Classes.* Newtown, CT: Motor Skills: Theory
into Practice, 1978, Table 2.3, p. 16. **10.4:** From
Goldberger, Michael, et al., ''The effects of
three styles of teaching on the psychomotor
performance and social skill development of
fifth grade children,'' in *Research Quarterly for
Exercise and Sport, 53* (1982): 116–124.
© 1982 American Alliance for Health, Physical
Education, Recreation and Dance. Reprinted
by permission. **10.5, 10.6,** and **10.7:** From
Mosston, M., *Teaching Physical Education.*
© 1981 Charles E. Merrill Publishing Co.,
Columbus, Ohio. Reprinted by permission of
the publisher.

Index

drug abuse, 364–65
specialization of athletes,
    361–62
teacher versus coach, 361
violence, 363–64
youth sports programs, 365
Issues in physical education,
    396–403, 411–18
apathy, of students, 411–12
burnout, teacher, 414,
    416–17
class size, 412
competency, teacher, 401
credit, athletic participation
    as physical education,
    397
discipline
    lack of, 411–12
    physical activity as,
        396–97
individualized instruction,
    414
legal liability, 417–18
motivation of students,
    413–14
objectives of physical
    education, 400–401
risk acceptance, 417
salaries, 401–2
status of physical
    education, 398–99
teaching/coaching, role
    conflict, 397–98
unionism, teacher, 402–3
violence in schools, 412
Ivory tower concept, 399

J

Jahn, F. L., 22
James, W., 23
Jefferson, T., 12
John, T., 18
Johnson, C. J., 356
Johnson Sportsmanship
    Scale, 324
Journals, 169–71
    research journals, 170–71
        abstracts of, 170
        types of, 171
    types of, 170
Junior college coach, 346–47
Junior high school coach, 345

K

Kennedy, J. F., 15
Kinematics, 93
Kinesiology, 93–94, 96
anatomical, 93
human motion analysis,
    93–94
    cinematography, 93
    electromyography, 93
    free-body diagrams,
        93–94
    mechanical, 93

qualitative analysis in, 94
quantitative analysis in, 94
Kinetics, 93
Knighthood, training for,
    11–12
Knowledge-based approach,
    teacher education,
    146–47
Knowledge of results (KR),
    96–97
    field experience and,
        156–57
Krathwohl, D., 257
Kraus-Weber test, 14

L

Laban, R., 35
Leadership, 63–64
    autocratic style, 63
    democratic style, 63
    people-oriented, 64
    task-oriented, 64
Leadership roles, 66–70
    aged, programs for, 68
    handicapped, programs for,
        70
    health and fitness
        programs, 67
    youth sports programs,
        67–68
Lead-up activities, 249, 254
Learner designed program,
    288–89
Learning, instructional aids,
    value of, 299
Learning approach, teaching,
    283
Learning environment
    importance of, 294–95
    least restrictive
        environment for
        handicapped students,
        265
    teaching skills, 224–28
        classroom management,
            227
        interpersonal
            relationships, 227–28
        knowledge aspects,
            225–26
        ludic-elements, 226–27
        modeling behaviors in,
            225
        rules, 227
        social behavior in, 225
        socialization of student
            in, 225
        successful, factors for,
            224
Lecture method, 283
Legal factors, liability, 417–18
Legislation
    physical education, 267–68
    Public Law 94–142, 25, 70,
        267

Leisure services. See
    Recreation
Leisure therapy, career of,
    160
Lesson planning, 291, 292–99
    instructional aids, 296–99
        benefits in learning, 299
        instructional needs and,
            297–98
        integration with lesson,
            298–99
        positive transfer in, 299
    organizational format, 292,
        296
        of activity variations, 294,
            296
        sequencing events, 294
        timing the lesson, 294
Lesson teaching, 299–303
    instructions, presentation,
        300–301
    teacher feedback, 301, 303
        motivation and, 303
        specificity of, 301, 303
Liability, 417–18
    negligence, 418
    product liability, 418
    tort liability, 418
Liddell, E., 31
Lieber, F., 22
Lifetime physical activity, 202
Lifetime sports, 202, 256
    advantages of, 256
Ling, P. H., 16, 264–65
Ling's system, 16–17
    gymnastic exercises in, 17
Locke, J., 21
Locomotor skills, basic, 252
Low organized games, 253
Luther, M., 21

M

McCloy, C. H., 17
Mager, R., 276
Magill, R., 221
Mahre, P., 18
Mainstreaming, 25, 405–6
    handicapped students, 265
    problems in, 406
Maslow, A., 154
Master's degree, 172
Mastery tests, 321
Mathematics, 85–86
    arithmetic, 86
    geometry, 86
Measurement, 308, 313–17.
    See also Validity
    objective measurement,
        313, 315
    reliability in, 317
    subjective measurement,
        314–15
    validity in, 315–16
Mechanical kinesiology, 93

Women in sports, 32–34
  attitudes about, 53–54
  coaching by men, 352, 354
  development of, 32, 33
  governance of, 32
  Olympics, initial
      participation, 28
  sex role behavior and, 54,
      56–57
  Title IX and, 34
Wood, D., 23, 24, 25
Written tests, 321
  discrimination tests, 321
  mastery tests, 321
  standardized tests, 321

Y

Young, C., 18
Youth sports programs
  issues in, 365
  leadership of, 67–68

Z

Zoology, 81